New York Jews and the Quest for Community

The Kehillah Experiment, 1908–1922

New York Jews and the Quest for Community

The Kehillah Experiment, 1908-1922

§

Arthur A. Goren

§

Columbia University Press
New York
The Jewish Publication Society of America
Philadelphia

Copyright © 1970 Columbia University Press
SBN: 231-03422-9
Library of Congress Catalog Card Number: 76-129961
Printed in the United States of America

To my parents
Lillian and Saul Gorenstein

Acknowledgments

I
N THE COURSE OF PREPARING THIS VOLUME, I HAVE INCURRED
many debts some of which I am at last able to acknowledge
publicly. A grant from the National Foundation for Jewish
Culture in 1965 enabled me to carry out a major part of the
research. In the fall of 1967, a grant from the Philip W. Lown Graduate Center for Contemporary Jewish Studies at Brandeis University
permitted me to complete my research on Judah Magnes' pacificism.
The Hebrew University in Jerusalem graciously freed me from my
obligations there, and a fellowship at the Charles Warren Center for
Studies in American History at Harvard University has allowed me
to complete the process of book making and to pursue further my
interest in ethnic groups.

I profited from a number of interviews with veterans of Jewish
communal life of half a century ago. They are listed in A Note on
Sources, but I would like to single out Mr. Bernard G. Richards, the
executive secretary of the Kehillah, who was especially helpful. Mrs.
Rachel Blumenthal, since deceased, archivist of the Jewish Historical
General Archives in Jerusalem was most helpful. Professor Stanley
F. Chyet of the American Jewish Archives assisted me beyond the
call of duty. Mr. James Marshall granted me permission to examine
the papers of his father. Professor Jonathan Magnes gave me access

to manuscript material which had been in the keeping of his mother, the late Mrs. Judah L. Magnes. Professor Mordecai Kaplan invited me into his home and opened his journals to me. Dr. Menahem Schmelczer of the Jewish Theological Seminary made the Israel Friedlaender Papers available. The staffs of the Columbia University Oral History Project, the Jewish Division of the New York Public Library, the Municipal Archives and Records Center of the City of New York, the Swarthmore College Peace Collection, and the Yivo Institute Archives, extended many courtesies to me. The original version of chapter two appeared as an article in the *YIVO Annual* and is used here with the kind permission of the publishers.

A number of scholars read the manuscript and made useful suggestions. They are Yehoshua Arieli, Sigmund Diamond, Robert M. Fogelson, Benjamin Halpern, Gerd Korman, and James P. Shenton. Gerson D. Cohen subjected an early draft of the manuscript to a searching criticism from which I learned much. I benefited greatly from David J. Rothman's reading of a final draft. Joan McQuary of the Columbia University Press was a wise and discerning editor.

To this good company of scholars, librarians and supporters of scholarship, my profound thanks.

My two greatest debts rest elsewhere. I was fortunate to study American social history with Robert D. Cross, then of Columbia University, whose sensitive treatment of immigrants was matched by his compassionate understanding of graduate students. As sponsor of my dissertation, his encouragement and his meticulous and shrewd criticism, were of inestimable benefit. Finally, Ayalah, and our sons, Avner and Amos—by their remarkable patience, good humor, and support—created the conditions that made the writing of this book possible.

Arthur A. Goren

Jerusalem, Israel
Cambridge, Massachusetts
January 1970

Contents

New York Jews and the Quest for Community

The Kehillah Experiment, 1908–1922

In blending Judaism with Americanism the edges and corners will have to be leveled on both sides. Compromises will be unavoidable. . . . But these compromises will never be such as to obliterate or mutilate the character of either party. . . . In the great palace of American civilization we shall occupy our own corner, which we will decorate and beautify to the best of our taste and ability, and make it not only a center of attraction for the members of our family, but also an object of admiration for all the dwellers of the palace. . . . We perceive a community . . . leading a new current into the stream of American civilization; not a formless crowd . . . but a sharply marked community, distinct and distinguished, trusted for its loyalty, respected for its dignity, esteemed for its traditions, valued for its aspirations, a community such as the Prophet of the Exile saw in his vision: "And marked will be their seed among the nations, and their offspring among the peoples. Everyone that will see them will point to them as a community blessed by the Lord."

Israel Friedlaender
Past and Present, pp. 276–78

The Kehillah in America must be that instrumentality through which the Jews of America exercise self-determination, exercise the right and the privilege of every group to determine what they want to become in this country, what they want to do, what their relationship shall be with one another. . . . The organization in America of such Kehillahs, upon a democratic basis, is a distinct contribution by the Jews to community life in America. Rightly used, it will come to be regarded . . . as one of the many group endeavors which may be of aid to the American people in understanding and furthering the development of so complex a unit as America.

Judah L. Magnes
Report to the Ninth Annual Convention of the Kehillah,
June 1, 1918

§ CHAPTER ONE §

The Tradition of Community

OST IMMIGRANTS BROUGHT TO AMERICA A TRADITION OF communal life. This body of folkways and institutional experience, nourished by ties of religion and language, and common life style, eased the immigrant's adjustment to the alien environment. For the newly arrived, it provided the first familiar landmarks in a strange country. When the continuing flow of immigration enlarged the group and taxed its beneficence, the settlers drew upon the communal tradition to stabilize and broaden their associational life. A loose network of communal agencies evolved—part transplanted, part indigenous—which supplied the immigrant settlement with social and welfare services, and above all with an ethnic identity.

The conditions of American society, however, particularly as they had unfolded by the end of the nineteenth century, profoundly affected the shape of ethnic-group life. A heterogeneous and democratic public had long ago eliminated the vestiges of a state church tradition and proscribed corporate recognition for national or religious minorities. More recently, the rapid economic and social changes wrought by an industrializing America had disrupted an older localism and sense of community. The immigrant, consequently, could hardly rely upon the authoritarianism and traditionalism which in

Europe had served him in maintaining his communal polity. Powerful assimilatory forces operated, moreover, on a personal plane. The expectations of self-advancement, free public education, and an open political system complemented a national ethos which frowned upon separatism. Indeed, for the larger public, which the immigrant became increasingly aware of, the efficacy of assimilation constituted an article of civic faith—a warranty of the ultimate achievement of homogeneity in American life. In this setting, ethnic organization had to depend upon voluntarism, with all its vagaries and risks. As a result, the option of personal withdrawal from the group, the presence of factional strife, and the threat of open rupture constantly and severely tested the viability of the ethnic entity.

Settlement in the expanding American city accelerated these centrifugal forces, but it opened, as well, opportunities for reordering group life. Thus the city encouraged occupational and residential mobility and disengagement from the group to a greater degree than town or countryside. Furthermore, the ecology of the metropolitan immigrant enclave gave free reign to Old Country localism, bane of collaborative activity. On the other hand, the populous ethnic settlement of the city possessed, in the aggregate, vast communal resources. It contained, too, a growing leadership element which was prepared to apply new techniques and strategies to ethnic organization and to fight immigrant provincialism in the name of a higher ethnic loyalty and institutional efficiency.

The immigrants and their offspring who in the early twentieth century lived in these urban enclaves occupied, for the most part, a middle range between the poles of self-segregation and rapid assimilation. They esteemed their new nationality and welcomed the prospect of social integration, but they also sought anchorage in their ethnic community and feared for its demise. The private person, bewildered by competing loyalties and saddled with his own burdens, might choose to drift or to abandon the group. Institutional life, however, compelled its participants to face openly the disparity between the dictates and inducements of inheritance and environment. Consequently, even as immigrants built institutions to preserve the solidarity of their particular group and to provide a measure of personal security, they endeavored to fit these institutions into the American social landscape.[1]

This dual process—the struggle to maintain ethnic integrity and to achieve social accommodation—is the ultimate concern of this book. At its heart, however, lies a relatively brief episode: the striving of key elements of New York Jewry during the second decade of the twentieth century to establish a comprehensive communal structure. The active sponsors of this endeavor envisioned a democratically governed polity which would unite the city's multifarious Jewish population, harness the group's intellectual and material resources, and build a model ethnic community. Order and coherence would then replace the turbulence and dislocation attending the mass migration. In addition to easing the social and economic adjustment of the newcomers, the organization would also contribute to their psychic well-being. It would overcome the apathy and ignorance—even the scorn —which many held for their ethnic heritage. This intellectual and spiritual "revival," the protagonists assumed, would invest the group with vitality, cultural distinction, and the will to survive. It would mitigate the generational conflict and redeem youth estranged from their immigrant parents and ancestral inheritance. In these ways, the ideologists of the movement declared, an organized Jewish community would contribute to the general welfare and direct the healthy and balanced Americanization of its constituents. They called their undertaking "the New York Kehillah." The Hebrew term "kehillah" —community—recalled the venerable, self-contained communal establishment of European Jewry.* It evoked an image of stability, comity, and collective responsibility. For nearly ten years, swayed by these old and new notions, the New York Kehillah functioned through its representative assembly, executive departments, and embryonic civil service. Then it began its precipitous decline, which its leaders were unable to check.

The few scholars who have taken note of the Kehillah have generally used it as a paradigm of the erosion of community: modernism

* When capitalized, "Kehillah" refers specifically to the New York Kehillah. When lower-case, "kehillah" refers to the local communal organization of European Jewry or, in a generic sense to the Jewish community in its East European context. "Kahal"—linguistically similiar to "kehillah"—was used in Eastern Europe to designate the Jewish communal administration. By extension it frequently replaced "kehillah" in daily usage. For the sake of clarity, this term is here avoided.

in Europe weakened the communal fabric; immigration to America's burgeoning urban society tore it to shreds; and new social conventions provided no adequate alternative. The insight is a valuable one, and this study explores its implications. But no less instructive than the breakdown of community was the endeavor to reconstruct one. In its brief but seminal existence the Kehillah posed the options and encouraged the experimentation which suggested some of the limits and possibilities of ethnic group life in America.[2]

To create a unified Jewish community in America required, in the first place, a new rationale for corporate action. No longer able to rely upon public law, and divided rather than bound together by religious practice, the Jewish public needed a concept of communal polity able to embrace a variety of institutional interests, conflicting ideologies, and provincial loyalties. In their formulations, the architects of the Kehillah drew heavily upon the American experience and upon the progressive ideas of the period. Pluralism, with its connotations of latitudinarianism, reciprocity, and salutary competition, was one cornerstone. Another was voluntarism itself, and Kehillah leaders stressed the uplifting effect of persuasion and consensus as instruments of public endeavor. They also held, like the progressive reformers whom they resembled, that planning, efficiency, and an "enlightened public opinion"—in short, "science and democracy"—were sureties of progress. So equipped, their Kehillah would overcome "the vested interests," the stumbling blocks to unity.

Needed, too, was an interpretation of the American creed sympathetic to ethnic group life. One circle of young intellectuals, zealous supporters of the Kehillah, presented ethnic pluralism as a permanent and desirable feature of American society. Dr. Judah L. Magnes, a young, American-born rabbi, gave succinct expression to this view on the eve of the Kehillah's founding convention in February, 1909. He titled a sermon delivered for the occasion, "A Republic of Nationalities." Nine months later he preached on Israel Zangwill's play, *The Melting Pot.* "The symphony of America," he remarked,

must be written by the various nationalities which keep their individual and characteristic note, and which sound this note in harmony with their sister nationalities. Then it will be a symphony of color, of picturesqueness, of character, of distinction—not the harmony of the Melting Pot, but rather the harmony of sturdiness and loyalty and joyous struggle.[3]

For Magnes and his friends, the Kehillah venture represented a step towards realizing that vision.

So singular an undertaking entailed considerable experimentation: it required synthesizing Old World practices and New World skills and handling situations for which few precedents existed. The Kehillah's most substantial achievement—its educational system—rested upon the attempt to apply modern pedagogical insights to an archaic but hallowed curriculum. The controversy it roused convulsed the community. In a parallel development, the Kehillah sought to improve Jewish welfare services by supporting—despite stubborn opposition—the establishment of a central philanthropic authority. In the garment trades, it created its own arbitration machinery with the intention of becoming the mediator of the city's "Jewish industry." When criminality in the Jewish quarter became a matter of public concern the Kehillah formed its own intelligence apparatus, entered into an understanding with the city administration, and proceeded to track down Jewish criminals.

There are, then, three dimensions to this account of the Kehillah. The first treats the undertaking as a challenge to the pattern of Jewish communal life as it stood at a critical juncture in its development. Because the Kehillah represented a well-defined alternative and was strikingly innovative, it prodded leaders and organizations to reappraise their ideas and methods. In this way, it promoted change and contributed to a clarification of communal goals.

The Kehillah episode also provides a particular focus for observing the interaction between the new immigrants and the metropolis. Since the organization wished to represent New York's largest ethnic group—one which was of an overwhelmingly immigrant cast—its range of interests coincided in part with the general urban predicament.

Finally, the decade of the Kehillah spanned a period of rapid change and intellectual ferment. Its beginning coincided with a frenzied but optimistic time of massive immigration and social reform. It disintegrated in the wave of disenchantment with social visions and experimentation which came in the war's aftermath—the years of the Red Scare and rampant nativism. Eager to fit into the American setting, the Kehillah registered some of these general developments.

To examine the Kehillah, therefore, is also to probe the effect of the American social system upon a new immigrant culture and the particular institutional response of Jews—so rich in minority group experience—to conditions of freedom and pluralism.

§

NEW YORK'S JEWS WERE WELL ENDOWED FOR THE TASK OF COMMUNITY-building. From Europe they brought, in addition to the economic and social skills of an urban people, a monumental experience as a minority. For a millennium and more they had accommodated themselves to the sovereign powers and majority cultures of the countries of their dispersion.

The interplay of historical development and public law set the terms of the encounter. Christendom's pervasive hostility toward the Jews, the corporate status assigned to them by medieval society, and then the marginal position they occupied as subjects of the rising national state, isolated and repressed them as a group. Viewed, however, through the prism of their religious inheritance, segregation had assured the integrity of the congregation and subjection had been interpreted as a token of divine election. The communal thrust of rabbinic Judaism—its faith in collective redemption, the emphasis it gave to the study of the sacred law and to charitable works—equipped generations of European Jewry with an acute sense of common fate and group discipline and with a unifying intellectual tradition.

These elements complemented one another and shaped the Jewish communal order. Rulers interested in the Jews for fiscal and financial reasons permitted them a measure of authority in arranging their communal life; governments thereby held the community accountable for the obligations of the individual. They granted Jews the right to self-taxation, limited juridical autonomy, and a free hand in the internal administration of the community. The leadership—lay and rabbinical—used this secular power to reinforce a body of religious precepts which, in its own right, claimed authority over the private and public life of the Jew.

In Poland, during the early seventeenth century, Jewish communal settlement reached its zenith. In size and density of population, it constituted the heartland of European Jewry. The key role the Jews played in Polish life in part accounts for this development. In a sharply divided and backward society of landlords and peasants, the Jews supplied needed services as entrepreneurs, tradesmen, and artisans. Communities expanded, achieved a modicum of stability and well-being and, in the process, enlarged and refined their authority. With the establishment of a network of regional and national councils and courts, Polish Jewry exercised a high degree of minority self-government. This golden age of kehillah, moreover, coincided with the flowering of rabbinic Judaism. The erudition of its interpreters, the fame of its academies, and its diffusion through the folk culture bore witness to this fact. The ascendency of rabbinic Judaism further solidified the kehillah.

The two million Jews who immigrated to the United States in the thirty years before World War I came from this center. A substantial number still subscribed to a communal tradition whose core reached back to Polish Jewry's creative age of kehillah. Indeed, for those who, like the founders of the New York Kehillah, were seeking to check the dissolution of community life, the kehillah heritage suggested continuity, the model for and chief determinant in reviving the community.

What, then, was the shape and quality of the kehillah polity both in its classic form and as it was modified by later and harsher times?

Structurally, the seventeenth century Polish kehillah combined, in its quintessence, a strong executive body and a wide-ranging network of voluntary associations. Elected elders, drawn from the wealthy and learned classes, operated within the well-defined bounds of communal regulations. Paid officials assisted them: the town rabbi, rabbinical judges, teachers, administrators, clerks, and inspectors. Meanwhile, the associations, products of individual initiative, enabled large numbers of the middle strata to participate in the life of the community.

The associations tended to specialize in given areas of public endeavor. They addressed themselves most frequently to such causes as: interring the dead, ministering to the sick, and supporting particular welfare services (i.e., care of orphans, loans to the distressed, free education to needy children, and maintenance of a hostelry for paupers

and wayfarers). Other societies—adult education circles, in essence—
dedicated their efforts to the study of Bible or Talmud. In addition,
artisans established guilds to protect their craft interests, while the
upkeep and management of the synagogue offered another range of
opportunities for societal activity. Beside its interest, however, each
society responded to the general needs of its own membership. Social
and religious activities and mutual aid provisions reinforced the associations and gave them a fraternal character. Yet despite their broad
scope and wide latitude, they remained under the close supervision of
the kehillah council. The latter certified the individual regulatory
codes, granted permission to solicit funds, mediated internal disputes,
and on occasion participated in the selection of association functionaries. Organizing a new body—the establishment of an additional
synagogue, for example—required the council's approval.

The kehillah's elders devoted considerable time to civic and economic problems. The Jewish quarter required municipal services, and
the kehillah administration either supplied them or negotiated for
them with the town's officials. In economic matters, the general welfare of the community provided the justification for intervention.
The council established guidelines for the Jewish merchant in his
dealings with the outside world. Within the community, it supervised the market, determined rights of domicile, imposed rent controls, and sought to prevent cutthroat competition. Individual insol-
vency, after all, imposed added burdens upon a kehillah facing the
fiscal claims of church, town, nobles, and king, in addition to its own
administrative needs.

In the middle of the seventeenth century, the Jewish settlement in
Eastern Europe entered its long, dark age of tribulation. Oppression
from without pauperized the group and, in moments of convulsion,
threatened its physical survival. Spiritual upheavals shook the be-
sieged community from within.

First came the disintegration of the Polish state: a century and a
half of disorder and anarchy, of invasions and pillage. For the Jews,
the period brought decimation, flight, or—at best—a perilous existence which imposed upon the community immense tasks of defense
and reconstruction. The kehillah regime buckled under the ordeal:
economic calamity reduced its fiscal resources; exorbitant new taxes

and extortionist practices drove it toward bankruptcy. The wealthy elders, themselves hard-pressed and no longer swayed by the moral constraints of an earlier age, frequently shifted the burden to an already impoverished and desperate commonalty. Aggressive leaders seized communal power and used it for self-aggrandizement. These developments affected the entire fabric of kehillah life. Standards of education and of rabbinical leadership declined, and class antagonism damaged group solidarity.

Hasidism, the pietistic movement of religious revival, constituted a disruptive force of another kind. Its emphasis on personal spontaneity rather than fixed practice, on faith rather than knowledge, on the prophetically inspired rather than the rabbinically ordained, challenged the rational and legalistic nature of the classic communal tradition. Indeed, the sect (which by the turn of the nineteenth century dominated the greater part of East European Jewry) either bypassed the existing kehillah or absorbed its institutions. This process was in large measure effected by the charismatic figure of the saddik, the Hasidic leader who, invested with divine grace, became the infallible guide of his flock. He dispensed charity, arbitrated disputes, trained disciples, and exalted public worship with his presence. For the zealots, faith in the saddik and attendance at his court replaced, in part, the institutions of the established community.[4]

In the course of the first half of the nineteenth century, forces operated to restore a measure of equilibrium. The bitter controversies between the followers of hasidism and rabbinic Judaism subsided. Areas of influence became fixed, and numerous hasidic circles moderated their positions. One could speak again of a homogeneous religious culture, though a culture of variegated styles and nuances. Regionalism, past feuds, the decline of kehillah authority, and doctrinal particularism had left their marks. (In a later period, in the new centers of immigrant settlement like New York, these muted and substantively minor disparities contributed to the disorganization of normative Judaism.) Nevertheless, external conditions had in the meantime strengthened Orthodoxy and community.

These conditions became manifest following Poland's final dismemberment as a sovereign state. East European Jewry then found itself divided between three absolutist monarchies: Prussia (in possession of Posen's Jews); Austria (holding the much larger Galician community); and Russia (ruling the remaining and greatest part of Polish Jewry). All three governments subscribed to the notion that the Jews represented an alien, harmful, and benighted element. They prepared Draconian "rehabilitation" programs to purge the group of its "antisocial ways" and prepare it for "fusion" with the native population. (Fusion, hopefully, would lead to conversion.) Consequently, the Jewish communities, confronted by centralized, bureaucratic powers, brutal in their methods and bent upon reordering if not eliminating Jewish life, responded by closing ranks and treating external innovations and influences as stratagems and heresies.

The most oppressive and persistent practitioner of assimilation-by-duress was czarist Russia. Convinced that the Jewish communal establishment was a major impediment to its program's success, the regime circumscribed communal autonomy. In 1844 it abolished kehillah self-government altogether. As this "reform" program and its long-standing discriminatory practices required an administrative apparatus, the government converted part of the old kehillah administration into a municipal bureau of Jewish affairs.

This policy tried the inner unity of the local community. Jewish notables, for example, were charged with enforcing the notorious conscription laws of Nicholas I even after the annulment of communal autonomy. Whenever the government's demands for recruits were unfilled—the term of military service was twenty-five years—juveniles as young as twelve were forcibly enlisted to meet the quotas. The system of exemptions placed nearly the entire burden of supplying conscripts upon the poorer classes. In another instance, kehillah worthies, acting as tax farmers and aides, continued to administer the burdensome and hated korobka, a sales tax levied primarily on meat. Instituted originally to meet the community's needs, the fund was placed under municipal control when kehillah self-government was abolished. The municipality now used the income to finance the government's Jewish program—so repugnant to the group—and to reduce the fiscal debt of the old kehillah establishment. Only then were appropriations made to the religious and welfare agencies of the community. Under such conditions, enmity for the Jewish "autocrats" and aversion for any supervisory authority crystallized into a formidable opposition. It was reinforced, in the last two decades of the nineteenth century, by secular Jewish movements which challenged Orthodoxy's communal hegemony by appealing to the disaffected intelligentsia and the lower strata of traditionalist society.

These movements, radical and nationalist in outlook, represented one response to the calamities of the 1880s and 1890s (the great migration westward constituted another). For the Jews who had embraced modernism, the events of those decades proved to be a shattering experience. Not only did the pogroms of 1881, and others which followed periodically, underscore once again the deep-seated antipathy the common people harbored for the Jews: they also indicated government collusion. Perhaps most depressing of all, they laid bare the apathy and even enmity of Russian intellectuals to the plight of the Jews. Russified Jews and *maskilim* (the latter had imbibed their "enlightenment" in Hebrew translation) were thus disabused of certain cherished notions: that the regime would reward those who had disengaged themselves from Orthodoxy in favor of Westernization; and that a progressive front, in which "enlightened" Jews were welcome, was laying the groundwork for a more tolerant and equitable society.

Economic factors widened the crisis. The increasing pace of industrialization, well underway by the 1870s, was playing havoc with the small artisans and petty tradesmen of the Pale. Now came expulsion from townlet and countryside, additional occupational restrictions, and the consequences of rapid, internal migration to the new industrial centers. The Orthodox had nothing to offer dislocated intellectuals and depressed proletarians except the traditional services of the Jewish community. The cosmopolitans and nationalists, identifiable as socialists and Zionists, proposed secular redemption.

By 1900, these socialists and Zionists—to mention the two main camps of what would shortly become an ideological patchwork of factions, splits, and alliances—had developed full-grown organizations. The economic, political, and cultural programs they offered were carried on, for the most part, outside the kehillah framework. The Zionists created fund-raising machinery, superintended agricultural settlements in Palestine, participated in political work through the World Zionist Congress, and inspired a prolific publicistic literature in Hebrew. The Jewish Labor Bund organized strikes and strike funds, co-operated with the general socialist parties, and operated underground cells which preached class consciousness, revolution and, incidentally, promoted popular Yiddish culture.

Secular causes unsettled Jewish institutional life and on occasion disrupted it altogether. Nevertheless, the old communal order remained, at least outwardly, a viable one. The largest part of East European Jewry continued to hold to traditional ways. In fact many may well have identified with their kehillah at the same time that they enlisted in a secular movement. Nor were all regions or settlements equally affected by the new intellectual currents and economic changes. Finally, the kehillah tradition was a flexible one. When the kehillah's governing body was formally abolished the group substituted other communal devices. The voluntary associations grew in importance, and sometimes a particularly strong one would, in effect, direct the affairs of the entire community. There were cases of kehillah rabbis or powerful laymen who enjoyed the prestige or wealth to establish an unofficial hegemony over the community, just as there were instances of welfare agency functionaries directing public affairs. In one section of Greater Russia—Congress Poland—the congregational councils created by the government soon appropriated to themselves the more extensive functions of the old kehillah.[5]

The great immigration to America during the three decades which preceded World War I brought, then, both uprooted kehillah men and earnest party workers. It brought, too, a multitude of tractable, pragmatic townspeople. Yet all did possess a single broad culture— the Yiddish-speaking culture of Eastern Europe, all had suffered from czarist oppression, and all now shared the common lot of the newcomer. In brief: the preconditions existed for a reconstruction of community or for its fragmentation.

The East European Jews (Russian Jews as they were generally called) who settled in New York City found a Jewish community in existence dominated by a group strikingly different in its cultural background, social standing, and communal outlook. Americanized and prosperous, it stemmed largely from the German-speaking areas of central Europe. By 1900, thirty years separated the colony from its own last wave of immigrating countrymen, though a trickle continued to come. Predominantly native-born by then, it was intent on casting Jewish life into a liberal, denominational mold, a task begun by the immigrant generation.

Old World origins prepared the way for the new communal outlook. The Jewish communities the older settlers left behind in the 1830s to 1850s were small, scattered, and located for the most part in the rural areas of southern and western Germany. Unlike the East European kehillahs, they boasted neither an abundant nor distinguished leadership. The folk who emigrated from these communities possessed hardly more than a perfunctory knowledge of the tradition. Moreover, the Enlightenment ideals of the eighteenth century and the political turmoils of the early nineteenth century corroded a religious–ethnic constancy that had been present until then. Immigration, in turn, nullified the formal constraints of community, permitted unhampered experimentation, and loosened group ties.

The Jewish arrivals of the middle decades of the nineteenth century also belonged to the great stream of German immigration. Despite prejudice and religious differences, they were drawn to the German cultural milieu. In their own Jewish circles and in German-American societies they cultivated the language, literature, and music of the fatherland. Until the crisis of World War I, Jews remained receptive to German intellectual currents and sympathetic to Germany's political ambitions. Nor were these ties merely emotional. In the cities, they lived in German neighborhoods or close by and drew upon a common language to build their business and professional clientele. Thus a double ethnicity operated which further diluted group solidarity.[6]

By 1900 a remarkable number of German Jews and their sons had won distinguished places in the economic and civic life of New York. Founders of the great department stores like the Straus, Stern, and Bloomingdale families, financiers like Jacob H. Schiff and Isaac N. Seligman, and corporation lawyers like Louis Marshall and Edward Lauterbach used their fortunes and prestige to champion civic reform movements, support philanthropic work, and wield political influence. For these notables Jewish matters comprized only one of their many interests, an interest, however, which was too important to be left to others.

Their Jewish affiliation manifested itself in two ways: membership in a Reform temple (by 1900 nearly all the prominent German-Jewish congregations were Reform); and sponsorship of Jewish welfare institutions. The first represented, to no small degree, an expression of middle-class propriety. The emphasis on prestigious externals bears this out: elaborate temple construction and the engagement of distinguished and well-paid rabbis contrasted sharply with an indifferent attendance at services and the paltry religious training offered the young. But membership in a temple was also an affirmation of Jewish identity, though in a manner intended to encourage integration in the wider community. Thus Reform Judaism inveighed against the "insularity" and "obscurantism" of the Orthodox regimen: the ancient ordinances were anachronistic and irrational; the notion of an exiled people awaiting redemption was false, if not dangerous. Probably with the Orthodox, Yiddish-speaking immigrants in mind, Kaufmann Kohler, minister of New York's Temple Beth El, asserted:

Judaism must drop its orientalism, and become truly American in spirit and form. . . . It will not do to offer our prayers in a tongue which only few scholars nowadays understand. We cannot afford any longer to pray for a return to Jerusalem. It is a blasphemy and lie upon the lips of every American Jew.[7]

Reform congregations conducted themselves as members of a religious denomination, in tone and form modeled upon liberal Protestantism. But Reform did all this, at least in theory, in the name of the authentic teachings of Judaism. Reform ministers exhorted their congregants to do good works and live uprightly. These were universal ideals, and conventional aphorisms, which bound good men of all faiths and placed preacher and congregation in the American mainstream.

More than any other institution, Temple Emanuel represented the older community's conception of the ultimate achievement of Judaism in America. When it moved to its new building on Fifth Avenue and Forty-third Street, the *Times* hailed the congregation as "the first to stand forward before the world and proclaim the dominion of reason over blind and bigoted faith." In the 1900s, its membership, celebrated for its wealth and public service, elected boards of trustees which regularly included banker James Seligman as president; Louis Stern, of department-store fame; Emanuel Lehman, a senior partner in the Lehman Brothers brokerage firm; Daniel Guggenheim, head of the American Smelting and Refining Corporation; and Louis Marshall (in 1916, Marshall succeeded Seligman as president). For the immigrants of the lower East Side, Emanuel and its Jews personified "uptown"—the territory of the wealthy and the Americanized. Their own "downtown" domain formed the other camp of a polarized New York Jewry.[8]

Philanthropy provided a useful, less problematical, and more congenial way of expressing one's Jewish ties. Patrician practice, moreover, commended it. These sentiments combined with a persistent sense of collective accountability for the group's dependents. The result was the creation, in the half century before 1900, of a number of large, efficient, and worthy institutions: general relief agencies, hospitals, old-age homes, orphan asylums, vocational training schools, and settlement houses. Prominent members of the community not only contributed handsomely to their support and attended the ceremonial gatherings, but they also served actively as directors. Mayer Lehman "consciously walked the wards" of Mount Sinai Hospital and "kept a vigilant eye on nurses and doctors." Jacob Schiff, for thirty-five years president of the Montefiore Home for Chronic Invalids, spent each Sunday morning at the home and knew all but the transient patients personally. In a similar fashion, Isidor Straus and Judge Samuel Greenbaum were identified with the Educational Alliance; Morris Loeb, son of Solomon Loeb, a founder of Kuhn, Loeb and Company investment bankers, with the Hebrew Technical Institute; and George Blumenthal, senior partner of the banking house of Lazard Freres, with Mount Sinai Hospital.

These welfare establishments, like the temples, were staunchly autonomous. A coterie of sponsors closely controlled each institution, a majority of whom opposed all efforts at collaboration. Beginning in 1895, agencies coordinating fund-raising activities (the charity federation movement) had proven their worth in a number of cities. In

New York, however, more than twenty years elapsed before the opposition of the larger institutions was completely overcome. Nevertheless, an informal liaison existed among the leaders of philanthropy. They belonged to the same German-Jewish social clubs and temples and met one another at meetings of the boards of directors of their philanthropies. Ties of marriage among the children of the elite further strengthened the group. The older settlement, moreover, had its dominant figure—Jacob Schiff, head of Kuhn, Loeb and Company.[9]

By the early years of the 1900s, Schiff had won his fame as a railroad organizer who had challenged J. P. Morgan, an international banker who refused loans to czarist Russia, and a power in the Republican Party and counselor to its leaders. His munificence toward a wide range of educational institutions and civic causes enhanced his influence. Morris D. Waldman, a young social worker at the time, recalled Schiff's standing in the Jewish community:

His appearance at a board meeting invariably caused a quiet stir and a sudden hush in conversation in deference not merely to his great wealth . . . but rather because of an aristocratic quality in his personality that palpably, yet subtly, distinguished him and, in a manner, separated him from them.

Schiff's warm attachment to Jewish learning and tradition, his own religious education in the Orthodox community of Frankfurt-am-Main, and a lineage that included rabbinical scholars and communal leaders, added a further dimension to his stature in the eyes of the Russian Jews. Schiff was the foremost figure of both communities.[10]

Uptown's charities reflected the receptivity of the established leadership to the social currents of the time no less than did its temples. Scientific philanthropy, with its condemnation of "open-handed but indiscriminate alms-giving," its insistence on the thorough investigation of the needy applicant, and its sociological view of poverty, also affected Jewish welfare work. The attention paid to administrative efficiency, the professionalization of welfare services, and the growing support of "preventive social work" (broadly based social reform)—these were other features borrowed from the general field of philanthropy.

In practice this progressive stance generated conflicting institutional policies. Some uptown philanthropists encouraged the communal, self-help endeavors of the affected public (i.e., downtown's Russian Jews). They assisted such immigrant-supported bodies as the Hebrew Sheltering and Immigrant Aid Society and the Hebrew Free Loan Society. They permitted the United Hebrew Charities to experiment with local participation in the management of specially organized district offices. The same line of thought led some uptown leaders to endorse the aims of the Jewish labor movement. However, there were also those who stressed other nuances of progressive social work philosophy. They condemned the inefficiency of duplicating organizations and the substandard services provided by the small and unprofessional immigrant bodies. Such establishments, these uptown critics claimed, merely perpetuated ghetto self-segregation and the concomitant vices of radicalism and Orthodoxy by handing the tutelage of the immigrants to the immigrants themselves.[11]

Both approaches represented, in fact, different expedients for achieving the identical goal: creating social controls to assure the efficient and unobtrusive integration of the newcomers. What the Americanized leadership would have to learn, however—and the Kehillah episode was part of this education—was that its frame of reference for dealing with downtown was unsuitable. The size of the immigrant settlement, its store of communal experience, its proud intelligentsia and independent temper of mind, severely limited the efficacy of uptown philanthropy and its oligarchic system.

In less than a generation the East European migration had produced a demographic and communal upheaval. It had transformed a fairly homogeneous community into a vast, volatile, and multifarious public. In 1880, Jews of German stock formed the majority of Greater New York's Jewish population of 85,000. Twenty years later they made up about a fifth of the city's half million Jews. By 1914, when the Jewish population had risen to 1,335,000, the German Jewish stock represented some 10 percent of the total. For seven of the eleven years which preceded the outbreak of World War I, over 100,000 Jews arrived annually from Eastern Europe. Those who remained in New York—and they may have been as many as 70 percent of the arrivals—poured into the Jewish immigrant districts of the city and most of all into the lower East Side, the preeminent Jewish quarter. In 1910, that area reached a peak of 542,061 inhabitants.[12]

By that time, the Jewish quarter had become, in a number of respects, a self-contained enclave. In the economic realm, the clothing industry bulked large as the single major source of employment for the immigrant Jews. The minute division of labor (which permitted the semiskilled and the unskilled to enter the industry), the proximity of the shops to the Jewish quarter (in 1900, 79.8 percent of the industry was located below Fourteenth Street), and their ethnic homogeneity, turned the needle trades into the most accessible field of employment. Workers were typically employed in small factory units or in the "outside shops" where contractors and subcontractors processed the cut garments received from the manufacturer. In 1913, the 16,552 factories in New York City's clothing industry employed an average of 18.8 workers per factory. In the important men's tailoring branch, however, 78 percent of the shops averaged five employees each. Though the contractor frequently fared no better than his worker, and the small manufacturer waged a relentless struggle to survive in a highly competitive industry, the apparel trades beckoned to the immigrant with ambitions to become an independent entrepreneur. As early as the 1890s, the industry began to pass from the hands of the German-Jewish manufacturer to those of the Russian Jew, a process which paralleled the rise of the contractor and the small manufacturer.[13]

This "Jewish economy" included other principal areas of activity. Branches of the food-processing industry—like baking and the slaughtering and dressing of meat—were "Jewish industries" due to the ritual requirements of kashruth. Cigar-making and the building trades also drew high concentrations of Russian-Jewish labor. In addition, a host of Yiddish-speaking professionals, merchants, and petty tradesmen made their living in the Jewish quarter. In 1907, one scholar estimates, 200 physicians, 115 pharmacists, and 175 dentists served downtown's Jews. The most densely populated Assembly District of the lower East Side, the Eighth, in 1899, numbered among its businesses

140 groceries, 131 butcher shops, 62 candy stores, and 36 bakeries. Isaac M. Rubinow, physician, economist, and statistician wrote in 1905 of the recent growth of "Russian Jewish fortunes in New York," many of which ranged between $25,000 and $200,000. "Almost every newly arrived Russian-Jewish laborer comes into contact with a Russian-Jewish employer, almost every Russian-Jewish tenement dweller must pay his exorbitant rent to a Russian-Jewish landlord." [14]

The Jewish trade union movement, which these laborers created, occupied an ambivalent position in the communal life of the quarter. Its most notable figures considered the Jewish East Side as one sector of the world struggle with capitalism. Most of the movement's leadership had broken with the traditional community in Europe and embraced the revolutionary doctrines of Russian radicalism. It now applied the idiom of class war and of anticlericalism to Jewish communal life. Jewish workers, the rhetoric went, had nothing in common with uptown philanthropists, who used charity and Americanization to silence social protest; nor could immigrant workers properly enter the conventional life of the Jewish quarter. Synagogues and lodges, the leadership declared, were irrelevant, wasteful, and a plaything for those seeking prestige and power. They were dominated by the class enemy—the very bosses against whom the unions struck with such passion. Moreover, the respected place accorded Zionism provided further indication of the gulf separating socialist and community. Nationalistic pipe-dreaming, they charged, flouted the cosmopolitan ideal and turned the heads of the Jewish public from the vital issue. To a considerable extent, then, the labor movement formed a community unto itself. By the early years of the 1900s it had created, in addition to its trade unions, a fraternal order (the Arbeiter Ring), an influential press (the Yiddish daily, the Forward, was the outstanding example), and a political platform (the downtown Socialist Party).[15]

Despite its cosmopolitanism and class-war vocabulary, the Jewish labor movement did not secede from the ethnic community. Language, a common past, present domicile, and group interests tied it to the larger public. The Forward differed little with its three competing dailies, one radical-nationalist and two Orthodox, in condemning manifestations of anti-Semitism, efforts to restrict immigration, and czarist ruthlessness. In its eagerness to increase its circulation, the *Forward* appealed to a broad ethnic public, and in succeeding, it played a major role in encouraging Yiddish letters. Moreover, the tactics of the Jewish labor movement presumed the existence of a bedrock of ethnic unity. When the trade unions called their strikes, they appealed for assistance to the good will of the entire community, a call which touched upon traditional charitable instincts. The unions, furthermore, accepted the mediation offered by uptown Jews in settling with the downtown manufacturers. Finally, as in the European kehillah, an indeterminate, but probably a considerable, number participated in the institutional life of both communities.

Ethnic attachments, then, operated even upon those who considered them harmful and passé. Indeed, the most pervasive force in the institutional life of the quarter was the *landsmanshaft*, the society of townsmen. In a census of Jewish organizations conducted in 1917, of 3,600 enumerated, 1,000 called themselves by the name of some locality in Eastern Europe. The glut of small associations bearing the town and regional names of emigration mirrored the poignant but parochial loyalties of the newcomers. Nostalgia for the town only recently left behind was coupled with a desire to assist newly arrived old neighbors.

These town loyalties reflected, as well, sectional variations of some moment. Galicians, Lithuanians, Ukranians, Poles, and Rumanians spoke Yiddish with different dialects and diverged from one another in minor matters of ritual and religious emphasis. Though the distinctions carried little substantive importance, they were nevertheless meaningful. In the initial adjustment to the shock of loneliness (even in a Yiddish-speaking quarter), the newcomers sought out the remnant of town and region.

The vast majority of the 326 permanent congregations which existed on the lower East Side in 1907 were *landsmanshaft* synagogues (by 1917, an additional 96 had been founded). Writing about them in 1905, Louis Lipsky described the downtown synagogues as "really institutional churches." They were actually microcosms, as far as conditions permitted, of the old kehillahs. Synagogues sponsored associations which owned burial plots or provided small funds for the needy or supported religious schools. If affluent enough the congregation supported a rabbi. Invariably he came from the old town or region.

The *landsmanshaft* principle carried well beyond the synagogue. The mutual aid societies, which provided sick and death benefits, were essentially associations of fellow townsmen. When these groups affiliated with a national fraternal order they generally retained their *landsmanshaft* identity and not even the socialist Arbeiter Ring significantly altered the pattern. The *landsmanshaft* motif also appeared in the economic life of the ghetto. The contractor or clothing manufacturer recruiting his workers from among the arrivals from the old town was a well-known feature of the industry. Whole branches of the apparel trades were identified with particular towns of Eastern Europe.[16]

The Americanized Jews observed this downtown world and were appalled at the jangle of provincial loyalties, religious "medievalism," and strident radicalism. To nativists its bizarreness personified the menace posed by the new breed of immigrants. Since the American public failed at times to discriminate between old-stock American Jews and new, the conspicuousness of the ghetto threatened the established settlement. Willy-nilly, the latter was becoming the upper stratum of the former. However, alongside the aversion for the immigrants as outlandish and perhaps unassimilable, there also existed pity for the victims of oppression. A number of uptowners went further and indicated their admiration for the dynamism of the ghetto. (Sympathetic gentile journalists, like Hutchins Hapgood and Lincoln Steffens, may have taught them this.) The immigrant's thirst for education was a byword. Progressives praised his political independence. Even the older generation's affecting loyalty to the tradition found its sympathetic observers. Thus ambivalence marked uptown's relationship to the Russian Jew: imperiousness coincided with compassion, disdain with engagement.[17]

The deterioration of conditions in Russia beginning in 1903, exemplified by the Kishinev pogrom, produced wide discussion of the need for more formal communal coordination. The precipitous rise in immigration, political activity in support of the Jews in Russia, and the raising of large funds on their behalf, dominated the interests of the Jewish public. Different elements of the community came together in ad hoc committees, protest meetings, and joint enterprises. A climate of mutual concern softened, for the moment, intergroup animosities. It led also to the creation in 1906 of a national body, the American Jewish Committee (AJC), among whose founders were the leaders of New York's German-Jewish group: Jacob Schiff, Oscar Straus, and Louis Marshall.

The negotiations and the public debate which accompanied them underscored both the durability of the elitist-populist, uptown-downtown syndrome, and the recognition of the need for a regulatory body. Only when the more liberal element among the notables—represented by Marshall, who favored a limited representative structure —retreated and agreed that the organization be established on a self-appointed basis and as a self-perpetuating body was a split avoided. The prestige and wisdom of its membership, men like Adolph Kraus and Oscar Straus held, was its mandate to act on behalf of American Jewry. In the press, the alternative proposal of a Jewish congress was debated. Indeed, the fear that others would create a popularly led body and preempt the field served as a major consideration in the establishment of the AJC. The leadership of the AJC was, nevertheless, sensitive to the cry of plutocracy levied against it. Marshall, in particular, continued to press for an arrangement which would broaden the base of the AJC and tie it to local constituencies.[18]

The quest for new institutional forms and strategies affected different sectors of the New York community itself. In 1907, the Council for Jewish Communal Institutions was established. It consisted of eleven of the largest philanthropic agencies in the city, ten of whom belonged to the uptown community. The Council acted merely as an advisory body to consider the "mutual betterment in methods and economies of administration." In the event of conditions arising "not cognizable by existing organizations," it undertook to recommend "ways and means" of dealing with the situation. Despite its very limited powers, the Council did represent a departure of sorts from institutional isolationism. The years between 1903 and 1908 witnessed, furthermore, the organization of three federations of landsman-shaftn: the Rumanian, Galician, and Russian-Polish groups. During this period, the Federation of Jewish Organizations was founded as well. It drew its support from the downtown community and operated primarily as a lobby group fighting immigration restriction.

There were also signs just before 1903 that uptown Jews were prepared to employ new approaches in dealing with the immigrant community. In 1901, Jacob Schiff, his son-in-law, Felix M. Warburg, Daniel Guggenheim, and Louis Marshall, among others, undertook to sponsor the reorganization of the Jewish Theological Seminary. The institution, it was hoped, would attract young Russian Jews and prepare them to be rabbis, faithful to the tradition yet leaders in the Americanization of the immigrant. Solomon Schechter—theologian and reader of rabbinics at Cambridge—was invited to head the Seminary and attract the young scholars deserting East Side Orthodoxy. In 1902, Louis Marshall experimented with a Yiddish newspaper in an effort to encourage a "responsible" press. Even the Educational Alliance, the German Jews' foremost Americanizing agency on the East Side, softened its antipathy to Yiddish culture about this time in an attempt to reach its constituents more effectively.[19]

A mediating force of another sort was the cultural Zionists. They called for the unification of the community as a desirable end in itself. As nationalists, they considered the preservation of the Jewish collectivity a value transcending in importance all particularistic conceptions of Judaism. This approach endowed them with a latitudinarianism which enabled them to treat sympathetically with the full range of groups and movements. Judah Magnes, associate rabbi of Tempel Emanuel and secretary of the Federation of American Zionists, best articulated this stand. Another forceful exponent of this approach was Israel Friedlaender, a professor of biblical literature at the Jewish Theological Seminary.

Apathy for the ethnic heritage so pervasive among the children of the immigrants deeply distressed both men. The group's survival, they held, depended upon a cultural revival. In this analysis, they were deeply moved by the views of Ahad Ha'am, the Russian Zionist, Hebraist, and publicist. Ahad Ha'am placed his version of Zionism in apposition to Theodor Herzl's political construction. For the Herzlians, anti-Semitism constituted the central problem to be confronted, and a Jewish state was the one honorable solution. The Ahad

Ha'amists placed the cultural predicament of the Jews at the heart of the debate. Assimilation loomed as the great danger. This description, to Magnes' and Friedlaender's minds, fit the American situation. Ahad Ha'am's nationalistic emphasis on the Hebrew language as preserver of the Jewish people and its spiritual values, and his concept of a Palestine center which would assist the Diaspora in its educational and cultural tasks, seemed relevant indeed. Only so inspired and so aided, Magnes and Friedlaender believed, would the forces arise to combat the cultural impoverishment of the community and assure its continuity.[20]

Thus before the actual proposal was made to create a unified and democratic communal polity, trends and attitudes were current which lent themselves to this end. Uptown Jews were seeking better ways to stem the social disorganization and expedite the integration of the immigrants. The Kehillah could be presented to them as a progressive philanthropic device or as a necessary cooption to their councils of downtown's responsible leadership. The immigrant Jews were bewildered by the communal anarchy and by the ineffectualness of their own traditional institutions. They would respond to the prospect of order, recognition, and financial assistance. Overburdened communal elders from all camps, observing the rising curve of immigration, would be receptive to a plea for a rational division of labor. Finally, a group of young intellectuals—influenced by Jewish national ideas and American progressive notions—were prepared to use these trends and communal developments in a grand experiment which would be meaningful for the Jewish group and American society at large.

The catalyst which brought these interests together in the fall of 1908 originated in a statement by a high city official that the crime rate among immigrant Jews far exceeded that of other groups. For the uptown leaders, the statistic, though exaggerated, confirmed their long-standing criticism of the East Side: delinquency was rising, a grim indication of the presence of moral dissolution. Sensitive downtown Jewry read the statement as bald anti-Semitism, a blot upon their name. The incident produced a virulent debate within the community over the course of Jewish communal life and prepared the ground for the emergence of the Kehillah movement.

CHAPTER TWO

The Emergence of the Kehillah Movement

O N SEPTEMBER 1, 1908, EVERY YIDDISH DAILY NEWSPAPER FEA-
tured the claim of New York's Police Commissioner
Theodore A. Bingham, that 50 percent of the criminal
classes in New York City were Jews.[1] The allegations appeared in the September issue of the *North American Review* in an
article entitled "Foreign Criminals in New York." The commissioner
wrote:

It is not astonishing that with a million Hebrews, mostly Russian, in the
city (one-quarter of the population) perhaps half of the criminals should
be of that race when we consider that ignorance of the language, more
particularly among men not physically fit for hard labor, is conducive to
crime. . . . They are burglars, firebugs, pickpockets and highway rob-
bers—when they have the courage; but though all crime is their province,
pocket-picking is the one to which they take most naturally. . . . Among
the most expert of all the street thieves are Hebrew boys under sixteen
who are brought up to lives of crime. . . . The juvenile Hebrew emu-
lates the adult in the matter of crime percentage.[2]

The high office the author held, the reputability of the publication,
and the statistical data invested the article with an aura of objectiv-
ity and authority. Its reverberations reached beyond the pale
of Jewish interest. The metropolitan press gave prominent coverage to

the article and to the barrage of counterstatements that followed.[3] Mayor George B. McClellan later recalled the "storm of indignation" that followed the police commissioner's "outburst of injustice" and which made necessary his own intervention. But it was from the accused, the outraged immigrant Jews of the East Side whose self-image as a law-abiding element in the city had been impugned, that the most tumultuous response came.[4]

The Yiddish press directed and colored that response by portraying the incident as a grave threat to the well-being of the community. The theme which it emphasized of attack from without and ineffectualness from within lent itself to the hyperbolizing of fiercely competitive newspapers which were divided on most issues by conflicting outlooks and by publishers eager for communal power.

All four dailies, then—the Orthodox and nationalistic *Tageblat*, the *Morgen Journal*, Orthodox but anti-Zionist and conservative on social issues, the radical and nationalistic *Warheit*, and the socialist *Forward*—branded the commissioner an anti-Semite and his article a fabrication. Never before, the *Tageblat* wrote, had the Jews of America suffered such an affront. Still more, the Bingham calumny would become grist in the mills of immigration restrictionists in America and of the czar's Black Hundred in Russia. Nothing less than the future of the Jews in America was at stake, the *Tageblat* and *Warheit* wrote, and an ineffective rebuttal would be tantamount to an admission of guilt. The circumstances brooked no delay.[5]   The ensuing parade of spokesmen, each appearing on behalf of the maligned Jews, coupled with the duplication in calls for conferences and protest meetings, confirmed the Yiddish press' worst premonitions of disunity. In the span of two weeks following the appearance of the Bingham article, sixteen prominent communal leaders issued statements to the press. Each leader offered his own statistical or polemical refutation of the Bingham charge, taking little notice of evidence or arguments already marshaled.[6] When a group of East Side functionaries convened on September 5, one of the two resolutions passed with much fanfare called for a thorough statistical study of Jewish criminality in New York.[7]

The champions of unity behaved no differently. The publishers of the very *Tageblat* which denounced the anarchy in Jewish communal affairs and repudiated the "self-appointed spokesmen" addressed the mayor in a private communication on behalf of "the tremendous [Jewish] population of New York" since "unfortunately there is no central organization that can talk or act" for them.[8] Nor did the Federation of Jewish Organizations—a name indicative of the body's aspirations rather than its substance—hesitate to dispatch a delegation to meet Bingham. For good measure, the Federation sponsored a public protest meeting where speakers demanded Bingham's resignation and urged a march on City Hall.[9]

In reporting the conflicting tactics and the ineptitude of the community's functionaries, the Yiddish press disregarded one strong bid for leadership. Of all the spokesmen who entered the lists against Bingham, Edward Lauterbach's public performance was the most fiery and best prepared. An "apparition of know-nothingness" is how he labeled Bingham's article at a press conference held the day following its appearance. "The leaders and protectors of Jewish interests," he announced, were preparing a plan "to check the mad career of a man who clothed with police authority makes random statements derogatory to a race . . . that is both thrifty and orderly." Lauterbach countered the commissioner's allegations with conclusions drawn from a detailed statistical analysis of Jewish crime. Months before, he had prudently initiated the study. Sponsored by the Council of Jewish Communal Institutions, the findings had appeared in the journal of the Federation of Jewish Organizations.[10] Lauterbach served as a director of both groups. His organizational credentials also included the presidency of the National Liberal Immigration League, an important pressure group fighting immigration restriction, and membership in the prestigious American Jewish Committee (AJC). The Committee, formed by the notables of the older, German-Jewish community, had preempted the field of Jewish defense work. Success as a corporation lawyer and prominence in state Republican affairs further enhanced Lauterbach's stature.[11] Here, then, were the qualities of leadership which the East Side critics demanded: bold rhetoric, farsightedness, aggressive tactics, and social standing. Yet the Yiddish press, the committees, and the conferences ignored Lauterbach's bid for a central role in mobilizing the community. Despite all his credentials, the East Side leaders knew that others occupied the principal seats of power.

Instead, the Yiddish press chided Louis Marshall and Jacob Schiff and the AJC, which the two men dominated, for what it chose to regard as their inexcusable passivity. In so doing, the journalists tacitly acknowledged the informal but nonetheless recognized hegemony of Marshall and Schiff in the direction of Jewish affairs. Unable to reply effectively in its own behalf, the immigrant community admitted its dependence on the "men of influence" whose motives it suspected and whose approach it questioned. At the same time that journalists berated the AJC circles as assimilationist, timid, and disdainful of the immigrant Jews, they called for their aid. "When someone refused to allow a [Jewish] aristocrat into a Gentile hotel," the *Tageblat* recalled, "the Jewish four hundred did not rest until the guilty party had been dismissed; and now——they are quiet! Is it because the ones insulted are Russian Jews?" Even the *Maccabaean*, the journal of the Federation of American Zionists, which had long challenged the right of the AJC to speak in the name of American Jewry, rebuked the Committee for lack of initiative. "The matter [of the Bingham affair] was clearly one which the American Jewish Committee should have taken up," the *Maccabaean* wrote, "but from all public sources of information it does not appear that the Committee considered it." [12]

It is in this context that we may understand the tone of rancor and self-flagellation which dominated the Yiddish press. The *Tageblat* and *Warheit*, in particular, combined with their acrimonious appraisal of the behavior of "the magnates" a scathing analysis of the disorganization among the immigrant masses. Turning to the "great mass of immigrant Jews," the *Warheit* editorialized: "And we, what have we done . . . so that we will be reckoned with and respected . . . so that in such situations we can protect ourselves . . . ?" The *Tageblat* commented in the same vein: "We have a million Jews in New York. Where is their power? Where is their organization? Where are their representatives?" Societies and associations of every description existed among the Jews of New York, the paper continued, but in the moment of crisis their voices went unheeded. Unable to claim any considerable following, these self-constituted committees and self-appointed spokesmen were ineffective. Furthermore, many were calloused to the immigrant Jew's feelings. A unified community of the million Jews of New York could alone marshal the moral force to undo the mischief.[13]

As the days passed in early September, with no public retraction by Bingham, the *Tageblat* and *Warheit* pitched their editorials on a more strident key. A raucous dialogue now developed with the uptown circles, who expressed their dissatisfaction with the frenzied protest activity on the East Side and the inflammatory role of the Yiddish press. New York's most prominent Anglo-Jewish weekly, the *American Hebrew*, in its initial reaction castigated the police commissioner for injecting "venom and prejudice" into his discussion when speaking of the Jews.[14] A week later a second editorial, under the caption "Jewish Sensitiveness," found the commotion over Bingham's statement uncalled for.

The cry goes up to heaven from all quarters that a serious insult has been put upon the Jews of New York, and some hotheads are even clamoring for the removal of the Commissioner. . . . The whole incident illustrates the excessive sensitiveness of Jews with regard to any statments derogatory to their highest claim. So many of them have passed their lives under the withering fact of repression, that in this land of liberty they tend to go to the other extreme and insist upon the right of freedom with undue emphasis.[15]

The indignant reply came quickly. "The *American Hebrew*," the *Tageblat* charged, "organ of the Jewish four-hundred," attacked the hotheads of the East Side and soft-pedaled Bingham. "Is this the Torah of Americanism which you teach us," the *Tageblat* asked. "Instead of teaching us to be proud citizens . . . of the land of freedom, you preach the old Torah of fawning, to bend the back quietly and be still." If the Jews should win this struggle with Bingham, the editorial continued, credit would be due not to the Jewish "magnates," but to the feeling of protest which swept the East Side.

Our magnates were cold to the entire question. They were more unhappy about our agitation against Bingham than over the insult Bingham so crudely flung at the Jews. . . . The purpose of this editorial is . . .

to arouse the great Jewish public. . . . We cannot be dependent on our grand moguls.[16]

The *Morgen Journal*, alone among the Yiddish dailies, took no part in berating the Committee. Bingham posed no threat that could not be met with authoritative statistics and a calm head, the *Morgen Journal* asserted. The real menace lay in the bombastic behavior of the Jewish demagogues thirsting for attention, whose rantings had grossly inflated the incident and provided the English press with daily copy that did the Jews no good. As the conservative newspaper of the Jewish quarter, the *Morgen Journal* echoed the position of the *American Hebrew*. Yet it, too, lamented the lack of a bona fide spokesman for the immigrant Jews.[17]

Opportunistic East Side journalists may well have overdrawn the issue and exaggerated the extent of disunity. Nevertheless, the agitation for effective community action was pervasive enough to prompt the first steps in the experiment in ethnic community organization which culminated in the Kehillah.

On September 3 the Jewish League, a group of young professionals affiliated with the Federation of American Zionists, met to discuss Bingham's allegations. The League appointed a committee to press Bingham for a public retraction and resolved, as well, to issue a call for a protest meeting. The decisions, thus far, were typical of similar ones independently arrived at by other societies. The following day, however, Joseph Barondess, the one-time labor leader and Socialist candidate for Congress, recently turned Zionist and popular figure in East Side communal affairs, persuaded the League to reverse its position. Barondess' suggestion was accepted: the establishment of a "nonpartisan preliminary committee" which would immediately convene a "conference to consist, as far as possible, of gentlemen representing different shades of opinion of the Jews of Greater New York." Dr. David Blaustein, superintendent of the Educational Alliance, was selected chairman and charged with implementing the program for broader community consultation. As head of the great community center of the East Side sponsored by uptown philanthropists,

Blaustein served as a link between the immigrant quarter and its benefactors.[18]

Those invited represented the full range of Jewish opinion. They included public figures identified with the uptown community, office-holders from East Side constituencies, heads of fraternal orders and *landsmanshaftn*, the Zionists and Jewish socialists, and the editors of the Yiddish press. On September 5, barely two days after the League's original decision for unilateral action, about a hundred persons gathered at Clinton Hall on the East Side. None of the uptown notables, all members of the AJC, attended. Absent, too, was Abraham Cahan, the editor of the *Forward* and the leading Jewish socialist. Nor did the representatives of the conservative *Morgen Journal* attend.[19] Thus the conference represented a broad, middle grouping of the Jewish organizational spectrum, an East Side affair with the conspicuous absence of the socialists. Yet to have achieved this much was an auspicious beginning.

Two views dominated the discussion. On the one hand, some delegates considered an alliance with uptown leaders, who had failed to attend the conference, as indispensable for effective action. The gravity of the situation, they hoped, would induce the distinguished men of the AJC to join with the East Side in a common stand. Hence any program liable to offend the AJC—and nearly all schemes for a permanent and representative central agency would—had to be avoided. But others, the Zionists in particular, believed that the circumstances demanded sweeping changes in the conduct of communal affairs. Given this unprecedented forum, the moment seemed propitious to press views heretofore indifferently received: proposals for a comprehensive, popular, community structure.[20]

In the name of unity and communal stability, Barondess attempted to reconcile these positions. His plan called for an association operating "in cooperation and in unison with the American Jewish Committee" enabling "it to speak authoritatively in the name of the organized Jews of Greater New York." Supported by the Zionists and the benevolent orders, Barondess proposed a series of conferences, each conference to encompass representatives of a different sector of the community. The various conferences were to elect delegates to a central body, which would appoint an executive committee "to work in conjunction with the American Jewish Committee." [21] In essence, Barondess projected a federation of the Russian Jewish immigrants and the elevation of their representatives to partnership, albeit a junior partnership, with the Americanized German-Jewish group in directing Jewish communal affairs.

The resolution, however, failed by three votes. Opposing it were General Sessions Judge Otto Rosalsky, Congressman Henry Goldfogle, and Samuel Dorf, Grandmaster of the Order Brith Abraham, one of the country's largest fraternal orders. Pillars of downtown society, all three subscribed to the approach of the uptown worthies on public matters. The plan which the conference accepted, and which they supported, instructed the chairman to appoint a committee of five empowered, in turn, to name a larger committee. This larger committee was "to comprise all the different elements" of New York's Jews. Undoubtedly, the sponsors of the majority resolution hoped for its readier acceptance in AJC circles. The Warheit evidently had this in mind when it wrote approvingly that "this committee . . . will most likely include many German Jews." [22]

The plan adopted represented the more restricted and conservative approach to community organization which had guided the establishment of the AJC. That principle held that a number of respected individuals were best qualified to select those to be entrusted with the task of protecting Jewish interests. This approach assumed the impracticality of a fully representative and democratic association of Jewish organizations. Furthermore, it viewed such a broad-based association as undesirable in so far as it delivered to the "unassimilated, inexperienced, and undisciplined" immigrant Jew of the East Side the direction of Jewish affairs. Moreover, there existed an uneasiness that the public would misconstrue the establishment of an all-inclusive Jewish community organization, viewing it as an attempt to create a quasi-governmental structure. Thus the East Side conference, seeking acceptance by the AJC, followed the Committee's method in erecting its structure. [23]

Yet the proponents of a community comprehensive in scope and democratic in government had gained much. The existence of the conference itself, with its hundred delegates representing diverse views and submitting to democratic procedures, demonstrated the maturity and self-discipline of the downtown leaders and attested to the credibility of a program previously ridiculed as visionary. Moreover, those present fully understood the considerations which prompted Barondess and his supporters to abandon the more comprehensive plan. Barondess himself related: "I could see plainly that had my motion been carried, Rosalsky, Goldfogle and Dorf would have left the meeting entirely dissatisfied. For that reason I left the room when the vote was taken, and did what I could to have my own motion defeated." [24] Barondess and his side gained thereby goodwill and supporters for their proposals. Once the Bingham affair would be formally terminated and the ad hoc committee disbanded, the idea of a permanent organization would receive continued attention.[25]

On September 6, Blaustein announced the decision to appoint two committees, one to collect statistical data on Jewish criminality and the second to select a large committee to represent New York's Jews in the troublesome situation. The *Morgen Journal* greeted the announcement with an editorial, "Statistics Rather Than Shouting," and emphasized the need for experts who would gather evidence to prove to the "great non-Jewish world" that the police commissioner had lied. The *Warheit* saw in the conference and in the East Side uproar laudable consequences of the Bingham affair. The *Tageblat* praised the prospect of united action and of recognition by the "magnates." Only the socialist *Forward* maintained editorial silence.[26] Apparently—later it was to be stated explicitly—Abe Cahan's *Forward*, and the Jewish socialists in general, viewed the movement as a plot by clerics and philanthropists to dominate Jewish communal life.

Little more was heard from the designated committees. Blaustein, occupied with personal matters, failed to provide the necessary direction. Nor did the call for unity retain its hold long. Active participants at the conference soon became involved in separate endeavors.[27] The high hopes raised by the Clinton Hall conference, it now appeared, would come to nothing.

During the two and a half weeks of tumult, from September 1, when the issue of the *North American Review* appeared, until September 16, when Bingham issued his retraction, Marshall and Schiff refrained as long as possible from involvement in the affair. To Dr. Paul Abelson of the Educational Alliance staff, Schiff wrote from his summer home that he was unprepared to take part in a "public discussion of the question of Jewish criminality in New York." Debating the question at all was, in fact, "unwise for obvious reasons." Two days later, on September 8, Marshall made his position explicit to Dr. Adolph Radin, the Jewish prison chaplain. He opposed "sensational methods." However, "if you are entirely sure," he wrote, "that the figures you have are correct and cannot be successfully impugned or criticized, then . . . write a letter to the New York *Times*." It should be couched in "temperate language, without in any way indulging in personalities. A clear and pointed statement of facts would be much more effective and convincing than a tirade." [28]

In his letter to Radin, Marshall gave no indication of his intention to intervene, but by September 13 he had done so. The threat of "sensational methods" could no longer be ignored. Behind a flurry of rumors of discussions on the highest level, Marshall began confidential negotiations with Deputy Police Commissioner Arthur Woods. The peace terms formulated called for a public retraction by Bingham of his charge of excessive criminality and an explanation of how he "came to use the expression which has been criticized." Upon publication of the retraction a committee from the East Side would "make a statement to the effect that they accept the explanation of Mr. Bingham and that they regard the incident as closed." Finally, Marshall and Schiff would issue similar statements. The price, then, for Bingham's retraction was to be the cessation of the East Side's anti-Bingham campaign, which, after two weeks of agitation, resounded with demands for his resignation. The committee established at the Clinton Hall conference now offered the one prospect of curbing the East Side protest movement. But to activate the committee, and then to mediate between it and uptown, required the intervention of a personality who enjoyed the confidence of all sides. Dr. Judah L. Magnes, the popular young Reform rabbi, stepped in to fill this role. Negotiations with Commissioner Woods were completed, therefore, only after Marshall discussed the terms with Magnes and the committee and received their approval.[29] For the moment, at least, a de facto directorate representing both communities had been created.

On September 16 Commissioner Bingham returned to New York from his vacation and on the same day withdrew "the statement challenged, frankly and without reservation." The East Side committee —newspaper accounts now referred to it as "the Jewish Council"— promptly announced its willingness "to allow the incident between Commissioner Bingham and the Jews of New York to be regarded as closed." Louis Marshall expressed his approval of "the manly and courageous manner in which [Bingham] . . . acknowledged his error . . . His frank recognition that he had unwittingly wronged the Jewish people will be accepted by them in the same frank and manly spirit." [30] All parties to the agreement had acted in good faith and the incident was considered terminated.

In Jewish circles the gleeful reception of the retraction failed to still the mutual recriminations over the handling of the incident. The post-mortems focused on the question of community leadership and organization. In a letter to the *Tageblat*, Marshall broke his public silence by rebuking the Jewish quarter for a twofold sin. In the first place, it had evinced little gratitude for the service rendered by saner heads in extricating the downtown Jews from a plight partly of their own making. The publication of Bingham's retraction had produced better results than "a thousand mass meetings" might have. Indeed, "so-called Jewish magnates whose coolness you deprecate," and not "indignant hot-blooded men," had influenced the "dignified solution of an unpleasant episode." But second, and more important, Marshall continued, the immigrant community had not kept its house in order.

What has the great east side, with all of its protests, done to obviate and cure the existing evils, and to eradicate the causes which have led to juvenile delinquency. . . . We have cried because a corn has been trodden on, and we are entirely indifferent to the cancer which is gnawing at our vitals.[31]

Galled by the reprimand, the *Tageblat* assailed Marshall by justifying once again the East Side firebrands and their tactics. "Had we on the East Side remained silent and awaited salvation from on high,

Bingham would not have taken his words back. If our prominent Jews from the upper circles used their influence, it was due to the storm we raised on the East Side." [32]

Underlying the angry polemic was a felt need for alliance with the uptown Jews, even a recognition of dependence on "the magnates." But the public debate also laid bare the complex of tangled emotions which influenced the newcomers in their attitude to the Americanized settlers. Proud and self-assertive, on the one hand, immigrant leaders revealed the depths of their insecurity, on the other hand, by their aggressive demands for recognition and their sensitivity to criticism. Every Jew on the East Side, the *Tageblat* wrote, acknowledged the importance of a Schiff and a Marshall. "But we seek self-recognition," the paper continued. "We seek recognition for eight times a hundred thousand souls, for a hundred thousand voters, for thousands of doctors and lawyers and for tens of thousands of businessmen. We want to give our famous Jews their honored place" but "in the measure that they have earned it." The Jewish quarter had its failings, the *Tageblat* admitted. However, a central communal authority could alone correct them, and such an authority would succeed only if the notables "worked with us and not over us." [33]

Thus reluctantly uptown's Louis Marshall had interceded, goaded by a raucous and impatient Jewish quarter. He did so believing the delinquency charge to be partly true and rejecting what he considered to be the self-righteousness of the immigrant leaders. Circumstances subsequently necessitated finding responsible East Side men. In the process Marshall helped turn a paper committee into a "Jewish Council." When that East Side committee met to approve the Marshall–Woods agreement, it went even further. It voted to convene a meeting of "representative Jews of the city" on October 12 for the "purpose of forming a permanent organization to foster the interests of the Jews in every proper way." Below Marshall's statement in the *Times* appeared a manifesto by Magnes. He, too, saw the Bingham incident as closed. But, he went on: "The one million of Jews of New York should draw the proper deductions from this incident. They need a permanent and representative organization that may speak on their behalf, that may defend their rights and liberties and that may also cope with the problems of criminality." [34] Marshall's strictures in the *Tageblat* led as surely to the same conclusion. The Jewish quarter had to organize to cope with its problems. Leaders of the older Jewish community, eager to reform the immigrants and fearful of leaving so crucial an enterprise to the immigrants themselves, would inevitably be drawn into the undertaking.

The emergence of Judah Magnes as leader of the downtown committee was a propitious event in the campaign for a community organization. At thirty-one, Magnes stood at the top of a meteoric career. More than any other personality of his time, his interests and influence spanned the cultural, social, and ideological chasm of Jewish society. On the one hand, as rabbi of Temple Emanuel he ministered to a congregation which included such wealthy German-Jewish families as the Schiffs, Warburgs, Guggenheims, and Lewisohns. In the fall of 1908, when he became Louis Marshall's brother-in-law, marriage reinforced his connection with the Jewish elite. At the same time, Magnes served as secretary of the Federation of American Zionists, with its mainly immigrant constituency. Born in San Francisco, educated at Reform Judaism's Hebrew Union College in Cincinnati, Magnes went on to Berlin and Heidelberg to complete his graduate studies.[35] Spiritually, the young Reform rabbi found kindred souls in Professors Solomon Schechter and Israel Friedlaender of the conservative Jewish Theological Seminary. Yet the Yiddish intellectual milieu of the East Side, secular and radical, also attracted him. He established close rapport with such bearers of Jewish nationalist and socialist programs as the essayist Dr. Chaim Zhitlowsky and the Yiddish playwright David Pinski. Little troubled by ideological inconsistencies—on one occasion Schechter rapped him hard for representing the Zionists at a memorial meeting honoring the Russian revolutionary hero Gregory Gershuni—Magnes often attended Orthodox services in the tenement-house basement synagogue of a Hasidic congregation. Similarly, while heading a fund initiated by Socialists and Zionists to aid clandestine Jewish self-defense units in Russia, he participated in the establishment of the patrician American Jewish Committee.[36] Eclectic and pragmatic in temper, he eagerly confronted and tolerated the conflicting ideologies and causes which crowded the Jewish intellectual world of his time. This added to his stature as the candid and broadminded young leader and gave him entree to all circles.

To his public activities, Magnes also brought a magnetic presence —many considered him the outstanding Jewish preacher of his time —and a courage braced by dramatic personal triumphs. In a protest march against Russian pogroms in December, 1905, Magnes led 150,000 Jews from the East Side up Fifth Avenue, an audacious demonstration for the time and one that endeared him to the immigrant quarter. Soon after, New York's most staid temple called him to its pulpit. When a wealthy trustee of the temple approved his daughter converting and marrying out of the faith, Magnes used the pulpit to inveigh against intermarriage. The indignant trustee offered his resignation and the issue threatened to split the congregation. But Magnes won accolades from religiously indifferent radicals and a vote of confidence from the temple's board of trustees.[37] His downtown following was an asset in the eyes of the uptown community. His prestigious connections, on the other hand, served him well in his relations with the immigrant community.

Joseph Barondess therefore turned to a close associate when he reported to Magnes on September 8 the details of the Clinton Hall meeting.[38] Magnes immediately returned to the city to mediate between Marshall and the East Side committee in negotiating an end to the Bingham affair. Seizing upon the momentum generated by the affair, he bent his efforts to achieve a permanent coalition between the immigrant quarter and the Americanized Jews of uptown.

It was, consequently, not unexpected when Magnes' name headed the committee which signed the "Appeal to the Jewish Organizations of New York City" announcing a conference for October 11 and 12, 1908. The other signatories included the ubiquitous Barondess; Gedaliah Bublick, editor of the *Tageblat*; Bernard Semel, president of the largest *landsmanshaft* organization, the Federation of Galician and Buckovinian Jews; and Judge Otto Rosalsky, the most prominent Russian-Jewish officeholder.[39] These East Side celebrities, drawn from the mainstream of the quarter's communal life, together with Magnes' forceful leadership, conferred a sense of urgency and distinction upon the impending conference.

In less than two weeks, through the press and in thousands of Yiddish and English brochures, the Jewish public was informed of the provisory rules governing the selection of delegates. Fraternal orders, federations of societies, and rabbinical associations were allowed ten delegates each; and synagogues, schools, and independent organizations, one delegate each. The committee also printed a "preliminary draft" of a constitution for the new organization.[40] But a letter printed in the *Tageblat* and *American Hebrew*, rather than the brochure and proposed constitution, best expressed the strategy of Magnes and his associates.

Using as his point of departure Marshall's letter in the *Tageblat* rebuking the Jewish quarter, Magnes praised the tumult Marshall criticized. "I am proud . . . of the indignation of our Jews and of their readiness at their mass meetings . . . to resent insult. This is the way every healthy and manly people gives expression to its elemental emotions." (Readers of the *Tageblat* undoubtedly thrilled at the rhetoric.) However, was it not the best part of wisdom, Magnes asked, "to try to organize the Jews so that their mass meetings and their power . . . may be turned to the general good?" He next addressed the East Side and portrayed the mutual dependence of the two sections.

Mr. Marshall represents, in some measure, that section of the community with leadership and wealth. You, Mr. Editor, represent in some measure, that section of the community with our masses and our hopes. An army without leaders is almost as absurd as leaders without an army. The opportunity is now at hand for leaders and soldiers to recognize the need they have of each other and to join ranks.

(The metaphor probably reassured the young rabbi's uptown parishioners.) Thus far, Magnes went on, the establishment of the AJC represented the first effective step out of chaos. But with no "mandate from the people" its usefulness was restricted. The next move, therefore, required the organization of the "Great East Side." Only then, if the AJC would be "alive to its great duty of leadership," could it come "into direct touch with the Jewish masses" and be assured of a "united Jewry" at its back.[41]

Two hundred and fifty representatives of the "Great East Side" gathered at Clinton Hall on October 11 and 12 for two boisterous sessions, which the *American Hebrew* described as "turbulent, eloquent, bitter, sentimental, and quite often practical." Most observers agreed that the gathering enormously advanced the idea of community organization. Even the rejection of the planning committee's draft constitution redounded to the conference's credit. The incident was hailed as proof of the democratic nature of the proceedings. Instead of accepting the committee's assumption that attendance at the meeting implied acceptance of the community idea (and hence a constitution should be the first order of business), the participants called for a discussion of the basic question: was a central organization necessary? [42]

Behind the demand stood the Federation of Jewish Organizations claiming recognition as the already existing central agency. In its three years of existence the Federation had been concerned mainly with issues which threatened the position of the Jews. It had attacked the federal government's acquiescence to Russia's discriminatory practices against Jews holding American passports. It had also campaigned against the movement to restrict immigration. In both instances—as in the case of the Bingham affair—the Federation relied upon mass public agitation. Essentially a lobby group, it made little impression upon the Jewish community.

Informed people also understood that the AJC looked upon the Federation and its sister organization, the National Liberal Immigration League, as maverick organizations. The AJC operated in the same field, and the aggressive tactics of the Federation and the League irritated the Committee's leaders. In rejecting, therefore, the Federation's demand for recognition, delegates demonstrated their preference for a community organization whose primary thrust would be the improvement of the internal conditions of Jewish life. Repudiating the Federation's bid, moreover, advanced the chances of cooperation with the powerful AJC.[43]

But in seeking to improve the quality of Jewish life which canons would guide the organization on its way? Divided on fundamental beliefs, downtown Jewry included secularists who rejected synagogue affiliation as the criterion of group loyalty, or who declared nationality, not religion, to be the basis of group cohesion. At the second session, on October 12, a steering committee after long deliberation offered two propositions to the conference:

. . . the purpose of this organization shall be the formation of a representative community, or kehillah, of the Jews of New York City:

. . . it shall have represented within it the Jews of New York City, and shall act for them as necessity requires; and it may promote and foster such organizations, institutions etc., as will fulfill its purposes.[44]

The innocuous formulation deliberately evaded a commitment to any persuasion.

The effort to avoid controversy failed, however, when Dr. Bernard Drachman, an American-born Orthodox rabbi of one of the city's most affluent congregations, challenged the neutral formula. A declaration of principles which did not affirm "the protection and care of the . . . interests of the Jewish faith" as its central purpose, the rabbi stated, degraded Judaism. The conference was in an uproar. Dr. Henry Moskowitz, leader of the Ethical Culture Society's Madison House settlement, and Dr. Nachman Syrkin, the theoretician of Socialist Zionism, responded for the secularist camp. They proposed an amendment excluding all political and religious issues from the organization's program: the Kehillah was to devote itself to those interests of "the Jewish people that are national, cultural, social, economical, etc."[45]

The ensuing debate threatened to wreck the conference. But in a singular performance, Magnes, who chaired the session, mixed cajolery, righteous indignation, and ardor for the Kehillah idea to persuade the opposing sides to withdraw their amendments. He, too, felt that an affirmation of Jewish religion, in some form, should be included in the objects of a Jewish organization. But others had different conceptions of Jewish life and their views had to be respected. Furthermore, Magnes continued, the refusal to commit the organization on this point quite properly avoided a premature declaration of policy. "The evident desire of [the conference] leaders," the *Maccabaean* commented, "was to avoid dissension. Union first, dissension after, seemed to be the policy. Yet the important question was just this, what would the Kehillah do once organized?"[46] Eloquence and adroit parliamentary maneuvering had resolved the issue only for the moment.

Nevertheless, the conference and Magnes' handling of it received wide praise. The *Tageblat*, despite its religious orientation, commended the neutralist resolution. The right way, it said, was the middle way. To be successful, the Jewish community had to be tolerant enough to embrace all who would join. The Committee of Twenty-five, which Magnes was instructed to appoint as the interim executive body, reflected this hope. Represented were the major *landsmanshaft* groups and fraternal orders. Well-known Orthodox rabbis appeared on the list alongside of intellectuals of radical and nationalist views. Appointed, too, were the immigrant quarter's own philanthropists.[47] One influential group of the "Great East Side," the socialist-led Jewish labor movement and the closely associated fraternal order, the Arbeiter Ring, followed the lead of the *Forward* and ignored the conference. But the positive accomplishments were significant. A broad coalition had been formed, and the emphasis had changed from protest and defense to community building.

§ CHAPTER THREE §

The Founding Convention

I N THE MONTHS THAT FOLLOWED THE CLINTON HALL CONFERENCE of October, 1908, advocates of the Kehillah broadened their coalition and drafted a constitution in preparation for a founding convention. They intended the convention to serve as a ratifying assembly where representatives of the city's Jewish associations would adopt the proposed constitution and proclaim the establishment of a unified democratic community.

Constitution-making, culminating in the convention itself, provided the vehicle for a remarkable dialectical exercise. Eminent founders of the American Jewish Committee (AJC), representatives of Reform and Orthodox Judaism, builders of immigrant fraternal orders and followers of secular movements brought to the task strikingly different conceptions of American society, of Judaism and of the desired synthesis. They produced a compromise plan which potentially could draw upon impressive organizational and human resources. In the parlance of the day, a partnership between "uptown" and "downtown" was about to be established. Partisans of the Kehillah idea believed a new epoch in American Jewish life was at hand. Some even held that the experiment was pregnant with meaning for American society at large.

§

EVEN BEFORE THE OCTOBER CONFERENCE, MAGNES MOVED TO ESTABLISH
an alliance with the AJC. His request, however, that the Clinton
Hall meeting be placed on the agenda of the AJC executive committee was not acted upon. Nor did members of the AJC accept invita-
tions to attend the conference. Both Schiff and Marshall in letters addressed to the gathering struck a decidedly reserved note in warning
against hasty action.[1] But the success of the meeting and the fact
that Magnes emerged as the dominant figure undoubtedly made the
AJC leaders more amenable to overtures from the conference committee. Moreover, permanent association with New York's Jewish
masses through a Kehillah promised to allay the resentment harbored
against the AJC in Russian-Jewish circles.[2]

This hostility had existed from the AJC's beginnings. Critics berated it as a self-constituted and self-perpetuating body. They bela-
bored its imperious manner and beclouded its genuine accomplishments. The danger existed that its opponents would coalesce and,
drawing support from the immigrant quarter, challenge the AJC's
hegemony in Jewish affairs. At its inception two years before, Marshall had sponsored, unsuccessfully, a plan which would have created
a popular base for the Committee and allowed for more democratic
methods in the selection of its executive committee. Efforts to activate regional councils, each with the right to elect representatives to
the general committee of the AJC, indicated continued sensitivity to
the problem.[3] The proposal, therefore, to link the Kehillah to the
AJC appeared to coincide with the self-interest of both sides: the
Kehillah would become the AJC's New York district, deferring to it
in all national and international affairs while retaining its autonomy
in local matters. As Marshall put it: If the plan is adopted, more
than one third of the AJC would be selected by those "Jews of New
York who are affiliated with the Kehillah." The same individuals,
Marshall continued, would constitute the executive committee of the
Kehillah. They would thus be kept in constant touch with the affairs
of American Jewry, and with those of the Jews in all parts of the

world. Not only would "the Jewish Community of New York" be self-governing in all local matters, but it would "exercise a potent influence upon all matters of general interest coming within the jurisdiction of the American Jewish Committee." Marshall also held out the prospect that the AJC would similarly recognize other local community organizations and so continue the process of democratization. For the downtown leaders the expectation that the enormous prestige, wealth, and ability of the AJC people would be immediately committed to the success of the Kehillah carried most weight.[4]

By mid-November the Clinton Hall conference Committee of Twenty-five and the annual meeting of the general committee of the AJC had ratified the "Memorandum of Tentative Agreement" governing the relations between the two groups. A joint committee then undertook the task of drafting a constitution for presentation to a convention. In the course of four formal and innumerable informal meetings, from December to February, the final draft slowly took shape.[5] A number of articles dealt with the relations between the AJC and the Kehillah. Equally detailed were the sections on representation to the annual conventions. But of particular significance were those additions and changes made in the original draft. The first article, the declaration of purpose, led to a renewed consideration of the nature of Jewish group life. This touched off a discussion, no less fundamental, of the place of ethnic organizations within American society.

The first two drafts stated merely that "the purpose of the Jewish Community of New York City shall be to represent the Jews of New York City with respect to all local matters of Jewish interest." [6]

The joint committee obviously intended to pursue the middle course, sustained by the Clinton Hall conference, hoping to estrange neither the secular nor the religious camp. But at its final meeting ten days before the convention the clause was amended to read: "The purpose of the Jewish Community of New York City shall be to further the cause of Judaism in New York City, and to represent the Jews." [7]

"The cause of Judaism" was no mere editorial flourish. Dr. Samuel Schulman of the New York Board of Rabbis had proposed the amendment. His appearance at the final meeting followed a threat by the Board to boycott the Kehillah convention unless its representative was invited to discuss the Kehillah platform with the joint committee. For Rabbi Schulman and his colleagues on the Board (most of whom were Reform and Orthodox rabbis who served the older settlement), the original statement of purpose meant a surrender to the secularists. Reports circulated, moreover, that the new Kehillah would forswear all religious activity. In the final days before the convention, delegates of East Side Orthodox congregations caucused to denounce the aberration of a godless Kehillah. The Kehillah's sponsors had certainly intended to include the community's religious institutions within its purview. Pluralistic and pragmatic in outlook, they sought only to avoid damaging ideological debates. But in the intellectually charged climate of the times, Schulman's bland phrase read like a party tract. Nevertheless, it was incorporated into the proposed constitution, though a cry would now rise from the nonreligious circles.[8]

This insistence that the statement of purpose be given a religious turn stemmed not merely from the doctrinal earnestness (or pedantry) of men like Drachman and Schulman. It reflected as well a strand of anxiety which marked the public discussions of the Kehillah idea. Dr. David de Sola Pool, rabbi of the venerable Spanish and Portuguese Synagogue, expressed this feeling succinctly in a sermon delivered in December shortly after the joint committee began its deliberations. Pool warned against the attempt "being made to organize the Jewish community in New York on national, but not necessarily religious, lines—an attempt which would create an *imperium in imperio*." [9]

Others, sensitive to the foreign character of the Jewish population, sounded similar warnings. Only days before the October Clinton Hall conference, Rabbi Schulman had devoted his Yom Kippur sermon to the need for the projected community organization. Danger existed, he warned, "in prolonging any longer than absolutely necessary the features of a foreign colony in the midst of American life." Unification of the Russian Jews with German Reform elements would encourage the desired process. This was the task of a Kehillah, but:

there is only one basis of unity and representation and that is the synagogue. Both from the point of view of inner development and outward safety and welfare we cannot organize New York Jewry on the basis of race or nationality. We exist in the non-Jewish world only as a *Knesseth Yisrael*, a congregation of Israel.[10]

At the final meeting of the joint committee this uneasiness over the public image of the future Kehillah found expression. In addition to Schulman's recommendations for changing the declaration of purposes, Jacob Schiff offered articles barring "political organizations" from membership and prohibiting the Kehillah from engaging in "any propaganda of a partisan political character." (An earlier meeting had accepted an amendment requiring delegates to be American citizens.) [11]

The emphasis on religion as the single legitimate basis for ethnic organization imperiled the notion of a comprehensive communal structure, one that would encompass the multifarious Jewish public. To defend this maximal position it now became necessary to formulate a rationale which would locate the Kehillah idea in the mainstream of American life and Jewish belief. In a sermon delivered on February 13, 1909, two weeks before the founding convention, Magnes undertook the task.

Americanization—the integration of the immigrant into American society—was his point of departure. The injunction that the immigrant assume the obligation of citizenship, "understand the spirit of [America's] history . . . [and] saturate himself with the dominant culture of the land," Magnes accepted as axiomatic. He rejected, however, a second meaning often ascribed to Americanism which, though it recognized loyalty to religion, called on the immigrant to abandon his nationality. Politically, Magnes agreed, "a man can be a member of but one nation at one time." But "when I speak of nationality here I mean, in particular, such elements of nationality as man can carry with him when he leaves his old home—his national language, his culture, his history, his traditions, his customs, his ideals." [12]

Magnes justified retaining nationality in this sense on a number of counts. It would alleviate, in the first place, the psychic stresses and social disorganization caused by immigration. "The hiatus between the traditional national culture and the new surroundings" was often so great that it led to "degeneracy." Children of "minority nationalities all too frequently were "not the equals of their parents in those things that have permanent value, because the chain of tradition has been broken and the accumulated wisdom and beauty of ages is set at naught." Recognition of a pluralistic society as not only normative but durable and desirable would, then, open the way for coping with the reality of the new life.[13]

Such recognition, Magnes believed, also promised to enrich the quality of American life in general. Democracy tended "to level all distinctions, to create the average type, and almost to demand uniformity." These weaknesses might be overcome by "reason of a variegated national culture." America, not yet a finished product, would then "become like a garden of blossoms of many colors rather than a field of flowers of the same size and color." [14]

From general considerations, Magnes moved to specifically Jewish ones which, he argued, enjoined Jews to embrace this view of America. "With us nationality and religion are so inextricably interwoven that . . . to allow the cultivation of our Jewish nationality to fall into neglect or disrepute" would endanger Judaism.

Our religion has its national element of race, of language, of literature, of history, of law and custom and tradition. If, therefore, we be not careful to preserve these Jewish national possessions, the purely religious elements of our lives as Jews will suffer. . . For the Jew there cannot, I think, be a permanent Jewish religion without Jewish nationality, nor can there be, I think, a permanent Jewish nationality without Jewish religion.[15]

Finally, in his peroration, Magnes offered this dictum in justification of his pluralistic conception of American society.

America is not the melting pot. It is not the Moloch demanding the sacrifice of national individuality. America is a land conceived in liberty and dedicated to the principle that all men are created free and equal. And a national soul is as precious and as God-given as is the individual soul.[16]

What made Magnes' formulation less distressing to Americanized Jews than the classic Zionist position was his blending of religion and nationality and his eschewal of messianic political hopes. Thus the Magnes rhetoric contained enough religious nomenclature to soften the ethnic, separatist nuances. America, after all, condoned religious self-segregation.[17] Consequently, all but the most rabid adherents of classical Reform Judaism, who rejected Jewish nationality in any combination, could tolerate his philosophy of Kehillah.[18]

On January 28, 1909, the call for the constituent convention was released to the press. Two groups signed the text, the New York members of the AJC and the Clinton Hall conference committee. Besides the press release, the call was issued as a brochure and distributed as widely as possible. Communicating, however, with the estimated 3,500 Jewish organizations of the city was a prodigious task. No reliable roster of organizations existed. And furthermore, the newness of the undertaking entailed negotiating with societies and institutions and launching an extensive publicity campaign. For such a task, neither the time was available (only four weeks remained from press announcement to the scheduled date of the convention), nor the personnel.[19]

The convention call also outlined the basis of representation: synagogues with a membership up to 250, one delegate; federations of societies, one delegate for every ten branches; independent organizations, one delegate for the first one hundred members and an additional one for each increment of 1,500; professional societies of rabbis, cantors, social workers, and Jewish colleges, one delegate each. Only American citizens were eligible to serve as delegates.[20]

The opening session of the convention took place at the United Hebrew Charities building on February 27. Three hundred delegates representing 222 organizations attended. Magnes estimated that 500 groups were actually represented, since federations were allowed only one delegate for every ten branches. Represented were: 74 synagogues, 18 charitable societies, 42 mutual benefit societies, 40 lodges, 12 educational institutions, 9 Zionist societies, 9 federations, and 9 religious societies. The *Morgen Journal* reported with approval that "the radicals who led the way at Clinton Hall" had absented themselves from the convention's opening.[21] The Orthodox newspaper undoubtedly had in mind Nachman Syrkin, who was not a citizen, and Henry Moskowitz. The absence of the latter, in particular, indicated the shift in the potential constituency of the Kehillah which had taken place in the months between the Clinton Hall conference and the opening of the convention.

Moskowitz represented a secularist element which had no formal ties to Jewish institutional life. However, as a product of the East Side and a leading social worker in the Jewish quarter, he favored the Clinton Hall undertaking. All indigenous communal enterprises were to be blessed. Since the October meeting, however, the proposed Kehillah had moved towards a religious definition of its purposes. Moreover, it had established ties with the aristocratic AJC. Both facts probably displeased Moskowitz.[22]

And indeed, Magnes dealt at length with both developments in his opening address. The Committee of Twenty-five appointed by the Clinton Hall conference, Magnes explained, entered into negotiations with the AJC for three reasons. The AJC was established for purposes similar to those of the projected Kehillah. Second, the Clinton Hall meeting was representative of the downtown Jews, whereas the AJC consisted primarily of uptown Jews. Finally, the possibility existed of democratizing the AJC and turning it into a national body representing Jewish public opinion. Not only would the Kehillah be the local arm of the AJC and benefit from its support, but members of the Kehillah's executive committee would serve on the governing board of the AJC. They would thereby play a considerable role in national Jewish affairs. A precedent would be set for Jewish communities throughout the country to follow suit.[23]

With a strong Orthodox delegation present and undecided about affiliation, Magnes next sought to meet its reservations. Downtown's Orthodox rabbis feared the influence of the non-Orthodox elements: Reform rabbis and "assimilationist" German Jews might use the new body to undermine the Orthodox institutions of the Jewish quarter. Magnes therefore assured the convention that the autonomy of all member organizations would be strictly observed. Moreover, the Kehillah, he asserted, would help establish the authority of the Orthodox rabbis within the Orthodox community. It would, furthermore, mobilize support for Jewish religious education. These were the two critical areas in which Orthodoxy had encountered vast difficulties.[24]

Rabbi Joseph M. Asher, the Orthodox spokesman, responded that

Magnes' address had allayed his fears. The *American Hebrew* noted that the speech had the opposite effect "upon certain other delegates." [25] For Magnes, aid to the Orthodox community did not mean capitulating to it, though that argument would become increasingly popular among Kehillah critics. Any program that fostered Jewish identity, or brought order to a sector of the community, deserved, Magnes held, the support of the Jewish public as a whole. In fact, just as ethnic survival in America was predicated on a pluralistic society, so a system of co-existence would have to obtain within the Jewish community if it would exist as an organized entity.

The opening session had its great moment as well. After several hours of desultory debate, the chairman called for a vote on Marshall's proposition that "it is the sense of this gathering that a Jewish Community of New York City be formed." The motion was carried and then Jacob Schiff took the floor.[26] "It was a unique event in Jewish communal affairs," the *American Hebrew* reported, "for a man to receive such an outburst of spontaneous, sincere, and enthusiastic applause, which had all the characteristics of a demonstration at a political meeting in the height of a campaign." [27] Schiff, the most influential leader in the Jewish community and its greatest philanthropist praised the convention. He then moved the acceptance of the first two articles of the proposed constitution: that "the purpose of the Jewish Community of New York City shall be to further the cause of Judaism . . . and to represent the Jews of this city;" and that "the organization shall not engage" in political activity "or interfere with the autonomy of a constituent organization." Rabbi Stephen S. Wise, the liberal and controversial minister of the Free Synagogue, seconded the motion. The resolution was carried unanimously.[28]

In his remarks Schiff agreed with all those who had stressed the need to organize the community along religious lines. But religion and dogma, he said, were not identical. What the Orthodox demanded had to be agreed to; what the reformers and nonobserving Jews claimed to be Judaism, also deserved respect and consideration. The important point, he emphasized, was launching the community organization. Thus the pragmatist eschewed the ideological discussion and offered a way for divergent elements to participate in the common undertaking. Even the radical *Warheit*, which had warned against the "conversion of the Kehillah into a religious community," echoed Schiff's stand: the practical accomplishments of the Kehillah would determine its nature and success.[29]

At its second session, on February 28, the convention completed its discussion of the constitution. The proposed text was adopted without substantive changes including the representation formula used for the constitutional convention. Two sections, however, elicited considerable opposition.[30]

The requirement that delegates be American citizens brought the warning that large numbers of newly arrived immigrants would thereby be "disfranchised." If the Kehillah was nonpolitical, some asked, and concerned mainly with internal, Jewish communal matters, why the citizenship requirement? They read into the proposal a deliberate attempt by the uptown group to reinforce their position. But the supporters of the clause emphasized the negative impression that would be made on the general public were the citizenship requirement to be eliminated. The clause was approved. Among those disqualified from serving as delegates were Solomon Schechter, president of the Jewish Theological Seminary, Rabbi David de Sola Pool, and Rabbi Joseph Asher.[31] Marshall wrote to Schechter explaining the decision:

Unless it were insisted that those who should become eligible to membership on the [executive] committee are citizens, a great peril would not only confront the entire movement [for a Kehillah], but the Jewish people of this country as well. Hostile criticism would be certain to be provoked. . . . The movement would be construed to be an attempt to erect an *imperium in imperio*. We should be charged with disloyalty to this country, and a powerful weapon would be placed in the hands of our enemies. . . . If the test of citizenship had not been adopted, a large percentage of the members of the executive committee would have consisted of non-citizens. . . . Those who have been in this country for a period of time insufficient to enable them to become citizens, do not adequately understand the relations of the Jews in this country to the state, and cannot, therefore, be safely entrusted to deal with the delicate problems with which the executive committee will have to grapple.[32]

Affiliation with the AJC, however, was expected to be the explosive issue. The opponents to affiliation carried into the convention debates a tradition of hostility to the AJC. The handful of self-appointed men, they said, unable to tolerate the democratically inspired Kehillah movement, were now conniving to control it through an alliance. The opposition, however, was partly disarmed by the apparently sincere move of the AJC leadership towards self-democratization. "The American Jewish Committee is not here to capture the Kehillah," Marshall said. "On the contrary, the members of that Committee have tendered their resignation to this convention, and are asking you to elect the men to fill their places."[33] The longstanding adversary of the AJC, Louis Lipsky, editor of the *Maccabaean*, still stood by his motion to strike out the relevant articles. But once they were accepted he expressed his guarded approval. Credit had to be given to the AJC "for its patriotic subordination of partisan interests to the cause of Jewish democracy." The AJC had "lacked the energy and ambition to realize a scheme of representation." When it was confronted, however, "by a convention of New York Jewry . . . moulded by the public opinion of the community," it had acquiesced.[34]

The election of the executive committee required two more sessions of the convention; one was held on March 6 and another on March 27. The struggle over the limited number of places on the executive committee led to the extra meeting. The constitution stipulated a committee of twenty-five with members serving for five years. At the first meeting of the executive, they were to draw lots dividing themselves into five classes of five members each, to hold office for one, two, three, four, and five years respectively. Thus at the annual convention only five places would be filled. This first election, therefore, was a particularly critical one when all twenty-five members would be elected. The framers of the provision supported the idea of a small efficient body and one that could withstand popular uprisings. The small size also gave the balance of power to the uptown aristocrats. Lesser-known figures of the East Side or the younger communal leaders stood little chance of defeating the notables.[35]

An abortive attempt was made to force a reconsideration of the article. On the evening of the balloting, the Orthodox group, fearing that Magnes' promises would be vitiated by an executive committee dominated by the anti-Orthodox, proposed a two-fold increase in the size of the executive committee. Magnes ruled the amendment out of order. The constitution stood: a document which met the stipulations of the AJC. Yet few withdrew from the convention, even though Stephen Wise inveighed against the "small coterie of men" who were "running matters according to their own sweet will." [36]

The results of the balloting bore out the fact that the assault on the Kehillah–AJC link as subverting democratic principles had made little impression on the commonalty. Jacob Schiff led the list with 177 votes. Louis Miller, the *Warheit*'s editor, who claimed to speak for the East Side masses, ran last, in forty-second place, with 22 votes. Of the twenty-five elected, ten were members of th AJC. Not one of the sixteen defeated candidates belonged to the AJC. The convention delegates, overwhelmingly from the immigrant quarter, wanted the most prestigious personages to head the Jewish community. Given an opportunity, the conservative *Morgen Journal* wrote, the public acknowledged the right of those who gave so much money and time to Jewish causes to remain at the helm.[37]

The elected included, too, a representative group of East Side communal leaders. Key members of the original Clinton Hall conference committee, Barondess, Dorf, and Semel, Russian Jewish philanthropists Harry Fischel, Sender Jarmulowsky, and Nathan Lamport, and one of the city's illustrious East European Orthodox rabbis, Moses Z. Margolies, made up part of the group. Two uptown Orthodox congregations, representing an increasingly important middle ground between the immigrant ghetto and the German-Jewish Americanized element, placed their rabbis, Dr. Bernard Drachman and Dr. Philip Klein, on the executive committee. Several heads of major *landsmanshaft* groups completed the slate.[38] But it was the AJC group that retained the dominant voice in the Kehillah movement.

The protagonists of the Kehillah movement had promised the democratization of Jewish communal life. To succeed, the participation of the men of the AJC was essential. In return for joining the movement, they had exacted two concessions: that hegemony in national affairs remain with the AJC; and, through institutional arrangements, that the conservative character of the Kehillah democracy be guaranteed. They thereby satisfied their fears of creating a democratic golem which they assumed would be directed at themselves.

But, ironically, the AJC men turned out to be the people's choice. Moreover, the presence of Schiff, Marshall, Sulzberger, and Magnes was, in itself, sufficient guarantee for the conservative and experienced direction which they considered imperative. Thus the guarantees they won were not only superfluous but, in fact, harmful. Stephen Wise's behavior should be viewed in this light. A sympathetic participant during the earlier meetings he became increasingly critical of the convention managers as the elections approached. The absence of Wise's name from the nominating committee's slate may account, at least in part, for his change of heart. Aspiring young communal workers as well as veteran functionaries found the Kehillah's highest council closed to them. Although an advisory council of seventy was elected at a final session of the convention in early April, this consolation prize mollified few.[39]

Despite the portents of difficulties ahead, the founding of the Kehillah emerges as a striking achievement. Momentarily, at least, an impressive number of groups overcame their irascibility and mutual suspicion. For four sessions stretching over a month, Zionists, Orthodox, Reform, and even a handful of radicals had discussed divisive issues, and none had seceded. Influential figures drawn from the first echelon of communal leadership had participated in the deliberations and accepted places on the governing body of the Kehillah. But it grossly exaggerated the case to announce, as some enthusiasts did, that New York's million Jews had in fact established a democratic community structure.[40] On the eve of the convention, Samuel Dorf, Grandmaster of the Order Brith Abraham, came closer to the truth. In a circular to his lodges, he wrote:

It is about time that the Jews in this country became American Jews, and not Russians, Galicians, Germans and Roumanians; let us all come together and possibly stop this terrible feeling that exists between one and the other.

The names you see attached to the circular . . . make me believe that the German Jew has at last opened his eyes to the necessity of getting closer together with the rest of us. What a grand thing it would be if we could accomplish such a union; whether we can accomplish it or not, I cannot tell, but it is certainly worth a trial; possibly we can succeed.[41]

Born from a sense of community in crisis the Kehillah movement had dramatized the problem, proclaimed its intention to refashion the community and persuaded wide circles that its proposals were "worth a trial."

§ CHAPTER FOUR §

Polity, Philanthropy, and Religion

EHILLAH LEADERS COULD CALL UPON A RICH COMMUNAL tradition in building their comprehensive community organization. Yet in one essential feature that tradition offered no guidance. Nowhere had so diverse and so large a number of institutions and factions voluntarily federated together in a single body. Indeed for two influential groups the new arrangements entailed yielding long-standing claims to communal preeminence. In Eastern Europe, Orthodox Jewry had retained considerable control over the institutional life of the local community—even after losing its social and cultural hegemony. For New York's Orthodox leadership, composed largely of recent arrivals, the Kehillah idea stirred hopes of retrieving communal power lost in the move to the New World. The Jewish notables—Americanized, wealthy, and patrons of the principal philanthropies—represented the second element. Self-denominated custodians of the community, their behavior fit the American notion of the stewardship of wealth and corresponded as well with older, European models of the *hofjude* and the *shtadlan*.

Nevertheless, the Kehillah, in its quest for order, unity, and a popular base, could overcome these obstacles, Magnes believed. Two approaches—inspired by the optimistic currents of the times—provided the key, he felt. Through its annual conventions the Kehillah would create a "Jewish public opinion." An informed public, by "supporting a good cause or condemning a bad one," would exert a decisive influence on communal affairs. And second, the Kehillah would establish "scientific bureaus." The scientific investigation of a problem would cut through ignorance, expose the "vested interests," and offer a rational basis for establishing communal policy. Together, these devices would produce a new force—an enlightened Jewish democracy—which would direct Jewish life. Nor did the lack of sovereign power, to Magnes' mind, handicap the undertaking. Success depended now entirely on the good will and good sense of the people.[1]

Fusing old and new world experiences entailed, then, creating a new communal polity. This called for an apparatus geared to winning the confidence of the conservative benefactors which at the same time was capable of holding the interest of the populace. A related problem centered on the feasibility of integrating into the Kehillah system the older, proudly independent philanthropic and religious institutions. These issues put to the test the major assumption of the theorists of an American Kehillah, for here their notion of the efficacy of an enlightened democracy confronted the prerogatives of the wealthy and the claims of the traditionalists.

§

IN THE SPRING OF 1909, FOLLOWING THE ADJOURNMENT OF THE FOUNDing convention, the Kehillah established its offices in the United Hebrew Charities building, an impressive and spacious building which suggested a Florentine Renaissance palace. The Charities, the largest society in the field of relief of the Jewish poor, coordinated the activities of a number of philanthropic bodies. The building housed, as well, the offices of the American Jewish Committee (AJC). The two agencies brought together the great German-Jewish magnates and philanthropists, the Schiffs, Strauses, Seligmans, Lewisohns, and Guggenheims. The Kehillah's first secretary, Bernard G. Richards, recalls how the advent of the Kehillah introduced a new element into the premises. "The opening of the offices of the Kehillah in a building

entirely devoted to Jewish charity and other public undertakings actually gave the Jews a headquarters." Heads of organizations affiliated
with the new body, as well as other aspiring leaders, visited the building regularly for consultation and assistance. "Uptown and downtown were coming together . . . in a unified communal organization," and members of the immigrant groups "were meeting on
common ground with the aristocrats." [2]

The Charities building had its own auditorium and accommodated
all but the largest of the Kehillah's conventions. It was also well located geographically. Situated on the corner of Second Avenue and
Twenty-first Street, it was close by fashionable Gramercy Park, yet it
was within easy reach of the Jewish quarter. Below Fourteenth Street,
Second Avenue was becoming one of the main thoroughfares of the
lower East Side.

The first executive committee meeting, in April, 1909, elected
Magnes chairman. Though he had been the active spirit behind the
movement, his election came only after other plans for filling the
position were defeated. One called for a rotating chairmanship and
another for a president to be elected by the convention. Instead, the
committee accepted the proposal that a chairman be elected annually
by the executive committee at the meeting following the convention.
Magnes was then elected unanimously, and he continued to be so
until the demise of the Kehillah.[3]

The first meeting of the executive committee also established
standing committees on religious organization, on Jewish education,
on finance, on social and philanthropic work, and on propaganda
and organization. In the course of the next five years other committees were added on conciliation and arbitration, on legislation, and on
industrial relations.[4]

In addition to current business (most committees reported on
their activities at the monthly meetings of the executive committee),
Magnes had the committees prepare plans for establishing permanent
bureaus in their fields. A considerable part of the early executive committee meetings were devoted to these plans and to the preliminary
investigations and surveys. In 1910, the first of the bureaus, on education, was formed. Two years later, in the wake of the notorious Herman Rosenthal murder, the Kehillah created the Bureau of Social

Morals to combat crime. It was followed in 1914 by the Bureau of Industry, which was concerned primarily with industrial mediation. In 1916, the Bureau of Philanthropic Research was established jointly with the Council of Jewish Communal Institutions, the association of large philanthropic institutions. The same year the Kehillah established the School for Jewish Communal Work. In addition to the bureaus and the School, the Kehillah organized in 1911 the Board of Orthodox Rabbis.[5]

All the bureaus and the Rabbinical Board had salaried staffs. In a speech he gave in 1915, Magnes spoke about the "regular meetings of the heads of departments—a kind of cabinet." At that time there were four full-time directors. Between 1915 and 1917, at the height of the Kehillah's activities, as many as seventy-five persons were employed in the various departments of the Kehillah. The largest, by far, was the Bureau of Education with sixty full-time and part-time employees.[6]

The question of popular control of the Kehillah's professional agencies created considerable controversy. Each bureau was directed by a board of trustees which administered the funds raised for that particular bureau. The executive committee approved the appointments of the trustees who were generally drawn from its own ranks. In the case of the Bureau of Education, they were appointed for a five-year term. The original standing committees, however, continued to function. While the board of trustees was conceived of as a small group responsible for a particular agency, the committee was envisioned as an advisory group alert to all problems in the field and prepared to initiate new activities. The chairmen of the boards of trustees were generally the chairmen of the parallel committees. A feature of every convention was the series of detailed statements presented by the chairmen or the bureau chiefs.[7]

From the ranks of the convention delegates (who were also called into session for consultative purposes from time to time) came the accusation that the Kehillah's ultimate authority, the convention, had no control over the bureaus. The *Maccabaean* commented acidly that the trustees appointed to supervise the Bureau of Education had "segregated and sterilized it against interference by the Kehillah convention."[8] At one delegates' meeting, in 1915, devoted solely to Kehillah administration, Magnes countered the criticism by comparing the Kehillah's structure to that of a city government. The elected officials, he argued, did not ask "at every step the opinion or the consent of the electorate." They carried on the affairs of the city by establishing departments and bureaus. Thus the members of the municipal Board of Education were appointed for a period of years "in order that the educational affairs of the community may not be mixed up in communal politics." Similarly, the elected executive committee of the Kehillah appointed trustees to its Bureau of Education. When their term was up, the Kehillah's constituency through its convention would have its say. The heart of the matter, as Magnes put it, was "to establish in the community authoritative leadership" that would be "accepted by the people in the community." The only way this could be done was by assuring that the Kehillah bureaus "act upon the sanction given them by the Jewish democracy of the community."

Magnes admitted that the Kehillah needed another bureau, this one to "strengthen the democratic basis of the Kehillah . . . [by] enlarging the number of societies" affiliated with it. Moreover, methods had to be found to bring each society into closer touch with the central organization. Only then could the Kehillah be truly responsive to its constituents.[9]

To those who sharply disagreed with the work of the bureaus, Magnes' discourse on representative government offered no immediate relief and little hope of ultimate change. Only five places on the executive committee were contested each year. But perhaps more important was the *Morgen Journal*'s caustic remark. In reporting one of Jacob Schiff's munificent gifts, the paper warned: "He who picks up the bill has the final say." [10]

The problem of financing went to the heart of Kehillah democracy. Who really had the final say? The hundreds of delegates who represented, in the main, the small organizations of the immigrants and contributed little to the financing of the Kehillah, or the large contributors?

Initially, the finance committee assumed that the five-dollar membership fee each delegate paid at the convention would provide most of the income needed for the organization's administrative expenses. Only a modest office was envisioned. Here the Kehillah would pursue its primary duties as mobilizer of public opinion and coordinator and expediter of community endeavors. Contingencies would be met by the direct benefactions of interested parties who had been alerted to the problem by the Kehillah. Thus, at the second meeting of the executive committee, the finance committee estimated the Kehillah's expenses for the first year at $2,500. Any deficit would be made up by contributions from the officers of the organization. In the summer of 1909, Cyrus Sulzberger financed a study of unemployment. When the Kehillah opened four temporary synagogues for the High Holy Days in September to relieve overcrowding, a collection made among the members of the executive committee covered the costs. Magnes, who first suggested the bureau system in his address at the founding convention, assumed that the institutions benefiting from a particular bureau would willingly bear the major part of its expenses. It became apparent, however, that the very groups who required the services of a bureau most were least able to sustain one financially. With the establishment of the first bureau, a method of financing crystallized which could best meet the demands of the large structure which began to evolve.[11]

The Kehillah attempted to attract donors on the basis of their particular interest in a given program. Hopefully, each undertaking would eventually have its group of underwriters. One prospective contributor to the Bureau of Education, for example, the treasurer-designate of a fund to build new schools, withdrew a promised contribution on discovering that the Bureau included the teaching of Hebrew in its curriculum. He opposed Hebrew instruction, he told Dr. Samson Benderly, director of the Bureau. He had assumed the Bureau to be a "civic movement" that taught "better American manners." The remark failed to upset Benderly's equanimity. In relating the incident to Magnes, the education chief explained that he then tried to interest the prospective contributor in the Kehillah's anti-crime work. "He did not take the bait. . . . Maybe some day in the future we can use him." Other elements, bitterly opposed to the Kehillah, did indeed "take the bait" and supported particular projects of the Kehillah like its efforts to combat crime. Financial decentralization had its advantages.[12]

In 1916, the potential contributor had a choice of six funds which supported various Kehillah projects: the Bureau of Education, the Bureau of Industry, the Bureau of Philanthropic Research, the proposed

School for Jewish Communal Work, and religious activities. The Kehillah also attempted to raise funds for its own administrative needs.[13]

Supporting an office, however, had little of the appeal that the other projects had. One attempt in 1912 to raise $10,000 for administrative purposes brought meager results indeed. A decision taken two years later to hire a field secretary to "secure the affiliation of societies and individuals" could not be implemented for lack of a suitable candidate. In the spring of 1916, the executive committee reactivated a dormant committee on organization and propaganda. It appointed a paid coordinator and voted him a three-month budget of $3,500 to launch a campaign to enroll unaffiliated groups. The committee sponsored neighborhood meetings and recruited volunteers to spread the Kehillah idea. Thousands of leaflets describing the organization's activities were distributed. By convention time in June, 115 groups had joined for the first time. Nevertheless, the finance committee—facing a mushrooming deficit and the severe criticism of the large donors— curtailed the campaign as an economy measure. The Kehillah's office was caught in a vicious circle of inadequate funds, though the number of affiliated organizations did reach 750 by 1916.[14]

The financial decentralization of the Kehillah is reflected in its records. Although extensive financial statements exist for the Bureau of Education and incomplete ones for other bureaus, only in the fall of 1915 do we find a comprehensive report for the Kehillah as a whole. A financial crisis led to the creation of a special committee under the chairmanship of Herbert H. Lehman. Magnes prepared a statement of the Kehillah's income for the committee for the year ending March 31, 1915. It showed the following: [15]

Bureau of Education	$68,069.40
Vice Fund	20,900.00
Bureau of Industry	9,850.00
Executive Office	6,854.31
Bureau of Religious Affairs	2,333.02
School of Jewish Communal Work	240.00
Miscellaneous	246.45
	$108,493.18

Financial decentralization, besides impairing the central administration of the Kehillah, raised a more fundamental question. The large contributors insisted on a stable and efficient administration of their bequests. They gave their money to Magnes knowing that he would appoint trustees, "responsible" men, who would manage the undertaking. (It would have required an extraordinary belief in the uplifting power of democracy for men who considered the immigrant community a major social charge to hand to it the agencies which their funds created.) Thus, though Magnes undoubtedly believed in the trustee system as a way of guarding the integrity of a public agency, he well knew (as did the community at large) that the philanthropists were also rejecting the notion of a communal purse popularly controlled. Consequently, a strand of frustration and bitterness ran through all the deliberations of the Kehillah. Critics asked if the convention was merely a sham, meeting in order to ceremonially approve decisions made elsewhere. Since the largest contributors were German-Jewish philanthropists and the great majority of the delegates East European Jews, all the animosities which that confrontation elicited suffused the debate.[16]

However, the East European Jews had their philanthropists as well. Though less affluent, they too contributed to the Kehillah's bureaus, accepted the trustee system, and served on the executive committee. The question, therefore, was more than one of lack of confidence in the ability of the Russian Jews who controlled the conventions. Men of wealth, regardless of origin, questioned the competency of the commonalty to direct the affairs of the group. Only if the multitude of organizations had mobilized large funds from its own ranks could it have gained a greater say in Kehillah deliberations. It would thereby have strengthened the central Kehillah administration and raised its own prestige in the eyes of the philanthropists. The need to make such efforts was recognized. The inability to translate that recognition into deeds proved to be the Kehillah's greatest shortcoming.

Yet the Kehillah's conventions, despite their limitations, were more than rubber-stamp affairs. The trustees of no other category of Jewish institutions were required to render an accounting to an assembly open to representatives of all Jewish organizations. The intensive debates and the extensive press coverage given the conventions created, in part, the organized public opinion Magnes had wanted.[17] Moreover, the debates influenced the Kehillah's executive body which, after all, did consist of responsible and respected leaders of up-town and downtown. Men like Bernard Semel, Samuel Dorf, and William Fischman (Russian Jews who headed a large *landsmanshaft* federation, fraternal order, and educational institution, respectively) occupied key places on the executive committee. Though the seats on the committee were frequently contested, the incumbents were generally reelected. This fact reflected more than administration power. Magnes and his close advisers knew the Jewish quarter, and their nominees included the most representative figures available.[18]

Nevertheless, the conflict, with its rancor, persisted, aggravated by swelling deficits. In 1917, Magnes suggested a reorganization of the Kehillah's structure. He spoke about the two methods which the Kehillah had employed to create "a conscious, organized, and united Jewish Community"—the "Democratic Method and the Scientific Method." The latter, the Kehillah's bureaus, had proven to be more successful than the former. Ideally, both were integral parts of the Kehillah. The burden, however, of maintaining the bureaus and the dissensions created in protecting their integrity had placed too great a strain on the "Democratic Method." The Kehillah democracy was "not yet alive to its obligations and powers," and it was unable to supply the funds for the bureaus. The best interests of the community, therefore, called for severing the bureaus from the Kehillah.[19]

The integration into a democratic polity of the commons with those of rank and wealth had not gone well, and in a move to salvage a remnant of the structure Magnes proposed a new tack: relieving the Kehillah of its institutional responsibilities. Freed of that yoke, the Kehillah would devote itself to "the democratic experiment without let or hindrance." The "Jewish democracy" would then "find itself," and in time a "mighty Jewish public opinion"—that coveted and elusive force—would compel "the coordination of all Jewish efforts." This would lead "inevitably" to a "genuine Jewish community." [20]

Magnes failed to see the flaw in his "two-method" construct. Divorcing the "democratic method" (the Kehillah as a public forum) from the "scientific method" (the Kehillah's service bureaus) blocked access to the levers of communal power, including those which the Kehillah itself had fashioned. While severing the connection with the bureaus promised financial relief, the decision also freed those benefactors who had supported the bureaus, from their Kehillah connection.

In 1912, when Magnes presented his report to the Kehillah convention, he introduced the discussion on philanthropic work with these remarks:

The Jews of New York City are highly organized if we consider their numerous and finely endowed philanthropic institutions. When some day a federation of these institutions is brought about, that will be another permanent basis for the organization of the Jews of the city. Meanwhile, lacking a federation of charities, the Kehillah feels itself called upon to engage upon philanthropic work, that would properly be within the province of a Federation of Jewish Charities.[21]

Five years later—and not unrelated to the reorganization of the Kehillah—the Federation came into existence.

Its establishment was a hotly debated topic in the first two decades of the century. The mass immigration from Eastern Europe had placed a heavy burden on the large welfare agencies which were supported and directed by German Jews. And in large measure, the federation idea developed in response to this need. Supporters of the plan pointed to the increased income that would accrue from coordinating the collection and distribution of the charitable funds. The prospect of eliminating the plethora of fund-raising activities by substituting an annual canvass of subscribers on behalf of all bona fide institutions promised, besides convenience, the elimination of unsavory practices.[22]

There was another facet to the interest in federation. The welfare activities of the immigrants themselves were multiplying. This meant not only duplication. In the eyes of many German Jews, the immigrant agencies were ineffectual and even harmful. Moreover, in the end, uptown was asked to finance them. Louis Marshall told the Kehillah convention in 1914:

A number of men get together. Because a certain person was not admitted into an institution, in five minutes, they decide that a new institution is necessary. They raise a few thousand dollars. Then they decide they will appeal to the public. Who is the public? They go to Mr. Schiff and ask for a contribution; they go to Mr. [Adolph] Lewisohn and ask for a contribution; they go to Mr. Felix Warburg and ask for a contribution. I tell you there are some of us whose backs are being broken under the ever-increasing burden. It is time to call a halt or else the entire charitable system of New York City will go bankrupt. . . . What we need is an organization to suppress unnecessary organizations. . . . Here is an orphan asylum being established in a thickly congested district. This is wrong. It is criminal! [23]

The main opposition to federation came, however, from a segment of Marshall's own social class. The discussion had become particularly intense at the time of the establishment of the Kehillah. Louis A. Heinsheimer, a partner in Kuhn, Loeb, and Company, had left a $1 million bequest to the larger philanthropic institutions provided a minimum number federated for money-raising purposes. The offer failed to move the supporters of a majority of those eligible.[24] More than loyalty to one's own charity was involved. The banker, James Speyer, a director of Mount Sinai Hospital, wrote to the *American Hebrew* in April, 1909:

It seems a remarkable coincidence that some of the prime movers and advocates of this [Kehillah] movement are the same who are so insistent on the great advantages to the poor of a sectarian Federation of Charities in New York, and that both movements are being promoted simultaneously. I do not think well of such a modified form of "Zionism in New York." [25]

Speyer eschewed any public activity predicated on ethnic-group identity. A federation of Jewish charities, to the banker, was such a movement. It was "sectarian" like the Kehillah, separatist in practice and hence "modified Zionism," the bête noire of Speyer and his associates. For them, religious needs construed in narrow institutional terms offered the single legitimate basis for segregated activity. Even then, centralization was suspect.

He was, of course, correct in asserting that advocates of Kehillah wanted federation. Cyrus L. Sulzberger, chairman of the Kehillah's committee on philanthropic work and at the time president of the United Hebrew Charities, was an early and staunch supporter of federation. Jacob Schiff and Felix Warburg welcomed all stabilizing forces. Both supported the Kehillah handsomely and pushed hard for federation; in 1917, Warburg became its first president.[26]

The Kehillah and its committee of social and philanthropic work took an active part in the agitation for federation. In his report to the 1912 convention, Magnes offered an example of the work federation should be doing. He related how the Kehillah had investigated the plans of several societies which had intended establishing new charitable agencies. Finding that the work of existing institutions would have been duplicated, the committee on philanthropic work dissuaded the promoters from continuing their project. The same convention appointed a commission to investigate ways and means of furthering the federation idea. And again in 1912, the Kehillah issued the *Jewish Communal Directory* listing the Jewish organizations of the city and including a study of its Jewish population. "In this way," Magnes commented, "we have laid the foundation of a Bureau of Jewish Statistics." [27] Such a bureau many considered to be an essential part of the future federation authority.

For the moment the Kehillah had no ambition to become that authority. It may be that its leaders realized that the established and wealthy institutions, unable to agree among themselves, would have rejected out-of-hand a Kehillah-led federation. But probably of equal import was the *sine qua non* of all federation plans: the contributors controlled the management. It was a league of philanthropists. For Magnes, this meant an improvement over present conditions, a force for order and hence a trend to be encouraged. But in this form, it remained alien to the Kehillah idea. Moreover, for Magnes and those who thought like him, other issues took precedence. Hospitals, orphan asylums, and relief for the indigent were necessary; the social and cultural needs of the community, however, appeared more urgent. Grappling with these questions first would create a true community, Kehillah stalwarts believed, able to cope with the anarchy in philanthropic affairs.[28]

Meanwhile, the Kehillah felt obligated to undertake welfare activity on an ad hoc basis. When a situation arose which fell outside the bounds of existing agencies, the committee on social and philanthropic work responded. A list of its undertakings suggests this catch-all character. It supervised a Kehillah employment office for the "handicapped." The term included Sabbath observers, referrals from the United Hebrew Charities, those who had served prison terms, as well as the physically handicapped.[29] The committee also played an active part in aiding the Arabic- and Ladino-speaking Jews, who began arriving in numbers in 1911. By 1913, two groups had been resettled outside of New York. Sulzberger, who also headed the Industrial Removal Office, arranged for their industrial training and employment in local plants. The Kehillah undertook to raise funds to bring a spiritual leader from Turkey. Negotiations were well advanced when the outbreak of World War I cut them short. The president of the Federation of Oriental Jews, in fact, served on the staff of the Kehillah's employment office.[30]

One final example of the Kehillah's role in meeting contingencies as they arose was its response to the bank closings which followed the declaration of war in August, 1914. Panic-sticken immigrants, anxious to send money to families in the Eastern war zone, created a rush on the four largest banks in the Jewish quarters of the city. The New York State Banking Department closed them as insolvent. An estimated 50,000 Jewish depositors and $11 million in savings were involved. Riots ensued. The depositors became prey to unprincipled lawyers, while the Yiddish press printed rumors and advice and compounded the confusion.[31] Magnes, Marshall, and members of the committee, after consulting with a group of financiers, established a depositors' protective committee. Eugene Lamb Richards, superintendent of the State Banking Department, agreed that the protective committee act as official liaison between him and the depositors. Through printed brochures, newspaper announcements, and meetings, the Kehillah brought some semblance of order into the situation.[32] By the end of August, less than three weeks after the bank closings, 8,742 depositors had registered their claims with the Kehillah. Since most of the assets of the banks were in real estate and mortgages, the Kehillah hired appraisers to examine the property and advise it on the best possible settlement. As part of the effort to aid the depositors, a loan fund was created. And in the spring and summer of 1915, Kehillah leaders studied and then endorsed proposals to establish an immigrant bank. Legal complications, however, led to the abandonment of the project.[33]

In 1916, after two years of strenous efforts to achieve a modicum of collaboration in the field of welfare services, the Kehillah moved a step closer to that goal. Jointly with the Council for Jewish Communal Institutions—who represented the well-established charities—it formed the Bureau of Philanthropic Research. During the first year of its existence, the Bureau proved its serviceability. It conducted an exhaustive survey of day nurseries, investigated credit unions, and examined charges brought against an East Side orphan asylum for soliciting funds under false pretenses. It supplied information to potential contributors. The Bureau also prepared a master plan for a federation of charities. Finally, it accepted responsibility for maintaining the "Black Book," an annual listing of all contributors to the Council's constituent institutions.[34]

The establishment of the Bureau of Philanthropic Research appeared to be, at first blush, a substantial advance for the Kehillah. Patrons of such institutions as the Educational Alliance and Mount Sinai Hospital had sufficiently overcome their antipathy for the Kehillah to cooperate with it. Moreover, the creation of a single planning authority for the community seemed, at last, within reach. But the prolonged negotiations which preceded the agreement also underscored the gap which separated the Kehillah from its reluctant collaborators in their approach to community.

As early as 1914, Morris D. Waldman, executive director of the United Hebrew Charities and secretary of the Kehillah's philanthropic committee, together with Sulzberger, Warburg, and Magnes, had prepared proposals for a "Laboratory of Philanthropic Research and Information." In April, the Kehillah convention approved the plan, and Magnes immediately began to solicit pledges of financial support for the projected $20,000 a year budget of the Bureau. "We could have done it ourselves," he recalled later, but participation of "the largest and oldest and best philanthropic institutions" was essential. Cosponsorship with the Council assured the representation of "all shades of belief and all sections of the community." Popularization of philanthropic control promised, for example, "recognition that the . . . masses of the people must help themselves philanthropically." This meant the "opening up of new sources of income." [35]

More than a question of utility was involved. "The community needs a department of philanthropy," the executive committee reported to the 1914 convention. "We need once and for all scientifically to determine what the philanthropic needs of the community are, how they are being met, how they ought to be met. Who are the poor? Do the institutions meet their needs? What are the causes of their distress? Who give to the institutions?" Was a federation of Jewish charities, in fact, desirable, and could a communal welfare policy be worked out? [36] These were "virtually problems of government, but in a free country such as ours," Magnes wrote, "the government must derive its powers from the people." Here was but another phase of the general problem of communal organization: "the establishment of authority or authoritative influence in the various phases of the Jewish life of the community." A philanthropic authority required "democratic sanction." [37]

Twice negotiations broke down. In June, 1915, when the Council submitted the Kehillah's proposal to its constituent organizations, the largest—the Educational Alliance—voted against the plan. It rejected cooperation with any "outside organization" in establishing a bureau of philanthropy. Such a task, if there was a need for a bureau, belonged to the supporters and directors of the principal charities, the Council group. Compromise, however, finally moved the most adamant members of the Council when the Kehillah agreed to accept four places on the governing board to the Council's five. Nor could the Council completely ignore the fact that the idea of a bureau had come from the Kehillah and that its followers had promised financial aid to the undertaking. Persuasive, too, was Adolph Lewisohn's pledge of a $5,000 annual subvention to the Bureau. Prominent in the city's civic affairs and a pillar of Jewish philanthropy (his wealth came from mining and copper smelting interests), Lewisohn requested Kehillah representation in the Bureau's management.[38]

Among the German-Jewish notables, Lewisohn occupied a middle ground in his attitude towards Jewish communal organization. Schiff and Marshall believed that strengthening the traditional institutions of the immigrants and fostering popular participation in communal matters would curb social dislocation and abet a sound integration into American society. Confident of their skill and power, they participated fully in the Kehillah. Judge Samuel Greenbaum, president of the Educational Alliance, like the banker James Speyer, had greeted the Kehillah in 1909 as a dangerous act of self-segregation, "uncalled for" and "un-American." A "democratic" community structure, the Greenbaum group pointed out, had to recognize all brands of Jewish activity, countenancing even those immigrant organizations which were incongruous in the American setting. Lewisohn—mainstay of the Hebrew Sheltering Guardian Society and the Hebrew Technical School for Girls, proven charities of the old community—agreed with Greenbaum and the Council that responsibility for a bureau of philanthropy belonged to it. The Council represented "coherence and permanence" and its patrons financed, in large part, the Jewish welfare services of the city. Moreover, Lewisohn asserted, the Kehillah represented those elements who "filled the orphan asylums" yet who wished a say in the direction of philanthropic policy. Nevertheless, "if the Kehillah or so-called Jewish Community of which I am a member, although inactive, can be . . . helpful in carrying out this work, it is of course desirable." [39]

For Lewisohn, the value of the Kehillah lay not in its aspirations to embrace the entire community but in its immigrant composition. "The Kehillah," he noted, "is in great part made up of congregations, lodges, and the newer societies representative of those of our faith who came to this country in comparatively recent years." It highlighted issues such as "downtown Jewish schools" and "Jewish affairs in general, particularly from the religious aspect," which hardly interested "the people who are represented by the Council." For these reasons and because the immigrant public had to be prepared for responsible participation in communal leadership, the Kehillah's presence in the Bureau was necessary.[40] So came grudging recognition by the uptown worthies that place had to be made in their counsels for representatives of the downtown Jews.

The Bureau of Philanthropic Research paved the way for the federation of charities. The insularity of the old-line welfare agencies—which had blocked the movement for a decade and a half—softened in the controversy over the Bureau. Functions of the new agency which dovetailed with those of the projected federation proved useful and tempered the long-harbored apprehensions over the dangers of a central authority. Certainly the war in Europe encouraged the federation movement. Unprecedented calls for overseas aid added heavy new burdens to the philanthropic conscience and pocket of the community. But of major significance was the Kehillah's perseverance. It had placed the question of the community's philanthropic policy before the public and kept it there, forcing leaders of all persuasions to search for a solution.

On January 1, 1917, the organizing committee—having fulfilled three conditions—declared the Federation for the Support of Jewish Philanthropic Societies operative. It had included rigorous guarantees in the by-laws assuring absolute autonomy in internal matters to the beneficiary institutions. It had limited eligibility to welfare agencies, excluding those construed as primarily religious in purpose (this denied support to Jewish religious schools and other cultural institutions). And in a preliminary campaign, the organizing committee had collected subscriptions for a sum greater than that raised independently by the participating societies during the previous year. A central fund-raising instrument had been established.[41]

What was to be the relationship between the Kehillah and the Federation? "The idea of the Kehillah, embracing as it does the various aspects of the Jewish problem in New York City, is larger than the idea of a federation of contributors to philanthropic institutions." So stated one member of the executive committee at a meeting devoted to the issue. The Kehillah was composed of representatives of a multiplicity of societies, others asserted, not of individual contributors. It did not conform to the normal pattern of philanthropic organization where a contribution brought membership which in turn carried a share of authority. Common to these views was that first notion of the Kehillah as the democratic polity of the Jewish community. Kehillah, not Federation, should encompass the other. From the Federation's pragmatic view, the Kehillah was disqualified from receiving aid on two counts: it was neither a charity nor a "nonsectarian" agency, since so much of its energies were devoted to Jewish education and religious affairs.[42]

Magnes' proposals in 1917 to restructure the Kehillah sought to resolve these problems and win Federation support for some of its activities. Detaching the bureaus and establishing them on an independent footing—each financed by its own supporters—likened them to other welfare institutions. (There would remain the task of convincing the Federation to lift its ban on aid to Jewish education, a feat described in chapter 5.) The reorganization plan represented, nevertheless, a sharp break with the Kehillah's grand theme: the creation of an "authoritative influence" sustained by the "democratic sanction" of the community. The "authoritative influence," the bureaus, were being turned over to the sole control of the philanthropists.

Constant emphasis on the need for a popularly governed, united community did leave its impress even on a Federation dominated by the large contributors and philanthropic institutions of the older settlement. (Only three of thirty-eight of the original trustees and four of fifty-four constituent societies belonged to the East European Jewish group.) From the start, the Federation felt constrained to seek the support of the Jewish commons. A subscription of $10 granted the contributor "membership" and made him eligible to vote for a small number of "trustees-at-large" on the governing board. In the fall of 1917, a massive house-to-house canvass resulted in 51,000 new subscriptions, tripling the number of subscribers. The average contribution was $4. Federation spokesmen prided themselves at the number of contributors. Participation, they said, was as important as the amount raised.[43] In 1918, I. Edwin Goldwasser, executive director of the Federation, summing up its first year, reported how "the entire community" had been "welded into a solid unit." No division of uptown and downtown nor any other sort of division existed within the Federation, Goldwasser boasted. The committees of the Federation were "considering the general problems of community welfare, and for the first time in the history of the Jewish community in New York City giving full consideration to the problems affecting its institutions." Not only had Goldwasser—never a supporter of the Kehillah or its philosophy—borrowed its rhetoric, but he had imbibed its unrestrained optimism as well.[44]

Ten years of Kehillah experience had convinced the philanthropists that some regulatory body was necessary. Even those most vehemently opposed to the Kehillah idea must have at last realized that the loose, informal arrangements were anachronistic. The Federation, ostensibly a coordinating device for fund-raising, appeared in Goldwasser's 1918 statement as an alternative form of communal control to Kehillah.

The idea of a professional school for training Jewish communal workers was closely related to the Kehillah's philanthropic program. It reflected Magnes' belief that the expert functioning as civil servant must be the keystone of the community structure. The idea of a professional school expressed, moreover, his faith that "scientific research" would help solve "the perplexing difficulties arising out of the transplantation of the Jews from an old to a new environment." Thus social research was assigned a central place in the activities of the school. Its establishment may have also stemmed from a desire to counter the unsympathetic view of ethnic survival shared by influential Jewish members of the social work profession. Those who took this stand doubted the desirability of attempting to preserve Jewish communal life. "The forces of the new environment are slowly but irresistibly making for the ultimate assimilation of the immigrants," one observer noted. Whatever "special social problems" existed because "of the transplantation from the old to the new environment" had to be met "as individual concrete problems." Training for Jewish communal work, consequently, "must be primarily for specific fields with no particular theory or bias in mind." [45]

The School for Jewish Communal Work began its first regular academic year in October, 1916, with thirty graduate students, a faculty of twelve, and six departments. Judge Irving Lehman headed the board of trustees, and Samson Benderly, the director of the Kehillah's Bureau of Education, was chairman of the administrative committee of the faculty. Julius Drachsler, a young sociologist of great promise (his Columbia University dissertation, *Democracy and Assimilation*, was published in 1920), served as secretary. The faculty was drawn from the Kehillah's staff as well as from the social work profession at large. Some of its courses were held jointly with Columbia University, which granted credit for work done at the school. Another feature of the school was the system of "institutes." Extension courses were offered in various fields of social work to those actively engaged in them. Dr. Paul Abelson, for example, the director of the Kehillah's Bureau of Industry, lectured on "The Administration of Trade Agreements." The course lasted for twenty sessions and attracted, in particular, the business managers of the trade unions.[46]

During the academic year of 1917–1918, the number of graduate students dropped to twenty-seven. In its third year, partly because of military conscription and partly because the entire venture had been too ambitiously conceived, the school closed. By that time, too, Magnes had ceased to play the role of initiator and gadfly.[47]

The Kehillah faced another element, the Orthodox Jews of Eastern Europe, whose communal tradition was one of self-segregation. Despite the corroding influences of modernism, a substantial number of the immigrants still adhered to the religious laws and folkways which had distinguished their self-contained society in Russia.

In America, however, circumstances unhinged the traditional system, confusing and disheartening the pious. The economic necessity which led many to violate the Sabbath was the most obvious example. More subtle was the effect of the public school with its promise of material rewards for the diligent. Alongside it the rudimentary religious classes of the Orthodox appeared ineffectual indeed. To add to their bewilderment, the Orthodox, like all immigrants, were grateful for those conditions of freedom and opportunity which, unhappily, also invited the erosion of their traditional way of life.[48]

Particularly demoralizing was the decline of the authoritative leaders and especially the rabbinate. In Eastern Europe, the rabbi's prestige and duties stemmed from his expertise as expounder of a code of religious law which regulated most of the civil life of the Jews. Scholarship (essential for the explication of the sacred law) and instruction (the obligation of the scholar) were esteemed functions of the office. Arbitrator in all manner of disputes and overseer of public institutions, the rabbi was a party to the major decisions taken by the community. Larger towns required several rabbis to fulfill these tasks, and generally specialization took place. Lesser figures like sextons, preachers, teachers, and supervisors of the ritual slaughtering of meat rounded out the cast of officials. These functionaries, who had been supported in Europe by communal arrangements, became in America private entrepreneurs of religious skills subject to the laws of the market place. No longer were they instruments of public authority, and no longer did the rabbi personify such authority. The latter at best found employment with a congregation which gave him little security and meager wages. (There were a handful of exceptions to this generalization.) Rabbis complained of the indignities they suffered at the hands of the affluent, ignorant, and often impious "pillars of the synagogue." Moreover, in the new locale—the lower East Side, for example—five hundred congregations existed. They represented the map of Russian-Jewish settlement with all of its sectional rivalries and regional peculiarities. This atomization was increased by the immigrants' geographic mobility. Though only a minority of the congregations had their own rabbis, staking out a hegemony under these conditions was difficult indeed. The rabbis' traditional, community-wide functions atrophied. They lost their independence and influence. Questions of prestige became acute and petty intrigues divided them into factions which militated against any common endeavor.[49]

Faced with their own struggle for a livelihood and confused by the new conditions, the rabbis placed little stock in plans to reestablish communal authority. Only seven years before the founding of the Kehillah, Chief Rabbi Jacob Joseph, the central figure in the most ambitious attempt to create a rabbinical authority for the city's Orthodox population, had died in poverty.[50] The rabbis, therefore, acquiesced in the laissez-faire organization of Orthodoxy.

These circumstances permitted all manner of abuse. Imposters acted as rabbis and no communal power existed to prevent it. Worship at times was exploited for commercial purposes. Many immigrants, unable or not interested enough to attend the synagogue regularly, flocked to services once a year during the High Holy Days. Since existing congregations were unable to cope with the numbers, entrepreneurs rented temporary quarters, sold tickets, and catered to the overflow crowds. A Kehillah study in 1912 reported that most of the 286 "mushroom synagogues" counted "were conducted in cheap dance halls, theaters, moving picture places, factory lofts, sweatshops, and meeting rooms which . . . are connected with saloons." [51]

Nor did the Orthodox leadership know how to cope with another new development. Functions, once solely within the purview of rabbinic authority, now belonged to the jurisdiction of the state. The religious divorce not only went unrecognized in the courts, its execution came perilously close to being a criminal act. The ritual bath, the *mikveh*, a public institution which in the Russian town was under rabbinic supervision, fell under the jurisdiction of the city's Department of Health for hygienic reasons, as did the rite of circumcision, *milah*.[52]

But another part of the Orthodox system presented even greater difficulties. It involved the ritual dietary laws, kashruth, and particularly the regulations governing the slaughtering and marketing of meat. This kashruth code required specialized workers who were well-versed in its ordinances and trained in the necessary skills. The codes also required that those handling the meat—wholesaler, *shochet* (ritual slaughterer), supervisor, and retailer—be observant Orthodox Jews. The requirement was intended to give the faithful some assurance that the minutiae of the law would be respected.[53]

Not only the Orthodox observed the ordinance of eating kosher meat. According to one estimate made in 1917, a million Jews, two-thirds of the total Jewish population of New York City, consumed 156 million pounds of kosher meat annually. Thus the kashruth code had created an immense Orthodox Jewish industry which supplied employment to a host of religious functionaries and served a public considerably larger than the Orthodox group. In fact, the Jewish population of New York made it economically expedient to slaughter beef intended for non-Jews, according to the kashruth code.[54]

In Europe, this industry was exploited for the benefit of the community. Since religious law required the public to use kosher meat, the community declared its right to regulate the industry and to divert some of its profits to communal purposes. Rabbinical overseers, *shochtim*, wholesalers, and retailers were thus often in the direct employ of the community. The *korobka* (a kosher meat excise tax), though frequently a cause of fraud and misappropriation by the Russian authorities, nevertheless provided the community with its principal source of funds.[55]

In America, this central religious institution, with its strong social and economic base, crumbled. One investigation in 1915, conducted under the aegis of the Kehillah, estimated that only 40 percent of the retail butchers claiming to sell kosher meat were in fact doing so. Most of the rabbinical supervisors and *shochtim* were in the direct employ of the slaughterhouses (a religious prohibition since it compromised the independence of the religious functionary). Finally, the entrepreneur benefited commercially from a product whose higher price derived from its religious value.[56]

In New York, the sheer dimension of the problem thwarted the attempts to resolve it. According to one estimate made in 1915, there were 5,000 retail butcher stores and over 1,000 *shochtim*. The proper administration of kashruth would have entailed inspecting these stores regularly and supervising the *shochtim*.[57] The industrial side was no less complex. The large slaughterhouses which handled steer and lamb belonged to such industrial giants as Armour and Swift. Here, at least, some stability existed. Beef and mutton were less affected by seasonal fluctuations in price, while the size of the companies allowed a more rational organization of the industry. Slaughtering cattle also required greater skills and physical strength than slaughtering poultry. Consequently, the cattle *shochtim* and supervisors were employed on a salary basis and enjoyed a measure of job security.

The poultry sector suffered from a multitude of small processing units, cutthroat competition, and depressed wages. Hundreds of middlemen, the so-called "speculators," provided credit for the small retailers and connived frequently in selling non-kosher meat. Complicating the problem further were the different classes of *shochtim*, each with its separate union and special interests. *Shochtim* struck against marketmen and retailers. Retailers, protesting the higher prices and harsh credit terms of the "speculators," struck against them, while consumers boycotted the retailers. Everyone blamed the meat trust. Meanwhile, underworld elements began to infiltrate the industry.[58]

Thus, fraud, scandal, and sacrilege were present in an important field of Orthodox endeavor. "The disorganization of kashruth," Magnes told a Kehillah convention, "being synonymous with the disorganization of the authoritative rabbis, ramifies into all parts of the community, and creates much of the confusion which plagues us. . . . [It] has led to grave public scandals in Jewish life. . . . Whether we like it or not, that is the situation among thousands of our brethren, and it becomes our duty as a Community to face this problem of disorganization." [59]

A solution held out the hope, as in Europe, of financial benefits for the community and the prospect of raising the dignity of the immigrant rabbis and reestablishing their authority. Dr. H. Pereira Mendes, senior rabbi of the Spanish and Portuguese Synagogue and chairman of the Kehillah's religious committee, outlined such a plan in the fall of 1909. He projected a large rabbinical commission consisting of all Orthodox rabbis "whose ordinances would be respected." Their income from ritual matters, especially from kashruth supervision, would go directly to the Kehillah, in return for which they would receive a fixed salary as "Kehillah rabbis." The Kehillah in turn, would tax the slaughterhouses and kosher butcher stores for the communal kashruth service they were receiving. If the 10,000 cattle slaughtered weekly in New York, Mendes pointed out, were taxed at the rate of twenty-five cents a carcass, and if the 5,000 kosher retail butchers paid one dollar a month for kashruth supervision, receipts would reach $190,000 a year. Eliminating the kashruth abuses would bring as its reward funds for providing a living for the rabbis and for other Orthodox needs, such as religious schools.[60]

This was essentially the idea of the Kehillah's Board of Orthodox Rabbis (Vaad ha'rabbanim), whose formation Magnes announced at the 1910 Kehillah convention. In an Orthodox public of so many communities, Kehillah leaders reasoned, no single personality could command the loyalty of all. A board, properly financed, might do so.[61]

The communalization of kashruth, however, threatened existing arrangements. Three of the most influential rabbis, Philip Klein, Moses Z. Margolies, and Shalom E. Jaffe, had divided up the supervision of the larger Manhattan steer slaughterhouses. Kashruth supervision gave the rabbis, besides a considerable income, patronage to dispense, since they passed on the qualifications, technical and moral, of their rabbinical assistants and the *shochtim*. As key figures in the complicated world of rabbinical relations, their participation was necessary. Klein and Margolies, in fact, were invited to choose the committee which would select the Board of Rabbis.[62]

In the spring of 1912, after two years of patient and delicate negotiations, the Board of Orthodox Rabbis began to function. Thirty-one "authoritative" rabbis, all ordained in Eastern Europe, were installed as members of the Board. The Kehillah could now claim the support of the most distinguished rabbis in the Jewish quarter. With their lay supporters and synagogues, the Board's rabbis raised hopes of a collaborative effort that would bring a measure of stability into Orthodox affairs.[63]

The achievement, however, was marred by one note of discord, a portent of the storm of contention to come. Rabbi Gabriel Zev Margolis ("Reb Velvele"), an eminent scholar and recent arrival to the city, refused to join the Board. Party to none of the informal kashruth arrangements of pre-Kehillah days, nor a participant in the creation of the Board, Reb Velvele gathered around himself the disaffected. He became the boisterous center of an Orthodox opposition which dogged the steps of the Kehillah and its rabbinical authority. Two elements which sponsored Reb Velvele rendered his forays particularly disruptive. The publisher of the *Morgen Journal*, Jacob Saphirstein, used the rabbi in a campaign to discredit the Kehillah. Beef "speculators" and chicken marketmen—members of the Adath Israel society which had engaged the rabbi—publicized Reb Velvele as the preferred authority in all ritual matters. Particularly regrettable was the countermovement's strident tone of sectarianism.[64] Shortly after the Board began to function, the *Morgen Journal* editorialized:

If the Board of Rabbis stands by its determined decision to elevate the Kehillah and be elevated by it, if those [Kehillah] rabbis wish to remain close kin to the Reformed and live with them under the same roof of religion . . . let them remember one thing. Though they are the majority . . . [in matters of] principle, majority plays no role. . . . Rabbis of the Kehillah! . . . Because we respect you, we cannot see you dese-

crate your honor and the honor of the Torah by your crowning a young-
ster with shaven whiskers, a graduate of the most freethinking seminary
[the reference was to Magnes], as your chief rabbi, for that is what your
recent acts have in effect done.[65]

Such a call was bound to heighten the irascibility and suspicion of
the rabbis in their relationship to the Kehillah.

The Rabbinical Board's interests included such areas as arbitration
and education. Its concern with religious education led to its insisting
on overseeing the Kehillah's Bureau of Education, an issue which
shook the relations between the rabbis and the Kehillah. Kashruth supervision, however, absorbed most of the Board's energies and became the touchstone of its success.

The Board accepted direct responsibility for only one phase of the
kashruth operation—the inspection of the kosher meat stores. Considering the limited financial resources available, the approach was a
wise one. Other considerations, evidently, also influenced the decision. The Board avoided a clash with its three leading members, who
continued to maintain their private kashruth arrangements as before.
Moreover, since this decision removed the threat of interference in
the internal arrangements of the large wholesale houses, Magnes was
able to approach them for financial support. Once kashruth inspection of the retail shops became widespread, he told the wholesalers,
public confidence would rise and so would the consumption of meat.
He offered another "business" reason for financing kashruth. Kehil-
lah-inspected stores would be allowed to carry only locally slaughtered
meat (an accepted practice in Europe), since only such meat could
be vouched for by its inspectors. A subvention on a trial basis was
forthcoming.[66]

In the fall of 1912, Magnes wrote to Dr. Cyrus Adler, president of
the Philadelphia Jewish Community (the Philadelphia organization,
modeled after the Kehillah, was established in 1912), of a plan to appoint "district *dayanim*." These rabbinical judges, supported by the
Kehillah, would answer questions on ritual matters "free of charge"
and adjudicate minor disputes. "Not alone is this good in itself,"
Magnes wrote, "but it will enable us to give some kind of position
with an income to a number of rabbis. This is . . . the crux of the
situation." In the kashruth experiment, the Kehillah had provided

positions for a number of men. "If we can in time get positions for most of those who consider themselves important and make them Kehillah rabbis, the problem will be brought near its solution." Nor was this to be regarded altogether in criticism of the rabbis. "Most of them, as a matter of fact, are paid a miserable wage." [67]

By the spring of 1913, 250 stores were under the supervision of the Board of Rabbis. Twenty-two rabbis were serving as rabbinical judges and six local kashruth boards, each with a staff and secretary, were in operation. Six months later the kashruth supervision structure had collapsed. The experiment had lasted about a year.[68]

The immediate cause was the withdrawal of financial aid by the meat packers. Such support, they claimed, might make them liable to antitrust prosecution. (Three years later the Kehillah was indeed involved in antitrust proceedings. In a renewed endeavor to bring some order into the chaotic poultry industry, the Kehillah participated in establishing an association of wholesalers, retailers, and *shochtim*. Dr. Paul A. Abelson, director of the Kehillah's Bureau of Industry, was indicted under New York State's Donnelly Antitrust Law. The indictment was later quashed and the association disbanded.) [69]

Magnes did not expect the meat industry's subsidies alone to finance Orthodox organization. From 1912 through 1916, he strove vainly to build an association of Orthodox congregations able to underwrite the Rabbinical Board. In December, 1912, a conference of congregational representatives laid the groundwork for a federation. Prominent laymen led by Meyer Jarmulowsky, the East Side banker and a member of the Kehillah's executive committee, headed the movement. The prospects seemed so promising in the spring of 1913 that the Kehillah's convention discussed the relationships between the two organizations. Magnes, for example, insisted that the Orthodox group be independent. Several days after the convention he wrote to Jarmulowsky congratulating him and the Orthodox Jews of the city on "what seems to be a happy solution of a difficult problem." [70]

The optimism proved misplaced. In his report to the Kehillah convention a year later, Magnes described the efforts that had been made to maintain the Rabbinical Board and encourage it in its work. He had hoped that the Board's activities would convince the Orthodox of the "necessity of organizing themselves into a strong and unified section of the community." But that strategy had failed, and so the convention voted to put the Rabbinical Board on an independent footing. Perhaps this would prod the Orthodox into facing their internal problems.[71]

In the spring of 1915, the kashruth issue stirred the Orthodox circles to their most sustained collective effort since the founding of the Board of Rabbis. The New York legislature passed the so-called Kosher Bill, which made it a misdemeanor to sell meat "falsely represented as kosher." Government fiat, it seemed, might now provide the basis and incentive for creating a workable system. The Kehillah's Religious Committee seized the initiative and formed a "committee of one hundred" which included nearly all factions. (Reb Velvele and his followers did not participate.) A contribution of $60,000 provided the means to guarantee the salaries of rabbis and shochtim participating in the program. The major meat-packers, however, ignored the new Board and a fall in meat prices reduced the expected income from kashruth. The entire subsidy went to cover the deficit, and it was not renewed the following year. Nor did the committee of one hundred enlist any significant support.[72] Even the defense of kashruth had failed to kindle a sustained collaborative effort by the Orthodox group.

Meanwhile, the Kehillah's religious committee attempted to cope with some of the less controversial problems. Nearly every year it sent representatives to Albany to lobby for legislation which would permit observant Jews to open their businesses or work on Sunday.[73] It inaugurated Kehillah-sponsored "provisional synagogues" to offset the "mushroom synagogues." In 1913, the peak year for this activity, seven such centers served 2,000 worshippers. The project apparently had some effect and encouraged established synagogues to sponsor annual supplementary services.[74] In 1914, the Kehillah established a Milah board in response to complaints made to the Department of Health. Incompetent mohelim (religious functionaries who performed the rite of circumcision), the Department had told Magnes, were threatening the health of the community. The Milah board, composed of medical doctors, rabbis, and representatives of the Association of Mohelim, instituted courses, prepared a medical and religious handbook (which was endorsed by Dr. Haven Emerson, Commissioner of Health), and examined prospective practitioners. By 1916, the Board had certified forty *mohelim*.[75] A similar instance involved the *mikva'ot*, where the Kehillah handled complaints of unsanitary conditions referred to it by the Department of Health. Emerson appreciated the fact that problems entailing sensitive religious questions were dealt with in an unobtrusive and responsible manner.[76] The Kehillah also sponsored a number of conferences to clarify the problem of rabbinical divorce.[77]

But these were peripheral matters. The main issue—the disorganization of Orthodoxy—remained unresolved. The Kehillah did bring together the Orthodox rabbis. But they were bewildered men torn between an attempt, on the one hand, to reestablish their Old World position in the community and, on the other hand, dependent in that very endeavor upon a Kehillah which was pluralistic and at whose head stood a Reform rabbi. In the kashruth question, the pluralistic Kehillah readily granted their preeminence, eager to revive a center of Orthodox authority around which the lay leadership could coalesce. The expectations of the rabbis rose. For the first time in their American experience a communal establishment existed, no matter how frail. Within it or against it the rabbis could now unite to insist upon their traditional prerogatives. These included not only kashruth and other ritual matters but overseeing Jewish education. For the Kehillah's leadership, the reconstruction of Jewish education was its major undertaking, and it transcended, in their view, denominational loyalties. Education, then, was bound to become another area of conflict between hostile social and religious creeds and clashing ambitions.

CHAPTER FIVE

Education as a Communal Responsibility

JEWISH EDUCATION OFFERED THE KEHILLAH AN UNMATCHED OPPOR-
tunity to elaborate and popularize its theories of Jewish group
life.[1] Assigning a high priority to educational activity meant
transforming the Kehillah into more than a public forum and
coordinating agency. Important as these functions were, they hardly
inspired the vision of building a culturally creative and purposeful
community. Educational work did. Men like Magnes equated the
problem of the unschooled and the poorly schooled with the question of group survival. This entailed, they asserted, reconstructing
Jewish education, an undertaking which provided scope for those
who spoke of a Jewish cultural renaissance.[2]

Kehillah leaders also presented religious education as necessary for
the successful integration of the immigrant masses into American society. In this respect, they shared the conviction of progressive educators that the school must play a decisive role in social betterment and
particularly in saving the young of the city's ghettos. But the thrust
of Americanization and its secularist commitment, Kehillah leaders
held, limited the public school in the performance of its mission.
The immigrant and his children, taken up in the feverish tempo of
transition and adjustment to American society, required the guidance
of a complementary educational force—religious training. It alone

could assure the transmission of the group's moral values to the young.[3] "How can we expect," Magnes wrote to Jacob Schiff, "young men and women growing up in crowded sections and working under unfavorable conditions to be pure and clean and honorable, if they are allowed to drift from the anchorage which the religion of their fathers might have given them?" Magnes saw the rift between parents and children as the nub of the problem. That gap could be bridged, he believed, only through a Judaism acceptable to the parents and made attractive to the children. An effective system of Jewish supplementary schools was therefore necessary. Such a system held out the hope that Jewish youth would grow into "American men and women who will prove not a menace to the Republic but a blessing to it." [4]

The field of education also offered to the newly established Kehillah the attractive possibility of a leap forward in organizational growth. A large patchwork of institutions did exist, inadequate and ineffective as many claimed them to be. Thus conditions seemed opportune to demonstrate the Kehillah's efficiency as a coordinating and policy-making agency. In his programmatic address to the founding convention, Magnes described the roles a "Board of Jewish Education" and a "Superintendent of Instruction" could play in creating an educational system out of the existing morass.[5]

§

UPON WHAT ASSETS COULD A COMMUNAL AGENCY DEVOTED TO JEWISH ethnic survival draw? Certainly the Russian-Jewish legacy of religious study was central. For three and a half centuries in the setting of the devout and socially isolated world of East European Jewry, educational activity had flourished. As an essential component of piety, it held a preeminent place in the hierarchy of Old World values. Hallowed by custom, supervised by communal authority, and all-pervasive in its social and cultural effects, the comprehensive system of religious education placed a common stamp upon Russian Jewry. True, the secular movements spawned by modernism challenged venerated ways and shook the established pattern of education. Nevertheless, the Russian-Jewish immigrants in the New World were largely products of that educational system.[6]

Despite the bruising experience of immigration and such startling new conditions as citizenship and free state education, many struggled to provide the young with religious training inspired by the "old country." One of the first major decisions of the newly organized Kehillah was to survey the results of the effort.[7]

In September, 1909, the executive committee of the Kehillah approved Dr. Mordecai M. Kaplan's proposal for a detailed survey of the conditions of Jewish education. By December, ten investigators under the supervision of a public school principal had canvassed the city's major areas of Jewish settlement. Two executive committee meetings discussed the preliminary findings and in February, 1910, Kaplan presented the final report to the first annual convention of the Kehillah.[8]

The investigation stirred interest on two counts: it was the first systematic study of its kind (research as the necessary first step in solving a problem became an article of faith for the Kehillah's leaders); and second, it revealed a wasteland of apathy for religious training, and ineptitude where it was offered. The scientific character of the investigation, its endorsement by a body fairly representative of organized Jewish life, and the convention setting of open debate roused the community. Overnight the study provided benchmarks in an unsurveyed field.[9] Heretofore, problems of religious education belonged to the province of small, isolated groups, motivated by personal philanthropy or private gain. The Kehillah at its 1910 convention transferred such discussion to the public realm.

Three-quarters of the Jewish children of school age, Kaplan reported, received no religious instruction. The quarter given some training hardly fared better. Incompetent teachers, shabby quarters, and a sterile approach to education combined to estrange many of the young. Of the approximately 51,954 children who received instruction, 27 percent (13,952) supplemented their public school session with daily attendance in 468 small, improvised, private schools, the "ignominious" *hadarim*. They were "conducted by one, two, or three men," who wished only to "eke out . . . a livelihood which they failed to obtain by another means." Classes met in the "basement or upper floor of some old dilapidated building" where rent was minimal. The provisional classrooms were "usually filthy, the light dim and [the] air stuffy." A single class included all ages and levels, and the turnover was large. Instruction seldom went beyond "the mechanical reading of the prayer book [in Hebrew] and the teaching of a few blessings by rote." Finally, since most teachers were recent arrivals, they employed Yiddish as the language of instruction.[10]

Beyond the statistical reach of the investigator, private itinerant tutors "peddled their wares." The majority, informed observers claimed, failed even more dismally than the proprietors of the *hadarim*. With no overhead and only a prayer book needed as a text, anyone desperate enough to be satisfied with an average annual income of $2.50 per student could enter the field. At best, private teaching supplemented a full day's work elsewhere. In making their rounds, perhaps a thousand such tutors reached ten thousand youngsters. Heder and tutor probably accounted for nearly half of those receiving religious instruction.[11]

At the other pole, the Sunday schools of the Reform temples and the congregational schools of the neo-Orthodox catered to the children of their members. Religious and cultural barriers, and a geographical and social gulf, separated these institutions from the great mass of immigrant Jews. Seventy-one such schools served 9,790 students. But judged even in their own terms, their performance provided little comfort. Though pedagogical standards were decent, in part because they employed large numbers of American-born, public school teachers, the fare they offered was meager.[12] Neither institutionally nor educationally did they provide a guide for dealing with the children of the immigrants. Jewish settlement houses and children's homes conducted religious schools which served the immigrant quarter. Supported by German-Jewish philanthropists, these institutions ignored the traditional methods and subject matter of the East European schools. The immigrant avoided them whenever possible. Thus the Americanized form of Jewish education, both in its own locale and in its downtown form, accounted for nearly a third of the children receiving instruction.[13]

Though the report drew a gloomy picture of the communally sponsored Talmud Torah schools, Kaplan and his associates at last sounded a note of hope. What distinguished these schools from the others was the element of public enterprise in their formation and operation. Originally intended only for the indigent (in Europe, parents who could possibly afford tuition preferred the private heder), the Talmud Torah provided not only religious training but it clothed and often fed its charges. Support of the Talmud Torah association in the East European town, like all charitable work, brought esteem and public recognition.[14] In America, the critics said, circumstances had transformed the individual heder master into a petty business-man. He battled for survival as any other East Side merchant did. Neither the watchful eye of fellow townsmen nor the discipline of convention could enforce Old World standards in the American metropolis. On the other hand, the Talmud Torah association as a charitable and communal undertaking not only survived the crossing but offered the best possibilities for a reconstruction of Jewish education.[15]

In the name of a charity well-remembered from Europe, associations succeeded in appealing for broad popular support. Good works also satisfied a social need. Kaplan reported the existence of twenty-four Talmud Torah schools. A study published a year later described the financial condition of the eight largest schools and confirmed the survey's generalizations of the broad base of Talmud Torah support. The eight sponsoring associations listed 6,641 dues-paying supporters, only 48 of whom contributed $25 or more.[16]

The Talmud Torah association's independence of synagogue affiliation added to its communal character. This feature especially appealed to the Kehillah's leaders. In seeking support and clients, the Talmud Torah transcended, at least in part, the rampant particularism of the immigrant ghetto. Where the number of landsmanshaftn helped account for the plethora of immigrant synagogues, it affected the Talmud Torah less.[17] Such institutions, hopefully, would be amenable to joining an educational system.

From these characteristics stemmed another encouraging prospect. The Talmud Torah association as a communal body owed an accounting to its supporting members; hence some degree of form and order was inevitable. This, in turn, implied rational, institutional management. Popular support, public accountability, and communal direction, Kehillah leaders believed, could lead to the modernization of the Jewish educational structure. Modernization would bring graded classes, a stable teaching staff, pedagogical supervision, decent salaries, textbooks and, eventually, even proper physical plants. In short, the charity school of the Russian-Jewish town would now become the supplementary Jewish public school.[18] Kaplan found trends in that direction in the Kehillah's survey.

The Talmud Torah school frequently occupied an entire building, and the larger schools contained from ten to twenty classrooms. There were 29 students attending the average heder, 98 the average congregational school, and 188 the average Sunday school. But 446 attended the average Talmud Torah, and if only the eight largest were considered the figure rose to 881 per school. Though salaries rarely reached $40 a month and often were as low as $25 (teachers generally taught twenty-two hours a week in the Talmud Torah schools), this wage scale exceeded that of any other type of school. Finally, half the pupils paid some tuition so that the Talmud Torah was losing the stigma of a charity school. The 10,710 students who attended these schools (20 percent of all those receiving instruction), Kaplan concluded, received the best education available. But what a far cry that was from a satisfactory level. Another statistic sums up conditions in this way: in 1909, all of New York contained but one building erected specifically as a Jewish religious school. But the building was a Talmud Torah.[19]

The Talmud Torah sector contained yet another asset. Dedicated pedagogues from among the immigrant intelligentsia, though relatively few in number, could be found scattered among its schools. They belonged, in the main, to that branch of the European Jewish enlightenment, the Haskala, which exalted Hebraic culture as the essence of "the Jewish renaissance." From Russia they brought a familiarity with the reforms in methodology and curriculum which formed part of the cultural and social ferment of the times. By 1910, such men had risen to controlling positions in a handful of institutions in New York. They attracted like-minded men and introduced changes inspired by their Jewish national commitment.[20]

Two events in the spring of 1909, shortly before the Kehillah raised the education question, testified to a disquiet shared in other circles. Lay and professional leaders of a number of Talmud Torah schools organized the Central Board of Jewish Education. Parallel but unrelated to the formation of the Central Board was an endowment fund of $50,000, established by Jacob Schiff, for the Teachers Institute of the Jewish Theological Seminary. In the summer of 1909, Mordecai Kaplan became principal, at the same time, entering actively into the Kehillah's deliberations on education. Before committing the Kehillah to the field of Jewish education, Magnes established close contact with both Schiff and the Central Board.[21] The latter could offer little more than moral support. Schiff offered money. At the Kehillah convention in February, 1910, the Jewish public learned not only of the distressing state of religious training. It also heard Magnes announce the philanthropist's gift of $50,000 to the Kehillah. The money, to be paid in five annual installments, was earmarked for the "improvement and promoting of Jewish religious primary education in this city." [22]

The assignment was awesome. Instruction for but half the Jewish children of school age required an expenditure of $1.5 million. Needed, too, were 1,500 capable teachers. "And in this country ability means that Hebrew teachers should possess, in addition to their intellectual and pedagogic equipment, a knowledge of our American Jewish youth; they should be imbued with American ideals, and they should know and love the Jewish people." [23] The promise of a flow of new financial resources and fresh organizational efforts into the field of Jewish education brought a surge of momentary elation. But above all, it heralded a totally new way of viewing the field itself.

In the course of several months, Magnes completed the foundation work for the new structure. The task entailed two fundamental decisions. The first turned on the most efficient way of using the Schiff donation. Many expected direct subventions for the hard-pressed schools. ("Fifty thousand dollars for *hadarim*," the *Morgen Journal* headline read.) [24] But rather than "prop up this or that institution," the executive committee accepted the approach which called for the creation of a "lever-like" apparatus. The institutional form was to be a bureau of Jewish education. With the available funds, such a bureau would study the existing educational forces, bring about "cooperation and the elimination of waste," organize teachers and supervisors "for both their material and their spiritual advancement," and undertake a vast campaign to "acquaint parents with the problem before them and with the means for solving it." [25]

Another phase of the program, the establishment of model schools, best illustrates the "lever" concept. Had unlimited funds been available, Kehillah leaders might well have established their own network of schools, or at least used subsidies to revamp, pedagogically, the existing institutions. But funds of this order did not exist. Consequently, they projected two experimental schools under the direct management of the bureau. Existing institutions, seeing the advantage of the new "textbooks, methods, appliances, etc., worked out in the model schools," and pressured by public opinion, would adopt the reforms. Moreover, in a second capacity, as preparatory schools, they would feed their superior students to the new Teachers Institute and provide laboratory experience for a generation of American-trained Jewish educators.[26]

The second question addressed itself to the locus of authority for the proposed bureau. Where did ultimate control lie? With Schiff, the donor? Or did it rest in the democratic institutions of the Kehillah, its executive committee, and ultimately the convention? How did one reconcile faith in the communal-democratic ideal of the Kehillah and the need for expertise and stability in the execution of the program? Obscurantists, partly responsible for present conditions, might conceivably seize control of rich endowments one day through the medium of Kehillah democracy. And of more immediate concern, the divisive interests of a heterogeneous population could paralyze the new agency.[27]

In the post-convention reorganization of the Kehillah's executive body, Magnes established his position clearly. The standing committee on education which he appointed reflected the full range of education opinion as well as specific institutional interests. The four Orthodox members included Dr. Joseph Bluestone, prime mover in the recent effort at Talmud Torah cooperation, and Rabbi Moses Z. Margolies, the distinguished Orthodox leader. Dr. Maurice H. Harris, a Reform rabbi, represented the liberal wing. Holding the middle ground (and the circle to which Magnes himself belonged), were Kaplan, Henrietta Szold, and the committee's chairman, Professor Israel Friedlaender. Magnes also appointed a public school principal, Dr. Bernard Cronson. "It might be useful to have a schoolman on our committee," Friedlaender advised Magnes, "one who could help us to regulate the relation between Jewish and secular education." Louis Marshall completed the committee. Schiff's close collaborator, this hardheaded, highly respected leader could be expected to keep a watchful eye on the youthful exuberance of the Magnes group.[28]

At the first meeting of the education committee, Magnes defined its responsibilities, and chief among them was supervision of the proposed bureau. But the executive committee was to remain the "final court of appeals." It approved budgets and its treasurer disbursed moneys. When Friedlaender dissented and protested the executive committee's lack of professional competence, Magnes extolled the arrangement as "ideal": the agency administering the private bequest should be subservient to a democratic body. For Kaplan, only the guiding hand of a democratic body assured a wide hearing for the bureau's ideas and the prospect of their eventual acceptance.[29]

In May, eight weeks after the convention and with the concurrence of all the principals, the Kehillah voted to establish a bureau of education and earmarked the Schiff fund for its use. The executive committee accepted the Magnes formula, which delegated routine supervision to the education committee but reserved final jurisdiction for itself. The satisfactory conclusion of the preliminary discussions brought a further indication of confidence in the Kehillah. The New York Foundation agreed to allocate $5,000 annually for five years to the Bureau. Behind the Foundation stood the family banking firm of Kuhn, Loeb and Company. The Foundation administered a million dollar legacy of Louis A. Heinsheimer, a late partner in the investment house. Professor Morris Loeb, son of a founder and the brother of Mrs. Jacob Schiff, served as its head. Thus Kuhn and Loeb accounted for the $15,000 annual subvention promised to the Kehillah's education arm. A year later, Felix Warburg, son-in-law of senior partner Jacob Schiff, joined in underwriting the bureau.[30]

In September, on the eve of the bureau's opening, second thoughts among the Kehillah's leaders led to a radical change in the supervisory arrangement. The executive committee, on Magnes' recommendation, appointed a board of trustees "with full power to administer the fund for five years." Lest there be a misunderstanding, the trustees, at their first meeting, defined their relationship to the Kehillah's education committee. The latter, the board decided, held only advisory functions in matters pertaining to the Bureau.[31]

Ostensibly, stability and efficiency dictated the change. However, the composition of the board of trustees suggests other considerations as well. Friedlaender, as chairman, joined by Kaplan, Magnes, Henrietta Szold, and Marshall, formed a well-knit group that shared much in common. The Jewish Theological Seminary provided one important bond. Either professionally, philanthropically, or intellectually, all five had a stake in the institution. It preached reverence for traditional Judaism and also upheld integration in American society. Thus it personified a middle way between a segregated East European Orthodoxy and the kind of Americanization that forswore all loyalties to the ancestral tradition.[32]

Leadership of the Zionist movement linked all the trustees but Marshall. In their Zionism, they further shared the emphasis on Jewish cultural activity identified with Ahad Ha'am. But unlike Ahad Ha'am, who was a secularist, the Magnes group assigned a central role to religion in their scheme of a Jewish national revival. With Solomon Schechter, president of the Jewish Theological Seminary, these young intellectuals saw Zionism as "the great bulwark against assimilation." Its success lay "in bringing back into the fold . . . those who otherwise would have been lost to Judaism."[33]

For Americanized Jews of German origin like Marshall and Schiff, this strain of Zionism, no less than the Herzlian political brand, contained the potential for exaggerated ethnicism. But though it was suspect, it was tolerable. The adherents of cultural Zionism, after all, saw education, not politics, as the decisive act. Consequently, the Bureau of Education, like the Jewish Theological Seminary, provided a field for collaboration in bringing enlightenment to the immigrant Jews. German-Jewish wealth financed the idealogues of cultural survivalism recognizing that no other group was similarly equipped to speak to the young men of the East Side. With its youth, American roots, talent, and determination to halt the growing alienation from

Judaism, the Magnes group would assure a balanced and healthy Americanization.[34]

Not a single member of the education committee identified with Orthodoxy was, consequently, promoted to the inner circle of policy-makers. Ignoring them meant disregarding the lay leaders of the largest schools. Even under the most auspicious beginnings, the enterprise would have been suspect in the eyes of the Orthodox. Magnes' imprudence (as Kehillah chairman and intermediary, the responsibility is his) undoubtedly increased their misgivings. When in time the Kehillah's opponents, for their own self-interest, fanned existing discontent into wild, damaging accusations, they were able to exploit these grievances.[35]

The Kehillah leaders also came to the 1910 convention with a candidate for director of the program. Dr. Samson Benderly, head of the Baltimore Hebrew Free School, had acquired a reputation as a brilliant educator and innovator. Born in Safed, Palestine, educated at the American College in Beirut, Benderly came to the United States in 1898 to complete his medical studies. But shortly after graduating, to the consternation of friends, he abandoned a medical career for the unpromising one of Jewish education.[36]

Even in his early work, Benderly disclosed those tendencies and traits which later characterized his guidance of the Bureau of Education. He sought to apply the new educational thought to Jewish religious training. His school became a laboratory. "In the mornings he would read," a former student recalled, "and in the afternoon he would test out these newly acquired theories. Then the fun began. We seldom did the same thing twice. We experimented with everything." Benderly taught Bible with a stereopticon and homemade slides. He instituted play periods, taught Hebrew through games, and employed the natural method of language instruction (avoiding the vernacular wherever possible). Student government, extracurricular activities, holiday celebrations, and attention to health standards were other indicators of the tendencies of his showcase school.[37]

Benderly preferred American-born teachers, despite their inadequate Judaic background, over the new immigrants who were steeped in Jewish knowledge, but strangers to American youth. Consequently, the informal training of teachers became part of the school program. The American experience, he believed, produced a malleable type, inherently sympathetic to the main intellectual currents of the times. To Benderly, science applied to education, given full reign in pragmatic, democratic America, provided the means for closing the gap between barren performance and the appalling need. When it was applied to teaching methods, curriculum, teacher training, and administration, even the circumscribed Jewish school with its limited hours and more limited budget became an effective instrument. The Hebrew teacher from Europe, he felt, could never wholly identify with this approach. Later, in New York, Benderly valued the professionally trained pedagogue more highly than the scholar immersed in Jewish lore.[38]

For Benderly, educational reform eliminated the need of the parochial school as guarantor of ethnic continuity. As an idealogue of survivalism, Benderly should have favored the more comprehensive system once he determined that the supplementary school was failing to raise a generation loyal to Judaism. The Orthodox yeshiva, with its daylong program and emphasis on Hebrew studies, did offer an example of the maximalist curriculum in operation. Catholic parochial schools, furthermore, provided massive proof that a considerable body of Americans had the courage to choose the way of separate education. Instead, Benderly urged, modernize the methods and improve the facilities of the supplementary schools. In fact, reduce the hours of Hebrew study even further. The physical and emotional strain the child endured attending two schools required it. The supplementary school curriculum, he continued, had to be "simplified and coordinated" with that of the public school "so that the child spends in the Hebrew school as little time as is actually needed." Then let the Hebrew school make its offerings "so interesting and stimulating as to get the response even of tired children." [39]

Benderly not only rejected the parochial school as unnecessary but as objectionable as well. He embraced the tenet of the public school as the *sine qua non* for a Jewish educational system. Jews in America formed an integral part of the Republic. They were "under an obligation to demonstrate that the principles [of Judaism] . . . are perfectly compatible with and essential to the fundamental principles upon which the American nation is building a wonderful structure of human liberty and happiness." Consequently, "as the great public school system is the rock bottom upon which this country is rearing its institutions, so we Jews must evolve here a system of Jewish education that shall be complementary to and harmonious with the public school system." [40]

And indeed, for the Jewish immigrant and his Americanized mentors, the public school was the great democratic institution, the bridge to the new society, and the key to self-improvement.[41] None but a handful chose the yeshiva over the free state school. Nor could the parochial school mobilize significant financial support. Anathema in the eyes of the uptown wealthy, the yeshiva received only little support from the downtown men of means. Kaplan failed even to mention, in his report to the convention, the existence of the East Side's one, well-established parochial school, though it had roused some attention in the Jewish quarter. At an education committee meeting in April, 1910, an Orthodox member asked Magnes whether that yeshiva would be eligible for aid. Until he had become acquainted with Benderly's "system," Magnes replied, he had been for parochial schools. Now he believed the implementation of Benderly's ideas made the parochial school unnecessary.[42]

For all these reasons, Magnes and Schiff found Benderly eminently suited to direct the projected bureau. Throughout the winter and spring of 1910, Magnes consulted Benderly on all stages of the discussions. The Baltimore educator attended the crucial meetings with Schiff and Loeb, and his formulation of aims and guiding principles became the official program of the new agency. In October, the Bureau officially opened its doors. A sense of resoluteness and clarity of purpose marked the occasion. Schiff's five-year financial commitment undoubtedly contributed to the mood of self-confidence. But careful preparation played its part as well. Kaplan's report, the convention debates, and Benderly's activity as planner and director-designate had all preceded the official launching of the enterprise. Benderly, in fact, spent much of the summer in New York immersed in the work.[43] Thus seven months of diligent activity preceded his public appearance in the fall of 1910. The preparatory phase seemed letter-perfect. Even the suspicious *Morgen Journal* applauded. Benderly, the paper wrote, "belongs to a class of persons rarely found among our people. He is a real specialist." His appointment alone justified the existence of the Kehillah. About to take place, the *Morgen Journal* noted, was "the first systematic attempt to bring order out of the chaos of Jewish education in America." Moreover, not only did Benderly possess great ability but he had the financial backing to carry out his plan. Those "who do not feel inclined to help," the paper hoped would not "hamper the work by . . . premature opposition." [44]

The first meeting of the board of trustees happily noted the "kindly feeling that existed toward the Bureau of Education" and ordered the *Morgen Journal's* editorial spread upon the minutes.[45]

By February, 1911, five months after the Bureau's opening, Benderly could report prodigious achievements. Two model schools were in operation. Textbooks prepared the previous summer were already in use. A talent search in the local colleges yielded the first of a highly motivated group of recruits for the field of Jewish education. Under the Bureau's tutelage, Benderly placed them in an apprenticeship program as teachers and learners. He succeeded, too, in convincing some schools to adopt his curriculum reforms and employ his teachers.[46] Nor had he neglected research. A study of the financial conditions and administrative procedures of the larger schools was nearly complete. And finally, under the Bureau chief's guidance, the principals of the largest Talmud Torah schools were meeting weekly to formulate a set of common goals and a common curriculum.[47]

These results, Benderly wrote to Magnes, "prompt me to lay a plan before you, the consequences [of which] may prove of great moment to Judaism in America." Benderly envisioned a permanent endowment that would provide the Bureau with an additional $100,000 annually. A fifth of the sum he earmarked for aid to new schools. Each year the Bureau would supervise the establishment of ten new schools with a capacity for 5,000 students, a beginning towards providing for the 150,000 unschooled. With two-fifths of the funds,

Benderly planned to improve those existing institutions amenable to change. This meant implementing the recommendations of the principals' conferences. The forward-looking schools and those with the largest enrollments, by implication the most efficient, would thereby be rewarded. The remaining two-fifths of the annual income Benderly budgeted for the training of one hundred teachers a year. Preparatory schools, subsidizing students to permit full-time study at the Teachers Institute, and special courses in education and English for immigrant teachers were some of the proposals for teacher training.[48]

Magnes endorsed the plan of an Education Fund enthusiastically and turned to Jacob Schiff. If the philanthropist would subscribe half the sum, the Kehillah chairman was prepared to turn to the community at large for the rest. "The Jewish community," he wrote, "has never been tested like this." Schiff rejected the endowment idea as impractical. A fund of $2 million, he said, would be required to provide an annual income of $100,000. Moreover, he objected to the idea in principle. This generation should not be asked "to provision for all times to come the needs of the community." How much he would give depended "upon the readiness with which our Russian-Jewish townsmen would come forward themselves in support of the scheme." Schiff finally agreed to subscribe $10,000 a year (in addition to his $10,000 annual subvention to the Bureau) provided the Kehillah would raise an additional $40,000.[49]

Not only did the financier halve the goal of $100,000, but he upset whatever hope Magnes entertained for a permanent endowment. A veto of this idea by the head of Kuhn, Loeb and Company precluded asking others to join in guaranteeing the financial security of the Bureau. Instead, the Kehillah chairman faced the task of financing the educational program with short-term contributions. Continued support would now require periodic solicitations and subject the Bureau to all the hazards of fund-raising. In the years ahead that chore became increasingly onerous. But in the spring of 1911, Magnes shouldered the burden with gusto. "Dr. Benderly, Dr. Friedlaender, Dr. Kaplan, and myself are young and hopeful," Magnes wrote to Schiff, "and we are willing to make a strong fight for Jewish education, because we feel that Judaism in this country is largely dependent for its strength upon the education this generation is able to give its children." [50]

Magnes turned for aid to three groups: German-Jewish financiers, largely members of Temple Emanuel; Russian-Jewish merchants and textile entrepreneurs, members of the newer and more affluent Orthodox synagogues (most of whom spent their summers at the Long Island resort town of Arverne); and the Cloak and Suit Manufacturers Association.[51] Two hundred and thirty-three donors pledged sums which ranged from Schiff's $10,000 and Felix Warburg's $5,000 to $10 and $25 subscriptions.[52] On January 31, 1912, in a victory statement to the general and Yiddish press, the Kehillah chairman announced that $50,000 per annum, "the first quota of the Jewish Education Fund of New York City," had been raised. Nearly all subscriptions covered a period of five years. Thus the $250,000 pledged, together with the moneys already at the disposal of the Bureau of Education, exceeded $300,000.[53]

For the Kehillah's partisans, this may have been their most gratifying hour. For Magnes, certainly, the moment was one of great personal triumph. He had brought together widely disparate elements in support of a radical innovation: the communal support of Jewish education. And implicit in the concept of an educational agency serving a Jewish public and all its factions was the idea of the Kehillah. In his press statement on the Education Fund, Magnes also announced his resignation from the pulpit.

With the aid of several men of this city, I shall have the opportunity of devoting myself to those problems of Jewish religious organization and Jewish education, without being attached to any particular snyagogue. A society for the advancement of Judaism has been formed and I expect through this society to be given complete freedom and added energy to devote myself to Jewish work in this city.[54]

Provided for financially by a group of admirers, the thirty-four-year-old rabbi chose the Kehillah as the most important public career open in Jewish life. The *Maccabaean*, among others, hailed the announcement. Freed of rabbinical obligations, Magnes could now devote himself to "building up Jewish life generally." [55]

The optimism of 1912 became the burden of 1914 and the despair of 1916. On the one hand, promises and half-promises remained unkept. On the other hand, Benderly, strong-willed, venturesome, and indefatigable, expanded the scope of the Bureau and demanded ever larger sums from Magnes. In October, 1914, the deficit reached $32,-182. Of the 233 contributors who pledged themselves in 1911 to donate a fixed sum annually for five years, only 89 met their obligations three years later. In January, 1916, Benderly estimated that the deficit would reach $49,797 by September 30, the end of the Bureau's fiscal year. Had he added the debt incurred by the Textbook Fund, which was treated as a separate account, total indebtedness would have amounted to $72,330.[56]

The Textbook Fund deserves attention as an illustration of one cause of the Bureau's predicament: the disparity between Benderly's soaring plans, the Bureau's financial limitations, and the badly neglected field to be worked.

From the outset, Benderly railed against the dearth of adequate educational material. "What we need," he wrote, "is a graded, well-printed, properly bound, illustrated series of text books that take into consideration the limited time at the disposal of our children." The books had to be as attractive and as pedagogically sound as those used in the public schools. He outlined a series of 28 volumes, 4 for each year of a seven-year curriculum, with 28 companion volumes for teachers. By 1915, 18 had appeared. Needed, too, were language charts (Benderly soon revised the estimated cost from $1,900 to $5,000), Hebrew maps (50,000 sets of a series of sixteen colored maps were printed), storybooks for home-reading, and slides for teaching biblical history. Since the initial grant did not cover these items, Benderly proposed borrowing $10,000 on commercial terms. Predicting a nation-wide demand for the material, he expected repayment of the loan within five years. Four years later the Textbook Fund owed $30,683. Its assets included $26,547 of inventory, and the original loan, with interest, now amounted to $11,460.[57]

Commercially, the undertaking was a disaster. But it marked the entrance of Jewish education into the modern age of pedagogy. "The attempt to produce a graded series of Jewish textbooks [and other educational material]," Benderly could well claim, "was unique in the history of Jewish education." In the spring of 1912, only weeks after the $10,000 loan had been arranged, three editors were engaged. By 1915, the number reached five (though the Bureau was in deep financial trouble that year). A children's magazine in English was proposed. Benderly approved the recommendation, hired special staff, and a weekly with a circulation of 15,000 soon appeared. A companion magazine in Hebrew was similarly issued. And, as in all his departments, Benderly succeeded in staffing his publications department with outstanding young men. (In 1915, the Bureau included the director, six department heads, and a total personnel of sixty-one, many of whom, however, were part-time employees.) [58] Members of the staff, who later became Benderly's severest critics, recalled the pervasive spirit of dedication and inventiveness which characterized the Bureau. But as the financial predicament worsened, Benderly "would not accept the edict of the budget," one memorialist recalls. "He was unable to master his own urge to initiate new enterprises, though no new sources of money existed." Payrolls went unmet and threatened the Bureau with demoralization.[59]

Nor was the board of trustees of much help. Strong on intellect but short on fund-raising acumen, it considered its primary function a policy-making one when the overriding problem was financial. As early as 1913, the treasurer, Henrietta Szold, asked to be relieved of signing checks. Financial arrangements had become so uncertain and fund-raising so important that she no longer could exercise any control over disbursements. A year later the trustees ceased meeting regularly. [60] Friedlaender put it bluntly when he, too, asked to resign in 1915. Owing to financial problems, the board had lost all control over the activities of the Bureau. Friedlaender was particularly disturbed because the Bureau "never paid salaries on time." Furthermore, Benderly ran things as he pleased. With all admiration for the Bureau chief, Friedlaender was unwilling to continue as a figurehead. "I feel like a rider who has been thrown off by his horse and, holding to the tail, is dragged along the street, with this difference that the rider in this case is not allowed to let go." [61]

In the spring of 1915, Herbert H. Lehman joined the executive committee and accepted the chairmanship of the Kehillah's finance committee. His primary assignment was to eliminate the $73,000 deficit of the Bureau of Education. A banker, not an educator, now supervised the budget. Magnes soon received the stern warning (though Benderly was the culprit) to live within his means and to cut back the Bureau's activities. Debts were canceled and some new

moneys raised, but the financial straits of the Bureau still weighed
heaviest on Magnes.[62] In a rare expression of personal feelings, he
wrote to Schiff in the summer of 1915:

After four years of work . . . the financial burden of the Bureau of
Education has rested primarily upon two persons—upon yourself and
upon me. . . . Not a day passes that, often after many difficulties and
much humiliation, I succeed in interviewing a number of people. Even
though these interviews often bring no financial results at first, they pave
the way for an understanding of the problem and for future contributions. . . . We have just received $1,000 from Eugene Meyer, Jr., with
whom, as an illustration of how things sometimes go, I have been laboring
for over three years.[63]

The letter begged Schiff to convince his son Mortimer to contribute $5,000. Mortimer refused. "I feel ashamed of the community,"
the elder Schiff wrote, "but we here [the Schiff family] have gone as
far as we should, and if others of wealth are unwilling to do their
duty, I am powerless to change this." A year later, Magnes pursued a
different tack. He asked the Schiff family, whose annual contributions now reached $35,000 a year, to guarantee a fixed sum for ten
years. With such a promise, Magnes hoped to convince other philanthropists to follow suit and finally provide the stability which the Bureau so desperately needed. He asked for himself "one whole year free
from daily worry as to how to meet the pay roll and the bills large
and small that plague us." [64] But by the fall of 1916, the establishment of a federation of charities appeared imminent. The possibility
that the new agency might accept financial responsibility for the Bureau brought Magnes' negotiations with Schiff to a near standstill. Attention shifted to the task of persuading the federation planners that
religious education was not a sectarian concern but constituted an integral part of a community welfare program. This meant convincing
philanthropists opposed to the Kehillah that Jewish education, most
of it in the hands of Orthodox and Zionists, was a communal responsibility which the new federation must support.

The question distressed not only uptown philanthropist-critics of
the Kehillah. It irritated no less the uptown sponsors of the Bu-

reau.[65] Dialectical and practical efforts to resolve the matter had, in fact, attended the Kehillah's educational activity from the start. The intellectual leaders and professionals of the Bureau were cultural Zionists, and precisely this ideological commitment suffused the educational work with the élan of a movement. Philanthropists like Schiff and Warburg were well aware of the sentiment shared by the Bureau's leadership. But what appeared to be a reasonable risk at the outset turned into concern and then anxiety as the Bureau grew, attracted exuberant young workers, and bred controversy. In February, 1914, replying to a request for increased support, Schiff expressed his dilemma to Friedlaender:

Dr. Magnes, of whom I am exceedingly fond and whose manly qualities and devotion to Jewish affairs I highly respect, but whose intense Jewish nationalism . . . makes him blind to everything outside of this, constitutes, in my opinion, a grave danger to many things we need hold dear.

What made Magnes particularly dangerous was his "magnetism . . . which, perhaps even unknown to him, hypnotizes many who come in closer touch with him." Yet, Schiff continued, should Magnes "eliminate himself from the situation, his loss to the cause of Jewish primary education and other problems, would be so great as to become almost fatal." [66]

Certainly the fear existed that zealots (Benderly, Friedlaender, Kaplan, and their disciples were of the same stripe as Magnes, if less "hypnotic") might use Jewish education to convert immigrant children segregated by circumstances into separatists by choice. To the philanthropists, their funds were, perhaps, stamping out one evil— the "obscurantism" of the heder master—by abetting another evil— the rampant ethnicism of Zionist educators.

Thus Felix Warburg queried the emphasis on Hebrew language instruction and the inclusion of Hebrew conversation in the Bureau's syllabus. Magnes' reply was only a half truth: it was pedagogically the most efficient means of teaching Judaism. "The Bureau is not interested in the least in making Hebrew a spoken language in this country," Benderly explained. "No sensible teacher would use this method in the Diaspora for such a purpose. The Bureau is merely searching for the shortest and most attractive road to the Bible and Prayer Book. The natural method is based on pedagogic principles." [67]

Benderly and his colleagues may have had no intention to make Hebrew a spoken language in America. But they were being less than candid. Surely, as cultural nationalists and disciples of Ahad Ha'am, their emphasis on Hebrew was more than a pedagogical device. For them, the language was the essence of Jewish education. It not only linked the child with his past, but it promised to win him for the movement for Jewish renaissance. In Palestine, Hebrew was a spoken language. And cultural Zionism, with its vision of a revived center in Palestine, offered, they believed, the best hope for ethnic survival.[68]

Lack of ingenuousness under the pressure of fund-raising did not prevent the Bureau's leaders from espousing cultural survivalism. The question of the Bureau's philosophy rose periodically and created storms of controversy.[69] A year after Warburg's letter, Lee Kohns, a trustee of the City College of New York and vice-chairman of the Educational Alliance, wrote to Friedlaender:

What certainly cannot be subscribed to . . . is the plan of the Kehillah which . . . states that the aim of Jewish education is to be: "The preservation of the Jews as a *distinct* [emphasis is Kohns's] people existing and developing in the spirit of the Jewish religion."

Certainly, this is an unwise provision. It does not seem to me to be a patriotic provision. . . .

What we need is more training in the ethical teachings of Judaism, and I do not think you can overdo this with our constituency [of the East Side]. If this were combined with the religious conception of the Fatherhood of one Supreme and Eternal Being, you have the essence of Judaism and the moral benefit of what it stands for. We need nothing more today.[70]

In two ways Magnes and his associates sought an accommodation with the philanthropists, despite their differing views. The Bureau of Education, they urged, was non-partisan. Magnes gave expression to this notion most succinctly in his address to the 1912 convention:

As a Kehillah Bureau, we feel we must be above all parties in Judaism. . . . We do not . . . emphasize this kind or that kind of Judaism. . . . Our chief aim is purely technical. . . . We find at hand a mass of material called Judaism. We find schools desirous of teaching this to children.

We come to them with expert advice as to what appears to us to be the best way of imparting this instruction. . . . It becomes the function . . . of each individual school to put its own stamp upon its teaching.[71]

Four years later, at another convention, Magnes used rhetoric that undoubtedly appealed to the uptown patricians. It came at a time when the Jewish Congress issue (which is discussed later) embroiled the community. That controversy was portrayed by some as the revolt of the East European masses against the hegemony of the German-Jewish aristocracy.

Our idea of expertness has been this: That whatever bureau we have established should be scientific, should be systematic, should be well ordered, should be nonpartisan, should be removed from the heat and dirt of Jewish politics. Just as in the larger community we are all eager to see our public school system out of the hands of the politicians, big and little, so have we in the Kehillah wanted our Bureau of Education to be out of the hands of the communal politicians. . . . We have done our educational work in a nonpartisan way, looking neither to the right nor to the left.[72]

The concept of a "bureau of experts," couched as it was in the contemporary idiom of good government, probably soothed the uneasiness of the moderates among the uptown philanthropists.

Presenting religious education as uplift was the second tactic which Bureau partisans used to win patrician support. The theme appeared in the first overtures to Jacob Schiff. "We must Americanize, in the higher sense, every Jew in this country," Benderly wrote in 1910, "infusing into him the spirit of self-reliance, fair play, and social cooperation." But as the need grew to seek funds more widely and more intensely and as the Bureau became more dependent on uptown philanthropists, Jewish education as a remedial device received greater emphasis.[73] "The horde of Jewish children who either do not receive at present any religious education whatsoever, or receive it in a manner not compatible with American conditions [are] a danger to the position of the Jew in communal and American life." This is how Schiff, Philip Lehman, and Paul M. Warburg formulated the problem in an invitation to New York's Jewish elite to consider the formation of a "general board of education" in support of the Bureau.

The statement of purposes they then drafted represented Jewish religious education as the necessary supplement of the public school in the struggle to save children from growing up in "ignorance, stultified by vice, or oppressed by the sordidness of things." [74]

Presenting the problem of Jewish education in this manner nettled the Bureau's leaders. "I loathe the argument which looks upon religion as a kind of police force," Friedlaender wrote privately. Yet, Friedlaender and his friends well knew that no other approach would impress uptown philanthropists. And for seven years their pragmatic and necessarily pluralistic strategy in fact yielded salutary results. From 1910 to 1917, about $380,000 was raised for the use of the community's central educational agency. Pew holders of Temple Emanuel placed large sums in the hands of Jewish professional educators (a new type), who then assisted Orthodox Talmud Torahs, among others. There never had been enough funds. Donors gave reluctantly and some of them perhaps for the wrong reasons. Only a handful of men carried the bulk of the burden. Nevertheless a principle had been forcefully stated: the education of the community's youth in any of its assorted forms deserved the support of all sections of the Jewish public. [75] Now, with the launching of the new Federation, the Kehillah could press the new body to accept this principle and to support its institutional expression.

In November, 1917, six educational bodies—the Bureau of Education among them—were declared affiliated with the Federation for the Support of Jewish Philanthropic Societies. All had worked closely with the Bureau, and even within the Federation they maintained their corporate identity. A measure of financial stability had been achieved at last. [76]

The event was notable on two accounts. It indicated a reversal of the Federation's initial decision made nine months before which excluded "philanthropic-religious activities" from its purview. The Federation existed, its leaders explained at the time, in order to alleviate distress and not to underwrite religious instruction. The latter constituted, they argued, a congregational service, not a community problem. But Benderly, Magnes, and the lay leaders they had drawn into the Bureau's activities—including those benefactors who viewed

Jewish religious education as social amelioration—were influential enough to win a reversal of the decision.[77]

The event was also portentous for the Kehillah. The idea of Kehillah had inspired the Bureau scheme. Seven pioneering years had won acceptance for the corollary of that idea—the communal responsibility for Jewish education. For this reason alone, the Kehillah could have hardly survived the admission that it no longer was capable of shouldering that burden. It was surrendering its most striking achievement.

CHAPTER SIX

Education: The Professionals and the Orthodox

THE BUREAU OF EDUCATION WAS NOT ALONE IN CLAIMING A principal share in the direction of Jewish educational work. So did the Orthodox. The latter's claim rested on the authority of religious law and custom, and on the premise that the religious instruction of immigrant youth, the object of concern, was its exclusive responsibility. To this end, Orthodox circles established Talmud Torahs, drawing upon the Old World experience for their model. Though overburdened by their maintenance, and distressed by poor results, the Orthodox rabbis, in particular, distrusted the calls for collaboration and innovation. An authoritative tradition rooted in the segregated Jewish world of Eastern Europe clashed with the modern liberal ethos of the Americanized part of the community.

Mediating influences were also present. The financial resources of the Bureau did induce hard-pressed Orthodox lay leaders to seek an accommodation with the non-Orthodox. No less important was the stand of the Bureau's directors. As cultural survivalists they valued Orthodoxy; it was the keeper of the group's inheritance. They recognized, moreover, the residual strength it possessed in the Jewish quarters of the city. The Bureau therefore assigned a central place to the Orthodox schools within its pluralistic system of education.

In shaping that system, the Bureau applied the methods and insights of progressive education to a variety of new situations testing their applicability to the peculiar problems of ethnic education. The Bureau also endeavored to establish the legitimacy of its approach in the minds of the Orthodox Jews. These efforts led to another development, no less significant. The program required educators of a sort that did not exist. They had to be recruited and trained. Sons of Russian immigrants responded, accepted the engagement as a calling, and in the course of fulfilling their mission, founded a profession and formulated a philosophy of American Jewish life.

$\int$

THE PRIMARY SCHOOL PROGRAM WHICH SAMSON BENDERLY, THE BU-reau's director, designed contained three major parts: model schools to be operated by the Bureau, "standardizing" (which also meant modernizing) the existing Talmud Torahs so that they would form the main supplementary school system, and extension work. The latter, based on the techniques of mass education, was intended as a means of bringing at least a superficial knowledge of Judaism to the large numbers of the unschooled. Each phase had its secondary functions, and the entire program was supported by the Bureau's departments of research, textbooks and educational materials, and teacher training.[1]

In the model schools, which soon became known as "preparatory schools," Benderly had the opportunity to evolve his own curriculum and methodology. Although originally intended as coeducational schools, they were quickly converted to schools for girls only. Two considerations influenced Benderly. The Orthodox community frowned upon mixed classes and was little concerned with the systematic education of its daughters. An all-girls school, therefore, avoided the censure that would have otherwise followed, and it permitted, too, wide latitude for experimentation.[2]

At the end of the Bureau's second year, the director reported to the trustees that a thousand students were attending its three preparatory schools. Four years later, in 1916, 2,500 were in attendance at five Bureau schools.[3] Strategically placed throughout the city, the schools held three sessions a week, two of which were on the weekend. The schedule reflected a reduction in hours from the Talmud Torah norm by one-half. More than any other deed or declaration, the reduced-hours feature underlined two tenets which Benderly had long held. First, since the primary commitment of the child was to the public school, Jewish education could not make undue demands on his time. Second, the child's healthy development required time for leisure and extracurricular activities. Religious instruction had to recognize these needs as well.[4] Translated into broader social terms, reduced hours meant that integration into American society held a paramount place. A modest field indeed remained for the survivalist to till.

Impressed as he was by progressive educational theory, Benderly introduced, on a wide scale, the experiments of his Baltimore days. Specialists in dramatics, music, and arts and crafts attached to the Bureau enriched the curriculum with their skills. And at the schools, the textbooks, educational materials, and stereopticon slides prepared by the Bureau were first tried out. Here, too, Benderly's recruits to the profession gained experience.[5]

Benderly expected his preparatory schools to fill a second function—preparation for teacher training. Impressed by the place women occupied in the public schools, he hoped to apply the lesson to Jewish education. The first-year classes of the preparatory schools, consequently, accepted girls from only the upper primary grades of public school. In three years they were expected to complete most of the seven-year Talmud Torah curriculum. The superior students would then continue with advanced Hebrew work and finally move on to the Teachers Institute of the Jewish Theological Seminary (JTS). By 1915, the Teachers Institute showed a marked improvement in the quality and the number of its entering students. Benderly's work was bearing fruit.[6]

The Bureau's director sought additional ways to speed the training of women. Why should not the older girls, Benderly asked a convention of the Kehillah, be directed to a course for Hebrew-school teachers rather than one for training stenographers? Soon, a staff member was assigned to search the high schools for those above the age of the preparatory classes who might form an elite group. Through intensive study, he expected to prepare them quickly for teacher training. High schools were canvassed. Candidates met to hear talks on Jewish teaching as a career. Parents were visited and special classes established. Benderly reported to the 1914 convention that five hundred girls "carefully selected [for] their mental fitness" were organized in intensive study groups. By 1915, the Bureau had established Hebrew high-school classes for boys in addition to the existing ones for girls. A small but comprehensive system of elementary and intermediate schools now existed.[7]

Benderly's incessant experimentation and his range of interests led to other ventures. What of the 150,000 receiving no religious training? From the time of the first survey in 1909, Bureau leaders had used that statistic as a battle cry. More than the accelerated training of teachers was necessary to meet that need. Why not use, he wrote in 1912, the theaters and halls located in the Jewish neighborhoods which on Sunday mornings could be rented at a nominal price. Children could be assembled in these halls and taught Jewish history, customs, and prayers. "To teach so many children in mass will of course be only possible by making ample use of the stereopticon." [8]

Thus a technical contrivance and a new organizational structure placed in the hands of the progressive educator would, in a measure, make up for lack of budget, lack of teachers, lack of time, even lack of interest on the part of the indifferent client.

To help further close the gap between means and needs, Benderly counted on the volunteer—college men and women would willingly work one morning a week without remuneration. For this reason and because of the large scale of the undertaking, the annual cost could be held to one dollar per capita, half to be borne by the Bureau and the other half by the children who would pay a small admission fee.[9]

Theaters and halls were rented. Groups of 500 to 900 children attended weekly assemblies, and Bureau specialists presented the weekly lesson in slide and song. Then, in smaller clubs, volunteer group leaders reviewed the material. By 1917, the extension activities had crystallized into two youth organizations: the Circle of Jewish Children, with an enrolled membership of 30,000, and the League of Jewish Youth, with a membership of 9,000.[10]

Meanwhile, in the fall of 1911, when the moneys from the new Education Fund became available, Benderly introduced another phase of his program, which in some respects was his most ambitious venture. He undertook to create the unified Talmud Torah system which had been projected at the founding convention and dramatically placed on the public agenda at the 1910 convention. What carried weight and aroused interest was the prospect of financial assistance for the Talmud Torahs. To those affiliating, the Bureau promised a grant of $1.25 per month for every child taught free of charge, provided the number of such children did not exceed one-third of the total attendance. Nearly all Talmud Torahs catered to a large percentage of tuition-free students. The Bureau formula meant, therefore, a monthly subsidy equivalent, in most cases, to half the school's payroll. The Bureau, however, whose intention was to create a centralized school system, set a series of conditions.[11]

Administratively, the affiliating school agreed to transfer tuition collections to the Bureau's office, as well as the right to investigate subsidized students and to visit the parents of truant students. The system eliminated some serious abuses, raised the income from tuition, and noticeably improved attendance. Where teachers had once collected weekly tuition fees in the classroom, a Bureau fieldworker canvassed each month a regular route of families. By 1915, the Department of Collection and Investigation had canvassed the homes of 40,000 children prior to their admission to school in addition to its regular visits. But aside from its main functions, Friedlaender told the convention that year,

the small army of young collegemen who carry on this work form a powerful medium of educational propaganda. . . . By acquainting the parents with the problem of Jewish education and with the work done by individual schools, our collectors and investigators establish a living contact between the parents and the schools . . . and serve to arouse in them a deeper sense of responsibility towards the demands of Jewish religious education.[12]

In his 1915 report to the American Jewish Committee, Magnes wrote that the Bureau was collecting $60,000 a year on behalf of thirteen schools. Six schools whose records permit comparison illustrate the advantages of the new system. Tuition collections for the school year

1912–1913 rose 79 percent and collection costs were reduced from 20 to 10 percent in comparison with the year 1910–1911, when the schools handled their collections individually.[13]

Eligibility for aid entailed changes in personnel policy. The Bureau set a minimum salary for teachers of $60 per month, which compared favorably with that for the lower grades in the public school system, and an annual increment until an $80 a month maximum was achieved. It required the teachers, on the other hand, to pass an examination by the Bureau's Board of License in the areas of Judaica, English, and pedagogy. Realizing that his American-educated men and his European teachers all were deficient in one area or another, Benderly arranged for temporary certification. Within three years, however, the candidate was to qualify for a permanent license.[14]

For his American teachers, Benderly urged attendance at the Teachers Institute. In a parallel move, he established intensive courses in English and pedagogy for the European teachers. Both he and Mordecai Kaplan, the Institute's principal, had planned to conduct these courses there as well. But President Solomon Schechter of the JTS refused permission and the Bureau sponsored the program on its own. Fifty teachers, Benderly reported to the 1912 convention, were attending twenty hours of classes a week.[15]

Benderly also required that the affiliating Talmud Torah adopt the Bureau-approved curriculum. In the fall of 1910, he had organized an association of Talmud Torah principals. Recalling the initial meeting Benderly wrote:

It is a characteristic indication of the disorganized state of Jewish education in America, and of New York in particular, that the principals of the largest Talmud Torahs of New York handling the same class of pupils and living in one and the same city were not acquainted with each other personally; most of them had to be introduced to one another on the occasion of the first meeting.[16]

The meeting also had its poignant side. For three hours the principals "poured out a tale of wasted love and effort on the part of the directors, principals, and teachers." They described "the indifference of parents, of the low estate of the teacher, and of the ignorance and godlessness of the rising generation." Later, discussions drew a fuller picture of ineffectual instruction, disorganized administration, inadequate facilities, and outmoded methods.[17]

In thirty-one wide-ranging sessions, which stretched over a ten-month period, the principals moved from point to point in Benderly's agenda. They produced, among other things, a standard curriculum which the Bureau immediately accepted. The aim of Jewish education was defined as "the preservation of the Jews as a distinct people existing and developing in the spirit of the Jewish religion." This formulation, together with the adoption of the natural method in teaching Hebrew, the introduction of history into the course of study, and the interest in educational aids, marked the dominant tendency. The principals who set the tone were Russian *maskilim*, modernists, and Hebraists.[18] In their partiality for Hebrew culture, in their readiness for pedagogic innovation, and in their need for professional recognition, the principals were Benderly's natural allies.[19]

The final requirement which Benderly set for joining the Bureau's system was size. "Since the present status of the Jewish Education Fund . . . forbids the standardization of all the Talmud Torahs," only the larger ones were eligible. Had his original request for $100,-000 a year been realized, Benderly said, most of the schools would have been included. But only half the amount had been pledged. After careful investigation, he concluded that the best results for the maximum number of students demanded the exclusion, for a time, of the smaller, less efficient, and less stable schools.[20]

Though the Bureau's main interest was the education of the immigrants' children, it also wished to maintain its position as a community-wide agency. This expressed itself in the interest it took in the Sunday Schools of the Reform movement. Temple Emanuel's school, for example, became a laboratory where the Bureau adapted methods and curriculum innovations to the needs of Reform Jewish education. Ten other temple schools followed Emanuel's lead. Sunday School teachers, notoriously weak in their knowledge of Hebrew, participated in classes organized for them by the Bureau.[21] In principle, at least, Magnes seemed ready to go further in his pursuit to embrace all factions. At one convention, representatives of the Socialist Zionist organization, sponsors of the National Radical schools, which emphasized Yiddish culture and secularism, scolded the Bureau for discriminating against the Yiddish language. Let the National Radical schools apply to the Bureau, Magnes answered, and they would get pedagogical assistance in carrying out their program. Finally, the Bureau included within its education and administrative system the larger institutional schools, like those sponsored by the Educational Alliance and the Hebrew Orphan Asylum.[22]

This new, many-sided enterprise required personnel. And it was in their manpower policy that the Bureau's leaders, and particularly Benderly, showed their intention to build a permanent structure. Benderly set out from the beginning to create, together with the Bureau, the profession of Jewish education. As early as the summer of 1910, before he had officially opened the Bureau, Benderly began recruiting young college men. Collaborating with him from the outset was Mordecai Kaplan. "He needed trained people," Kaplan later wrote, "and the Teachers Institute was looking for students to train." [23]

Interested in encouraging Jewish cultural activities on campus, Kaplan had established ties with the Zionist and Menorah societies at City College. (Subsequently, Friedlaender and Magnes joined Kaplan in sponsoring the Intercollegiate Menorah Association, and their influence spread to other universities.) The societies were oases of Jewish interest admidst the indifference to Jewish affairs which prevailed among the college sons of the immigrants. Those who joined the Zionist and Menorah societies saw themselves, in a sense, as part of the "saving remnant," the still loyal sons of their people. Small in number, they were highly motivated and receptive. Kaplan and his colleagues responded to their warm interest by creating informal ties of fellowship with the active circle. Study groups at Kaplan's and Friedlaender's homes, for example, and 7:00 A.M. summer classes with Benderly followed and exerted further influence on what became a band of eager disciples and trainees.[24]

Kaplan, Friedlaender, Magnes, and Benderly provided the intellectual stimulation, the instruction, and the camaraderie of a common cause. They may have also served as models to be emulated. All four had the highest academic credentials, a gift for influencing their fellows, and a sense of mission. With great success, it seemed, they combined vocation with public service. Moreover, they had discarded the customary professions in doing so. Benderly had left medicine for Jewish education. Friedlaender, the academician, took an active part in public life to the detriment of his career. Kaplan had recently left the active rabbinate, and Magnes would soon resign his third and last pulpit, both feeling suffocated by the intellectual aridity and sterile parochialism of a congregational position. Nor did the field of Jewish social work mean much to men with visions of a "Jewish cultural renaissance." A career confined to the framework of welfare agencies, governed by German-Jewish philanthropists, surely dealt primarily with trivia and the mundane.[25] Here were four distinguished personalities, on the other hand, whose cause embraced the entire community and who agreed that the vital task to be performed was the education of youth. Jewish public service, it seemed, did offer, after all, scope and room for nobility of purpose.

Finally, the period from 1910 to 1915 was a heady time in the history of the Bureau. Despite budgetary problems at the end of the period, the outlook seemed bright. Powerful backers had shown their interest, and presumably would continue to do so. Thus Benderly's vision of a career in Jewish education promised a decent livelihood as well. And, as Benderly outlined that career, it required the highest scientific training. A mission, a living, academic training—all were combined.[26]

Benderly guided his neophytes masterfully in a three-part program. There were teaching and administrative assignments under the Bureau director's close guidance. One of the first recruits, for example, began as a teacher in a Bureau school in 1910, became principal a year later, and by 1914 headed the Department of Research and Appraisal. Meanwhile, he taught an experimental Sunday School class, edited *The Jewish Child* and later the Bureau's professional journal, *The Jewish Teacher*.[27]

In addition, the young apprentices continued their own Judaic studies mainly under Kaplan's and Friedlaender's direction. Benderly ran a special class in pedagogy. By 1912, 110 college men were preparing themselves for teaching positions. Of that number, 25 held Bureau staff positions. A salary scale slightly higher than the public school's, together with tuition aid, made graduate study feasible.[28] This was the third phase of Benderly's training program.

He expected his trainees to pursue graduate work at Teachers College, not merely as an investment for the future, but to meet current experimental and research needs of the Bureau. The Bureau inspired a cluster of significant doctoral dissertations which were researched and debated within its precincts. And at Teachers College, Benderly's protégés were recognized as a distinctive group preparing to work in the field of Jewish education.[29] William Heard Kilpatrick sponsored a number of their dissertations, knew the work of the Bureau, and sympathized with its goals. His influence was considerable. But in John Dewey, the Bureau group found not only justification for educational change but sanction for ethnic survival in democratic America.[30]

In one sense, the young professionals of the Bureau replaced scriptural authority with Dewey's educational philosophy. The ancient, Old World imperative of Torah-study as a paramount religious obligation had lost its grip on parent, child, and community. No longer could a movement for a Jewish educational revival draw upon common sentiments and values. A new educational canon, however, addressing itself to society in general, might, when applied to the Jewish community, pull together its divided groups. In Dewey's writings and teachings, Benderly's protégés did find such a rationale. Here were compelling new reasons, "American reasons," for returning Jewish education to its traditionally preeminent place. Ironically, Dewey served to justify reforms which led, as well, to a diluted curriculum shorn of its traditionally high intellectual goals.[31]

In January, 1916, the first issue of *The Jewish Teacher* appeared, subsidized by the Bureau and published by the Jewish Teachers Association. The Association, established two years before by Benderly's trainees, aimed to raise Jewish teaching "to the level of a recognized profession." The opening statement of *The Jewish Teacher*, the first professional journal concerned with Jewish education, read:

This magazine is to take part in the solution of the fundamental problem in the creation of a wholesome Jewish life in America—the problem of identifying the Jewish child with the Jewish people, of attaching him in loyalty to it, and of effectively transmitting to him its traditions and ideals. Education has probably never meant as much to the preservation of any group life, as Jewish education means at this moment to the continued life of our people. . . . The home and the synagogue, the communal life and the forces of social control, look to the Jewish school for their vitalization and strengthening. The burden of the world's work is being redistributed, and the school, both the secular and the religious, must be ready to undertake many functions not hitherto assigned to them.[32]

Under the new conditions of industrialism, Dewey no longer counted on the family and the neighborhood to perform the range of educative functions both had fulfilled in the older agrarian society. His and Benderly's students regarded the religious folkways of Russian-Jewish life as a second victim of industrialism. For Dewey the school now carried the burden of recreating the "harmonious society."[33] Jews, the Bureau men echoed, encountering America in addition to industrialism, required a supplementary institution, the Jewish religious school. Alexander Dushkin, the Bureau's first student at Teachers College to receive his doctorate, wrote an appeal to college men to enter the field of Jewish education: "With the decreasing power of the home, with the breakdown of communal authority . . . the function of the school is assuming an importance even greater than that hitherto assigned to it. In a new sense of the term must the Jewish teacher stand now *in loco parentis* to many a Jewish child."[34]

More relevant to the Bureau's pedagogical policies was child-centered education that emphasized the needs and interests of the learner. The reformers asked that content and presentation of curriculum be continually and critically evaluated. The criterion was their usefulness in creating "a desire for continued growth" and "making that desire effective in fact." The pursuit of "breadth and richness of experience" allowed no room for the reverential treatment of subject matter. "The curriculum," Dewey warned, "is always getting loaded down with purely inherited traditional matter."[35] Dushkin, in his dissertation, applied the master's dictum to Jewish education:

The change of educational viewpoint which the reorganization of the curricula should try to express, is the shifting of the center of attention from the *subject matter* to be taught, as handed down through the generations, to the great body of American Jewish *children*, whose needs are the ultimate guide of the schools. Instead of teaching Hebrew or Bible or Prayers or Talmud, the Jewish schools should teach Jewish children, and for this purpose the selections from the religious-national treasure house of the Jewish people should be such as will best prepare these children for their life as American Jews.[36]

For second-generation Americans who were preparing for a career in the service of their ethnic group, Dewey's recognition of diversity as an irrevocable condition of American life made the most telling impression. His ideal of the untrammeled growth of the child they linked with a pivotal concern for the individual. The fate of the individual in society, therefore, became the test of democracy. "The measure of progress in a democracy," Dushkin wrote, "is individual progress, and the enrichment of individual personality. The individual human being in his social relationships is the primary concern of the democratic state." [37]

Dewey, as the survivalists read him, not only granted the necessity of recognizing heterogeneity, but extolled a pluralistic society as the essence of a democratic community.

Diversity of stimulation means novelty, and novelty means challenge to thought. The more activity is restricted to a few definite lines—as it is when there are rigid class lines preventing adequate interplay of experiences—the more action tends to become routine on the part of the class at a disadvantage, and capricious, aimless, and explosive on the part of the class having the materially fortunate position.[38]

Dewey posited a second condition for democracy which his disciples in Jewish education took to heart as well. A social group must reject isolation and exclusivity and willingly enter a "mode of associated living, a conjoint communicated experience." Interdependence, "so that each has to refer his own action to that of others, and to consider the action of others to give point and direction to his own," weakened the "barriers of class, race, and national territory which kept men from perceiving the full import of their activity." [39]

These guidelines dominated the educational planning of the Bureau. But their influence went even further. In the stimulating and optimistic milieu of Teachers College and the Bureau of Education, the new principles of education promised fresh solutions to broad social questions. The new breed of Jewish educator, caught up in his child-oriented world of vocation and intellectual study, placed the child at the center of Jewish organizational life.

Isaac B. Berkson gave formal expression to this attitude. One of Benderly's first recruits, Berkson, like Dushkin, had held a variety of positions in the Bureau and studied under Dewey and Kilpatrick at Teachers College. In 1919 he received his doctorate, and the following year his dissertation, *Theories of Americanization*, was published. "I was attempting," he later wrote, "to express the viewpoint not of myself alone but of the group that had joined the Bureau in the historic endeavor to establish Jewish education in the United States on an autonomous noncongregational basis." [40]

Berkson, like his fellows, leaned heavily on Dewey's vision of a mobile, many-sided, but interdependent society. "One finds democracy," Berkson wrote, "where there is a progressive consideration of uniqueness, a multiplication of diverse possibilities [and] a growing consciousness of man's interdependence." Thus by way of Dewey's educational theories, or at least as his Bureau students understood them, ethnic survival entered the mainstream of American democracy. [41]

Yet Dewey had sounded a warning. His larger purpose was "the widening of the area of shared concern, and the liberation of a greater diversity of personal capacities." He wanted "greater individualization on one hand, and a broader community of interest on the other." The thrust, moreover, of his discussion of "The Democratic Conception in Education" was toward the breaking down of barriers between classes and groups. [42] How was one to attain both ends, "greater shared concern" and "greater diversity"? And furthermore, how could the truly democratic ethnic educator also fulfill Dewey's highest prescription, the uninhibited educational growth of the child?

Dushkin and Berkson responded by rejecting parochial school education. It failed, in the first place, "to fulfill the demands of the democratic idea that the school system must be representative of the community at large." In addition, it tended to "segregation and indoctrination" and "an undue exaltation of the place of the ethnic culture." On these grounds Berkson attacked Horace Kallen's call for "a democracy of nationalities, cooperating voluntarily and autonomously." Ethnic autonomy, Berkson said, would lead to "partial segregation and power over the school system." It meant, in short, "indoctrination" which would prevent, to use Dewey's phrase, "the adequate interplay of experience." [43] The Bureau's formula, on the other hand, offered a model for all ethnic and religious groups. The afternoon supplementary school, sponsored and supported on a voluntary basis by the ethnic community, was within the democratic guidelines set by Dewey. Dushkin indeed argued that the Jewish model was a compromise between the inadequacy of the Protestant Sunday School and the "dangerous" segregation of the Catholic parochial school.[44]

Berkson developed this line of reasoning into a program for ethnic survival which he called the "Community Theory." Culture, the "spiritual aspiration" of the group, he described as the mainspring of the ethnic society. In the case of the Jewish group, he identified its "cultural and spiritual aspirations" with Torah. So broad an interpretation of the traditional meaning (the sacred code and covenant with God) became necessary if Berkson's community was to embrace the multiplicity of factions in Jewish life. With culture "the raison d'être of the preservation of the life of the group, the [communal Jewish] school becomes the central agency around which the ethnic group builds its life." Institutions whose main functions were philanthropic, social, economic, and religious played a secondary role or none at all in Berkson's conception of the community.[45]

Unstated but implicit in his views was a further change. The American Jewish educator replaced rabbi, philanthropist, and advocate as the dominant figure in the community. Motivated by the ethical and professional standards of modern educational practice, he would guard the integrity of the ethnic community's central enterprise, its school. As the scientifically trained professional, the Jewish educator would stand above faction, and as a devoted democrat, he would recognize diversity within the ethnic group. His community theory, Berkson wrote, satisfied the basic notion of democracy that "the individual be left free to develop through forces selected by the laws of his own nature." It conceived of the individual as "creator of and participant in the culture to be evolved," and thus it allowed "a great degree of individual diversification." [46]

Yet Berkson admitted that such a philosophy, faithful as it was to Dewey's humanistic teachings, would be unable to generate sufficient cultural powers to sustain the group. In this instance, the master offered no guidance.

Dewey's sympathy for "diversity" did not stem from historical considerations. It was not the merit of an ethnic group's past which interested him particularly. In a pro-Zionist essay, in October, 1917, he said:

The concept of uniformity and unanimity in culture is rather repellent. . . . Variety is the spice of life, and the richness and the attractiveness of social institutions depends upon cultural diversity among separate units. . . . The theory of the Melting Pot always gave me rather a pang. . . . Where there are many sorts of independent vigorous life, one provides nationality for interchange, for give and take of culture. If this is not carried to a point which prevents a flexible and easy give and take between groups, it stimulates the cultural creativeness of each group.[47]

Not the drama of national renewal engaged him, then, but the social-psychological benefits to be derived from the phenomenon. Suppose one had to work hard to be "diverse"? This contingency Dewey's *Democracy and Education* did not account for.

Dewey was not enough. The young Jewish educators, consequently, complemented his teachings with those of Ahad Ha'am, the idealogue of cultural Zionism who had so decisively influenced their Kehillah mentors.

Ahad Ha'am stood squarely in the Jewish tradition which placed a high value on historical memory. Hebrew culture and the Hebrew language, Ahad Ha'am wrote, were "inseparably and eternally" part of the Jewish people; the language was the medium which tied the generations. Moreover, Ahad Ha'am's conception of a spiritual center in Palestine seemed to answer the question of how, in a mobile and democratic society, cultural diversity could be maintained. "A vital ethnic culture in the diaspora," Berkson wrote, "is dependent upon the existence of a cultural center to serve as a source of spiritual replenishment and to prevent the ethnic spirit from becoming the petrified relic of an ancient grandeur." [48]

The extraordinary exertion necessary to "replenish the ethnic spirit" was transferred to the cultural center in Palestine. In America, therefore, there was no need for the Jewish ethnic group to "segregate and indoctrinate," and to "exalt the place of the ethnic culture unduly." One remained faithful to Dewey's concept of democracy. In a sense, Berkson and his associates had transferred the function of the parochial school to Palestine.

Now Jewish education could serve democracy and America with an easy conscience. It "enriched the personality [of the Jewish citizen], widened his interests, and deepened his emotions." Full harmony, consequently, existed between true Americanization and a movement for Jewish cultural-religious reconstruction and revival.[49]

The Bureau's establishment in the fall of 1910 marked the appearance in the Jewish quarter of a novel agency of apparently commanding power. The legendary figure of Jacob Schiff was identified with it. Its director, praised by the Orthodox press during his first year as a brilliant executive, had gathered a large staff and introduced, in rapid succession, startling innovations. Now, in the fall of 1911, came the capstone of the Bureau's system, the "standardization" of the Talmud Torahs. Taken together with the Kehillah's attempts to reform kashruth supervision (during the fall of 1911 and spring of 1912, the final organization of the Board of Rabbis took place), suspicious leaders, religious zealots, and threatened functionaries raised the cry of a diabolical plot. The Reform Jews of uptown were entering the sacred domain of the Orthodox in order to capture two of its sustaining institutions.

A portent of the onslaught to come was evident even at the time of the announcement of Schiff's original gift at the 1910 convention. Philanthropists who can afford $50,000 gifts, the *Morgen Journal* wrote, are usually "far from us ideologically and religiously." Such donors, furthermore, invariably place conditions on their gifts. Can "education which is run only as the philanthropist wishes," the *Tageblat* asked, "carry weight with the Jews of New York, and will that [education] be worth anything?" [50]

These critics, nevertheless, considered themselves parties to the Kehillah, and for a time their criticism came from within. On the eve of the 1911 convention, in February, the Morgen Journal attacked the Bureau by describing it as Jacob Schiff's property. Yet it considered the condition remediable. Once a greater democratization of the Kehillah was achieved, control would pass to the "conservative, pious, Orthodox Jews." In the opinion of the Morgen Journal, they made up the largest part of the community.[51]

Even the weak Talmud Torah federation, the Central Board of Jewish Education, recognized the primacy of the Kehillah's Bureau of Education. Established a year before the Bureau, the Central Board watched the latter's rapid rise to prominence with some envy. After all, over the years, in the face of the poverty, social dislocation, and institutional fragmentation of the Jewish quarter, the men of the Central Board, and others like them, had steadfastly built twenty-four Talmud Torahs. Now outsiders suddenly discovered the need for religious training and the Talmud Torahs' role in meeting that need. But they then proceeded, so it seemed, to mobilize new funds by dramatizing unfairly the weaknesses of the existing institutions. The small band of functionaries who had striven valiantly for the cause of traditional education felt maligned. "The assertion," Gedaliah Bublick, the Tageblat's editor, declared, "that all was chaos prior to the establishment of the Bureau of Education is an outrage against the Talmud Torahs who have made such great efforts on behalf of Jewish education." Little wonder that the Central Board resented Benderly's, Friedlaender's, and Magnes' critique, and even more so, the fact that these men controlled the new funds.[52]

Yet, though relations deteriorated, both sides hoped for accord. Side by side with suspicion and friction there existed the recognition on the part of the Talmud Torah leaders that the Kehillah and its Bureau had access to desperately needed pedagogic and material resources. Dangerous as Schiff and Benderly loomed in the convention oratory of the East Side's Rabbi Shalom Jaffe, to harried directors of struggling Talmud Torahs, those two men held the keys of salvation.[53]

For the traditionalists, moreover, Kehillah and Kehillah-control of education evoked the memory of a time when congregation and community reinforced one another. Though spokesmen for the Orthodox, like the *Morgen Journal* and *Tageblat*, well knew that in the present pluralism they represented only one view among many, some coordinating structure, no matter how defective, seemed better than none. It provided a useful platform and created offices and posts worth fighting for.[54]

One more element within the traditionalist camp served the cause of concord. By 1910, a modern Orthodox group had emerged among the Russian Jews. They were affluent (their money coming primarily from textiles and real estate). They had moved out of the lower East Side, settled in Yorkville, West Harlem, and the upper West Side of Manhattan, and there they built their opulent synagogues based on similar class and status rather than *landsmanshaft*. The English-speaking rabbi served as a further indicator of the Americanization of their Orthodoxy. This segment of the Russian-Jewish community provided key leaders of the large communal institutions of the Jewish quarter. Magnes early achieved an excellent rapport with the group. Bernard Semel, Israel Unterberg, William Fischman, and Harry Fischel collaborated with him from the outset. In the resort town of Arverne, where many of them spent their summers, Magnes, in the summer of 1911, raised $70,000 in pledges for the new Education Fund.[55]

The Talmud Torahs these men supported, and they were among the largest, joined the Bureau's standardization program from the outset. One of them, the Downtown Talmud Torah, became a pilot school for the Bureau. The institution's president, William Fischman, was also the treasurer of the Kehillah. He and Semel and Fischel performed prodigious services in meeting the more violent assaults on the Bureau.[56] The Kehillah could claim, therefore, that responsible Orthodox elements supported its actions.

In the fall of 1911, however, these mediating forces were unable to prevent the Orthodox irreconcilables from mounting a frenzied campaign against the Bureau. Meetings of the Kehillah's Advisory Council broke up in pandemonium. The dormant Central Board of Talmud Torahs came to life as Kehillah adversaries promoted it as an alternative to the Bureau. Meanwhile, the powerful *Morgen Journal* cultivated local fears and resentment.[57]

The Bureau's dream, the *Morgen Journal* wrote, was to create an "educational trust." Benderly's lack of tact, his dictatorial methods, and his crude offer of uptown's gold in return for the Talmud Torahs' subservience had exposed his true intentions. His goal was nothing less than full dominion over Orthodox Jewry's most precious possession.[58]

The *Morgen Journal* portrayed the horror of that possibility by playing on the worst fears of the pious Russian Jew. In a report of a Kehillah delegates meeting, the headline read: "Dr. Benderly Accused of Apostasy." Another news report related that, under the pretext of supplying educational aids, the Bureau had smuggled a book on Christianity into one Talmud Torah.[59]

As the activities of the Bureau broadened, so did this type of attack. Not only had the Kehillah interferred in the Talmud Torahs, the *Morgen Journal* raged, but, referring to the extension work of the Bureau, it "kidnapped our young students." It then exposed the youngsters, the paper continued, to an exercise in blasphemy. The Bureau men

made a "show" of the Torah and our holy prophets. They changed these spiritual giants into moving picture heroes. From some gentile artist they borrowed an Isaiah and a Jeremiah and projected them onto a bed-sheet . . . one without a hat, the second without a beard but with a shaved mustache, exactly like a genuine Yankee "sport." And the old faithful Talmud Torah workers who gave their lives to build up these schools [the Bureau] threw out . . . when they refused to turn their institutions into moving picture houses and nests of Reform.[60]

The "bed-sheet," the improvised projection screen, was as great an abomination as the beardless prophet. Ephraim Kaplan, the *Morgen Journal's* educational reporter, treated "methods" and "systems" as synonymous with "free thinker" and "heretic." [61]

Kehillah leaders, failing to look beyond the surface noise, ascribed the frenetic strain and the wild charges to obscurantism and perfidy. Due to "violent hostility to the Kehillah and its chairman," Friedlaender told the executive committee, a Yiddish newspaper chose the Bureau as a "proper means to strike at the Kehillah." The attacks had proceeded almost entirely from "irresponsible and unscrupulous elements" who preferred "chaos to order." These elements had then found favorable soil in the Advisory Council of the Kehillah, "which frets under the restrictions imposed upon it by the constitution of the Kehillah." [62]

And indeed, Bureau opponents raised the cry of democracy. The Bureau, they said, was run by a small coterie of professional Jews who did Jacob Schiff's bidding. No convention had approved Benderly's five-year contract making him czar of Jewish education, nor had the delegates discussed the creation of the control body, the board of trustees. Dr. Joseph Bluestone, a director of the city's oldest Talmud Torah and prime mover of the first attempt at collaboration, reminded a Kehillah meeting of the early changes in Bureau management. The larger and more representative education committee of the Kehillah was originally entrusted with the supervision of the proposed Bureau. Soon after, however, it had been replaced by five trustees appointed for five years. The executive committee had ignored every orthodox member of the education committee in selecting those trustees.[63]

Thus the controversy thrived on the grievances of a number of active and ambitious men who wished recognition. Unable to break into the inner circle of the twenty-five–man executive committee, they had made the Advisory Council their platform. (In September, 1911, they changed its name to "Kehillah Council of Seventy.") They fought for a greater say in Kehillah affairs, proposed constitutional amendments, and provided the "favorable soil" for the Kehillah's critics.[64] But rather than recognize that critics, given responsibility, could well become confederates (and the Kehillah needed all the activists it could find), Magnes and his colleagues saw the Advisory Council as a populist, irresponsible, body thirsting for power.

The standardization plan also impinged on institutional prerogatives. Benderly's announcement that only licensed teachers would be eligible for employment in Bureau-affiliated schools frightened the European teacher. Fear at being unable to pass a test in English or pedagogy was coupled with anger at the indignity of appearing before a board of examiners. Some of the examiners knew less about the traditional subject matter than the applicant. In the past only one qualification had ever mattered, mastery of the sacred literature. No precedent existed for a bureaucratic device, such as a Board of License.

"The five distinguished authorities of the Board of License," one critic wrote caustically, "will not seek to determine, God forbid, if the teacher possesses too much idle knowledge. . . . They will ask him to show where on the map Jerusalem is. Then he gets a permit for six months." [65]

A large school like Machzikey Talmud Torah rejected the Bureau's setting a minimum wage for teachers. No outside agency would dare dictate wage policies to the directors, the institution's president wrote. Nor would the Talmud Torah tolerate Benderly's incitement of their principals. He "pounded into their heads the great wisdom that they, the principals, are the real 'big shots.' Were we to accede to their gracious recommendations we would have to close down every Talmud Torah." Indeed, now that the principals were organized in an association they were asking for a "union salary" and even threatened to boycott those Talmud Torahs not accepting the Bureau's standards.[66]

The small schools, on the other hand—precisely those that most needed help—were left out altogether. To qualify for Bureau aid, one functionary wrote, we need a building of our own. When we ask a philanthropist for a donation to our building fund he says, "Go to the Kehillah. I gave them money." But the small school's woes did not end there. Ineligibility for Bureau assistance implied an inferior school, and parents preferred a "recognized" institution. The Bureau's program, consequently, brought harm to those least able to bear it.[67]

Moderates among the Orthodox discriminated between the *Morgen Journal*'s calumnies and the reasonable fears that found expression in its pages. Thus some among the Kehillah's supporters demanded that it withdraw completely from the field of education. In its first stages of growth the Kehillah should avoid the controversial, they argued, for it possessed as yet neither the stature nor the moral force to cope with rabid partisanship. Others pointed to the subsidy plan as the source of the difficulty. When it comes to money, they urged, either give to all or give to none. Still other voices suggested that the Bureau concern itself solely with the unschooled. Let it establish its own model Talmud Torahs, so long as it left the existing ones alone.[68] For Magnes and the Bureau men, this would have meant defeat by the obscurantists. Where the spiritual activity of the community was taking place, there the Kehillah had to be.

In November, 1911, when the full details of the standardization program for Talmud Torahs were announced, Orthodoxy's most prominent rabbis joined in condemning it. They insisted that the smaller schools be given financial aid and that the decision for shorter hours be rescinded. They also demanded that a special rabbinical authority be appointed to supervise the Orthodoxy of the schools. Throughout the spring and summer of 1912, Rabbis Margolies and Klein engaged Magnes in long and tiring negotiations. Margolies resigned from the Board of License of the Bureau. He and Klein delayed the activization of the newly formed Board of Orthodox Rabbis and threatened to resign from it and from the executive committee of the Kehillah.[69]

The actions of the rabbis represented an attempt on their part to reassert their traditional position, one which they had lost in America. Magnes needed their participation in solving the kashruth problem. They demanded, in return, a share in directing the Talmud Torah program. By the early fall of 1912, an uneasy truce was achieved. The rabbis accepted the Bureau's word that in ritual matters it would consult a rabbi acceptable to both the Board and the Bureau. Magnes had meanwhile found the funds to launch the kashruth experiment. By 1914, however, the kashruth program was dead and no funds were available for financing the Board of Rabbis. At that point, the truce ended. The rabbis neither had a bargaining position nor an interest in the Kehillah.[70]

At a national gathering of Orthodox rabbis in May, 1914, they led an all-out attack on the Bureau of Education. During the final session, Margolies accused the Bureau of the most abhorrent of all transgressions. Two and a half years before, Margolies reported, the rabbis had received reliable evidence that a principal of a Bureau school had served in Europe as a Christian missionary. They had brought the information to Magnes but to no avail. (The *Tageblat* captioned the revelation: "Rabbinical Meeting Declares War on the Kehillah's Bureau of Education.") [71]

A resolution condemning the Kehillah's Bureau of Education pointed to the following transgressions: it was not under rabbinical surveillance; despite the prohibition of the rabbis, the Bureau's schools shortened their hours of study and diluted their program of instruction; many of the teachers were heretics, and the suspicion of apostasy clung to a number of these.[72]

Why had the rabbis, the Yiddish press asked, kept silent for two and a half years? They offered no answer. But one possibility suggests itself. So long as the Kehillah had given them hope, through its Board of Rabbis and its Talmud Torah program, of winning back their preeminence, they had refrained from pressing the apostasy charge. Embittered now, they publicized the charge, abandoned a policy of collaboration, and called on the faithful to adandon the Kehillah and boycott its Bureau of Education. Their call did not materially weaken either. Influential enough to evoke controversy and sap energy away from constructive efforts, the rabbis were too weak and bewildered to offer a viable alternative.[73]

The Bureau's leaders believed that they had created an instrument of the community with which to reorder its educational system. They saw themselves as civil servants, experts in their calling, and impartial in their actions. The Kehillah, which the Bureau would help build, was to be a microcosm of an ideal America with its multifariousness, its tolerance, its encouragement of self-improvement and personal fulfillment, its pragmatic and scientific thrust, and its democracy.

What is noteworthy is that on an institutional level an impressive beginning was made. Even in the short time of seven years, its founders sensed that a sharp and crucial corner had been turned. The profession of Jewish education was created. Young American-educated men had answered the call, and many of them had completed their novitiate. Devoted disciples now shared the responsibility with the generation of founders. Moreover, all but the Bureau's most benighted adversaries admitted that it had demonstrated the efficacy of modern methods, administration and research, and the advantages that accrued from centralization.

Other innovations of this seminal period were also apparent. Education for girls, preparatory work for teacher training, textbooks and teaching aids, Hebrew high schools, extension work for youth, and professional associations for teachers and principals were all new departures. Even statistically the accomplishments are impressive. "The Bureau directs, supervises, or cooperates with 179 schools, 521 teachers and 31,700 pupils," so Benderly summarized his report to the 1915 convention. The figures included peripheral contacts and somewhat exaggerated the effective range of the Bureau's work. In 1916, at the height of the Bureau's activities, about fifteen schools—which included Talmud Torahs, Bureau preparatory schools, and settlement schools—belonged to the Kehillah's centralized educational system.[74]

Finally, Magnes had gained the cooperation of important Orthodox elements. The perplexity of the times and the place confounded the authoritative religious leaders steeped in the East European experience, and they became separatists. The modern Orthodox lay leaders ignored the sectarian message of the European rabbis and chose, instead, to cooperate with the uptown moderates.

Yet by 1917, the movement to communalize Jewish education had lost its momentum, although periodic attempts to renew the effort took place. Support by the Federation of Philanthropies carried with it recognition by the uptown community, but it limited the scope and chilled the spirit of the Bureau. It became, as some had predicted, another client agency of the Federation. The difficulty was not only, as Kehillah leaders said in 1917, a financial one. The very concept of a Bureau of Education was inextricably tied to the idea of a Kehillah polity.

CHAPTER SEVEN

Crime in the Jewish Quarter

F OR A DECADE PRIOR TO POLICE COMMISSIONER BINGHAM'S ALLE-
gations in 1908 of a high crime rate among immigrant Jews,
Jewish philanthropists and social workers had been wrestling
with the problem. Their concern had been first aroused by
the disclosures made by civic reformers and their political allies during the 1890s. The widely publicized Lexow and Mazet investigations
in 1894 and 1899, exposing the ties between crime, the police, and
Tammany Hall, also implicated Jews. In 1897, Frank Moss in a study
of New York City devoted nearly a hundred pages to a harshly drawn
portrait of organized crime in the city's Jewish districts.[1] His experience as counsel for the Lexow and Mazet committees and as a member of the Police Board under reform Mayor William L. Strong gave
his description the ring of authority. By 1902, German-Jewish donors
had founded the Jewish Protectory and Aid Scociety to fill the need
for prison work and rehabilitation of delinquents. Four years later the
Protectory opened the Hawthorne School. And in 1908, the Council
of Jewish Women established the Lakeview Home for wayward girls.
Meanwhile, discussions of delinquency appeared regularly in the Jewish social service journals and in reports of charitable institutions.[2]

Active interest in the problem, however, remained limited to the
small group of financial supporters and professional workers. When a

dramatic event occasionally placed the topic before the public, the Jewish quarter faced the issue in terms of an external attack upon the group as a whole. The lesson it drew from Bingham's charges was the need for a powerful and aggressive voice to defend the Jewish name; it expected the Kehillah to be that voice. But for uptown Jews, who tacitly admitted the existence of criminality, the antidote was the development of a more healthy community. Hopefully, the Kehillah would help create that community.

Beginning in 1909 and reaching a climax in 1912, widely publicized disclosures of vice and crime among Jews created dismay and then alarm in Jewish circles. Protests of innocence were now impossible. Social amelioration and education offered no immediate relief. The debate that ensued over remedies and tactics raised the fundamental question of the relationship of the Jewish group and the general polity. Was the group accountable for those whose ties to it were founded on little more than accident of birth? Or was the problem a nonsectarian one, in which case Jews should join with all civic-minded citizens in an assault on the city's evils? Finally, crime and vice belonged to the domain of the state. At a time when these issues dominated municipal affairs, could the Kehillah avoid being swept into the political interplay of the period?

5

THE COMMUNITY'S ACHIEVEMENT IN FORCING POLICE COMMISSIONER Bingham to retract his statement on Jewish criminality in September, 1908, brought neither vindication for the Jewish quarter nor the tranquility which the uptown community desired. The East Side's stigmatization of the Police Commissioner as an anti-Semite and its reading of his retraction as exonerating the Jewish quarter of all taint of crime left progressive circles unmoved. Rarely, if ever, the *Evening Post* declared, had the Jewish race been charged with exceptional lawlessness; to be called a criminal was a new experience. "But those who follow the trend of Jewish life in this country are not at all sure that this boasted ethical preeminence . . . stands unimpaired." [3]

The Bingham incident quickly faded from public view, dismissed as a quarrel, now resolved, between hypersensitive immigrant Jews and an undiplomatic city official.[4] However, it was not the end of the affair in its broader significance. Eight months later the controversial commissioner again became the subject of contention. But this new embroilment, city-wide and political, signaled the start of a surge of reform sentiment which entangled Jewish criminality with politics.

In early July, 1909, Mayor McClellan, after a month of investigations and hearings, dismissed Commissioner Bingham for inefficiency and maladministration. The charges were instigated in part by Judge William E. Gaynor's attacks on the commissioner's "lawlessness" and "Russian methods." Immediately reform leaders and nearly the entire metropolitan press came to Bingham's defense. General Bingham, the New York *Times* editorialized, has proven to be "absolutely honest and of inflexible courage . . . unapproachable by the politicians. . . . [His] indefatigable labors have accomplished more for the Department than almost any other Commissioner within memory." [5]

The day following his dismissal a distinguished delegation representing the newly formed Committee of One Hundred called on the general. He was invited to enlist in the fight against "the alliance between Tammany Hall and organized crime." William J. Schieffelin, chairman of the Citizens Union and Robert S. Binkerd, secretary of the City Club, led the delegation. In dismissing Bingham, Schieffelin announced, the mayor had provided the Committee of One Hundred with the great moral issue it needed to win the forthcoming mayoralty campaign.[6]

At hand was a new and long season of reform. Gaining momentum in the municipal elections that fall, the climate of exposé continued well into Mayor Gaynor's term of office. Muckraking articles, government reports, published investigations by respected private agencies, and the findings of a special Grand Jury spelled out the details of a vast complex of prostitution and gambling. The near invincibility of "the system," reformers claimed, stemmed from the collusion between the Tammany organization, the police, and criminal gangs. Nevertheless, despite the disclosures of scandal and crime, by 1912 the recurrent absorption with lawlessness and immorality appeared to have run its course. In July of that year, however, interest revived on the heels of the murder of the notorious gambler, Herman Rosenthal. In the course of three murder trials, the testimony of thugs, gang chiefs, and gambling entrepreneurs revealed the sordid details of the operations of "the system." The crusade against evil reached and sustained a new pitch of intensity, prompting, in turn, new investigations.[7]

Local and state election campaigns from 1909 through 1916 fed on the themes of crime and corruption. Political careers were launched, high electoral office attained, and party fortunes rejuvenated by skillfully riding the crest of public indignation. Charles S. Whitman undoubtedly achieved the most notable success in this respect. Elected district attorney for New York County in 1909, he ran uncontested for reelection in 1913 and went on to win the governorship in 1914 and 1916. The Fusion victories in the municipal elections of 1909 and 1913 serve as further indicators of the city's preoccupation with scandal.[8]

This pervasive concern with crime inevitably fastened public attention on the East Side as the preeminent recruiting ground for young criminals and as the domain of gambling, prostitution, and narcotics. Here the gangs charged with regulating and sustaining "the system" found shelter. But the East Side also embraced ethnic enclaves and the frequency with which Jews appeared in the well-publicized accounts of crime and corruption gave the Jewish East Side a newly found notoriety. Behind such *noms de guerre* as Kid Twist (gang leader), Yuski Nigger ("king of the horse poisoners"), Big Jack Zelig (gang leader), Dopey Benny (leader of labor union strong-arm gangs), Kid Dropper (gang leader) and Gyp the Blood (bouncer and gangster), appeared the East European Jewish names, respectively, of Max Zweibach, Joseph Toblinsky, William Albert, Benjamin Fein, Nathan Kaplan, and Harry Horowitz.[9] Even the highly praised penchant for establishing mutual aid societies produced its monstrous aberration in the New York Independent Benevolent Association. Created by brothel owners and procurers the Association provided its members, unwelcome in other Jewish societies, with traditional health and death benefits rendering "assistance in case of necessity." [10]

The image of the Jewish quarter as the "ideal slum," with its sense of community, "consuming passion" for liberty, and craving for education, clashed with the painful disclosure of decadence and communal helplessness.[11] Men of good will generalized and spoke with increasing concern about criminality as a phenomenon prevalent among the sons of immigrant Russian Jews.

Yet few, indeed, contended that delinquency among the downtown youth reflected inbred character defects.[12] Rather, social reformers attributed the emergence of a problematic second generation to the conditions of the immigrant quarter. The harsh struggle for a livelihood forced the immigrant family into overcrowded and unsanitary tenements where the entire environment conspired to create prime conditions for delinquency. Precisely because of the perils of the slums, a particularly heavy burden rested on the family. And tragically, social workers noted, the very upheaval connected with emigration and the perplexities of urban life crippled the efforts of immigrant parents to provide the firm direction for their young. Old World customs and institutions helped little.[13]

But above all else, the reformers pointed to the entrenched Tammany organization as the promoter of evil. In its fight for survival, the organization had spun a giant conspiracy which linked the local club with the recruitment and management of gangs of election repeaters, and then sold police and court immunity to finance these operations. No diagnosis of the sources of criminality among immigrant youth received such wide acceptance as the view that the Tammany professional allowed vice to thrive on the East Side and raised thereby an American-born generation of procurers, gamblers, and gunmen. This was the horrendous process which Samuel S. McClure labeled "The Tammanyizing of a Civilization." [14]

Ten days before election day, 1909, one of the most sensational journalistic treatments of crime in New York appeared. Three articles in the November issue of McClure's Magazine undertook to expose Tammany as purveyor of a massive vice operation; in passing, the articles implicated large numbers of Jews. Of all the aspects of commercialized crime, the authors deliberately stressed prostitution as the most effective way of winning attention for their primary object, the defeat of Tammany. Portraying an efficient business complex systematically feeding upon the mass of chaste and defenseless immigrant girls, the authors played upon widely shared anxieties of the times: the fear of organized conspiracy by amoral business and political interests and the debauching of the "primitive peoples," the immigrants, who had "suddenly" been handed "the domination of American city life." [15]

The magazine's bill of indictment immediately assumed a pivotal position in the wide-open, three-cornered race for mayor. A fully mobilized Fusion organization backing banker Otto Bannard turned from its slogan, "a businessman in city hall," to exploit the material in *McClure's*. William Randolph Hearst made the most of the new emphasis, and the Tammany nominee, the colorful polemicist Judge Gaynor, accepted the challenge.[16]

In his article, Police Commissioner Bingham depicted the region "south of Fourteenth Street" as a criminal camp "thoroughly organized financially, politically, and legally for offense and defense." S. S. McClure, the magazine's editor, proclaimed Tammany a national menace. To a string of extracts from the muckraking literature on municipal misgovernment, McClure added choice bits from investigations past and present to describe the tenement-house prostitution, the "cadet" system of professional seducers, and the "merchandizing of women." [17]

However, as the *pièce de résistance* of the issue, McClure offered George Kibbe Turner's "The Daughters of the Poor." Turner traced the transfer of a vast empire of prostitution from its European base to the East Side of New York. There, in the dancing academies, employment agencies, political balls, and picnics, the ignorant and innocent immigrant girls were trapped into "white slavery." Moreover, the agents of the nefarious trade were their own countrymen, who operated hand-in-hand with "slum politicians." The New York *Sun*, reviewing the repercussions a week after the magazine appeared, wrote: "The sudden astonishment, horror, shame, provoked by the illuminating disclosures of Mr. George Kibbe Turner is of itself one of the most affecting spectacles in recent local history." [18]

The muckraker sacrificed accuracy and balance for the sake of sensationalism, and thereby struck a blow at the arch villain, Tammany. Fusion forces applauded the blow and took little notice of the distortions.[19] For the Jewish readers, however, the identity of the procurers, magnates, and victims of the white-slave trade was, for the moment, more important than establishing the ultimate cause of the evil, and the cases Turner and McClure cited referred mainly to immigrant Jews. In predictable fashion the Yiddish newspapers challenged the veracity of the evidence. Turner, they claimed, had offered no statistical evidence to support his allegations. The authorities he and McClure quoted, like Bingham and Moss, were flagrantly biased. The Yiddish press countered with authorities favorable to its views, some of whom Tammany employed as well in its political countermove.[20]

Turner's imagery and inferences particularly incensed the East Side editors. A Yiddish translation of the following passage, for example, appeared in several newspapers:

Out of this racial slum of Europe has come for unnumbered years the Jewish kaftan, leading the miserable Jewish girl from European civilization into Asia. . . . To this day he comes out of Galicia and Russian Poland, with his white face and his long beard—the badge of his ancient faith—and wanders across the face of this earth.[21]

Even the Jewish immigrant's passion for education, a virtue so lauded by the observer of ghetto life, when touched by the muckraker turned into an abomination.

The chief ambition of the new family in America [Turner explained and the Yiddish press translated] is to educate its sons. To do this, the girls must go to work at the earliest possible date. . . . The exploitation of young women as money-earning machines . . . [is] not equalled anywhere in the world. . . . Thousands of women have sacrificed themselves uselessly to give the boys of the family an education.[22]

The Jews had been humiliated, their "chaste women slandered," the proud tradition of learning discredited, and all for the sake of gaining cheap political profit, the Yiddish press insisted. Papers which normally supported Republican candidates quoted Tammany men in defense of the Jewish East Side. And when confronted with the conclusions of the United Hebrew Charities that "vice and crime . . . are daily growing more pronounced," the *Morgen Journal* spurned the report as the sanctimonious preaching of uptown Jews. The *Tageblat*, meanwhile, sharply rapped the United Hebrew Charities for printing such a remark, true or not, in the first place.[23] Thus the uncompromising and self-righteous assault on Turner's exaggerations precluded winnowing hard facts from offensive rhetoric. Political interests influenced the pitch of the protest as well. The *Warheit*, always sensitive to the *Forward's* charge that it had "sold out to Tammany" and hence hesitant to endorse the straight Democratic ticket, now felt no compunctions in doing so. "It is no longer important for Jews whether Gaynor, or Bannard, or Hearst win," Louis Miller, the *Warheit* editor wrote: "It is only important if the Jews win or their defamers. . . . [The only question is] whose election will strengthen most the new calumnies against the Jews." [24]

The answer was self-evident: if *McClure's* demanded Tammany's defeat, honor required a Tammany victory. The socialist *Forward*, on the other hand, anxious to use the Turner exposé against all "capitalist parties," warned its readers that Tammany had cunningly cast the entire controversy into a Jewish issue in order to evade Turner's damning indictment and to pander to the Jewish vote. In the end, this most cosmopolitan of Yiddish papers criticized Turner, too, though in relatively gentle terms, for having written unfairly on the Jews. [25]

The Americanized leaders of the community with wider interests failed, as well, to face the issue resolutely. Committed to a Fusion victory, they feared the boomerang effect of the articles in *McClure's*. They felt constrained to bend every effort to prevent a massive Jewish vote for Tammany. Congressman William E. Bennett, campaign manager for Bannard, promptly furnished them with the opportunity. Turner's article, he declared, had been brought to him before publication with the suggestion that the Fusion organization print it as a campaign document. "Though true in all its hideous details he [Turner] sacrificed accuracy to picturesqueness in his story about Jewish kaftans and as I could not endorse such an article as a whole I would not touch it." Two days later, Louis Marshall, in a published letter, commended Bennett for his "admirable statement concerning the article in *McClure's* Magazine, which is now, with great cunning, sought to be contorted by the opponents of Mr. Bannard into an attack by him upon the Jews." While the motives of Turner could not be questioned, "he had doubtless been led into exaggeration by the rounding of his periods and by the supposed requirements of literary composition." As chairman of the recent New York State Immigration Commission investigation, Marshall wrote with authority. Some Jews, his investigation had shown, participated in the traffic, but the Jewish community had taken "measures to aid in the suppression of that crime." The following day another statement appeared, and among the signatories besides Marshall were Jacob Schiff, Lillian Wald, Stephen S. Wise, and Felix Adler.

No reflection [they declared] is intended [by the articles in *McClure's*] against the character or the morality of any race or of the people of any section of the city. The notion that such a charge has been made has been spread by the politicians as one of their means of deceiving the people.[26]

In this setting the Kehillah also raised its voice. On October 26, while agitation over the November issue of *McClure's* was at its height, a special meeting of the executive committee of the Kehillah debated the text of a public announcement. The statement finally issued to the press declared that the evidence at hand offered no justification for the "slanderous statements and inferences in [Turner's] article." However, an investigation into the extent of the white-slave traffic among Jews was underway, and the Kehillah promised to inform the authorities promptly of all data uncovered.[27] Thus an admission that an inquiry into the matter, at the least, was necessary accompanied the indignant tones of protest.

The general press gave the statement passing coverage, the Yiddish press hardly any, and little came from the investigation. In the months following, a paid investigator reported encountering grave difficulties securing evidence usable in court. Finally, in February, 1910, he concluded that no proof existed of organized groups of Jews directing the white-slave traffic. At the annual convention of the Kehillah the end of February, the chairman reported the findings of the investigation. "One cannot deny," he added, "that certain phases of the social evil present us with difficult problems, and it is our duty to fight them energetically." But these problems were not only Jewish ones. "All men of good will" had to join together to solve them.[28]

Supporters of the Kehillah compared the response to Bingham's article in the *North American Review* a year before with the Kehillah's handling of Turner's article in *McClure's*. "In the former case," the *American Hebrew* wrote, "the newspapers were lured with the statements from a thousand and one injured representatives of the Jews. In the latter case, feeling that the community would speak for them, they were content to let the duty rest there and accepted the one calm statement that was issued as the only one that was necessary." [29]

Notable as the change in temper was, the same self-righteous posture with its hints of guilt marked the Kehillah's reply as it had the discordant outburst the year before. Nowhere was this position made clearer than in a well-publicized address Dr. Judah L. Magnes delivered at Temple Emanuel in November, 1909. The traditional Sabbath Bible portion, the Life of Sarah, provided the text for his sermon. The Jew, he said, had never trafficked on his women. "They have been for him the symbol of all chastity and holiness." So today, "under conditions of poverty or in the midst of luxury, the Jewish women are still worthy descendents of a fine and continent people." However, the "ancient bulwarks of our religion" were largely destroyed for many. Together with poverty, the social dislocation attendant upon immigration and the compelling need for women to work in factory and shop, it was

small wonder that in this terrifying struggle for life, some children of our ancient mother Sarah have gone astray. . . . It is for us to burn this desolation of abomination out of our midst. . . . All this, however, is but incidental to the orderly course of our lives, and, alas, that it becomes necessary to assure ourselves and the world that such happenings are but rare among us. . . . And therefore I say it to you, that the women of Israel are pure, clean, womanly women.[30]

In meeting the issue of Jewish criminality for the first time, the Kehillah had broken no new ground nor commanded wide public attention as communal spokesman. Two of its sources of strength, the Americanized Jewish leadership and the Yiddish newspaper publishers, dealt with the problem separately and in essentially apologetic and political terms. The mayoralty campaign had publicized the subject of Jewish criminality, to the embarrassment of all. But, paradoxically, political considerations, and not the "one calm statement" of the Kehillah, had muffled the debate. No candidate could afford to offend the sensibilities of a large ethnic group. By election day, most nominees for office had done their best to dull the sharp thrusts of the November *McClure's*.[31] This, after all, was what uptown and downtown alike wanted. For the militant spokesmen of the Jewish quarter, throttling the controversy once again implied vindication. For the leaders of the older, German-Jewish community, it ended public embarrassment and permitted normal institutional work to continue undistracted.

The discussion of Jewish criminality in the fall of 1909 brought, therefore, no major change in communal policy. Some minor expansion of social services for delinquents occurred. However, the growing alarm felt by the well-established Jews did contribute, indirectly, to a new and ambitious program of uplift. Led by Jacob Schiff, distinguished members of the older community now gave time and money to revamp and revitalize Jewish religious education. Moral decline, they held, had followed the failure of traditional religious education to inculcate in the young the precepts of Judaism. The 1910 Kehillah convention that rejected Turner's allegations accepted Schiff's bequest to endow a bureau of Jewish education.[32]

The ritual of self-exoneration did not hide, at least among some, deep-seated uneasiness. Yet two and a half more years passed, from the appearance of Turner's article to the murder of Herman Rosenthal, before the Kehillah confronted the problem of Jewish criminality directly. Under the new circumstances of 1912, the education of delinquents appeared too circumscribed, and education as a prophylaxis against delinquency too uncertain. The far different response of the Kehillah and the new methods it used in 1912 can be understood only after considering the response of the community at large to the problem of crime.

As much as *McClure's* of November, 1909, influenced a particular political campaign, it reflected the rising anxiety over immigration and crime. A month after the election the United States Immigration Commission, the Dillingham Commission, presented to Congress the report of its special investigation into the white-slave traffic.

A large part of the report described conditions in New York. Directed by Professor Jeremiah Jenks and assisted by high officials of the New York Police Department and a special staff of undercover agents, the findings once more indicated the considerable role Jews played in the commercial vice of the city.[33] The discussion that followed centered, however, on the committee's legislative proposals. A year later another volume of the Dillingham Commission appeared, this one dealing with immigration and crime. The commission's staff abstracted statistics from a variety of court sources and also collected its own limited data on the relationship between crime and ethnic origin in New York.[34]

Of more immediate bearing on the city was the special grand jury headed by John D. Rockefeller Jr., which was impaneled in January, 1910, to investigate "the alleged . . . organized traffic in women." Charles S. Whitman, the new district attorney, and his assistant, James B. Reynolds, conducted a painstaking investigation that lasted five months. One result of the grand jury investigation was Rockefeller's decision to create a private "permanent organization . . . which would not be dependent upon a temporary wave of reform [interest]." [35]

The Bureau of Social Hygiene, organized in 1911, was that organization, and it immediately undertook yet another investigation of prostitution. Police collusion received special attention. The probe continued from January to November, 1912, and elaborate reports were prepared from information supplied by informers and agents who infiltrated the vice complex. In May, 1913, the Bureau published its findings.[36]

The Bureau of Social Hygiene was not the only private organization that assumed quasi-governmental functions. The grand jury investigation that led to the formation of the Bureau also induced the Committee of Fourteen to revive and enlarge its activities. Organized in 1900, the committee concentrated on research into the problems of prostitution, and on lobbying for more stringent laws in the field of vice prevention.[37] It published three influential studies during the next decade and was instrumental in securing laws holding tenement-house owners responsible for prostitution practiced on their property. Unexpectedly, the committee became a clearing office as well for complaints by citizens unable to obtain relief from the authorities. In 1907, when the committee reorganized, it placed new emphasis on crime prevention and crime detection. Additional impetus to this phase of the work came with the expansion of the committee in 1911. Its policy of refraining from public criticism of city officials won for it a close working relationship with the district attorney's office, the Police Department, the courts, the Excise Board, and the Mayor's License Bureau.[38] It succeeded in cajoling the brewers into an agreement whereby they extended credit only to establishments meeting the committee's standards; some centers of gambling and procuring were thereby eliminated. Other groups operating in related fields collaborated with the committee. Mrs. Charles H. Israels headed the Committee on Amusement Resources for Working Girls. (Mrs. Israels later remarried and became better known as Belle Moskowitz, the wife of Dr. Henry Moskowitz.) The committee's agents collected information on the dance halls, movie houses, and amusement parks frequented by the immigrant girls. The Bureau of Social Hygiene shared its information with the committee.[39]

Thus private civic agencies apparently found a formula that brought significant results: exerting economic pressure, continually prodding the authorities with carefully collected evidence, offering the police legal assistance in court proceedings, and publishing scholarly studies. As the condition for success, these groups shunned publicity. They thereby gained the confidence of Police Department officials. When the time came, the Kehillah adapted some of these ways for its own purposes. It established ties with all the groups mentioned and selected as its chief investigator a person who had served on the staff of Rockefeller's Bureau of Social Hygiene.

The heightened concern with crime that sent organizations into the streets to track down vice also directed attention to the statistics of crime. At the core of the investigations, public and private, lay elaborate statistical analyses which conveyed the impression of scientific truth. Undoubtedly, a contributing factor to the intensity of the Jewish community's outburst following Bingham's 1908 article was his use of statistics to support his argument. A statistical indictment could be rebutted only by assembling other figures in return. This obsession with statistical data marked the response to the public discussion of Jewish criminality in 1908 and 1909. It reached a ludicrous extreme when, in the midst of the agitation over Turner's article, the *Warheit* published daily lists of the names of prostitutes convicted at the night court. In triumphant headlines the paper proclaimed that only 27 or 28 percent were Jewish, while the Jews formed more than one-third of the population of the borough.[40]

However, for the more professional statisticians and interested laymen, the obstacles in the way of proper statistical work were considerable. The peculiar difficulties in handling criminal data were compounded when attempts were made to manipulate the data to show ethnic crime rates. The most substantial study used to refute Bingham showed, for example, that of 2,848 convictions in the Court of General Sessions for New York County in 1907, 460, or 16.1 percent, were Jews. On the basis of an estimated Jewish population in New York County of 750,000, the ratio of convictions per 10,000 Jews was 6.1. For non-Jews it was 12.3, or twice as large as the Jewish rate.[41] Jewish leaders hailed the study in press releases as proof of the low crime rate among Jews. Privately, however, at least one student of the problem found the study totally misleading. Dr. Paul Abelson pointed out that the estimate of Jewish population was too crude for statistical purposes, and there was no assurance that among those classified as gentiles there might not be Jews. Furthermore, the purely legal test of convictions did not reflect the extent of the "criminal class." To these criticisms one could add that the convictions represented felonies and did not take into consideration the misdemeanor and vagrancy cases handled by the lower courts, where the proportion of Jews tried rose sharply.[42]

The most comprehensive studies, however, those sponsored by the United States Immigration Commission, were as open to criticism. One Yiddish paper recognized what criminologists pointed out in later years, that the crowded, confined immigrant neighborhoods made crime more visible, not necessarily more prevalent, than elsewhere. The better-off prostitutes of the Tenderloin, the *Warheit* remarked, operated with a minimum fear of arrest. It was the Jewish streetwalkers on the East Side who were most vulnerable and consequently appeared in the statistics of the night courts.[43]

Government studies failed to provide conclusive answers. In nearly all instances the data precluded the analysis the Jewish leaders were most interested in. The most extensive study of the problem, the United States Immigration Commission's volume on *Immigration and Crime*, used elaborate data on crime as a means of studying the acculturation of the immigrant. From the mass of studies a Jewish crime rate lower than that of the general population could be extrapolated, but so could the leap in criminal offenses among the children of Jewish immigrants. Katharine Bement Davis' careful investigation into the ethnic backgrounds of prostitutes at several New York correctional institutions found the Jewish rate "normal" for the size of the Jewish population. But the Immigration Commission's report on vice presented figures for one four-month period from the city's night court which showed that Russian-born women (and in New York City the assumption was they were all Jewesses) were far in the lead in convictions for soliciting.[44]

By 1912 the anxiety to prove that Jewish criminality had not exceeded some permissible level seemed to have been stilled. The Yiddish press, in catering to the Jewish quarter's sensitivity, continued to resort to statistical apologetics from time to time. It would appear, however, that the stream of investigations, studies, and articles from 1909 to 1912 had focused attention on the problem itself. Jewish criminality, in Louis Marshall's words, was "a cancer . . . gnawing at our vitals" whatever the rate might be.[45]

Beginning in July, 1912, new figures agitated the Jewish community. The cast of characters which appeared on the front pages of the city's newspapers in the wake of the Rosenthal murder was overwhelmingly Jewish. Yet hardly a voice was raised to urge that the make-up of the accomplices in the murder trial did not reflect a proper sample. Instead, the most heterogeneous and antagonistic groups in the Jewish community agreed that an entirely new approach was needed. The activities of privately endowed civic organizations provided the example.

In a journalistic coup the New York *World* on July 13, 1912, published an affidavit by the gambler, Herman Rosenthal, chronicling his business dealings with Lieutenant Charles Becker, head of the Police Department's antigambling, strong-arm squad. Becker had aided Rosenthal, originally a minor operator on the East Side, first with a loan, and then with a guarantee of immunity from police and court harassment. In return he had become Rosenthal's silent partner. Under pressure from superiors, Becker had raided and then closed Rosenthal's gambling house. In addition he had failed to quash charges against the gambler. Rosenthal then turned to the courts and to the district attorney, demanding relief from "police oppression." Piqued by the Police Lieutenant's reneging on an agreement, Rosenthal promised a detailed account of the "system." His statement in the *World*, an artless and brazen presentation of graft and gambling as subject to normal commercial practice, signaled the beginning of another storm of protest. Three days later, on the evening before a scheduled grand jury appearance, Rosenthal was gunned down on a brightly lit street, steps away from Times Square, in the most heavily patrolled section of the city. The judicious *Evening Post* called it "the culminating act of a series of outrages." Together with less-temperate rivals, the paper named the police as the prime suspect in planning, assisting, and ordering Rosenthal's "execution." [46] Neither did District Attorney Whitman hesitate to blame the Police Department for plotting Rosenthal's murder: "The time and place selected were such as to inspire terror in the hearts of those the system had most to fear. It was intended to be a lesson to any who might have thought of exposing the alliance between the police and crime." [47]

The district attorney built his case on the confessions of gambler-clients of Becker who stated that on the lieutenant's order they had plotted the murder and hired the thugs. Three and a half weeks after the crime, the last two of the hired gangsters suspected of committing the actual murder were apprehended. Soon after, Becker was indicted for ordering Rosenthal's death. Of all the major figures in the case—gangsters, accomplices, witnesses—only Becker and one of the hired gangsters were not Jewish. [48]

The public outburst that followed surpassed in intensity and longevity the response to all exposés of the previous decade and a half. The heightened activity by civic organizations during the two preceding years and their support by men and women of eminence had well prepared the ground for such a moment. Moreover, many leaders of the current protest movement had served in the reform surges of the 1890s and at the turn of the century.[49]

For forty-one consecutive days following the murder, the New York *Times* featured the episode on its front page. During Becker's trial in October, only the wounding of Theodore Roosevelt in Milwaukee forced the proceedings from the front page. The paper's daily coverage frequently spread over seven and eight columns and included transcriptions of the principal trial testimony and minutiae of the careers of major and minor underworld figures. This absorption in the case indicated more than reform sentiment. Sheer fascination with the racy drama of pursuit, trial, conspiracy, and punishment fixed the city's attention on the affair.[50]

Becker's trial was followed by the trial of the "four gunmen" and by a retrial of Becker himself. Intermittently, in the wake of legal appeals, petitions for clemency, the uncovering of alleged new evidence, and the execution of the "four gunmen," the press revived the story. Only following the execution of Becker in July, 1915, did interest wane. For three years, then, spectacle combined with civic conscience. The popular imagination saw "the system on trial" and in no mere figurative sense: judicial procedure assured a rigorous search for the truth, and the guilty surrogate for "the system" was to be punished not by a mere political setback but by paying the supreme penalty.[51]

One further element, politics, swelled the extent and scope of popular indignation. For two and a half years, Mayor Gaynor had made the Police Department his personal province. He had emphasized the enforcement of "outward order and decency" rather than attempting total repression of vice. The related sins of prostitution, gambling, and Sunday sale of liquor, the mayor believed, could not be completely suppressed by police methods in a great urban and immigrant center like New York. To attempt to do so, he repeatedly said, created those conditions which tempted and then corrupted the police. Prevailing opinion in patrician circles held otherwise, and Gaynor's political opponents exploited the issue for their own purposes.[52]

In 1909, the patrician-reform nexus, which included independent Democrats like John Purroy Mitchel, had coalesced with the regular

Republican organization. Under a Fusion banner, they had defeated the entire Tammany ticket except Gaynor. Now, as the last year of the mayor's term approached, the Rosenthal–Becker episode provided the opportunity to repudiate the mayor's police policy and hold him personally responsible for corruption.[53]

Two investigations into police corruption and organized crime were launched. A Republican, Henry A. Curran, headed a special committee of the Board of Aldermen. With Emory H. Buckner as chief counsel and a $40,000 budget, the committee's investigation lasted from September, 1912, to March, 1913. During eighty public sessions Curran and Buckner called 224 witnesses and evidenced as much concern for the banner headline as for the unvarnished truth. An ad hoc citizens' committee of reformers, social workers, and wealthy contributors sponsored its own mass-meeting at Cooper Union in mid-August to arouse public interest and to endorse a second, nonpartisan investigation.[54] The political factor, in addition to establishing the Rosenthal–Becker affair firmly on the city scene, had its ethnic aspect.

Gaynor was a popular figure among the Jewish immigrant masses. As a judge he had vigorously denounced highhanded and arbitrary police procedures. His criticism of Police Commissioner Bingham, moreover, had led to the latter's resignation. In his 1909 campaign speeches on the East Side, he had stressed "personal liberty," denounced police harassment of pushcart peddlers, and interpreted the law as allowing work on Sunday. No one had attacked the *McClure's* articles more caustically than he.[55] As mayor he had sharply warned the police against the use of clubs or making arrests for trivial offenses. Total arrests and summonses in the first inspection district, which included all of the downtown precincts, dropped from 25,060 in 1909 to 16,710 in 1910, the first year of Gaynor's term.[56] Finally, his approach to the vice problem seemed more realistic and understanding of immigrant sensibilities. His suspicion of those who called for well-publicized crusades, his feud with preacher-critics Dr. Charles H. Parkhurst and Dr. Stephen S. Wise over these very questions, matched the sentiments on the East Side. Such crusades, the immigrants felt, blackened the name of an entire district and an entire group because of the sins of a few. However, as we have seen, the type of muted reform activity so congenial to Gaynor was replaced by a policy of maximum exposure following the Rosenthal murder. Ready to provide vigorous direction for such a policy was the district attorney, Charles Whitman.[57]

The one regular Republican elected in the 1909 Fusion victory, Whitman had rejected Gaynor's emphasis on the primacy of personal liberties in law enforcement. Instead he had pledged himself to a massive campaign to expose vice. His response to the Turner article was to promise a grand jury investigation with Turner as first witness. He redeemed his pledge during his first week in office. Greatly expanding his staff, Whitman appointed two of the most knowledgeable men in vice work, James B. Reynolds and Frank Moss, as his assistants. The forceful and publicity-conscious district attorney made unprecedented use of grand juries and liberally offered immunity from prosecution to informers. He antagonized the mayor not only with his methods but threatened him politically with the resultant acclaim.[58]

In July 1912, Whitman's great opportunity came when Gaynor refused to take any extraordinary measures in handling the Rosenthal affair. The mayor declined to order an investigation of the Police Department or to remove Police Commissioner Rhinelander Waldo despite evidence of shortcomings and widespread demand for the commissioner's resignation. Whitman, Curran, the Citizens' Committee, the ministry, and the press, he charged, were leagued against him and his reforms. Whitman responded by treating Gaynor and the Police Department command as allies of "the system." He circumvented the detective bureau, hired his own private agents to pursue the fugitives, and charged the Department with harboring suspects and witnesses. Henry Curran, the chairman of the newly formed aldermanic investigating committee, complemented Whitman's word and deed. Refusing Gaynor's offer of assistance, he denied the right of the corporation counsel to participate in the investigation.[59]

By the time the Citizens Committee's mass meeting at Cooper Union took place in mid-August, a month after Rosenthal's murder, Whitman stood at the summit of his popularity. Magnes, who participated in planning the meeting and who was scheduled to speak after Whitman, refused to do so. Later he explained angrily that the meeting had been used for the "illegitimate ends" of "advancing the political fortunes of the district attorney." Whitman, Curran, and Buckner had all spoken, and an enthusiastic demonstration greeted the district attorney. Though it was ostensibly a nonpartisan gathering, no one had invited the mayor. Magnes remained wary that political considerations would subvert the declared purposes of the committees and investigations. Gaynor entertained no other possibility.[60]

The *Warheit*, too, criticized the Cooper Union gathering for besmirching the mayor and degenerating into a campaign rally to launch Whitman's gubernatorial candidacy. Moreover, editor Miller chose to defend Gaynor and attack Whitman by making Jacob Schiff the whipping boy. Schiff, by serving as treasurer of the Cooper Union meeting and of the permanent committee organized that evening, Miller wrote, had given his support to the anti-Gaynor cabal. The financier had thereby shown ingratitude for the mayor's solicitous interest in the Jews and his redoubtable defense of the Schiff family in the Foulke Brandt case.[61]

A former servant of Schiff's son, Mortimer, Brandt had been sentenced to thirty years for attacking and robbing the younger Schiff in his home. In a petition for executive clemency in January, 1912, Brandt claimed that he had knowingly pleaded guilty to trumped-up charges. Surprised during an illicit meeting with Mrs. Mortimer Schiff, Brandt said, he had gallantly staged the attack and robbery to protect Mrs. Schiff's reputation. The Hearst press gave wide currency to the story and soon, in competition with Pulitzer's *World*, supplied a salacious diet of innuendo and slander, attacking the millionaire Schiffs for "railroading" their ex-servant to prison. Whitman, despite decisive evidence to the contrary, supported Brandt and instituted a grand jury investigation into the charges of conspiracy to subvert justice. The *cause célèbre* continued into 1913.[62]

Gaynor upbraided the district attorney for his role in abetting sensationalism, and criticized the judicial proceedings. In his first statement following the Rosenthal murder, Gaynor again referred to Whitman's behavior in the Brandt case as an example of recklessness and unbridled ambition. On the front page of the *Warheit* the day following the Cooper Union meeting, a cartoon showed the biblical Mordecai, Jacob Schiff, saving Haman, District Attorney Whitman, from the gallows. In private letters to Miller, Schiff replied to the *Warheit* criticism by disclaiming all knowledge of the turn the Cooper Union meeting had taken. Not present at Cooper Union, Schiff expressed his indignation that his name had been associated with a move inimical to the Gaynor administration. Miller immediately informed the mayor of Schiff's disclaimer. Scarred by the Brandt episode and disturbed by Whitman's apparent demagoguery, Schiff supported Gaynor.[63]

Politics broadened the scope of the Rosenthal–Becker affair, raised the pitch of controversy, and thereby magnified the notoriety achieved by the Jewish criminals. It also isolated Gaynor further. Estranged from Tammany Hall, alienated now from the reformers, the mayor soon discovered in Schiff, Magnes, and the Kehillah, trusted allies. They, too, found little rapport with the temper of the reform agitation and its central figure, District Attorney Whitman. In time, behind a veil of secrecy, the Kehillah undertook, with the mayor's personal help and Schiff's financial and moral aid, to rid the Jewish East Side of organized crime.

The Rosenthal murder, with its revelations and reverberations, shocked the Jewish community profoundly. The appalling fact was that the underworld segment which the trials and the indefatigable press had so thoroughly laid bare consisted almost entirely of Jewish gangsters and gamblers. No longer could Jewish apologists find comfort in viewing the phenomenon as a rare deviation from the norm. In the accounts, the criminals appeared as commonplace East Side figures. Sons of hard-working parents, most had been exposed as children to religious training and had led average family lives. Even considering the hired gangsters apart, one could point to exceptional and touching instances of family loyalty, pride in one's ethnic group, and knowledge of and affection for Jewish religious tradition. The Yiddish press might have responded as in the past and pointed out that by chance the particular criminal complex uncovered consisted of Jews. The Rosenthal–Becker scandal in fact did not touch the more affluent networks of gambling and vice.[64] However, it is precisely the abandonment of this line of defense which underscores the depth of the distress and dismay felt in all parts of the Jewish community. "For hundreds of years we were proud of our high ethics and morality," the *Morgen Journal* editorialized. "No matter how bitter it may be, we must recognize the fact that among Jews we can find all kinds of bandits." And Gedaliah Bublick, the *Tageblat*'s editor, confessed his shame on seeing the police circulars of the wanted men. Distributed throughout the country and reproduced in the English newspapers were the photographs of the fugitives, he wrote, and the descriptions appended to them began with the words, "American Hebrew." "The divine word, 'I chose you among the peoples of the earth,'" Bublick continued, "ends this way!" [65]

In the weeks which followed Rosenthal's murder, the Yiddish press led the Jewish quarter in agonizing self-examination. The discussion focused on the children of the immigrant generation. From the ranks of "the first generation to grow up under the free sky of America with all the privileges and opportunities of young America" came the vast majority of criminals. In their despair, journalists placed in apposition the idyllic "old country" where tradition and its values guided the young and where delinquency was rarely met, and materialistic America which "left no room for God or ideals." [66]

Each paper stressed its particular variation of this common theme. The *Warheit* cast the blame squarely upon the Jewish quarter: the Jewish criminal, born on the Jewish East Side, operated freely in its streets; America allowed unlimited freedom to organize; the people of the Jewish districts therefore had to take steps to root out the criminal element. For the Orthodox *Tageblat*, the immigrant generation carried responsibility for the sins of the young: parents, confused by the siren call of Americanization, had jettisoned their religious practices and lost all moral influence over their young. But most of all, radicalism had bred a generation of godless Jews. Consequently, the Jews were accountable for the gangsters and gamblers they had produced. Self-respect and Jewish honor required establishing order in one's own house.[67]

For the socialist *Forward* as well, the phenomenon of Jewish criminality indicated a breakdown of the social order. However, capitalism, not godlessness, was the cause. Where honest work failed to bring its just reward, men were enticed to the stuss houses (a popular game of chance played for small stakes) and young girls inveigled into prostitution. From Wall Street on down, American society operated as a giant gambling house with the passion "to get rich" its compelling feature. Yet, its class bias enabled the *Forward* to offer some discriminating insights. In an editorial entitled "Is America Responsible for Jewish Children Becoming Gangsters?" the *Forward* replied with an emphatic "no." Jewish criminality was a phenomenon of the large cities. Odessa and Warsaw, like New York, have their gangs of Jewish culprits.[68] In describing the implications of urbanization, the *Forward* placed the onus of responsibility for social disintegration not on the Jewish community but on capitalism. It rejected "the narrow nationalistic explanation" of Jewish criminality. Hence it opposed, on principle, specifically Jewish group activity to fight crime. As in every other Jewish community undertaking, the Kehillah could expect no support from the *Forward*.[69]

On the other hand, the *Morgen Journal*, conservative and religiously orthodox, employing a different rhetoric, reached the same practical conclusion as the *Forward*. American-born criminals of Jewish parents had not learned crime from their elders but from the American environment with its corrupt politicians and police. Nowhere could one find an observant Jew embarking on a career of crime. Therefore, no specifically Jewish mold marked the criminal of Jewish parentage. The *Morgen Journal*, consequently, rebuked the Kehillah for undertaking anti-crime work on its own. In an editorial labeled "As Citizens, Not as Jews," the paper urged its readers to join the general movement seeking to bring order to the city.[70]

The opposition by two of the four Yiddish dailies to the principle of Jewish communal accountability misrepresents the temper of the Jewish quarter. Once the *Forward* announced its doctrinal position, it offered no alternate course of action for aroused East Side Jews. Some leading Jewish socialists actually joined with the Kehillah in the first stages of its vice work, and while the *Forward* ignored the work editorially its news coverage was fair. The *Morgen Journal's* criticism of the projected communal undertaking was so vitriolic that the Jewish public well understood that other grievances lay behind the attacks. Publisher Jacob Saphirstein's jaundiced view of the Kehillah's policy on Jewish education and religious organization distorted the paper's judgment of all Kehillah endeavors. With the *Tageblat*, the other religious daily, a powerful supporter of the Kehillah's decision to combat crime, the *Morgen Journal*'s opposition reflected no position of principle. Besides, events in the paper's own news columns and in the community at large muffled the shrillness of its editorial dissent.

Outside the immigrant ghetto, American-bred Jews, through their publications, presented a moderate and balanced view of the Rosenthal affair. The *American Hebrew* blamed "American economic and political influences and the crisis in municipal government" for creating the conditions which bred delinquency. It shared the position held by municipal and social reformers. On the other hand, the paper pointed to the lack of moral and religious education and the failure of the traditional religious school, the heder, to fill that want.[71]

However, in the first flush of chagrin and indignation, Louis Marshall may have given the most faithful expression of the true feelings of uptown Jewry. In a private letter to Magnes, Marshall wrote:

. . . the real cause . . . lies in the utter neglect by the East Side synagogues and their rabbis of the essence of religion, their failure to educate the young and to draw them to the synagogue by making it attractive, the failure to understand that what was effective in Russia is utterly useless, nay, pernicious here. . . . We close our eyes and ears to unpalatable truths, and Judaism here in New York, and especially on the East Side, is in greater peril than it is amid the persecutions of Russia, simply because it has escaped from all discipline and restraints, and is passing through an orgy of materialism, license, and indifference. . . . conditions here are entirely unlike those amid which they [the immigrant leaders of Orthodox Judaism] were brought up. They cannot maintain their hold upon the young by their methods. They become mere objects of derision, and the religion which they profess thereby becomes hateful to those who might be saved, if they were brought under proper influences, and were taught by methods which appeal to their minds and to their understanding. A heavy responsibility rests upon the heads of the New York congregations and their rabbis, whose sole ideal is to Russianize American Judaism, when all that they can accomplish is to drive their children to atheism.[72]

Marshall gave vent to all the frustrations he had encountered in three years of aiding the Kehillah's promising educational and religious programs. The fruits of the petty intrigues, as he saw them, the willful obstructionism in the name of benighted methods, the maneuvering for personal profit, had contributed their share to the Rosenthal scandals. In July, 1912, he wrote to the "Organization of Orthodox Rabbis, whatever the name may be" (a letter which he probably never sent):

You have closed your eyes to the departure of the children of a race, that justly prided itself on the purity of its moral life, to adopt the career of gamblers, thugs, gangsters, thieves and prostitutes, and to become a byword and a hissing. You have remained silent witnesses to the degradation of Judaism, to the alienation from it of the new generation. . . . You have clung to the shadow, while the vivifying spirit has departed.[73]

He reproached the rabbis and through them their way of life. A gulf separated Marshall and the immigrant Jews of the East Side. But a calamity had struck. Though responsibility for it perhaps lay elsewhere, all sections of the community had to aid in repairing the breach. Marshall, like the great majority of communal leaders, left theories of Jewish life aside and gave unqualified support for a community effort to root out "the cancer."

CHAPTER EIGHT

Crime Fighting

FOR FIVE YEARS, BEGINNING IN AUGUST, 1912, THE KEHILLAH maintained a Bureau of Social Morals, a euphemism for a secret service which fought crime and vice in the Jewish quarter. The undertaking presented the Kehillah with a number of problems. Should it build a broad civic movement out of the alarm which most Jewish circles felt following the Rosenthal murder? Or was the crime problem a task for professionals, to be handled discreetly and as far from public attention as possible? Once the scandal faded, Kehillah leaders faced the question of the permanency of the Bureau. Did this type of activity belong to a Jewish community organization? Was it a model other groups could emulate? The undertaking required, moreover, the approbation of the city's highest officials. Two mayors, Gaynor and Mitchel, reacted differently to the anti-crime activities of the Kehillah. They faced a political decision, but they also faced a question of basic policy. Was there a place for voluntarism in the operation of law-enforcement agencies?

§

ON JULY 28, 1912, THE EXECUTIVE COMMITTEE AND THE ADVISORY council of the Kehillah acted upon Magnes' recommendation to organize a "vigilance committee" and a "bureau of information and investigation." The meeting incorporated his suggestions in a series of resolutions.

As citizens of the city and as Jews [one resolution stated], we view with profound indignation the profanation of the Jewish name brought about by these events, and the implication of Jews in practices of vices which have, up to very recent years, been proverbially unknown among our people.

Other resolutions pledged the Kehillah's support to all "public and private agencies . . . desirous of laying bare all the ramifications of the crime." But of greater moment was the Kehillah's decision to conduct its own, independent activity. In so doing, however, the Kehillah sought the cooperation of all Jewish groups. The nature of the projected activities and the sense of urgency called for the broadest possible coalition.[1]

During the next three weeks, Magnes succeeded in enlisting the participation of groups who represented a range of interests and views heretofore indifferent or antagonistic to the Kehillah. In addition to Kehillah stalwarts like the financier Felix Warburg and the young Orthodox leader Isaac Allen, representatives of all the Yiddish dailies, except for the *Morgen Journal*, attended the first planning meetings in early August. This in itself was a feat. But the presence of Mrs. Charles H. Israels, Dr. Henry Moskowitz, and Meyer London best expressed the mood of crisis. It suggested, as well, a potential widening of the Kehillah's base.[2]

All three were representative of those Jews who though intimately connected with the East Side maintained only nominal ties with Jewish institutional life. Mrs. Israels, once associated with the Educational Alliance, had risen to prominence in general charitable activities as a member of the staff of *The Survey*. Her activities as chairman of the Committee on Amusement Resources of Working Girls and then as field secretary of the Playground and Recreation Association had added to her standing. Dr. Moskowitz, head worker of Madison House Settlement and leader of the Downtown Ethical Culture Society, occupied by 1912 an important place, together with Mrs. Israels, in the arbitration machinery of the clothing industry. Meyer London's great popularity on the East Side stemmed from his representation of the garment workers unions. He was also the most effective vote-getter of the Socialist Party.[3]

The presence of such key figures attracted East Siders who hitherto had rejected the Kehillah as parochial and a tool of the wealthy German Jews. Among those who responded to the first public call were two young lawyers, Jonah J. Goldstein and Alexander H. Kaminsky. The civic movement the Kehillah promised to launch offered a vehicle for both service and personal advancement. Goldstein had served as Al Smith's assistant and in 1912 joined the University Settlement as a resident. Kaminsky, a director of the Young Men's Benevolent Association, a neighborhood social and civic club, had been instrumental in founding the Jewish Big Brother movement.[4] Both men volunteered to head district offices whose function would be to gather confidential information on crime. Two hundred more offered their help to the Kehillah in the first wave of interest. In early September, when Magnes reviewed the progress of the vigilance committee before a meeting of the Kehillah's executive committee, he reported that the number of volunteers had reached over three hundred.[5]

At the first and most successful neighborhood rally held at the East Side's Educational Alliance on August 19, London shared the platform with Magnes, Moskowitz, and Goldstein. In reporting the event, the Orthodox *Tageblat* singled out socialist London for his powerful speech. The socialist *Forward* described the enthusiastic reception given to the talk by Temple Emanuel's rabbi, Dr. Judah Magnes. The *American Hebrew*, meanwhile, quoted Ethical Culture leader Moskowitz, telling the audience that the meeting was a family gathering of Jews to devise means "for saving our fair name." [6] The Kehillah had reached a rare moment in its career when its goal of representing New York's diverse Jewry seemed possible of fulfillment.

In preparing the neighborhood meetings, the planning committee decided that the neighborhood or district's Bureau of Information would be supervised by an executive committee made up in the following manner: "a rabbi, a professional man, a merchant, a settlement worker, a labor man, a representative of the general executive [of the Kehillah] and a newspaper man: the additional eight to be selected at the first district mass meeting." [7] Out of the anarchy of Jewish communal life was to emerge a grass-roots democratic order.

During August the Kehillah announced the opening of bureaus of information in Harlem, Brownsville, and the East Side in addition to a central clearing office. Information on vice and gambling streamed in. In an interview published in the *World*, Magnes announced that a lawyer had been retained who would review all evidence received and channel the important data either to the district attorney, the aldermanic investigating committee, or the citizens committee. "Hereafter," he concluded, "we shall have nothing to give out to the press. Our work must be done quietly and among ourselves." [8]

Gratifying as the initial response was, Magnes and his collaborators soon decided that the enterprise required a professional staff of investigators. This in turn called for sizable financial backing.[9] Cyrus Sulzberger, the chairman of the Kehillah's committee on philanthropic work, suggested raising $100,000. "Say nothing to the authorities," he wrote, "but engage Burns [the private detective] to study the whole question of criminality on the East Side, prepare his cases himself and then prosecute them."

As much as a year would be required to complete the investigation. Sulzberger however was in Europe at the time and, from New York, Magnes replied: "Our best men have again been led off by the goyim. They are contributing to the fund of the Citizens Committee organized at the Cooper Union mass meeting, so that it is impossible to approach them now for the large sums needed in order to make such an investigation."

Schiff and Warburg, however, had promptly given a "respectable sum" which enabled Magnes to hire "an excellent young Jewish man with considerable experience." If his work proved effective, Magnes wrote Sulzberger, it would be possible to appeal for more funds.[10]

Meanwhile, Magnes encouraged the one functioning bureau manned by volunteers to operate as originally planned. The bureau, located at the Educational Alliance, was headed by Jonah Goldstein. In the months ahead, a sharp conflict developed between the confidential, professional apparatus and the local East Side volunteers.[11]

The "excellent young . . . man with . . . experience" whom Magnes hired in August, 1912, was Abe Shoenfeld, son of a well-known labor leader of the 1890s who later was active in the East Side Civic Club. The younger Shoenfeld had joined the staff of the Rockefeller-financed Bureau of Social Hygiene as an investigator under

George J. Kneeland. He had participated in the extensive study of commercialized vice in New York City in the early part of 1912. When Shoenfeld accepted the position of chief investigator for the Kehillah's Bureau of Social Morals (the name that eventually replaced such initial designations as "vigilance committee," "vice committee," "Bureau of Information," or "welfare committee"), he brought with him a familiarity with the most comprehensive private investigation into vice conditions the city had known. He used his knowledge of the city's underworld to establish a network of undercover agents and informers.[12]

Shortly after Shoenfeld began work, Harry W. Newburger was appointed counsel. Socially, Newburger belonged to the uptown community. A Columbia University graduate, he served his law clerkship with the distinguished firm of Simpson, Werner, and Cardozo, and married into one of New York's most aristocratic Jewish families.[13]

By October, Newburger and Shoenfeld had compiled a comprehensive list of stuss houses and *weisbierstubes* (a curtained, store-front resort located in the tenement-house stoops and frequented by gamblers, prostitutes, and pickpockets). Despite a limited budget, they gathered information on the full spectrum of commercialized crime. Intelligence reports prepared almost daily reported the location, management, and frequenters of gambling resorts, brothels, and gang hangouts. The mere awareness that an investigation conducted by well-informed agents was in progress, a fact that could not be kept from the underworld, brought some results. One police inspector, for example, warned the stuss houses in his area to close because he was being observed by "Jewish societies." [14]

However, the one effective course called for a massive harassment of the various types of gambling resorts through police surveillance, suspension of licenses, and criminal prosecutions. Hopefully, such measures would disrupt an important economic base of organized crime on the East Side.[15] Success, consequently, depended on close cooperation with the law enforcement agencies. Now that the Kehillah's professional staff had proven its proficiency, the Kehillah leaders confronted the question of seeking collaboration with the authorities. On October 21, 1912, Magnes wrote to Mayor William J. Gaynor asking that he receive a delegation consisting of Judge Samuel Greenbaum, Marshall, Schiff, Sulzberger, and himself. The decision, evidently, had been made to proceed with crime work provided the city's collaboration could be obtained. The letter to Gaynor confined the proposed discussion to "police conditions especially in the first inspection district," the police precincts of the East Side.[16]

The meeting with Gaynor took place two days later. The alacrity with which both the mayor and Magnes embarked upon the arrangements reached at the meeting suggested the high degree of mutual confidence. Directly following the conference, Magnes sent to the mayor a list of vice resorts which included detailed descriptions of the offenses committed at each address and recommendations for action. Gaynor replied the same day:

I have had a personal interview with the commissioner [Police Commissioner Rhinelander Waldo] about the matter. I am quite certain you will find that he will work with you. . . . I shall be glad, as I told you yesterday, to have you call here at any time if I can aid in any way.[17]

The closing phrase was no mere amenity. Two weeks later the mayor wrote again and on his own initiative:

Now that the election is over, I would like to hear from you about the disorderly places. Are the commissioner and the officers under him giving you full help? Might it not be well for me some day to go down with you and look over the ground? Since you have taken the trouble to help us I want to help you all that I can.[18]

While the mayor, his chief law-enforcement officers, and the Kehillah's staff established the operating procedures of their coordinated drive against crime on the East Side, Magnes confronted the question of community support. The composition of the delegation that met with the mayor indicated his approach. The presence of Schiff, Marshall, and Sulzberger, the most eminent of the Kehillah's leaders, was to be expected in a matter of such importance. However, the absence of anyone who might have represented that East Side public, which two months before had responded to Magnes' call, is notable. The inclusion, on the other hand, of Judge Samuel Greenbaum, president of the Educational Alliance, clearly marked the direction in which Magnes sought aid.

Judge Greenbaum, as we have seen, opposed the Kehillah idea in principle. He belonged to that group of Reform Jewry which justified segregated activity for religious purposes alone. The mere existence of the Kehillah ascribed to the Jews common interests beyond the purely religious sphere and evoked associations of the European Jewish community with its autonomous powers. To the officers of the Alliance, legitimizing ethnic solidarity was anathema. Yet, ironically, in the fall of 1912, Greenbaum joined the Kehillah delegation to arrange a pact with the city government for joint police operations. The cumulative impact of the Rosenthal affair and the fear of losing the hegemony over the East Side to the Kehillah most likely produced the uneasy partnership.

At the November meeting of the Alliance's board of directors, Greenbaum presented a formal request from the Kehillah for financial aid in combatting vice on the East Side. Negotiations continued through January, 1913, and at one point they appeared to have collapsed. Finally, the directors of the Educational Alliance appropriated $5,000 and agreed to assist in raising the $20,000 which Magnes estimated as necessary to assure the work for one year. In return, Magnes agreed that supervisory control would rest in the Alliance's committee on legal affairs and that a committee of nine chosen by Magnes from among the contributors would retain final authority.[19]

The formula of the agreement conformed with Magnes' conception of the Kehillah as the initiator and coordinator of community action. The joint undertaking, moreover, promised access to financial and leadership resources heretofore closed to the Kehillah. More than half the contributors at the fund-raising meeting for "selected persons" had never previously aided any of the Kehillah's projects. Schiff, Warburg, Adolph Lewisohn, and Marshall—the financial mainstays of the Kehillah—still accounted for 60 percent of the money pledged. But the banker William Salomon, for example, treasurer of the Educational Alliance, contributed $2,500 to the vice fund. The hope, however, that the Eucational Alliance leaders would be drawn into Kehillah work in general did not materialize.[20]

Nor was Magnes able to exploit the initial surge of authentic, local interest which the Kehillah had encountered in the wake of the Rosenthal murder. Those good omens for a broadly based Kehillah-led movement proved even more disappointing. Within four months, the "Welfare Committee of the Jewish Community (Kehillah)," the product of that movement, repudiated the Kehillah and established a separate and competitive anti-crime campaign. Though larger social questions were involved, they were confused as well as influenced by an exasperating embroilment between Jonah Goldstein and Magnes.[21]

While Magnes relied on his professional staff of Newburger and Shoenfeld, Jonah Goldstein continued to manage the welfare committee on a volunteer basis. This was in keeping with the plans formulated at the August conferences. Magnes refused repeated requests from Goldstein for a budget to hire paid investigators and relented only when Goldstein threatened to resign. The Kehillah chairman also declined to share with the welfare committee information collected by his professional agents.[22] With Magnes' encouragement, the stablemen of the East Side had organized the Horse Owners Protective Association to combat the plague of extortions and horse-poisoning which had inundated the Jewish quarter. But Magnes insisted that Newburger serve as paid counsel of the Association rather than Goldstein who had volunteered his services. Magnes clearly lacked confidence in the young, native East Sider. His suspicions stemmed from information supplied by Newburger and Shoenfeld which portrayed Goldstein as a Tammany flunky who associated with untrustworthy characters. Goldstein, they reported, represented figures of dubious reputation in questionable legal actions. Some of the evidence was hearsay, and some of it incriminating only on the puritanical scales of the young rabbi.[23]

For three months Magnes permitted Goldstein to manage the welfare committee without confronting him with the evidence at hand. It may never have occurred to Magnes, confident in the integrity of his immediate coworkers and certain of his own moral judgment, that either mitigating circumstances existed or his own views were unfair. With all of Magnes' compassion for the Russian Jew, he lacked an indulgence for the ambitious young man trying to rise in the ghetto.[24] He deprecated the East Side lawyer who, in his pursuit of advancement and a livelihood, attached himself to the local Tammany assemblyman, represented allegedly disreputable saloons in eviction proceedings, and joined, in the same breath, the Kehillah's antivice campaign. Magnes described a meeting with Goldstein in which the latter complained that "he was not getting enough out of his position" as manager of the welfare committee. Access to secret information, court work, contact with police and city officials, all that would bolster his position and advance his political career, were being denied him. Like a patrician reformer, Magnes had difficulty sympathizing with someone who had been brought up in the Tammany world below Fourteenth Street.[25]

But it must also be remembered, in Magnes' favor, that the Rosenthal affair had sown the seeds of suspicion widely. One did not have to join the wild campaign against Gaynor to be painfully aware of the extent of political and police corruption on the precinct level. Magnes' straitlaced handling of the problem, on the other hand, gained him the confidence of a person like Gaynor. Magnes had decided to direct the vice work as a purely professional operation.

At the end of November, 1912, Goldstein resigned as manager of the Kehillah's welfare committee. He notified Magnes that an organization to be called the East Side Neighborhood Association was in the process of formation. Dr. Henry Moskowitz had agreed to serve as chairman and he, Goldstein, would act as executive secretary and counsel with headquarters at the University Settlement. In his letter of resignation, Goldstein presented a full account of his grievances.[26]

What had started out so auspiciously with the participation of representative East Siders like Moskowitz and London, Goldstein wrote, had ended in "suspicion of everyone and everything that smacked of the lower East Side." The Kehillah's chairman had given him scant encouragement. He had never visited the welfare committee's office and never consulted with its manager. Instead, he had appointed Newburger, an outsider who did not speak the language of the ghetto, as his confidant. Magnes behaved, Goldstein charged, as though only he and his "small coterie" could "render real service to the community. The downtown Jews," he continued, "hoped to find in you a mediator with his snobbish and unsympathetic German brother uptown, has found that you are now trying to discourage every bit of independent spirit." Magnes' way was "the old Parkhurst kind of reform," a reform "percolating downward from Gramercy Park." [27]

The East Side Neighborhood Association (ESNA), from its inception in December, 1912, until its demise at the end of 1915, failed to seriously challenge the preeminence of the Kehillah's Bureau of Social Morals. With men like Jacob Schiff, Felix Warburg, Judge Greenbaum, and Adolph Lewisohn endorsing the Kehillah's antivice work and supporting it financially, the ESNA remained an interloper. Magnes' close supervision of the operation assured its nonpartisan character. In his eight years as one of the city's foremost Jewish preachers, Magnes had eschewed political controversy. Thus his position as rabbi, his association with conservative German Jews (so great a handicap in Goldstein's eyes), and his determination to avoid publicity had won for him the confidence of Mayor Gaynor and his aides.

Meanwhile, Goldstein's tireless labors to establish working relations with the city administration and reform groups brought only a perfunctory response. The ESNA did gather evidence of gambling and tenement-house prostitution through its own investigators, which it funneled to the appropriate authorities. And Goldstein appeared before the Aldermanic Investigating Committee (the Curran Committee) and lobbied in Albany for legislation favorable to the East Side. He also consulted with the Committee of Fourteen and participated in City Club deliberations.[28]

But with the investigatory-type of activity preempted by the Kehillah, the ESNA soon turned to the more visible kind of community undertaking. Here, too, lay the chance for public recognition. Meetings were arranged with proprietors of dance halls, movie houses, and pool parlors to discuss voluntary codes which would eliminate the objectionable practices associated with these amusement centers. At local rallies, Goldstein wrote, East Side residents were exhorted "to stand together, fight the terrorizing influence of gangsters, and withhold tribute from them." Henry Moskowitz addressed the best-publicized meeting in these words: "If housecleaning is to be done we want to do it ourselves. We assert that we have the ability and the power to take care of our own problem." Probably the most successful undertaking of the Association was the promotion of the East Side Forum. During the winter of 1914 and the spring of 1915, large audiences attended weekly discussions of civic problems.[29]

The Yiddish press applauded the ESNA's stress on the need for an exclusively indigenous organization to undertake the task of "cleaning up the East Side." Meanwhile, the ESNA's location at the University Settlement and the presidency of Dr. Henry Moskowitz brought the approbation of settlement workers. However, no ground swell of local support followed. By 1914 the Association offered little more than its adult education project.[30]

By the end of January, 1913, the Kehillah's anticrime effort had attained nearly its maximum momentum and scope. An assured income of $22,500 for the coming year, more than Magnes requested, permitted an expansion of the staff. In addition to his chief investigator, Newburger added another full-time and three part-time agents. A young lawyer, Lawrence S. Greenbaum, son of Judge Samuel Greenbaum, joined in February to assist Newburger with the legal work.[31] At the same time, a separate branch, variously designated as the "welfare committee" and the "anti-oppression office of the Jewish community," began functioning at the Educational Alliance. The office dealt with labor problems, particularly acts of criminal violence, and hence collaborated closely with Newburger. Thus a minimum of eight paid investigators, of whom at least four served on a full-time basis, staffed the Kehillah's anti-crime operation. The entire undertaking was focused on the First Inspection District, the six police precincts of the lower East Side.[32]

Eager for quick results, Magnes and Newburger devised methods to cut through the maze of legal, administrative, and police procedures which encumbered law-enforcement officers in their prosecution of offenders. Such problems as conducting legitimate but effective gambling raids or establishing the criteria and strategies for closing public places catering to criminals brought the Kehillah's staff into daily consultation with a whole range of municipal officials. Requiring immediate attention, too, were the Inferior Court proceedings. There, police officers untrained in the law were pitted against experienced and oftentimes unscrupulous lawyers. Magnes and New-burger met with Gaynor, exchanged legal opinions, and hammered out a joint strategy. They brought to the mayor's attention the most prosaic details of criminal conditions. The practice developed of sub-mitting to the mayor from time to time lists of selected resorts which the Kehillah was especially anxious to close. Gaynor invariably inter-vened with the police and often obtained the harsher enforcement the Kehillah sought. On one occasion at least, he himself visited the suspected hangout. With a Kehillah lawyer present in all criminal court cases which involved the lower East Side, police officers were assured legal assistance.[33]

In situations beyond the mayor's jurisdiction, the Kehillah was less successful. When the Kehillah fought extortion and the related scourge of horse-poisoning, it encountered the indifference of the dis-trict attorney's office. In addition to organizing the Horse Owners' Protective Association, the Kehillah's counsel gathered evidence, pro-secuted perjured witnesses, initiated court actions, and only then per-suaded the district attorney to enter the affair. Magnes himself brought about a confrontation between "Yuski Nigger" (Joseph Tob-linsky), the leader of the band of extortioners, and members of the Horse Owners' Association. Stenographic minutes of the meeting helped convict the "King of the Horse-poisoners" and his lieutenants. The conviction ended a six-year reign of terror among the East Side stablemen by the so-called Yiddish Blackhand Association.[34]

The heart of the Kehillah's anti-crime apparatus was its excellent intelligence network. Kehillah agents supplied the detailed informa-tion that led to gambling raids, revocation of licenses, and the ar-raignment of individual criminals. The knowledge that a nonpolitical, powerfully backed organization scrutinized all facets of local law en-forcement apparently raised the level of police and court work. Fifty years later the chief investigator, Abe Shoenfeld, recalled the initial exploit following the mayor's acceptance of Kehillah collaboration. Data on four stuss houses prepared by the investigator were handed to Police Inspector Cornelius F. Cahalane, in charge of the First Inspection District. By order of the mayor he was instructed to "put them out of business." Cahalane called on Magnes and insisted that the latter's information was erroneous. In the presence of the inspector, Magnes telephoned his chief investigator.

You tell Inspector Cahalane [Shoenfeld remembers saying] that his graft collector, Bob Clifford, can be found right now at the Sagamore Hotel . . . [and] that he gets $125 a month from each stuss house and I say he [Cahalane] is a grafter and I say he also has a graft collector, Mass, . . . who sells the bottled beer to all the stuss houses.

The following day the inspector raided and closed the four stuss houses.[35]

In November, 1913, after a year of full-blown activity, Magnes submitted a confidential, sixty-page report prepared by Shoenfeld to the sponsoring Committee of Nine. At the end of his report, Shoenfeld tabulated the information he and his agents had collected. His statistics can be summarized as follows: 750 stories covering 1,922 typed, single-spaced, pages (each story containing repeated entries detailing all information known about a given resort or person); and a card file containing 2,516 names and addresses drawn from the stories. The latter included the locations of 914 hangouts, 423 disorderly houses, and 374 pool parlors.[36]

The quantitative dimension, however, does not do full justice to the sweep of the undertaking. In describing one troublesome poker house which had been running for fifteen years (the incident was one of a hundred selected cases illustrating the Kehillah's success in closing such resorts), Shoenfeld wrote:

The information would come from the Investigator, would be written out, sent and phoned to Mr. Newburger and Dr. Magnes and the police would be gotten after immediately. There was no two ways about it. They had to go. These poker houses were carried in our list for months. Daily reports from four investigators were submitted on these places. Very few places can withstand this sort of activity.[37]

And about "Dollar John Langer" who had been forced to move his gambling house from place to place the report stated:

When we knew that he was going to open up a particular place, before he was opened, while carpenters were fixing in the ice-box doors [double-doors installed against police raids], and while the painters were cleaning up—we were phoning the information to Mr. H. W. New-

burger . . . and he immediately got word to the Inspector—and the
two of them walked into the place before the owners had a chance to
do so.[38]

In explaining their success in ridding the East Side of stuss houses
which had been operating unimpeded despite the crusades of the previous twenty years, the chief investigator commented:

When the Inspector went to anyone of these places, he went armed
with a complete history of the place and every man therein. Alongside
of him was Mr. Newburger or Mr. Greenbaum ready with legal books
and the strength of the Committee [of the Kehillah] behind them.[39]

Another example was the downfall of Mother Rosie Hertz, whose
brothel was finally closed after thirty years on the same street.

It was our Committee that gave the Police Department the dope upon
which to work, and it was our Committee that forced them to do it.
About 15 pages of the inside history and life of the Hertz family, including the cousins, and everyone else working on the premises, and
daily reports on their actions—and how they were running were submitted until finally "we put it over." [40]

The Hertz establishment was one of 103 listed as closed through the
efforts of the Kehillah.

The report also contained a section on the fate of 200 East Side
thieves whose names had been submitted to the mayor in January,
1913. There were sections, too, on drug peddling (16 opium and co-
caine "dives" were reported "broken up"), immoral behavior in
movie houses, use of gangsters in labor strikes (eight strikes were reported and only one gang-leader supplying hoodlums had been apprehended), dishonest lawyers and "fixers" operating in the courts, and
the report on horse-poisoners.[41] In a kind of peroration, Shoenfeld
wrote:

It can easily be seen how closely our investigators are in touch with
the condition—we creep right into their home affairs—into their
lawyers' offices, and we know what goes on. There is not a time we
cannot lay our hands on them, and there is not a man on our lists who
is not known to one or more of our investigators.[42]

In early February, 1913, the mayor offered the Third Deputy Commissionership of Police to Newburger. After consultation with

Magnes he accepted on condition that, in Magnes' words, "everything affecting the First Inspection District would go through him." The Kehillah's chief investigator followed Newburger to police headquarters to serve as his secretary.[43]

For eleven months, until the new administration under Mayor John Purroy Mitchel took office in January, 1914, both men continued the same work employing essentially the same methods they had developed in the previous period. The staff of Kehillah agents continued to operate under the personal direction of Newburger and Shoenfeld. Greenbaum handled the bulk of the legal work as Kehillah counsel and received his instructions from Newburger as well as from Magnes. In one letter Magnes outlined the procedure to be followed: Greenbaum and the deputy police commissioner were to determine the addresses to be "closed out"; Greenbaum was to turn these over to the inspector as "coming from us [the Kehillah] directly and not from Deputy Police Commissioner Newburger"; then Greenbaum was to obtain another list of addresses for similar action. In the fall of 1913, when an agreement was reached with the Committee of Fourteen whereby that organization followed up certain categories of crime, Kehillah procedures required revision once again. Newburger recommended that in cases where he, Magnes, Greenbaum, and Shoenfeld felt proper action had not been taken, Greenbaum "on behalf of the Jewish Community" was to take up the case with the mayor. "It is most urgent," Newburger wrote, "that Mr. G[reenbaum] be allowed to use Kehillah stationery as was done originally by myself, on which stationery it would be indicated that he is acting as counsel. I cannot lay too much stress on this." Thus the jurisdictional problem was neatly evaded.[44]

With its men in the Police Department holding a mandate over the First Inspection District, the Kehillah's anti-crime effort reached its zenith. The deputy police commissioner ordered and led raids and his secretary, Shoenfeld, commanded one of the two roving "strong arm" squads. In one sense the commissionership merely recognized *de jure* the *de facto* situation which had developed out of the informal understanding Gaynor had reached with the Kehillah leaders in October, 1912.[45]

However, though the impetus behind the Kehillah's involvement rested on ethnic considerations, in the eyes of the city's chief magistrate crime had no ethnic boundaries. Deputy Police Commissioner Newburger's assignment included wider responsibilities than Jewish criminals on the East Side. His primary obligation, nominally at least, was that of chief examiner responsible for internal investigations of the department. If a particular significance attached itself to East Side crime and this drove the commissioner and his associates to proffer their aid in dealing with that problem, Gaynor had no objection.[46]

But the financial supporters associated with the Educational Alliance, skeptical partners from the first, viewed the Kehillah's deepening involvement in police activity with misgiving. In the spring of 1913, the supervising Committee of Nine instructed Newburger to prepare recommendations for improved law enforcement. The committee thereby joined municipal reformers in emphasizing the need for police reorganization. The Curran Committee and Citizens Committee had completed investigations and presented their findings, and now the Kehillah followed suit.[47]

Judge Greenbaum's keen interest in the drafting of the Kehillah's recommendations stemmed from two considerations central to the thinking of the Educational Alliance people: deemphasize the Kehillah's police work; and solve the problem of Jewish criminality by participating in the general movement for police reform.[48]

By September the recommendations were ready for submission to the mayor. On September 10, however, Gaynor suddenly died. Acting Mayor Ardolph Kline pledged himself to adhere to his predecessor's policies. But the intimate ties that linked the late mayor and the Kehillah leaders could not be transferred to a lame-duck, acting mayor. Magnes' prodding gained no serious hearing for the Kehillah's plan. Nevertheless consultations over the recommendations continued. Magnes and Newburger canvassed the police commissioner, the district attorney, Chief Magistrate William McAdoo, and the Committee of Fourteen for their views and endorsements. And the committee prepared to press its views on the new administration.[49]

For Magnes, beneficial as police reform might ultimately be, it in no way replaced the need for continued and direct action by the Jewish community. Accordingly, in November, 1913, when the Kehillah chairman sent the first yearly report of crime work to the contributors (at the same time he pressed the committee's program for police reform), he advocated an expansion of the vice bureau. Magnes pleaded for more financial aid and new subscribers. William Salomon, the Educational Alliance's largest contributor, replied that he doubted whether existing contributors would renew their subscriptions, let alone mobilize additional resources. Further support meant, Salomon said, that the contributors would "constitute themselves a permanent organization for the cleansing of the First Inspection District, [an] auxiliary to the Police Department who ordinarily should perform the work." [50]

Though Salomon and others reduced their pledges of financial aid (contributions fell by 32 percent the second year), the Kehillah's vice bureau remained intact and viable.[51] Action as Jews in a purely secular matter disturbed men of Judge Greenbaum's and Salomon's views. But the situation which had induced the Educational Alliance leaders to join the Kehillah undertaking still existed. Moreover, the city's chief executive had welcomed the Jewish community's help and elevated a Kehillah functionary to a high police post. When, however, a new administration "which knew not Joseph" took office in January, 1914, the novel arrangements developed under Gaynor dissolved. As the leaders of the Educational Alliance became aware of this, one inhibiting factor to their withdrawal from the vice work fell. Yet, for three more years Magnes kept the Bureau alive.

Mayor Mitchel never declared his intention to discontinue Gaynor's arrangements with the Kehillah. Rather, he achieved that end by procrastination and indifference.[52]

During Mitchel's second week in office he received a delegation composed of Judge Greenbaum, Adolph Lewisohn, Marshall, Schiff, Samuel Strauss, Sulzberger, and Magnes. In addition to its comprehensive plan for police reform, the delegation submitted to the mayor a second set of recommendations hastily prepared by Newburger. This second plan advocated the establishment of a "Bureau of Public Assistance" to be headed by a Fifth Deputy Police Commissioner. The projected Bureau was to have jurisdiction over all complaints relative to vice and gambling. Also, the public and "accredited bodies or societies organized for the purpose of suppressing vice or cooperating with the Police Department" were to be invited to cooperate with the Bureau.[53]

The proposal to replace personal understandings and informal procedures with a legally recognized framework revealed, most probably, an uneasiness as to Mitchel's intentions. In the final days of the outgoing administration, Schiff had publicly and forcefully called for the reappointment of Police Commissioner Waldo. But Mitchel neither retained Waldo nor Third Deputy Commissioner Newburger. Unable to assure continuity through the reappointment of key personnel, the committee sought instead to preserve the Kehillah's position by means of structural innovations. Possibly the Kehillah leaders hoped that Newburger would be appointed to the proposed new commissionership. But in any event, the suggested Bureau would serve as the official vehicle for continued Kehillah–Police Department collaboration.[54]

The plan was dropped when the Kehillah's delegation received assurances from the mayor of his intention to continue Gaynor's policies. In a public statement Mitchel commended the Kehillah for the "excellent help" rendered the police. "When the proffer came to assist this administration similarly, I was glad to accept it," he wrote.[55]

Magnes accepted the mayor's statement on its face value as an invitation to pursue the tactics which had proven so successful under Gaynor. A year and a half of probing East Side crime and Newburger's eleven months at police headquarters had armed both men with an expertise which few, if any, in the new administration possessed. The criticism among the Kehillah sponsors only raised Magnes' ardor for renewed activity. Self-confident and impatient, convinced of the importance of his mission and the efficacy of his organization, Magnes confronted an administration still in the process of formation. It also had good reason to be wary of vice issues. The encounter, if only for reasons of temperament, was bound to be a rankling one.[56]

Almost from the outset an attitude of nonchalance marked Mitchel's relations with the Kehillah. A member of his staff, usually Arthur Woods, soon to become police commissioner, handled all communications with the Kehillah. A monthly roster of vice resorts and criminals submitted by Newburger to the mayor for his personal attention (a practice which exemplified the Kehillah's preferential status under Gaynor) received only perfunctory notice or none at all. Complaints addressed to him of Police Department inaction brought no redress. Twice during Mitchel's first year in office, Magnes attempted to arrange appointments between Newburger and the mayor to discuss the lack of rapport which had developed. On neither occasion did Mitchel find time for Newburger. Nor is there a record of Magnes meeting the mayor at any time following the conference the second week of his term.[57] Yet though Mitchel was primarily responsible for the deterioration of relations, his police commissioner contributed to the changed climate.

Mitchel appointed Woods to the post in April, 1914. The new commissioner brought rare attributes to the position. After having been graduated from Harvard and teaching at Groton, Woods came to New York attracted by the reform movement. Police work, and especially its broader, sociological setting, led to an association with the research-oriented Committee of Fourteen. The committee sponsored a study trip to Europe which enabled him to observe police systems on the continent. After his return, as a deputy police commissioner under Bingham, Woods revamped the detective force and made his mark as a diplomat as well. During the Bingham affair in September, 1908, Woods mediated between Bingham and Louis Marshall. The new police commissioner, the *Times* wrote, intends to emphasize preventative work and invite the aid of philanthropic societies. In a word, the department was to become an instrument of uplift.[58]

It is remarkable, therefore, that no improvement in Kehillah relations followed. Magnes recommended, to mention one of his concerns, a more stringent supervision of suspected gambling places. He suggested a harsher policy on licensing pool parlors. Under the prior administration a similar strategy had proven effective in ridding the East Side of stuss houses and *weisbierstubes*. With Gaynor's approval, a steady stream of reports on these resorts and their clientele had forced the police to conduct frequent raids. Officers were stationed at suspected addresses. Few resorts had survived the harassment. But the new commissioner apparently resented the close scrutiny of self-appointed and ever-present critics. On June 16, 1914, for example, Newburger wrote to Woods, with a copy sent to Mitchel, enclosing lists of addresses. One group consisted of complaints forwarded to the Police Department from May 1 to June 1 for which no report of police action had been received. A second group included complaints for which reports of police action had been received, but further action was deemed advisable by the Kehillah's bureau. Newburger sent such letters monthly, a course of conduct which was perfectly acceptable in the Gaynor days.[59]

Increasing tension finally led to a Newburger–Woods confrontation in early July, 1914. The Kehillah, Woods complained, failed to provide hard, court evidence. Newburger replied that such a course meant exposing Kehillah agents to public view, which would necessitate their frequent replacement. For similar reasons he declined the commissioner's request that police officers be allowed to operate alongside the Kehillah's agents. Woods then stated that Kehillah complaints had caused "some irritation" in his office. Henceforth, other duties would prevent him from personally handling the Kehillah's complaints. An assistant with more time for Newburger, Woods felt, would expedite the action the Kehillah desired. In Newburger's words, the commissioner assigned a "nice young man who knows nothing" to serve as liaison officer. A month later Magnes wrote to Woods that the new arrangement had failed. By the end of the year, relations had reached their nadir.[60]

In a letter to Woods written in December, 1914, Magnes presented the Kehillah's grievances. Drafted with great care (the final version included changes by Marshall), the letter has the ring of both a final accounting and an ultimatum. The Kehillah chairman appended a 17-page list of selected names and addresses which had been submitted to Woods during the previous seven months. The list included "only those disreputable and disorderly places in the First Inspection District where we have claimed that thieves, cadets (procurers), gangmen, drug dealers and fiends, and prostitutes hang out, and which we thought should be closed on that account." It also included the names of the criminals, their "descriptions, records and activities . . . and the places where . . . they have been hanging out [which] we have given you during the six months mentioned."

Only a small percentage of the resorts had been suppressed, Magnes wrote, and few of the persons complained of were apprehended.

Our efforts to cooperate with the Department have seemingly been futile. . . . We are in no way desirous of embarrassing the Department. . . . We feel, however, that our duty to our fellow-citizens compels us to insist that the conditions of which we have complained be dealt with more energetically and efficiently than hitherto.[61]

In the months that followed, Magnes labored under increasing difficulties to reestablish some satisfactory relationship. To obtain the renewal of the annual contributions, he had to convince his sponsors that the police commissioner desired and needed continued Kehillah assistance. Equally difficult, he had to dispel the deepening conviction among the contributors that little lasting good had come of the two and a half years of effort. In early January, 1915, Magnes made efforts to call together the contributors to the vice fund but with no success. Indeed Judge Greenbaum, the nominal co-chairman of the Committee of Nine, ignored Magnes' request to summon such a meeting.[62]

In his negotiations with Woods, Magnes represented, in fact, an organization in disarray. The change of administration and the sense of frustration also left its mark on his able lieutenant. Newburger, in mid-January, asked to be released, pointing to Woods's hostility toward him.[63]

Yet by the end of April, 1915, Magnes reached an understanding with Woods and could report to the vice fund contributors that he had delayed writing "because for a time we had a little difficulty in arranging satisfactory methods of cooperation with the Police Department." Then came the balance sheet. As to gambling, regular houses of prostitution, and gangsters, the situation was better than at any time since the work had begun. But in regard to thieves and tenement-house prostitution, conditions had worsened. The Kehillah's rolls contained the names of 600 Jewish thieves operating on the lower East Side. Moreover, never "even in the palmiest days of the red light district" had prostitutes "so thoroughly infested" the tenement houses of the Jewish quarter. "The Police Commissioner," Magnes concluded, "is exceedingly anxious for our cooperation." [64]

Here was the formula that twice before had raised large sums. But this third appeal brought meager returns indeed. Another year of activity implied a permanent organization. The reluctant supporters rebelled. Salomon reduced his contribution to $250 with the clear proviso that the work be terminated as quickly as possible. In 1913 he had contributed $2,500. Lewisohn postponed payment of his annual $5,000 to an undetermined date. Schiff cut his contribution from $5,000 to $1,000. Total income (exact figures are unavailable) fell by approximately two-thirds from the previous year's total of $15,400. In October, 1915, Magnes, stung by a report of Judge Greenbaum's criticism of the vice activities, wrote to him demanding an immediate decision on the future of the vice bureau. It was the first communication between the two men in nine months.[65]

In his reply Judge Greenbaum reiterated positions that he and Salomon had espoused from the outset. The Educational Alliance had enlisted to rid the East Side of vice through cooperation with public authorities, to secure the effective execution of the law, and to gather data for the study of the causes of vice and crime. Instead, the judge told Magnes bluntly, the Bureau had done police work.[66]

The appraisal contains much truth. Magnes' posture in his dispute with Woods, as evidenced in his letter of December, 1914, approaches that of the vigilante.

The information conveyed to us has been gathered by responsible agents and has been specific. We have endeavored to provide this great city gratuitously with a secret service. . . . We have gathered at large expense and considerable risk the many details which you have been furnished, so that the Department might be facilitated in terminating the unpardonable conditions particularized. Our object has been to check crime, and to disperse professional criminals by informing the Police Department of facts, which it has ignored.[67]

In the turbulent months following the Rosenthal murder, a hard-pressed mayor had coopted the Kehillah's leaders to battle vice and with excellent results. Greenbaum reluctantly joined the dramatic pursuit. But when the storm center passed with Gaynor's death, and a rousing Fusion victory cooled the public's sense of outrage, the extraordinary times of Kehillah police work were over. Magnes quite correctly held that only continued anti-crime activity would guaran-

tee whatever gains had been made. But the new administration, bearing the stamp of reform and respectability, stood to gain nothing
from a vigilance committee fishing in the politically dangerous waters
of commercial crime. Accordingly, Magnes found himself caught between his rebellious supporters opposed to a permanent organization
and a city government desirous of disassociating itself from the notoriety of the Gaynor days. Gaynor's volunteers in the fight against
crime became, under Mitchel, vigilantes isolated from their supporters, dislocated in a body politic returned to normal, and an irritant to
a police commissioner of Woods's stature.

The political factor intruded as well in this final phase of the vice
bureau. Much as Kehillah leaders wished to avoid political entangle-
ment, Jewish criminality, viewed as a problem of law enforcement,
led to such involvement. Police maladministration and corruption
continued to be the most potent municipal campaign text of the
times. Consequently, a civic organization immersed in police matters
found political neutrality difficult to maintain. Moreover, eminent
members of the Kehillah participated in the political life of the city;
this in turn influenced their attitude in shaping the Kehillah's policy
on crime. The 1909 mayoralty campaign, and particularly Gaynor's alliance with the Kehillah in 1912 showed, as we have seen, the correla-
tion between the problem of Jewish criminality and politics. The re-
nomination of Gaynor, which dominated the New York political
scene from July until his death in early September, 1913, drew the
Kehillah's leaders into the vortex of the storm.[68]

The mayor's alienation from Tammany had precluded a regular
party nomination. A Fusion endorsement, therefore, became crucial,
and Jacob Schiff emerged as the mayor's chief advocate. He presented
Gaynor's case to a hostile Fusion nominations committee, fought
hard, and lost. Measured in customary political terms, Schiff's continued sponsorship of Gaynor's candidacy seemed foolhardy. He had opposed Gaynor in 1909. The mayor in 1913 claimed no organized following. And finally, Schiff, a financial pillar of the reform movement,
stood to forfeit his influence in choosing the Fusion nominee from

among the three prominent candidates. Here Schiff had a clear stake. Given District Attorney Whitman, ex-President of the Board of Aldermen Mitchel, and Borough President George McAneny, Schiff clearly favored McAneny.[69]

Ten years older than the young and temperamental Mitchel, McAneny had made an excellent record as borough president and served with distinction as president of the City Club. But most important, on the central economic question of the Gaynor administration, the long-debated subway construction issue, McAneny had staunchly opposed municipal ownership. He had negotiated the dual subway contracts which Schiff, the financier, desired. Mitchel's dissenting views had won him the adulation of the Hearst press and the taint of radicalism.[70] Schiff's distaste for Whitman, considered the strongest contender of the three, called for the financier's return to the Fusion council table once Gaynor had been rejected. Yet he remained with his candidate, broke with Fusion, and joined in the task of organizing an independent campaign for Gaynor. "Go right ahead with the campaign and do not give a thought to finances," Schiff instructed Gaynor's manager. "All of the money that will be needed will be forthcoming." [71]

This loyalty to Gaynor becomes explicable when the maze of emotions and reactions produced by the problem of Jewish criminality is placed in the balance. Gaynor's contempt for the sensation seekers (at whose hands Schiff's family had suffered personal indignities) must have won Schiff's admiration. His discreetness and temperance in dealing with the vice scandals placed Schiff and other leaders of a sensitive group in his debt. Even following the mayor's death, Schiff did not immediately move to Mitchel's support despite his Fusion endorsement. Instead, he rallied the Gaynor campaign organization behind McAneny. Only when the latter refused the nomination and Mitchel publicly apologized for his attacks on Gaynor did he receive Schiff's endorsement.[72]

The fleeting independent campaign in support of Gaynor also provided an opportunity for the mayor's East Side partisans to declare themselves. In early August, a Gaynor League for Foreign-Born Citizens made its appearance. "Jews First to Come Out for Gaynor," a *Warheit* headline read. The chairman was Joseph Barondess, a founder of the Kehillah and one of its central figures. A letter to Barondess indicates that Magnes himself had a hand in the discussions which led to the League's formation. Had Gaynor lived, Kehillah leaders might well have played a significant role in the mayoralty campaign.[73]

Not all Jewish leaders supported the mayor. Dr. Henry Moskowitz served as close adviser to Mitchel. Rabbi Stephen Wise and Jacob Saphirstein, publisher of the *Morgen Journal*, supported Whitman's candidacy for the Fusion nomination.[74] These persons had criticized the Kehillah's vice work. The mayor's cooperation with the Kehillah was the bond between him and Schiff, Magnes, and their followers.

The new mayor knew that he had been Schiff's third choice. This may in part explain his apathy to Magnes' year-long endeavors to reestablish the rapport that had once existed with the Police Department. However, men like Schiff and Lewisohn, eminent figures in the civic and business life of the city, would naturally strive for cordial relations with the city's chief executive. Fragmentary and circumstantial evidence suggests that they achieved this end in part by curbing the Kehillah's vice bureau.[75]

In June, 1915, the Kehillah's chief investigator reminded Magnes that at the outset of the Mitchel administration he had told the Kehillah chairman "[that] when Woods became Police Commissioner he will ignore Kehillah vice and crime work and silence it." Shoenfeld based his prediction on his "reliable sources." These sources also claimed that "the administration had prevailed upon the wealthy Jews to permanently discontinue all vice work because it embarrasses Woods." The information, if correct, would explain Schiff's and Lewisohn's dramatic reduction of their contributions in 1915. Both men, and especially Schiff, had supported Magnes fully, despite the criticism of the Educational Alliance group. Both men moved from a cool if not hostile attitude toward Mitchel to one of cooperation at a time when they withdrew their financial support from the vice bureau. In January, 1915, as Magnes labored to mend relations with his contributors, Police Commissioner Woods, in a seemingly independent move, invited all East Side organizations to a conference to discuss cooperation between the Department and interested societies. Such a conference may well have had as its purpose ending the hegemony of the Kehillah with the tacit agreement of its most powerful financial backers.[76]

Yet despite the frustrations which attended the changes under Mitchel's administration, Magnes remained committed to his program. The Committee of Nine had taken no firm resolution to disband the vice bureau. Only the Educational Alliance group had formally defected. Nor had Schiff and Lewisohn, the principal contributors, though sharply cutting their support, asked for a termination of the bureau's activities. Moreover, men like Marshall and Warburg, in renewing their contributions, certainly encouraged Magnes' espousal of a permanent Bureau of Social Morals. Finally, the apparent resolution of his quarrel with Commissioner Woods in the spring of 1915 hopefully paved the way for renewed cooperation with the Police Department. In his opening address to the Kehillah's Sixth Annual Convention in April, 1915, Magnes spoke about the "unfortunate" necessity for a Bureau of Social Morals.[77]

Thus the drastically reduced budget that resulted from the 1915 canvass for funds did not shake Magnes' determination. A year later, when the vice bureau's activities had shrunk even further, the Kehillah chairman requested Newburger to prepare a five-year "development plan." In Magnes' programmatic address several months later at the Kehillah's 1916 convention, he echoed the sweeping proposals made by Newburger.[78]

Early in 1917 Magnes undertook to reorganize the vice bureau. He proceeded along familiar lines setting a goal of $20,000 to finance the first year of work, launching the enterprise without waiting for the full sum, and projecting a supervisory committee from among the contributors. By May, Magnes had received $7,600 in contributions, Herbert Lehman, Schiff, and Warburg contributing two-thirds of that amount. Most of the donors had supported the earlier fund. Surprisingly, the subscribers included William Salomon who had so staunchly opposed a permanent vice bureau.[79]

Magnes' conception of a permanent bureau had not swayed the contributors; indications of a new crime wave had. The reports prepared during the period of the bureau's reactivization, from May to September, 1917, all describe the illicit traffic in drugs. Once again lists of names, descriptions, and addresses were submitted to the police commissioner. And those names, together with an undated report, prepared most likely at the start of the reorganization effort, all pointed to the fact that Jews were active in the traffic. During December, 1916, State Senator George H. Whitney's legislative committee held hearings in New York City on the problems of drug peddling and addiction. All through 1917 the public paid increasing attention to the problem particularly since it now involved servicemen. These conditions enabled Magnes to gain renewed support for the Kehillah's crime work.[80]

In June, 1917, Newburger was gravely injured in an automobile accident. Raising the funds and administering the bureau presented too great a burden for Magnes. He was now embroiled in a storm of controversy over his pacifist stand. These developments, furthermore, coincided with the precipitous decline of the Kehillah. However, above all else, the climate of 1917 precluded the success of a project dependent on the collaboration of a pacifist spokesman with city and federal law-enforcement agencies. Like other projects with which Magnes was associated, no one could or would replace him.

In 1916 when Newburger pleaded for an enlarged vice bureau, he linked the need with the overarching necessity that Jews "keep their house in order." The fact that "we are first American citizens," he wrote, "and then Jews" and that "the community as a whole is responsible for such things as crime is of course technically true. However, it is lovely fiction and we all know it." [81]

The exhortation to clean one's house, then, emanated from a deep-felt sense of belonging to a group at bay. Even those communal leaders who attributed delinquency to the upheaval of immigration and the stresses of urbanization, who blamed the evils of ward politics or the predatory nature of the American business ethic, responded in predictable fashion to the discovery of a crime problem in the Jewish quarter. They joined together "to burn the abomination out of our midst." They were heirs, after all, to a tradition which sought to reduce group vulnerability in a hostile environment by insisting on a well-ordered house.

CHAPTER NINE

The Jewish Labor Movement and the Kehillah

THE KEHILLAH'S PURSUIT OF "ORDER OUT OF CHAOS" COINCIDED with a central theme of the progressive era. Consequently, when ethnic interest led the Kehillah to concern itself with industrial relations—the most disruptive social and economic feature of New York in the 1910s—that activity dovetailed with the public interest. For the reformers, industrial strife represented a major obstacle in the quest for social harmony and efficiency; "scientific methods" of mediation, the first step to industrial democracy, pointed a way out of the impasse. Group-conscious Kehillah leaders also noted, with chagrin and anxiety, the ethnic make-up of the contending parties and were doubly moved to intervene.

Within the Jewish community some, nevertheless, questioned the propriety and others the validity of presenting the industrial question as one calling for Jewish communal involvement. "What has industry got to do with Jews," Magnes asked rhetorically before a meeting of Kehillah delegates. "Are their fingers Jewish when they make a coat?" In answering, the Kehillah's chairman brushed aside "theory." Facts and experience provided their own logic. "Because we are the Kehillah . . . we are in a position to come into touch with the Jewish worker and with the Jewish employer a little more expeditiously, with a little more understanding than a non-Jewish organization." And indeed, the lion's share of the 300,000 employees and the 15,000 employers in the dominant apparel trades were immigrant Russian Jews. Industrial strife, therefore, touched the livelihood of thousands of Jews and, as any disaster might have, called for communal action.[1]

An additional consideration prompted the Kehillah to undertake industrial arbitration (eventually formalized in the establishment of the Bureau of Industry). An opportunity now existed of establishing ties with the leadership of the Jewish labor movement. Mentors of the movement, those immigrant intellectuals who were imbued with socialist cosmopolitanism, had advanced an alternative to ethnic community. Working-class solidarity and the vision of a new society, socialist and nonethnic, preempted the place of a kehillah. Connections with the organized Jewish community were pointless, if not absurd. Yet in one luminous instance—the "Great Revolt" of the cloakmakers in 1910—class war had been suspended by a "protocol of peace." Jewish employers and employees had faced each other across the conference table, accepted the mediation of Jewish notables, and formulated a new and enlightened system of industrial relations. Surely a Jewish determinant had influenced the parties to the accord; the welfare of the group and sensitivity for its good name required industrial peace between Jewish bosses and their workers.[2] If the Kehillah took over this task, won recognition for the unions and stability for the industry, might it not go further and win the alienated Jewish labor movement back to the communal fold? In essence, would not the Kehillah be fulfilling, in the modern garb of labor mediator, the ancient role of public conciliator, recapturing thereby a measure of social control over its schismatics?

§

THE FOUNDING YEAR OF THE KEHILLAH, 1909, MARKED THE BEGINNING of a new era for those trade unions, mainly in the garment industry, populated and led by Jewish immigrant workers.[3] Massive and often brutal strikes in the course of the next five years transformed them into powerful and aggressive organizations. Not only did they win many of their demands, but they benefited, too, from the good will of patrician reform circles. The period, furthermore, gave full play to those qualities which to the devotee, transfigured weak, fragmented trade unions into an "*arbeiter bavegung*," a crusading labor movement, radical and messianic in temper.[4] The "uprising of the twenty thousand" is how contemporaries referred to the strike of the waistmakers in November, 1909. When the cloakmakers struck half a year later, the event was styled "the Great Revolt." "The seventy thousand cloakmakers were a nonentity, fair game in the eyes of the boss," Abraham Liessin, the Yiddish poet, wrote. "The seventy thousand weaklings have now become seventy thousand battlers, stubborn and resolute battlers." [5] The chairman of the general strike committee recalled how the workers poured out of their shops in response to the strike notice: "Many of our most devoted members cried for joy at the idea that their lifelong labors had at last been crowned with success. In my mind I could only picture to myself such a scene taking place when the Jews were led out of Egypt." [6]

Meanwhile, union orators, the socialist *Forward* and even the general press transformed picket-line and courtroom incident into proletarian legends. ("There was Esther Lobetkin," the story of one 1909 waistmaker heroine went. "Food or sleep did not seem to be part of her daily needs. All day long she kept strict watch of 'her' strikers and then would appear at headquarters . . . to attend the meetings till the wee hours of the morning. . . . She was arrested time and again, and every time she would shout from the patrol wagon: 'Do not lose courage. We'll win yet.' ") [7]

While astute union lawyers like Meyer London and Morris Hillquit bargained for the possible, radical journalists and orators addressed the laboring public in the strident voice of class struggle. The revolutionary rhetoric little influenced the former in their negotiations. It did, however, greatly add to the mistrust and enmity which separated the proponents of an all-embracing Jewish community from the militant exponents of the Jewish labor movement.[8] Thus Dr. Karl Fornberg, an editor of the highly respected socialist monthly, the *Zukunft*, reviewed the events of the year 1909: the "great strike of pantsmakers" opened the year; in the middle came the "great strike of the bakers"; the year closed with the "great strike of the waistmakers."

So much fighting courage, so much movement, so much class struggle, the Jewish public has not lived through in a long time. . . . Where such infectious class struggles are carried on, class feelings and class consciousness are planted deep in the soul [of the Jewish workers]. Eventually they must produce powerful and enduring structures.[9]

Fornberg also touched upon events among the "nonproletarian classes." "Philanthropists and politicians, *Yahudim*" (a pejorative for German-Jews), at last carried through "their old plan." They created a Kehillah and thereby claimed to speak for the great Jewish public. Editor Fornberg dismissed it as a "paper" organization which did some "chancellery work" and published resolutions.[10]

This view of the Jewish world assumed the existence of a self-conscious "Jewish labor community." [11] Trade-union activity, embracing most immigrant Jews after 1909 and directed almost exclusively against Jewish bosses, bore this out. But in addition to the economic phase, there were other manifestations of a self-contained, "proletarian" society.

The 1910s witnessed the great flowering of Yiddish literary activity. Most of the poets, novelists, and chroniclers wrote for this labor community, partly because few secular, nonradical periodicals existed. The *Forward* reached a circulation of about 150,000 in 1917, a threefold increase in ten years. Weeklies and monthlies, from the anarchist *Freie Arbeiter Shtimme* to the Socialist-Zionist *Yiddisher Kemfer*, accounted for most radical schools of thought. Impelled by their own version of the apocalypse, these journals were catholic in interest though sectarian in origin. Their intellectual breadth reflected the high standard of the Jewish radical press in Europe. None were purely house organs. Each offered belles-lettres and literary criticism in addition to political discourses and intramural polemics. The labor community thus attracted the intellectuals and provided them with a public. They, in return, encouraged a cultural autonomy which was Yiddish, secular, and proletarian.[12]

Politics, manifested in the rites of Socialist election campaigns, strengthened the labor movements' class and ethnic self-consciousness. Even though the Socialist Party formally spurned "racial" politics, the Yiddish milieu of the East Side precincts set the terms of the political encounter. Jewish union leaders and union lawyers ran for office on the Socialist ticket against the Jewish candidates of the "capitalist" parties, while local campaign news, laced with ethnic issues and ethnocentric distortions, dominated the front pages of the Yiddish press. In one East Side campaign, Meyer London, the Party's candidate for Congress, outran his Gentile running-mate, the gubernatorial candidate, by a two-to-one vote. The results proved, wrote Louis Boudin, an eminent Socialist writer, that local Party functionaries had appealed to the "racial and subracial prejudices of voters. . . . Russian-Jews were appealed to because Comrade London was a Russian-Jew." This "pestilential atmosphere," he added, had informed most Socialist campaigns in the Jewish quarter. And indeed, in 1914, London went to Congress from the lower East Side for the first of three terms, no less an ethnic hero than a Socialist one.[13]

Ward politics in the Jewish quarter, confining as it was, offered the militant radicals an outlet for their activism. "During the campaign weeks," one observer noted, "the East Side districts rocked with socialist agitation. The Socialist candidates were hailed as Messiahs. The open-air meetings were monster demonstrations of public confidence and affection." Opportunity for "direct action" also existed. Street corner rallies and poll-watching, like picketing, brought in their wake physical engagements with the "capitalist" police or the hired shtarke, the professional thugs. These East Side campaigns won wide attention and contributed to the élan of the labor movement.[14]

The Arbeiter Ring, a fast-growing fraternal order of workers, completed the interlocking institutional system. It appropriated the popular form of the mutual aid society and thereby offered the immigrant worker those social benefits which he sought. No need existed, therefore, to go beyond the labor community for these services. The Arbeiter Ring, however, did more than provide Jewish workers with sick benefits. It added an element of constancy to the volatile organizational conditions of the immigrant quarter.[15]

Because such societies as the Arbeiter Ring handled insurance, they came under state supervision. Imperfect as that supervision was, it did encourage financial and administrative responsibility. Managing an insurance department and operating a sanitarium and cemeteries required a bureaucratic apparatus, centralization, and a degree of efficiency. Moreover, since members paid relatively high assessments for these benefits, they had a serious economic stake in their fraternal order. Compared with other types of immigrant organizations the fraternal order probably enjoyed a high degree of membership participation and stability.[16] Where, as in the case of the Arbeiter Ring, the fraternal order considered itself part of a social movement, it could place a disciplined organization at the disposal of the cause.

Thus the Arbeiter Ring's membership assessments included a tax for the support of the revolutionary parties in Russia. In 1906, when William Randolph Hearst's gubernatorial campaign met with a warm response among Jewish radicals, the Arbeiter Ring convention warned its New York branches: members openly supporting "capitalist" candidates are to be denied all offices in the Order. On another occasion, in preparing for the 1910 cloakmakers' strike, 180 Arbeiter Ring delegates met in March, 1909, to discuss trade-union strategy and finances. But not surprisingly, only a single delegate representing one Arbeiter Ring branch attended the Kehillah's convention which took place the same month.[17]

Summarizing the Order's activities on the eve of its 1913 convention, the *Freint*, journal of the Arbeiter Ring, stated: "Lectures, discussions, labor lyceums, Sunday Schools and libraries, on the one hand; loan funds, aid and succor for needy and depressed members and a supporting arm for all strikes and [Socialist] Party calls on the other—this is the essence of the report to the convention." [18] At the close of 1908, 102 branches with a membership of 10,233 existed in the city. Ten years later the number of branches had risen to 250 with 25,000 members.[19]

Though the many groups and institutions of the labor movement shared common interests and passions, they possessed no central authority. The *Forward* filled this role, informally but with considerable success. As the workers' primary medium of information and communication—exerting a powerful cultural influence upon its readers—it imposed a measure of coherence and moderation upon the flow of debate within the labor community. It possessed, furthermore, material and manpower resources of consequence. Its management, treasury, and fund-raising capacity served all institutions of the labor movement. Adolph Held, Benjamin Schlesinger, Max Pine, and Benjamin Feigenbaum are central figures in the Forward Association who also filled positions in the trade unions, Socialist Party, and Arbeiter Ring.

Editor Abraham Cahan's influence seemed all pervasive.[20] At strike time, daily appeals from the *Forward*'s pages and the theater benefits it sponsored provided much of the funds. Of $246,403 collected during the 1910 cloakmakers' strike, the *Forward*'s share was $62,018. The *Forward* building itself (completed in 1912), ten stories high and overlooking the heart of the Jewish quarter, served as nerve-center of the Jewish working class. The United Hebrew Trades, the Jewish Socialist Federation, and the Arbeiter Ring had their offices in the building. Election Day, thousands of the Party faithful gathered in front of the building—the crowd often overflowed into Seward Park—to watch the returns which were projected on a huge screen. Here, too, the great strike victories were celebrated.[21]

Two tendencies coexisted uneasily within the Jewish labor community. One anticipated complete assimilation into American society. To the supporters of this view, socialist scripture rejected the "chauvinism of nationality" in favor of the "brotherhood of workers." The other position, with a variety of nuances, tempered the prospect of such integration with an element of ethnic continuity. Both drew upon socialist ideologies which emerged in Russia during the 1890s and which found their fullest expression in the Bund (the General League of Jewish Workers). By 1910, most Jewish socialists had been in America for no more than a decade and a half. They had witnessed the genesis of the Jewish revolutionary movement and followed the debates within the Bund and between the Bund and the Russian Social Democrats over the legitimacy of a Jewish national and cultural program. To a great extent the controversy turned on the status of the Yiddish language. Was it a transitory phenomenon, a convenient means of communicating with the Jewish worker until the new society brought acceptance and then assimilation? Or did Yiddish represent the folk-genius of the ascendent Jewish proletariat and proof of nationality? (Both sides rejected Hebrew culture as an anachronism, the province of clerics or reactionary Zionists.) With the outburst of pogroms after 1903 the controversy gained a new urgency.[22]

The arrival of new waves of refugees following the 1905 Russian revolution brought important reinforcements. Numbers, the presence of revered leaders, the perils and hardships of the mother movement, and a socialist martyrology suffused the debate with emotion and prevented a clear analysis of the American condition. Like so much else about the Jewish quarter in 1910, both tendencies drew strength from the flood tide of immigration.[23]

For the "cosmopolitans," those who ignored or were antagonistic to Jewish enthnicism, the garment strikes of the 1910s confirmed their belief that through the unions the Jews were taking their place in the mainstream of progressive America. Contemporaries, after all, hailed the "protocol of peace" as the beginning of the new era of industrial relations. They spoke, too, of the new genre of union leader, the "industrial statesman." Students of the problem, meanwhile, praised the mediation machinery and the trade agreements as preludes to "industrial democracy." The unions were making their mark on the American body politic.[24]

What must have further impressed the union leaders was the outpouring of good will. The sight of young women facing hired toughs, suffering further at the hands of allegedly brutal policemen, and finding neither justice nor compassion from Tammany magistrates won wide sympathy. In the 1909 waistmakers' strike, Mary Dreier and her comrades in the Women's Trade Union League addressed strike meetings, led protest marches, and some were arrested on the picket line. Columbia Law School's dean, George W. Kirchway, joined other respected lawyers to defend the arrested strikers. J. Pierpont Morgan's daughter helped arrange a money-raising affair at the Colony Club. During the general strike of wrapper and kimono workers in 1913, Theodore Roosevelt visited the strike halls. "This is crushing the future motherhood of the country," the *Times* quoted him.[25]

The exigencies of trade-union work provided no opportunity for a confrontation between the ethnic survivalists and the cosmopolitans. Within the Socialist Party, however, substantive policy questions forced a debate. On a national level, the issues of unrestricted immigration and recognition of autonomous ethnic federations divided the Jewish socialists. Building a great movement demanded a public posture that would appeal to the native worker. Those who saw that goal as central could not sanction free immigration or the legitimization of foreign enclaves within the organization. In the 1908 and 1910 socialist conventions these issues were debated. Morris Hillquit, by then a leader of American socialism, opposed Jews whose socialism included a large measure of Jewish group interests and sentiments.[26] Campaigning for Congress from the Jewish East Side in 1908, Hillquit told his audience:

The interests of the workingmen of the Ninth Congressional District are . . . identical with those of the workingmen of the rest of the country, and if elected to Congress, I will not consider myself the special representative of the alleged special interests of this district, but the representative of the Socialist Party and the interests of the working class of the country.[27]

Hillquit and Abe Cahan's *Forward* fought the efforts to create a Jewish section of the Socialist Party. In New York they defeated attempts by the ethnically oriented to gain a measure of autonomy. And even after a Jewish Socialist Federation was organized in 1912, the *Forward* treated it with contempt.[28]

However, besides socialist dogma and political pragmatism, another factor motivated the cosmopolitans. In czarist Russia, socialism promised human dignity. For the Jew it meant, above all, the end of segregation. In America, the law of the land—if not always the practice of the land—guaranteed those rights. Thus one could interpret any expression of Jewish sectarianism as "ghettoization," a rejection of America's revolutionary opportunity.

Even the organization in 1907 of a Jewish Agitation Bureau for the purpose of conducting propaganda activities in Yiddish was suspect. Samuel Peskin, editor of the *Forward*'s weekly, the *Tzeitgeist*, argued that a bureau disseminating propaganda in Yiddish ran counter to the country's social development. "The psychology" of all nationality groups, Peskin wrote, led to amalgamation in the "cosmopolitan American nation." Moreover, Jewish comrades had a vital task to perform within the Socialist Party which clashed with ethnic activity. The Party's stand on Negroes, the Japanese, and immigration revealed a "heavy ballast of bigotry and narrow-mindedness." Jewish Socialists had to devote themselves to fighting bigotry within the Party.[29]

Michael Zametkin, one of the most respected intellectuals of the movement and a leading socialist since the early 1880s, cut through the sophistry of the mission argument. His rhetoric stemmed from the humiliation of his Russian past and the new opportunities of America. "Self-isolation," he wrote, "in any form is a sickness which can and must be cured. Only the carriers of an epidemic should be quarantined. Lepers are put in isolation." [30]

Significantly, the Arbeiter Ring responded most positively to the influence of the Yiddish culturalists. The Order had its great debate, too. (An interlinking leadership, in fact, meant that so pervasive a question would penetrate all the institutions of the labor community.) But unlike the trade unions or the Socialist Party, the Arbeiter Ring had no expectation of serving anyone outside the Jewish quarter. Nevertheless, until 1917 opposing views struggled for ascendency. The practical issues were two: whether or not to vastly increase the cultural activities of the Order by establishing a publishing house and launching an extensive adult education program, and the establishment of Arbeiter Ring supplementary schools which would emphasize socialist thought and Yiddish culture. Both issues were finally resolved in favor of Yiddish cultural activity. [31]

The debate between the cosmopolitans and the Yiddishists over the desirability and possibility of Jewish survival in America engrossed intellectuals and party functionaries to a far greater degree than it affected the broad immigrant mass. Some recent observers claim that a considerable part of the rank and file voted for socialist candidates, belonged to socialist-led unions, read the *Forward,* and yet remained loyal to the folk traditions. [32] Evidence exists to support this view. On the High Holy Days, the congregations in the immigrant neighborhoods could not accommodate all who wished to attend services. Provisionary arrangements became necessary for the large numbers who, on these days of penitence, streamed back to the synagogue. In 1917, a Kehillah study found 343 such "temporary synagogues" with a seating capacity of 163,638. The Arbeiter Ring offers another instance which suggests that a gap existed between the socialist purist and the sentiment of the mass. In 1909, at a time when the Order's leadership was largely cosmopolitan in outlook, 53 New York branches were installed, of which 25 were *landsmanshaftn.* [33] For these groups at least, old-town friendships, as a principle of organization, proved as important as class solidarity.

From the viewpoint of the Kehillah, however, the leaders of the labor movement prevented tapping this grass-roots sentiment for Jewish public endeavor. Despite differences among themselves, they agreed that the labor community had nothing in common with the Jewish community. A *Forward* reporter at the time of the founding convention of the Kehillah explained the organization's constitution as an antidemocratic device. Lest readers conclude that revising it would remove the barrier to participation, editor Cahan appended this note to the report:

No more ground exists today for bridging the deep distinctions of class interest, class consciousness and origin than [existed] for the thousands of years until now. On the contrary, the differences today are even greater because of the progress of free thought and especially [because of] the class struggle and political antagonism.[34]

Yiddish cultural-nationalists among the radicals held out no more hope than Cahan. Ben Zion Hoffman, one of their most important publicists, joyfully greeted the trend within the Arbeiter Ring towards stronger ethnic interest. No longer would the organization "stand aside and gaze upon all that was happening in the Jewish quarter with . . . cosmopolitan indifference." It had to take its stand on questions relevant to Jewish life. As an example of such interest, Hoffman offered the case of the Kehillah. The Arbeiter Ring did not ignore the question of affiliation as irrelevant. It considered the matter and only then refused to join. "And in this case, the issue was properly handled. Not in a Kehillah such as this . . . can the Arbeiter Ring take part." Conceivably, Hoffman continued, the Order one day would join a Kehillah. But only if it were based on other principles and prove itself truly democratic.[35]

Labor conciliation offered one possibility of bypassing ideological rifts and establishing a viable, if limited, relationship with the leadership of the Jewish labor movement. Such a prospect emerged in the course of the 1909 and 1910 strikes when a confluence of interests swept industrial mediation to a place of central civic importance. Widespread sympathy for the strikers and their unprecedented militancy compelled management to enter into industry-wide collective bargaining. Meanwhile, reformers—exponents of labor arbitration— urged their good offices upon both sides.

The efforts of Marcus M. Marks, president of the National Association of Clothiers, and John Mitchel, former president of the United Mine Workers, reflect this development. In the 1909 waistmakers' strike both men intervened on behalf of the National Civic Federation. Mitchel headed its Trade Agreements Department and Marks, also a founder of the East Side's Educational Alliance, served as one of the Federation's star conciliators. From its inception in 1900, the Federation popularized the need for enlightened industrial relations. Oscar Strauss, together with Mark Hanna and Samuel Gompers, were instrumental in establishing the organization, and banker Isaac N. Seligman served for some time as national treasurer. The New York branch included ex-mayor Seth Low, Felix Adler, leader of the Ethical Culture Society, and publisher Hamilton Holt. Louis D. Brandeis and A. Lincoln Filene, the merchant reformer, belonged to the Boston branch (both had collaborated in introducing employee-participation programs in the management of the Filene family's department store). Settlement-house work provided additional recruits for the mediation cause. Henry Moskowitz, Lillian Wald, Paul Abelson, and Walter E. Weyl are the oustanding names.[36]

From these ranks of downtown social workers and uptown patricians came the peacemakers. At the height of the cloakmakers' strike, during the summer of 1910, Moskowitz, Filene, and Meyer Bloomfield—a Boston social worker—prepared the way for Louis Brandeis' intervention. Several weeks later, at another critical juncture in the dispute, Moskowitz and Filene prevailed upon Jacob Schiff and Louis Marshall to intercede. While Marshall replaced Brandeis in conducting the negotiations, Schiff coerced recalcitrant members of the manufacturers' association into resuming talks. Under the "protocol of peace," management and labor created standing committees to investigate and settle shop grievances and forestall major conflicts. Besides their own representatives and a paid investigating staff, both sides named mutually acceptable "public representatives" to the committees. Brandeis became chairman of the board of Arbitration while

Holt and Weyl served on it for various lengths of time. The Joint Board of Sanitary Control—a landmark innovation in the industry—included William Jay Schieffelin, president of the Citizens Union, Moskowitz, and Wald.[37]

Certainly the ethnic factor also affected the shape of events in the New York garment industry. Peacemakers and adversaries were largely of Jewish origin. To what extent, however, and in what way was this component responsible for "protocolism"? Some observers have explained the ready acceptance of collective bargaining and the principle of continuous mediation as inspired by Jewish communal experience. They have also ascribed to this tradition the innovations in arbitration procedures which quickly spread throughout the industry. "These immigrants came from parts of Europe where arbitration was an accepted method of settling disputes," Julius Henry Cohen, chief counsel for the manufacturers, wrote. "The early successful development of arbitration boards in the needle trades can be traced directly to this experience. Moreover, every Orthodox Jew had a thorough training in Jewish law—the Torah. His rabbi was for him always the final arbitrator." [38]

The tradition of arbitration certainly occupied a respected place in the European Jewish community. Through the centuries community leaders bargained hard with their hosts for the right to maintain their own courts (one of whose primary functions was arbitration). A main theme of Jewish communal history is the repeated religious injunctions and political manipulations resorted to in order to prevent Jews from taking their differences to "the courts of the gentiles." [39]

In an attenuated way, the Jewish tradition of mediation endured in America. Some of the fraternal orders and landsmanshaft groups provided means for adjudicating disputes between members. Moreover, formally, Orthodox rabbis continued to function as judges and mediators. In practice, however, they served a dwindling public, their judicial activities increasingly limited to questions of ritual.[40]

The Kehillah did attempt to revitalize the custom of voluntary mediation. It created a "committee on conciliation" composed of distinguished Orthodox rabbis and lay leaders. In the fall of 1909, the committee prevented a threatened strike of poultry shochtim (ritual slaughterers). During the following years claims against a benevolent order, factional struggles for control of a burial society, periodic revolts and splits within the Roumanian Federation, complaints by Sabbath-observing cloakmakers against their union, occupied the attention of the committee.[41] In 1914, the Kehillah reorganized its mediation machinery with a view toward establishing a network of arbitration courts staffed by volunteer lawyers, rabbis, and lay leaders. Through its initiative the legislature amended municipal court procedures and defined more clearly the legal status of voluntary arbitration. For a brief time only and on a local level was the plan implemented.[42]

The efforts to establish a communal arbitration service brought, then, meager results. These, moreover, were limited almost exclusively to religious institutions or the religiously observant. In the light of this experience, it is unlikely that men of Brandeis' and Julius Cohen's secular and liberal background drew upon traditions rooted in Jewish religious law and communal self-segregation. Nor is it likely that the manufacturers and the rabidly antireligious union leaders, many of whom remembered the Jewish town in Europe with repugnance, came to the conference table favorably conditioned by that experience.

The ethnic factor that influenced all three parties was social and psychological rather than institutional and religious. For men of Schiff's outlook, the labor problem of New York's immigrant Jews belonged to the colossal undertaking of settling the newcomers. Spiritual adjustment formed only a part of the process. The evident need was for economic rehabilitation. Schiff, for example, hailed the work of the Hebrew Free Loan Society. Interest-free loans enabled recipients "to become or remain self-supporting instead of becoming subjects for charitable relief." In a like manner, Schiff and Cyrus Sulzberger supported the Industrial Removal Office. Dispersing immigrants westward reduced overcrowding which many blamed for the conditions in the garment industry. Getting strikers back to work and arriving at a more rational organization of the industry through collective bargaining belonged to this larger conception of "constructive" charity.[43]

On their part, union leaders stood to gain from the intervention of the Jewish notables. They faced the problem of bringing the manufacturers to the conference table (which meant de facto recognition of the unions). For this purpose no one was better suited than the pillars of the Jewish community. This lesson labor learned during the cloakmakers' strike when Marshall's and Schiff's prestige proved decisive in reaching a settlement. When the general strike in the men's clothing industry erupted in January, 1913, the United Garment Workers Union presented a list of acceptable mediators. It included, besides Charles P. Neill, Federal Mediation Commissioner, Louis Brandeis, Oscar Straus, and Jacob Schiff.[44] But perhaps the most dramatic instance of labor profiting from the sympathy and anxiety of the Jewish worthies came two years later when the five-year-old "protocol of peace" in the cloak and suit trade appeared to be on the verge of dissolution. In a public letter to the manufacturers' association in early July, 1915, Schiff, Marshall, Magnes, Straus, and Sulzberger demanded that the manufacturers submit to arbitration. Six weeks of maneuvering directed by Magnes and Dr. Paul Abelson, the director of the Kehillah's Bureau of Industry, led to the statement. In the face of such an array of signatories, the association yielded.[45]

The vulnerability to pressure by at least some of the clothing manufacturers turned upon the role they sought to play in the Jewish community. Wealth, they acknowledged, brought prestige in equal measure with the burdens of communal responsibility. In this respect the values of the Russian-Jewish town resembled America's doctrine of stewardship. And for the immigrant nouveaux riches, the Schiff group served as a model of both traditions. Schiff, himself, was their inspiration. The lustrous moment for the Russian-Jewish philanthropists came when the head of Kuhn and Loeb visited their institutions. A contribution usually followed, but no less important was the prestige and approbation which his presence brought. Schiff's practice of making the amount of his contribution to a Russian-Jewish charity contingent on the sum pledged by his downtown counterparts offers further insight into his role as arbiter of the community. Other patricians, on a more modest plane, filled a similar function. The Kehillah facilitated this process by providing the opportunity for contact between the two elements through common undertakings.[46]

In this way, immigrant philanthropists crystallized into an informal group emulating the Jewish aristocracy of uptown and amenable to its influence. In 1911 when Schiff made his second large contribution to the Kehillah's Education Bureau contingent on downtown raising its share, the burden fell on William Fischman, the treasurer of the Kehillah. He turned to his colleagues of the Cloak and Skirt Manufacturers Association for support. Years later Julius Cohen, the Association's counsel, recalled Fischman's behavior during the great strikes. He was one of those manufacturers who "carried out a policy of appeasement." Together with Joseph H. Cohen, also close to the Kehillah, and Reuben Sadowsky, "their charitable impulses led them to bring pressure to bear almost always for peace." Communal leadership necessitated a policy of compromise just as surely as community building called for peace in the needle trades.[47]

The general strike of the fur industry during the summer of 1912 marked Magnes' first intervention in a major labor dispute, and it led to the Kehillah accepting responsibility for administering the arbitration agreement which he helped formulate. Kehillah coworkers, like Marshall and Fischman, had participated in earlier settlements, but they had done so as private persons. In the fur industry case, Magnes stressed the Kehillah's sponsorship of his intervention. Industrial relations involving thousands of Jews, he explained, was a legitimate concern of the organized Jewish community. In offering his good offices as chairman of the Kehillah, he was, therefore, bringing to bear the moral leverage of the most representative Jewish body in the city.[48]

The fur industry and the story of the strike itself paralleled, in broad outline, developments in other branches of the apparel trades. Changes in taste and technological advances had made the mass production of ready-made garments possible. New entrepreneurs entered the field and tapped the supply of cheap immigrant labor. While a minority of the shops were fair-sized establishments where relatively decent working conditions prevailed, the rest consisted of small units located in tenements. Conditions here compared with the worst in the needle trades. Abuses flourished. Large manufacturers contracted to have garments finished by small entrepreneurs whose margin of profit depended upon a low overhead and sweating employees. The seasonal character of the fur trade (September to December were the busy months) added to the instability and further depressed labor conditions. The furriers suffered from an additional disability. Working with fur, especially in the smaller shops where ventilation was poor, resulted in a high incidence of respiratory ailments.[49]

The furriers union had suffered a crushing defeat in a 1907 general strike. Factionalism, introduced by the Industrial Workers of the World, and the separate organization of the skilled German craftsmen further sapped union strength. But following the waistmakers' and cloakmakers' successes in 1909 and 1910, preparations began in earnest to reorganize the union. The United Hebrew Trades provided some financial help and organizers, and on June 20, 1912, a reconstituted Furriers Union struck the entire industry.[50]

The twelve-week, bitterly fought strike involved 9,000 furriers and 600 shops, and nearly all the employers and about 75 percent of the employees were Jews. Once again, the Jewish labor movement succeeded in casting the dispute in epic form. The furs they trimmed, cried the poet, Morris Rosenfeld, had given the furriers no warmth, but only hunger and tears.

> No longer shall we be bondmen
> And sleep our gifts away
> For this curse'd fur!

So he concluded his "hymn" for the striking furriers.[51] Mass meetings, parades, arrests on the picket line, and public fund-raising touched all parts of the labor community. As the summer months passed and the union did not break, the approach of the busy season undermined the implacable position of the manufacturers. In the early hours of September 8, news spread of a settlement. The weeks of arduous negotiations—even at the final all-night session the manufacturers refused to enter the same room with union representatives —Magnes had handled with skill and energy. The triumphant furriers marched to the *Forward* building and then to the home of the union's chief negotiator, Meyer London, to be told of the "heroic chapter" they had written in the history of the Jewish labor movement. The strike settlement also lifted Magnes to the front rank of peacemakers and thrust him into the thicket of industrial relations.[52]

The agreement marked another remarkable gain for labor. A stable union emerged and rational relations with the manufacturers were established. The terms included a 49-hour week, no homework, ten paid holidays which could be exchanged for Jewish holidays, a joint board of sanitary control, and the determination of the wage scales semiannually. The last point was an important concession to the union. It prevented the employers from negotiating pay rates whenever they wished, a practice which they resorted to especially during the slack season. A two-year limit to the contract was also agreed upon. (The 1910 cloakmakers' "protocol of peace," the prototype for the garment industry, contained no time limit.) The fur industry agreement, furthermore, established a conference committee with five representatives from each side and an umpire who had the right to cast the determining vote in the event of a tie. All unsettled issues were left to this committee including the establishment of procedures for handling disputes. Magnes agreed to serve as the neutral chairman of the committee.[53]

Six months of hard negotiating filled out the details of the agreement. A preferential union shop was ratified. (In engaging or retaining help, union members were to be given preference.) The employers, however, retained the right to discharge employees for "business reasons," a power which labor later claimed the manufacturers grossly abused. On the other hand, union shop stewards were granted the right to propagandize for the union and collect dues during lunch hours. Finally, the employers pledged to use only contractors whose shops observed the standards set by the agreement.[54]

In July, 1914, well before the expiration date, a new agreement for an additional three years was successfully negotiated with the large manufacturers. By August most of the smaller employers had fallen in line. The advances which had accrued as a result of the conference committee's work were incorporated in the new agreement, as were some substantive new demands made by the union. The arbitration machinery was improved with the creation of a committee on immediate action, composed of a representative of each side and the impartial chairman. The committee was instructed to mediate all minor differences within forty-eight hours of their being reported. The agreement, furthermore, recognized the desirability of a standard wage scale and referred its implementation to the conference committee. An attempt was also made to root out at least some of the evils of the contracting system. Manufacturers sometimes contracted with employees within their establishment to produce part of the garment. These "inside contractors" then hired the workers. Thus the onus of organizing and paying the labor force fell on the contractors. They and their workers, though they functioned on the premises of the manufacturer, were outside the pale of union control. This form of contracting was outlawed, but the union had to concede the legitimacy of the outside contractors. The provision requiring manufacturers to use only those outside contractors whose shops met union standards was one of the clauses most difficult to enforce.[55]

In the spring of 1917, for the third successive time, an industrywide agreement was reached without a strike. A wage scale which included moderate wage increases was incorporated in the settlement and reflected the improved economic conditions of the war period and a much stronger union. The union also won a 48-hour week and a full union shop. The agreement was to be in force until January 31, 1919. Magnes was again elected chairman of the conference committee and the staff of the Kehillah's Bureau of Industry (discussed below) continued to supervise the day-to-day implementation of the agreement. In 1919, surveying the Kehillah's work in the industrial field, Magnes spoke about the need that still existed for a communal agency to further the "orderly relations between Capital and Labor within the Jewish community." The fur industry conference he considered a model beginning for bringing industrial relations "within the range of communal inspection and responsibility." [56]

Magnes' early success as a mediator made him a prime candidate for additional assignments. When industrial strife of even greater magnitude shook the city only four months after the settlement of the 1912 furriers' strike, Magnes immersed himself in the mediation efforts emphasizing once more his role as Kehillah chairman.

From January to March, 1913, nearly 150,000 workers struck the different branches of the apparel trades. Poorly organized sections of the women's garment industry—like the kimono, waist, and white goods (underwear) divisions—showed unexpected militancy. The men's clothing industry, however, was the eye of the storm. There the Brotherhood of Tailors, chafing under the conservative leadership of its parent union, found the time propitious for a general strike. (In the fall of 1914, the Brotherhood left the United Garment Workers Union and participated in the formation of the Amalgamated Clothing Workers Union.) [57]

The sheer magnitude of the confrontation between workers and bosses, together with the cumulative effect of labor's recent successes and the rhetoric of the radical leadership, infused the strikes with a secular eschatology. "Swear under God's blue sky that none of you will return to work until the union has been recognized," cried Jacob Panken, counselor for the Brotherhood of Tailors. "Let your hands, which you have just raised [so Panken paraphrased the Psalmist], become paralyzed if you touch a needle or machine under non-union conditions! Let your tongue which uttered 'yes' be cut off if you ask your bosses for work under non-union conditions." [58]

Support of the strikers by the Jewish labor community and by sympathetic progressive elements (particularly the Women's Trade Union League) surpassed past achievements. Food commissaries manned by settlement-house workers and Arbeiter Ring members distributed provisions to the strikers' families. The Bakers Union supplied truckloads of bread each morning, and the Socialist Party opened free kitchens. A depot located in Clinton Hall offered clothes to the needy. Contributions by organizations like the *Forward*, returns from bazaars, theater benefits and concerts, and assessment of employed workers produced the income which financed the strike. [59]

In his mediation work, Magnes concentrated on the men's clothing industry. By mid-February of 1913, he had arranged a settlement between one group of East Side manufacturers and the union. [60] But the general situation remained unresolved. Two weeks later the national officers of the United Garment Workers accepted the terms for an industry-wide settlement offered by the manufacturers, only to have them repudiated by the union's rank and file. Finally, on March 11, an agreement was ratified by the strikers. Magnes had figured prominently in both the abortive settlement and in the final one. (Marcus M. Marks and R. Fulton Cutting, founder and chairman of the Bureau of Municipal Research, were the other conciliators.) To enforce the agreement, Marks, Meyer London, and Magnes were appointed to a Clothing Trades Commission.[61]

The strike brought only minor benefits to the union and failed to stabilize relations in the men's clothing trades. For the next three years, Magnes headed various mediation commissions and directed the arbitration machinery in this volatile branch of the industry. Henry Moskowitz, Charles C. Bernheimer, chairman of the Arbitration Committee of the Chamber of Commerce, and Paul Abelson worked with him.[62]

The Kehillah's interest in industrial matters coincided with the initiative it displayed in the aftermath of the Rosenthal murder. During the summer of 1912 Magnes met London not only at arbitration sessions but also at Kehillah meetings which dealt with Jewish criminality. Moskowitz also participated in these Kehillah parleys.[63] Civic and social problems offered, it seemed, a field for common endeavor.

Thus encouraged, Magnes made a concerted effort to bring the radical groups into the Kehillah. No doubt his contacts with leaders of the Jewish labor movement gave him some expectation of success. The documentation of the effort, unfortunately, is scanty. But on January 19, 1913, Magnes wrote to London:

Despite the fact that you were kind enough to tell me that I need not remind you of my hope that the radical Jews of this city will see the need and the advantages of interesting themselves in problems of Jewish organization through the Kehillah, I am writing to ask you if you will take this matter up as soon as possible. Our fourth Annual Convention takes place at the end of April, and I am in hopes that by that time you will have been able to persuade at least the most thoughtful among your friends of the wisdom of the course you and I have discussed. It will be an element of great strength to the whole community if the radical element will take up the problem of Jewish communal organization together with the rest of the community. We are, after all, one people—whether we wish it or not, and whatever our views of things may be.[64]

No reply, if indeed London bothered to answer, was found in the Kehillah's files. At the Arbeiter Ring convention in May, 1913, however, the National Executive Board reported on an invitation to join the Kehillah. In his letter, the Kehillah's chairman anticipated the cries of partisanship and Orthodox domination which were so often leveled against the Kehillah. He explained the Kehillah's interest in kosher meat supervision (in the eyes of the radicals, the sign of subservience to Orthodox interests) as a desire to replace chaos and fraud with order and integrity. Similarly, he described the Kehillah's interest in labor mediation as a wish to restore harmony and mutual respect within an organized Jewish community. Magnes requested permission to appear at a National Board meeting and discuss the matter further. The request went unanswered. So did an announcement inviting the Arbeiter Ring to send delegates to the Kehillah's convention in April.[65]

The Kehillah failed to translate common civic interests into identification with the Jewish community. At the convention of the International Fur Workers in 1915, among the resolutions passed, was one extending the union's appreciation to the Kehillah and to Magnes for "their valuable assistance." Magnes was gratified at the gesture. In the list of resolutions, following the one of the Kehillah, appeared a similar expression of esteem for the Hebrew Immigrant and Sheltering Aid Society. This time, however, the union also urged its members and locals to affiliate with the Society.[66]

The Jewish labor movement was prepared to avail itself of the Kehillah's good offices just as it accepted the intervention of Brandeis or Schiff. But mediation failed to lead to affiliation.

The Kehillah's arbitration activity, Magnes told the annual convention in April, 1914, "leads inevitably to the thought that there should be connected with the Kehillah a permanent machinery looking to the adjustment of all industrial disputes brought to our attention." The machinery, Magnes added, would be self-sustaining, financed by the parties having recourse to it.[67]

In the weeks that followed, Magnes approached a select group for the initial sums to launch the "committee on industrial relations." He wrote to Herbert Lehman, who he hoped would become treasurer, that the committee offered "the opportunity for an important piece of constructive work of benefit to the state and to the good name of the Jews of the community." Moreover, Magnes continued, "I have thought of turning to you because I know of your interest in public affairs." Lehman joined the committee and contributed substantially in time and money. Similarly, Charles Bernheimer and Louis B. Schram, both prominent in arbitration activities, and Maurice Wertheim, banker and member of the New York Industrial Board, joined the committee. Kehillah stalwarts, Bernard Semel and Cyrus Sulzberger, took an active part as well, and Felix Warburg and Adolph Lewisohn made large contributions.[68]

A year later success and an imaginative director led to ambitious new plans and a change in nomenclature. The committee became the Bureau of Industry with a supervisory body now known as the Board of Managers. Bernard Semel accepted the chairmanship of the Bureau's Board. One of Magnes' closest collaborators and an important woolen merchant, Semel was intimately associated with the East Side communal institutions. He took a hand in the mediation work and won praise as an effective arbitrator.[69]

While organizing the committee of sponsors in May, 1914, Magnes hired the two men who placed the entire undertaking on the highest professional plane. Magnes succeeded in recruiting Dr. Paul Abelson as director, and Dr. Leo Mannheimer as secretary.[70]

From 1911 to 1914, Abelson served professionally on the conciliation staff established under the protocol plan of the cloak and suit industry. An assistant to the Chief Clerk of the Manufacturers Protective Association, he was instrumental in convincing employers to support the union's membership drives, which tacitly transformed the preferential shop into a closed shop. Abelson's interest in labor arbitration stemmed from an East Side social reform background. At the turn of the century, he belonged to a group of young East Siders who came under Felix Adler's influence. Abelson participated in the establishment of the Downtown Ethical Culture Society and its Madison Street Settlement House, and he also served as secretary of the East Side Civic Club, hailed by reformers as a model of grass-roots civic spirit. In 1906, Abelson received his doctorate at Columbia for a dissertation in the field of medieval history. After several years of teaching high school, he left for the Educational Alliance, where he directed the adult education program prior to entering the arbitration field.[71]

Mannheimer, the son and brother of reform rabbis, was graduated from the Hebrew Union College with Magnes and studied at the University of Berlin before entering the active rabbinate. In the spring of 1913, he gained fame briefly when he was summarily dismissed from his post as rabbi of a Paterson, New Jersey, temple. His mediation efforts in the silk industry strike angered conservative members of the temple, and when he continued his peacemaking, the trustees terminated his service.[72]

The Kehillah's Bureau of Industry reached its maximum effectiveness during the years 1915 to 1917. The two full-time mediators in addition to Magnes and Semel formed a concilation staff of high competence. Abelson assumed much of Magnes' day-to-day burdens. He administered the fur industry's Committee on Immediate Action, which entailed his frequent presence. (During one two-month span, thirty-one complaints came before the committee, half of which required investigations on the shop premises.) When a new collective agreement was approved between the Amalgamated Clothing Workers and the East Side Clothing Manufacturers, in February, 1915, Abelson was selected chairman of the Committee on Immediate Action. Magnes became chairman of the Permanent Board of Arbitration, which also included Bernard Semel and the union's Abraham Shiplakoff. Meetings of the committees took place in the offices of the Kehillah.[73] Abelson also acted as secretary of the other major mediation boards which Magnes headed, the Clothing Trades Commission and the Council of Moderators of the men's clothing industry. In July, 1915, when a protracted strike that would have involved 80,-000 workers was averted, Abelson reported to the Kehillah's executive committee:

This agreement lays the foundation for what we all hope will be a peaceful solution of the problems confronting the clothing trade. In the preparation of this agreement, the chairman of the [Kehillah's] Executive Committee took a leading part and the Director of the Bureau of Industry acted as secretary of a committee and the subcommittees. . . .

While the conflict was terminated after a short period of negotiations

. . . the fact is that preparatory work which made possible the settlement . . . had been done by the Bureau of Industry for more than
a year. The present settlement is but a fruition of the plans and energies put into the clothing situation since July 1914.[74]

In January, 1916, a strike of 40,000 workers in the same industry
was once more averted. Four months later the situation had grown
more tense. Constant attention was required, Abelson reported.
Magnes and the committee of conciliation resigned in May, 1916, in
protest over the behavior of the manufacturers' association. But the
Bureau of Industry continued to maintain contact with both sides to
salvage at least a semblance of the arbitration machinery.[75]

The Bureau expanded its mediation activities beyond the industries
with which Magnes had established contact. It moved, first of all,
into fields peripheral to the fur industry. In the spring of 1915, the
Bureau mediated the dispute in the largest fur dressing and dyeing
plant in the industry, the A. Hollander Company of Newark. The
five-week strike was accompanied by continuous violence, including
the fatal shooting of two union leaders. In the tense aftermath,
Mannheimer acted as chairman of the committee on adjustment.
When an allied industry, the muff bed workers, struck, both sides
naturally turned to the Kehillah. Here, too, continuous arbitration
was established.[76]

At the end of 1915, the Bureau prevented a strike in the millinery
industry that involved 12,000 workers. The settlement led to arrangements similar to those in the fur industry. The Bureau took complete
charge of enforcing the agreement. Under Abelson's guidance as impartial chairman of the committee on adjustment, both the manufacturers' association and the union solidified their organizations. In
1919, Abelson praised the industry for its no-strike record. Only the
fur industry surpassed it.[77]

The Bureau served the smaller industries as well. In a routine report in April, 1916, Abelson mentioned the following parties to disputes who had had recourse to the Bureau's services: Children Dress
Workers Union, Division Street cloak-store clerks, Waiters Union.
The report also mentioned the strikes which the Bureau had been
unable to terminate. These included the men's shirt strike, the cloakmakers' strike, the jewelry workers' strike, and affected 15,000 work-

ers. The embroidery industry, bakers, and leather-bag and suitcase industry also came within the purview of the Bureau. On invitation, Bureau mediators intervened in disputes in the fur or men's clothes industries of Boston, Philadelphia, Rochester, and Chicago.[78]

Abelson, like Samson Benderly, conceived of his Bureau as a turning point in the social development of New York's Jews. Achieving some modicum of harmony in industrial relations occupied, of course, a fundamental place in his program. But there were other facets to the "industrial problem of the Jew." Abelson's detailed plans envisioned three additional spheres of activity. Besides a Division of Industrial Relations, the Bureau of Industry needed a Division of Surveys, of Vocational Guidance and Industrial Education, and of Employment. These proposals were, in fact, adopted by the executive committee, and parallel with the mediation work, Kehillah leaders undertook to implement the total program.[79]

The Division of Surveys, intended as the research arm of the Bureau, was the first casualty. The vocational guidance program hardly moved beyond the discussion stage. Some funds were raised for a study of existing facilities, and a consultant was employed for a time. The two abortive attempts offer some insight into the thinking of the Kehillah leaders.[80]

In proposing a vocational guidance program, Abelson first explained the Jewish element in the problem:

The children of an immigrant Jew are obliged to find their places in an entirely new environment. The natural placements which in a settled community exists through the established relations which the parents and family have to the industries in the community are, in a large measure, nonexistent for the children of the Jewish immigrant. Race prejudice is an important element. The Jewish children drift unguided into vocations, the possibilities and opportunities of which are unknown.

The adult Jew in industry was maladjusted as well, Abelson continued. Either he was inadequately trained or he had no training. Abelson then anticipated the criticism of his associates: "The needs of the

Jewish adult immigrants and of their children are too pressing, and the distress resulting from this maladjustment is so great, that the Jewish community as a whole cannot afford to wait until the whole problem of vocational education will be solved by the City of New York.[81] If community meant collective responsibility for the well-being of fellow members, it followed that where the larger polity failed to act the group, apparently, was obligated to fill the void.

The implications of Abelson's grand design elicted no substantive debate. But an unspoken built-in veto did operate. His plans, though sanctioned by the Kehillah, won no fiscal support from either the broad Jewish public or its men of wealth.

The fourth area of Bureau activity, employment, produced some modest successes. As early as June, 1909, Cyrus Sulzberger proposed that the Kehillah establish an employment agency for the handicapped. The term covered not only those with physical disabilities, but included, too, were Sabbath observers and persons unable to speak English. The agency began to function in mid-1910 and handled primarily referrals from the United Hebrew Charities and the Jewish Protectory. Thus juvenile delinquents and ex-convicts were added to the clientele. The Protectory and the Charities provide the funds. It was the one Kehillah institution never in want. In February, 1911, Magnes reported to the Kehillah convention that 500 cases were handled during the previous six months. The figure rose to 1,633 in 1912 and the following year, reflecting economic conditions, the number increased threefold.[82]

With the creation of the Bureau of Industry, the employment agency was transferred to the Bureau. Abelson attempted to coordinate the activities of the multiple agencies which by then were in the field. He succeeded, finally, in establishing a central office in the fall of 1916 which served as a clearinghouse for the four Jewish agencies. The Kehillah's branch remained the largest, and in 1916 it had a staff of five. In that year, 3,000 persons were registered with the agency, and over 1,100 were placed in permanent positions.[83]

During 1917, with the reorganization of the Kehillah, the Bureau was established on an independent footing. Magnes and Semel still maintained their affiliation with it. The Bureau, however, curtailed its activities and functioned primarily as professional arbitrator for the fur and millinery industries.[84]

In the 1920s, another turbulent era began in the garment industry which reminded some of the time a decade before when Magnes, at the head of the Kehillah, had entered the field. But the new strife found Magnes in Jerusalem. Abelson urged him to return and create a new version of the Bureau of Industry. He reminded Magnes of the "unique sphere that you and I worked for almost a decade." [85]

For the Kehillah that decade of struggle for industrial peace—constructive in itself—had paved, at most, a one-way street to the Jewish labor movement. Like the progressives who had hoped that industrial conciliation would contribute to a revived sense of community, so the Jewish progressives of the Kehillah found themselves and their institutions overwhelmed, at the decade's end, by new heights of industrial tumult.

§ CHAPTER TEN §

Decline: The War and the Democracy

THE OUTBREAK OF WAR IN 1914 MAGNIFIED THE DIFFICULTIES of the Kehillah. The Jewish public, alarmed over the fate of millions of kinsmen, now channeled its best energies into overseas relief. The war also roused hopes that a peace settlement would redress the age-old grievances of East European Jewry. Eager to lend political and moral support to that end, American Jewry plunged into a great debate over the form and the direction such support should have. When the cataclysmic events of 1917 came—America's entry into the war, the fall of czarism, and Britain's recognition of Zionist aspirations—interest shifted almost exclusively to international events. Local communal affairs, in comparison, seemed onerous if not sterile.

This time of high emotionalism and extraordinary events witnessed, within the Jewish community, the launching of new movements and the emergence of new personalities who challenged the hegemony of the established leadership. Louis Brandeis' sudden rise to eminence as the head of the Provisional Executive Committee for General Zionist Affairs (a coordinating agency created in August, 1914) is one such example. The Joint Distribution Committee (JDC) in the field of overseas relief and the movement for an American Jewish Congress in the political realm are other instances. In both cases an impatient public cried out for unified action and prodded contending factions into uneasy coalitions.[1]

The war years also changed the temper of American society, which further complicated the inner life of an ethnic group composed overwhelmingly of recent arrivals. True, the Wilsonian watchwords of democracy and self-determination for small nations, in addition to their general significance, tended to legitimize ethnic self-consciousness and to justify supporting the aspirations of the ancestral center. But "hyphenism" also came into usage and cast suspicion on ethnic activity.[2] The Kehillah idea celebrating pluralism became embarrassing if not suspect.

These changes in the climate of opinion, in the concerns of the Jewish public, in the communal structure and in the power balance came upon a Kehillah grappling with the prosaic but complex problem of molding heterogeneous institutions and contentious groups into an organized community. They came upon an organization still seeking stability and acceptance.

§

IN OCTOBER, 1914, LOUIS MARSHALL, AS HEAD OF THE AMERICAN JEWISH Committee (AJC), invited all national Jewish organizations to a conference for the purpose of facilitating the collection and distribution of relief funds. Earlier that month the Orthodox groups had set up a Central Relief Committee and the Zionists at a conference in August had launched their Palestine Relief Fund.[3]

At the AJC's conference, the end of October, in which forty organizations participated, a committee of five was appointed, which in turn selected the governing committee of one hundred. The former consisted of Oscar Straus, Julian W. Mack, Louis D. Brandeis, Harry Fischel, and Meyer London. London the socialist, Fischel the Orthodox Jew, Brandeis the Zionist and proponent of democracy in Jewish life, Mack the Midwestern communal leader, and Straus, a member of the German-Jewish aristocracy, joined together in the emergency.[4] The newly formed American Jewish Relief Committee, dominated by AJC circles and with Marshall as president, federated with the

Central Relief Committee of the Orthodox to form the JDC. In the summer of 1915, Jewish socialist and trade-union leaders, prodded by the Socialist-Zionists, established the People's Relief Committee, with Meyer London as chairman. In the fall of that year the socialist group affiliated with the JDC.[5]

Authentic differences had dictated the organization of separate relief committees. Orthodox Jewry, with its venerable tradition of charity and its parochial institutions, served a particular public in a distinctive way. On the other hand, collecting funds from immigrant workmen and activating Jewish trade unions called for arrangements and criteria of achievement far different than those appropriate for the Orthodox or the wealthy uptown donors. Neither monetary return nor the conferment of divine approbation could serve as the measure of success. A rationale was necessary which emphasized the moral worth of mass participation. The "democratization of philanthropy" became, then, the slogan, and it enabled the People's Relief to appeal to class pride. The number of workers that pledged a day's wages or the number of canvassers on the streets during a "tag-day" —these were the essential statistics. Proletarian philanthropists also entertained strong views on the distribution of overseas relief. They emphasized economic and social rehabilitation and the reconstruction of communal and cultural institutions—a policy they called "constructive relief"—rather than the amelioration of personal distress. Finally, both the Orthodox and the radicals understood the advantages which accrued from maintaining separate relief organizations. The dispensers of funds were also the wielders of influence.[6]

Pragmatic considerations, nevertheless, produced a semblance of unity. Affiliation with the AJC-dominated JDC meant, for the financially weak People's Relief Committee and Orthodoxy's Central Relief Committee, an opportunity to influence the policies of the wealthy, general agency. Where the stakes had been less palpable— joining the Kehillah—the radicals had refused to cross class lines or to cooperate with the "benighted" Orthodox.

On their part, the leaders of the AJC agreed to maintain the coalition despite the "irresponsibility" and the "reprehensible attitude" of the radicals. "The principal contributors have been bullied by this so-called democracy," Marshall wrote to Felix Warburg. But "it is always better to keep men of this kind within an organization than to deal with them when they are on the outside." [7] Yet brittle as the unity in relief work was, an institution representing all groups in American Jewry had been created. Significantly, it dealt exclusively with overseas relief work.

By the end of 1915, the JDC announced a $5 million goal for the coming year, which entailed developing new fund-raising devices and the creation of communal machinery. In New York, for example, the People's Relief Committee organized periodic mass canvassing of the Jewish neighborhoods. In December, 1915, at Carnegie Hall, the American Jewish Relief Committee held the first of a series of mass meetings. Magnes made the appeal for funds.[8] "As he spoke," one newspaper account went, "women, and then men, wept and sobbed. . . . And then a dozen, and then hundreds, rushed forward to pour their offerings at his feet." In the next two years, the JDC raised over $16 million, and Magnes, the speaker most in demand, duplicated his Carnegie Hall feat a score of times.[9]

Overseas charity work forced the JDC into the sensitive area of politics. The transfer of funds in wartime, dealing with the belligerent governments and coping with the complex needs of war-torn communities, created suspicion and dissension. Magnes, for example, served on the JDC's key Subcommittee of Eight, which studied the reports from overseas and recommended the priority of allotments. This involved, among other duties, negotiating with the Provisional Zionist Committee on the relative apportionment of funds to Palestine and Europe. In the summer of 1916, Magnes was sent on a four-month mission to Poland to investigate the problem of transferring and distributing relief. Germany permitted him entry to the Polish territory under its control, while Russia refused a similar request. This, combined with his conclusion that German-Jewish organizations offered the most expeditious way of channeling relief funds to the war zone, led to accusations of being pro-German and favoring the philanthropies directed by assimilationist German Jews.[10]

Like Magnes, the majority of the Kehillah's executive committee was immersed in fund-raising and in the politics of overseas relief. (Since the headquarters of most national societies were located in New York, nearly all members of the Kehillah's executive committee were also national leaders.) There is no way of measuring the extent that these multiple responsibilities diverted attention from the Kehillah. Samson Benderly believed that his educational work did indeed suffer as a consequence. "We have been completely taken up with the problem of relief," he told the 1916 convention; "while the problem of relief is undoubtedly essential and cannot be postponed, the provision of a fund for the erection of school buildings is also urgent and should not be postponed." [11]

More than a conflict of competing commitments was involved. As the European war came to dominate the interests of the public, these men dealt increasingly—in their capacity as national leaders—with issues connected with the emergency. The clear division which the Kehillah constitution made between its local and the AJC's national jurisdictions became difficult to maintain. Moreover, so long as the AJC's leadership had been tacitly accepted in most circles, the original formula, despite inner stresses, had proved viable. But extraordinary conditions had encouraged new forces to rise and challenge the hegemony of the AJC. The Kehillah, because of its democratic format, became first the scene, and then the victim, of that confrontation.

From the fall of 1914 and for the following two years, the negotiations connected with the calling of an American Jewish Congress agitated the community.[12] Congress advocates—and they were the Jewish nationalists and particularly the Zionists—projected the establishment of a democratically chosen body which would speak authoritatively "on all issues involved in the Jewish Problem." War, the partisans of the congress-idea wrote, had placed a heavy responsibility upon American Jews. They were citizens of a neutral, democratic, and powerful nation. They possessed important economic and political resources. Moreover, they asserted, "our fellow Americans are infused with a high and generous spirit, which insures the approval of our struggle to ennoble, liberate, and otherwise improve the conditions of an important part of the human race." Only spokesmen elected by a body representing the popular will would be able to claim and mobilize the support of a united, 3,000,000-strong community.[13]

The congress partisans believed, moreover, that a representative body would adopt their program, which called for the granting of minority rights to the Jews of Europe and for the recognition of a Jewish national interest in Palestine. Thus American Jewry, they reasoned, would tacitly commit itself to a pro-Zionist position. But above all, militants like Louis Lipsky, Bernard G. Richards, and Baruch Zuckerman—joined in mid-1915 by Brandeis—viewed the congress movement as a struggle over first principles: in the name of democracy the organized multitude would defeat the German-Jewish oligarchy and discredit the overcautious policies and "assimilationist" philosophy of the AJC.[14] "Jewish Wall Street does not want this congress," Nachman Syrkin, leader of the Socialist-Zionists, told a pro-congress rally: "those men are standing against democracy, and they are not only treacherous to the Jewish people, but to the spirit of America." In more measured tones, Louis Brandeis informed a Carnegie Hall audience in January of 1916 that the congress "is not to be an exalted mass-meeting." It is to be, rather, "the most effective instrument of organized Jewry of America." Two months later the popular, aggressive Rabbi Stephen S. Wise added his voice to those of the militants. About to replace Brandeis as the movement's chief, Wise paid him this tribute: "He has moved his people to repossess themselves of the spirit of self-determination and to loose themselves from a long-endured bondage of eleeymosynary patronage." Thus in the eyes of the congress leadership the crisis overseas offered, in the first instance, an extraordinary opportunity to revamp the communal order of American Jewry.[15]

This position, however, others viewed as opportunism. It jarred moderates like Israel Friedlaender and Moredecai Kaplan. What the congress supporters want, Kaplan wrote in his journal, "is to establish here a semi-autonomous Jewish group life. They are using the congress idea simply as a means of getting the Jews together for that purpose. They want to utilize the predicament of the Jews in Europe as a means of organizing the Jews of America." [16] As idealogues of the Kehillah movement and of ethnic continuity in America, Friedlaender and Kaplan sympathized with the congress notion. But as Kehillah leaders they stood committed to the slow pace of building a consensus.

To AJC leaders Marshall, Schiff, and Cyrus Adler, it seemed that behind the undertaking stood men "actuated by selfish motives or by fanaticism," who imbued the masses with false hopes. The congress movement—in Marshall's words—gave "blatant and flamboyant orators an opportunity to make themselves conspicuous for a moment irrespective of the permanent injury which they inflict upon Jewry." Officeholders can be elected, not true leaders, Schiff told an East Side audience; true leaders must develop and prove their value. The AJC, he declared, was the best qualified group to represent Jewish interests, and its notable eight-year record bore this out. It had, furthermore, taken into account the heterogeneity of Jewish life and coopted persons representative of the different strands of the community (though the real power, Schiff might have added, was still exercised by a small group within the AJC's executive committee). In August, 1914, when Brandeis, in the name of the Zionists, invited AJC cooperation in calling an emergency conference, Marshall replied that the Committee had "taken such action as it has deemed proper in the circumstances." [17] Nor did a year of widespread, pro-congress agitation move the AJC substantially. In a letter to Brandeis which he knew would be published, Adler wrote in August of 1915:

You seem to take for granted that in a matter of this kind [the calling of a congress] the American Jewish Committee stands upon a footing exactly similar to that of the Federation of American Zionists, or of other national bodies. . . . This interpretation can hardly be maintained. . . . Among the approximately forty Jewish organizations of national scope in the United States, the great majority were founded for specific purposes. . . . Now, if you will contrast these special purposes with those of the American Jewish Committee as recited in its charter . . . I think you will be constrained to admit that it is incumbent upon the American Jewish Committee to do exactly that which it is now doing.[18]

The term "congress" frightened the AJC leaders. It meant elections, parties, campaigns, open debates, and it raised the spectre of misunderstanding among non-Jews. "This proposition for an American Jewish Congress," Schiff wrote to Magnes, "is nothing less than an attempt to weld together the Jewish population of this country into a racial or nationalistic organization. . . . Let this attempt succeed and it will not be long before we shall witness in this country an anti-Semitism which does not now exist, and which in time will make the lot of the Jew throughout the United States well nigh unbearable." [19] This was in May, 1915. Marshall, writing at the same time in the shadow of the diplomatic crisis which followed the sinking of the *Lusitania,* said:

At this juncture, when every American citizen is subordinating every thought to the welfare of his country, when the hyphen has disappeared from every description of American citizenship, when we, of all people in the world, owe to the United States the utmost gratitude and the duty of permitting nothing to intervene between us and the obligation which we owe to our country, we are about to enter into a debate with respect to the holding of a Jewish congress . . . the very holding of which will give aid and comfort to Germany, a potential enemy of our government.

At such a congress, Marshall predicted, impolitic, emotional, ethnocentric leaders of the immigrant masses would flay the czarist government (a potential ally of the United States), praise Germany (a potential enemy), and support Zionist demands in Palestine (challenging Ottoman sovereignty and endangering thereby the local Jewish populace). Even those "bitten by the congress craze," Marshall wrote, knew "in their heart of hearts that the whole idea was ridiculous." But they were governed by "false pride," and they were "afraid of the Yiddish newspapers which they have themselves set in motion." [20]

The congress movement, however, was more than a power struggle for the leadership of the American Jewish community or the proving ground for a principle. The congress movement reflected the deeply felt needs of a broad public. Distraught immigrants, still close to the old home, sought an appropriate forum to express their anxieties, to receive information of conditions in Europe, and to hear plans for their amelioration. The term "congress" evoked the image of an august body, politically strong and sagacious. The democratic basis of congress implied the marshaling of the people's best talents. Finally, at a time when so little could be done, convening a congress meant doing something.[21] In a sense, the congress was a psychological necessity. Magnes understood this and bent all of his energies to convince his colleagues on the AJC that the congress idea was not fraught with danger. Large numbers of organizations, he told Marshall in January, 1915, were planning to join the congress movement. A forum was necessary to enable the people to express "in forms of resolutions and in other ways sentiments which naturally and justly animate them." Israel Friedlaender expressed the same thought to Brandeis six months later. The AJC had blundered in opposing a congress, not that it would have brought any tangible results, he wrote. But "the Jewish masses felt the burning need of crying out in their despair, and it was the duty of the American Jewish Committee to provide a suitable opportunity for this irrepressible need of expression." [22]

Meetings of Kehillah delegates in January and February, 1915, pressed the executive committee to use its influence with the AJC. Let the AJC, they urged, take the initative in calling together a representative general committee and let it stand at the head of such an endeavor. Suppose the AJC, Magnes argued in a memorandum to Marshall, decided that a policy of neutrality and silence was best in the light of present international conditions. How could it implement such a policy without the participation and agreement of the masses. In a joint letter to Marshall, Schiff and Oscar Straus, Magnes pleaded:

Whatever be the method employed [to choose delegates to a conference or congress] most of the men now at the head of the American Jewish Committee, together with a few other responsible men who might easily be mentioned, will, under all circumstances, be looked to for leadership.

"Let us have confidence in the people," Magnes concluded, "and they will have confidence in us. An authoritative leadership will be established, and its work will be made as effective as a united American Israel can make it." [23]

The problem was reminiscent of one six years before. At that time the AJC leadership had seen the Kehillah movement as a potential democratic behemoth controlled by impulsive, untutored immigrants. But the AJC had also recognized the greater danger of leaving such a creature to its own devices. Out of this ambivalence had come the uneasy Kehillah coalition of uptown "Hofjude" and downtown functionaries, which Magnes and his coworkers had so assiduously nurtured. True, immigrant leaders had been obliged to defer to the AJC and grant it a senior partnership in the enterprise. Nevertheless, to Israel Friedlaender's mind, the institutional collaboration had produced a softening of antagonisms and even a blending of values between the rich Reform Jew of German origin and assimilatory tendencies, and the immigrant Russian Jew possessed of an intensive, ethnic life and Zionist propensity. A period of regression had then set in. But now, out of the present upheaval, pleaded Freidlaender in a penetrating and moving letter to Brandeis, must come a "return to that synthesis" which would produce an indigenous and balanced "American Israel." "The Provisional Zionist Committee may defeat the American Jewish Committee," he wrote, "it can never replace it." The times cried out for mediation and compromise, for pragmatists rather than dogmatists.[24] At hand was the Kehillah model, and in the spring of 1915, its annual convention offered the opportunity for compromise or a factional test of strength.

The sixth convention of the Kehillah, held in April, 1915, was attended by 534 delegates who represented 341 organizations. The convention was larger by two-thirds than the founding one. Representatives of the nationalist radical groups, like the Jewish National Workers Alliance, returned after an absence of four years. The Zionists sent a strong delegation. Even branches of the socialist Arbeiter Ring and trade unions participated.[25] The executive committee well understood the opportunity that had presented itself of enlarging its constituency in directions hitherto blocked. More printed material, for example, was prepared for the delegates than at any other convention. The executive also proposed structural changes. The executive committee was expanded from twenty-five to thirty-six so that a total of sixteen members were elected at the convention. A reorganization plan for the management of the Bureau of Education was presented. The proposals recommended a more representative council to set education policy.[26] But the influx of new delegates had come for one purpose. The Kehillah offered the only public forum where the congress issue could be discussed, the AJC leadership confronted in open debate, and a decision registered. Whatever the ulterior motives were for the large attendance, the Kehillah never came closer to fulfilling its democratic role.

The main debate centered on Marshall's review of the activities of the AJC—his rejection of a congress but his willingness (a concession) to call a conference of national organizations. In a grand debate that was almost always passionate and frequently statesmanlike, representatives of different factions groped for conciliation. They sought to bridge the gap between "conference" and "congress," "plutocracy" and "democracy," an open agenda and a strictly limited one. Then Marshall rose in rebuttal. He began by citing the Kehillah's constitution, which gave to the AJC "exclusive jurisdiction over all questions affecting the Jews generally." Whatever decision the Kehillah might reach, therefore, would be in the form of a recommendation. Moving to the substantive question, Marshall ridiculed the prospective accomplishments of a congress.

One of the gentlemen says, "We will not beg a gift, we will ask for nothing, we will demand!" Now that is the very thing which I fear with respect to any Congress of the Jews. There will be those who will demand; there will be those who will accompany their demands with the most extraordinary arguments and with the most ineffectual assertions. And demand from whom, and demand what, and demand how? People who demand must have some sanction for that demand. . . . We have no armies, we have no country of our own, we have no power. . . . What can we accomplish by the passage of resolutions? Who will listen to them, who will present them to the leaders of the armed bands that are perpetrating [the pogroms]? Will you send a committee of the Congress to present them and ask them to desist from their unlawful actions?

The congress, Marshall believed, would bring only "infinite mischief."

If you run counter to our [the AJC's] best judgment, if you desire to take the . . . terrible risks which I see and which you apparently do not behold, of the inevitable consequences of holding a congress which nobody can restrain because it is incapable of being held in check by anybody when it once bursts forth in all of its exuberance of eloquence and rhetoric—I say, if you shall persist in this course, let yours be the responsibility. I will have none of it.

Magnes answered:

The people simply ask that in these moments of crises, at this historic moment, that they and their representatives be taken into the confidence of the leaders of the people.[27]

The *Maccabaean*, however, was less solicitious. "The reactionary forces in the Kehillah," represented by the leading officers of the AJC, "utilized . . . their position and wealth to deter action and to stifle the freedom of the Jews of this community." Marshall's performance was proof of this "reactionary temper." "He threatened and scolded, concluding with the undemocratic and un-American declaration: 'If you insist and persist in calling a congress, I'll have none of it.' "[28]

The pro-congress delegates, who were in the majority, agreed to postpone further discussion for one month. In the four intervening weeks Magnes labored over a compromise. Meetings were arranged between subcommittees of the AJC, the Kehillah, and the congress faction. The executives of the AJC, the Kehillah, and the Provisional Zionist Committee reviewed the compromise proposals in preparation for the reconvening of the convention. The Kehillah had become, for a moment, the mediating framework for the American Jewish community.[29]

The resolution prepared by the Kehillah leaders favored "a conference of delegates of Jewish societies . . . chosen by their membership, for the sole purpose of considering the Jewish question as it affects our brethren in belligerent lands." Thus "conference" was substituted for "congress" and some popular electoral arrangement was included. Finally, American Jewish affairs were excluded from the scope of the future gathering. The resolution "recommended" to the AJC that it consider "the advisability of calling a conference of the character favored by this convention" in lieu of a more restricted one which the AJC was then planning.[30]

At the reassembled convention, Dr. Isaac Hourwich, a nationalist and radical, presented the resolution, and Jacob Schiff seconded it. The Kehillah, it seemed, had successfully contained the most explosive and divisive issue then before the Jewish public.

But this moment of triumph for the Kehillah, and for Magnes personally, was shortlived. Were the members of the Kehillah's executive committee (who by virtue of that office served on the AJC) bound in AJC deliberations by the convention's decision? The delegates answered in the affirmative. In a second test, a resolution stating that the convention did not intend "to force any member of the AJC to vote against his will," failed in a dramatic roll-call vote. The Kehillah was binding Louis Marshall to its democratic will. When Marshall ridiculed the convention's decision and announced he would not be bound by the compromise forumla he dealt the Kehillah a heavy blow indeed, crushing its bid to be the great democratic forum of the community.[31]

A year later, in June, 1916, the congress issue seemed no closer to a solution. Pro-congress forces participated in the Kehillah convention once more but this time only to harass its leaders and mock the AJC. Louis Lipsky, the Zionist leader and spokesman of the opposition, reminded the convention that its mildly pro-congress resolution of the year before had been ignored by the executive committee. ("The Kehillah as such has committed moral suicide," he said.) Nevertheless, he and his associates had returned in a last attempt "to secure a new lease on life for the Kehillah." This could be achieved only by freeing the organization from "entanglements" that prevented it from responding to "the will of the people." The "entanglements" were the ties to the AJC.[32]

The pro-congress group, as it anticipated, was throttled at the convention. Its resolution to sever relations with the AJC was declared unconstitutional. A resolution reiterating the 1915 convention stand on the congress was declared out of order, "since the Kehillah had no authority with regard to national Jewish affairs." The organization, Lipsky concluded, has practically admitted that it "cannot affect Jewish life." In view of the "tremendous problems" of the hour, we must create, he announced, "an organization that is responsive to the ideals and duties of the Jewish people. We feel that the participation of nationalists and Zionists [in the Kehillah] is at an end." [33]

Wherever the blame for the impasse is placed—and Magnes and

Friedlaender also recognized Marshall's and Schiff's intransigence—the victims were Magnes and the Kehillah. For Schiff, Magnes had become a demagogue. The Bureau of Education he suspected of being under the control of the nationalists. If the Kehillah continued to abet the congress movement, Schiff warned Magnes in 1915, he would withdraw all support.[34] Three months later when Magnes appeared before the Zionist convention to fight against a congress resolution and to plead for unity, he was treated as a turncoat, the paid man of Schiff. That summer Magnes resigned from the Provisional Zionist Committee. (In resigning he argued that the Zionists, by concentrating their efforts on the congress movement, had departed from their principal objective—the upbuilding of Palestine as a national home and spiritual center. This he saw as partisan politics, a naked power struggle which would only split American Jewry.) An accommodation was finally reached between the AJC and the congress party in the fall of 1916. However, neither Magnes, Friedlaender, nor the Kehillah had a hand in the matter.[35]

A third party to the agreement on holding a congress was the National Workmen's Committee on Jewish Rights, the socialists. They had allied themselves with the AJC in the year of intensive negotiations which led to the settlement. A common animus against the Jewish nationalists had linked the two.[36] Had the accommodation taken place as a result of the 1915 convention of the Kehillah, as it might well have, it could have brought new prestige and energies into the Kehillah. It would have won back alienated elements and perhaps converted old opponents. A year and a half later, the agreement showed how ineffectual the Kehillah had been, and how completely the AJC had ignored its democratic constituency.

Two years of ferment over the congress issue coupled with arduous efforts on behalf of overseas relief contributed to the Kehillah's loss of standing and to its straitened circumstances. But in the early months of 1917, there were indications that reorganization might lead to revitalization. A cluster of fortuitous events created, at least for the moment, a new and favorable milieu.

In the communal realm, divisive issues of the recent past appeared to be well on the way to adjustment. The long-festering question of holding a Jewish congress was settled. The first meeting of the executive committee representing all factions took place on December 25, 1916. Four months later, dates and procedures for the election of delegates and for the convening of the congress itself were agreed upon. (After further postponements the congress eventually met in December, 1918.) The cumulative effect of the campaigns for overseas relief also contributed indirectly to the more congenial setting. In the pursuit of funds, the relentless appeal to group sentiments and individual conscience sensitized the Jewish public to other calls for succor. The newly launched Federation for the Support of Jewish Philanthropies benefited from this frame of mind. In its appeals for funds, the Federation focused attention on local needs once again and with unprecedented results. It stressed, moreover, the merits of a central body, though one limited to assisting the community's welfare institutions. All these notions harked back to the Kehillah leitmotiv of communal unity, coordination, and democratic control.[37]

The stirring events of the spring of 1917 quickened the growing sense of solidarity. In March, the Russian Revolution lifted the entire Jewish public to a state of near euphoria. "The Jewish Troubles Are At An End," a *Forward* headline read. "Every Jew hails free Russia's advent with prayer, thanksgiving, and pledges for cooperation," Louis Marshall cabled the Provisional Government; "the voice of liberty has caused the horrible spectre of absolution to vanish forever."[38] A British army advancing on Jerusalem (the army was no farther away than Yonkers from New York, a Kehillah convention was told), gave special meaning to reports that the British government would soon issue a favorable statement on Palestine. Jacob Schiff greeted the prospect warmly and hinted that he might join the Zionist organization.[39]

Finally, America's entry into the war created stresses and exigencies best handled within an ethnic framework. In the first place, much of the patriotic surge which marked the crisis moved in sectarian channels. Days before the declaration of war, journalists of the Yiddish press, for example, organized a League of Jewish Patriots. Soon after, the preliminary organization of the Jewish Welfare Board (a service organization for Jews in the military) was announced. This kind of voluntarism called for communal coordination and encouragement. Also demanding the attention of the community was the presence in the immigrant quarter of a vociferous antiwar element.

Indeed, the most eminent leaders among the Jews felt particularly vulnerable in the new climate of wartime nationalism. Two and half years of war in Europe had heightened the collective consciousness of the Jewish public, and Old World ties—uptown Jewry's German origins and downtown's hatred of czarism—had stamped it as pro-German. The Americanized community had resisted, for the most part, the pull of old loyalties in its eagerness to be included in the national consensus. (From the beginning of the war, men of Central European origin like Marshall and Stephen Wise had considered "German autocracy" as the enemy.) Among the Russian immigrants, however, some influential elements responded differently. They failed to comprehend the degree of conformity expected of them by an American society newly embarked upon a world crusade which treated dissenters as apostates. True, the fall of the czarist regime removed a major obstacle to enlisting in the American mission. But it also awakened a sympathy for Russia's desire for an immediate peace, a position inimical to United States policy. The end of hostilities on the Russian front meant relief for the war-torn areas of dense Jewish settlement and an opportunity for the new government, which inspired so much hope in the spring of 1917, to consolidate its position. Antiwar and radical circles fed upon these sentiments and upon the immigrant's repugnance for compulsory military service.[40] Two days after the declaration of war, in a moment of patriotic exhilaration, Stephen Wise told his congregation:

Yesterday, we were divided; today we are united with every surviving vestige of hyphenism gone. We are become a united and indivisible people fused together . . . in order to have part in a war, which if rightly waged, will liberate humanity everywhere and establish democracy as the norm of the nations of earth great and small.[41]

Wise's rhetoric aside, the hyphenated group actually provided a vehicle for immigrant participation in the common cause and a way for coping with deviationists—a fact civic and ethnic leaders quickly recognized.

Thus a variety of circumstances—some long in developing, like the organization of the Federation of Philanthropies, and others more spontaneous, like the response to the nation's entry into war—had created a propitious moment for the Kehillah to reassert its leadership and stake its claim as the representative agency of New York Jewry.

Such an opportunity the Kehillah convention presented when it assembled on April 28, 1917, the first large convocation of American Jews following America's entry into the war. The agenda included the full range of Kehillah and community problems: the reorganization of the Kehillah structure, the support of Jewish education by the Federation of Philanthropies, new proposals for meeting the still anarchic conditions in the kosher meat industry, and the activities of the Kehillah's bureaus. But, as the *American Hebrew* succinctly put it, the "themes uppermost in the hearts and minds of the 347 delegates" were the "prospect of Palestine for the Jews, the new era in Russia, and loyalty to America." Jacob Schiff introduced the resolution "reaffirming . . . the loyalty and devotion [of the Jews] to the great American Republic in these days of war." Voicing sentiments that many of his listeners undoubtedly shared, he said:

Had we been called upon to show our Americanism under conditions that existed in Russia two months ago, we no doubt would have followed the call of duty, but . . . with a heavy heart. Thank our God, the God of Israel, that things have turned out otherwise, that we can feel today that we are fighting for democracy in alliance with democratic governments, fighting against absolutism and autocracy.[42]

Marshall, in turn, praised the February Revolution. "Russia must know," he pointedly remarked, "that American Jews are unanimous against a separate peace." The Palestine resolution, which Israel Friedlaender introduced, called upon the United States and its Allies to aid in the "re-establishment of a free and publicly recognized homeland." Never in eight years, wrote the *American Hebrew*, had the Kehillah held a convention so harmonious. "It was a manifestation of the conscious, organized, united Jewish community as a truly democratic body, asserting itself in these great times." [43] So the com-

munal body satisfied the need to solemnly endorse the national purpose and to proclaim its particular goals.

The revered young Magnes of an earlier year was needed to turn
this moment of elation and dedication to good account. But to the
consternation of friends and the community at large, he now took up
the cause of pacificism and radicalism, jeopardizing the very institution with which he was so thoroughly identified. The controversy he
precipitated also transcended the particular question of the Kehillah's
fate. It forced the ethnic group to confront the wartime dilemmas
and conflicts faced by the larger society.[44]

In November, 1916, Magnes first indicated an interest in the peace
movement. Three months later, following the break in diplomatic relations with Germany, he offered his services to the Emergency Peace
Federation. At rallies held at the end of March in New York and in
Washington the night Woodrow Wilson delivered his war message,
Magnes emerged as a powerful spokesman for the peace forces. On
their behalf he appealed to Schiff for $10,000 to help finance a march
on the capital—a last effort to stave off the expected declaration of
war. Schiff, until then a supporter of the peace movement, refused.[45]
Rabbi Stephen S. Wise, a key figure in the American Union Against
Militarism, also abandoned his antiwar position. A year before, Wise
had toured the West in Wilson's wake and challenged the President's
preparedness program. In April, 1917, Magnes remained the sole
peace advocate of national eminence in the Jewish ministry.[46]

In the months that followed, Magnes drew close to a group of progressives of pacifist background who distrusted the Wilsonian rhetoric and decried Allied intentions as punitive and imperialistic. From
this circle—which included, among others, Amos Pinchot, Emily G.
Balch, Louis Lochner, Norman Thomas, Walter Weyl, Roger Bald-
win, and Oswald Garrison Villard—came the public critics of United
States policy and the defenders of domestic civil liberties. In the
spring and summer of 1917, Magnes participated in their efforts to
formulate a coherent and effective program. That fall he joined other
war critics and social reformers to support Morris Hillquit, the Socialist candidate in the New York mayoralty election. For Villard's *Evening Post* he wrote a notable series on international affairs under the

signature "Observer." Nor did Magnes shirk institutional responsibilities. He served on the executive board of the National Civil Liberties Bureau and was a member of the Bureau's delegation which met with Attorney General A. Mitchell Palmer in April, 1919, to request amnesty for "political prisoners." [47]

What brought him into disrepute, however, was his association with the People's Council of America, a group which absorbed the Emergency Peace Federation and attracted to its ranks antiwar Socialists like Scott Nearing and Morris Hillquit. The Conference for Democracy and Terms of Peace, which met in New York on May 30 and 31, 1917, provided the occasion for the establishment of the council. Both conference and council fixed upon the peace terms of the Petrograd Soviet—no forced annexations, no punitive indemnities, self-determination for all nationalities—as the basis for immediate peace negotiations. America was called upon to join "Free Russia" in repudiating the imperialistic aims and the intransigence of ally as well as enemy. On the home front, the People's Council remonstrated against the conscription laws as a manifestation of "the very Prussianism which America proposes to stamp out." To assure "democratic control of foreign policy" it urged legislation making mandatory a referendum vote on questions of war and peace. Through a national network of branches, the council hoped to provide a great popular forum for dissenting views. Despite harassment —its meetings were broken up, its speakers beaten, Scott Nearing, the organization's chairman, indicted for sedition—the People's Council maintained a precarious existence until mid-1919.[48]

From its beginning, Magnes shared all the notoriety of the organization, although within its councils he advocated moderation. During the May 1917, conference, he delivered the keynote address at the Madison Square Garden rally. An overflow crowd of thousands filled the streets, he recalled later. Troops with fixed bayonets were stationed on the sidewalks. "At each corner of the Garden block there was also a wagon containing a machine gun and a great searchlight pointed toward the exits." Inside, opposite the speaker, a group of recruits in uniform "endeavored to shout the meeting down." Three months later in Chicago, at the first convention of the People's Council, Magnes again delivered the principal address. National

Guard units arrived shortly after to disperse the meeting. Even at the last major undertaking of the People's Council, Magnes won special notice. In May, 1919, the Council sponsored a mass meeting to protest Allied intervention in Russia. Lincoln Colcord, John Haynes Holmes, Frederick C. Howe, and Amos Pinchot shared the rostrum with Magnes. But the "climax was reached," the *Times* story went, "when the crowd indulged in a series of tremendous 'boos' as Rabbi J. L. Magnes coupled the name of President Wilson with Prince Leopold, Kolchak, Lloyd George, Clemenceau, Orlando, and Makino as being 'all of one mould, the children of a dying generation.' " [49]

In 1920, the New York State Lusk Committee investigating seditious activities noted that the *Fur Worker* (organ of the International Fur Workers Union) praised Soviet Russia, demanded amnesty for "political prisoners," supported socialist Eugene V. Debs for president, and solicited funds for the defense of Scott Nearing. "Another indication of the character of the organization," the report continued, "may be gathered from the fact that Dr. Judah L. Magnes is chairman of the conference committee of the fur industry." All these causes were indeed his. For the Lusk Committee, Magnes was the measure of subversive radicalism.[50]

Thus the Jewish community faced the chagrin of having one of its most forceful spokesmen embrace a cause—though he stressed that he did so as a private citizen—which some equated with disloyalty to the nation.

The dismay and fear which the established leadership must have shared, Marshall expressed privately as early as the spring of 1917. Magnes' course, his brother-in-law told him bluntly, was "giving aid and comfort to the enemy." He was attending meetings which "go almost to the very verge of sedition and treason." Moreover,

By taking such a prominent position as you are in this agitation, you are jeopardizing other interests . . . which you have no right to imperil. You are the head of the Kehillah. You are a leader in the cause of Jewish education. You are one of the principal workers in the effort to bring relief to our brethren in the war zone. What right have you, therefore, merely for the purpose of voicing your personal views on a matter as to which the overwhelming opinion of America is opposed to you, to injure these great causes in which you are concerned, and not only to injure them, but to injure the Jewish people of America with whom you are so actively identified? [51]

Magnes faced the moral dilemma of choosing between his communal responsibility and the dictates of conscience. In 1919, brooding over the problem, he wrote in a personal memoir:

The organization needed as chairman some respectable, distinguished representative citizen who could always be depended upon to say the right thing. . . . I was too much a preacher to be that chairman. I was too interested in popular movements for justice and liberty and truth to be safe and sane for the Kehillah. I was gratified that during the war I had the *z'chut* [privilege] and the *z'chiya* [merit] to have said the things I did, to have taken the stand I did. Would it not have been a disgrace to the Jewish people had none—particularly no Jewish teacher of religion—taken the pacifist and radical stand? Yet I realized that this was harmful to the Kehillah as an organization. [52]

There were demands that he leave Jewish public life. From his pulpit Stephen Wise chided Magnes—without mentioning him by name —as one of the "impromptu peace advocates." He had come "to aid the cause of peace"—the phrase was Magnes'—"for the sake of Pax Germanica," Wise stated. [53] Six months later, again from the pulpit, Wise inveighed against Magnes:

The only decent thing for any Jew invested with any place of responsibility in Jewish life who chooses to espouse the Bolshevist program with all its fateful consequences to American life is voluntarily to withdraw . . . from Jewish life. If he refuses, . . . his withdrawal ought to be made inevitable by that great number of American Jews who abhor the Bolshevist propaganda, who are first and last and ever Americans, who know that any compromise with Prussianism would be fatal to the Republic. [54]

Privately, long-standing admirers of Magnes reacted similarly. In his journal, Mordecai Kaplan recorded Judge Irving Lehman's attitude. At a meeting of the executive committee of the Young Men's Hebrew Association, in April, 1918, the question had arisen of participating in the reorganized Kehillah. Lehman, who professed his deep affection for Magnes and acknowledged him as his spiritual guide, opposed participation. To support the Kehillah was impossible without compromising one's Americanism, in the light of Magnes' attitude towards the war. Would Lehman invite Magnes to his home, someone asked. He certainly would, Lehman replied, but he would not want strangers present, to whom he would have to explain.[55]

Both the Kehillah and Magnes were trapped. He offered to resign, but that would only have highlighted the community's embarrassment. It would have "raised public issues which it was deemed advisable not to raise." "I doubt the wisdom of making any statement on behalf of the Kehillah," Marshall told Professor Richard Gottheil in May, 1917, "the least said the soonest mended." Under this cloud Magnes continued to serve as the Kehillah's head. "He has incapacitated himself entirely for Jewish work as a result of his new interests," Mordecai Kaplan wrote two years later; "but instead of cutting his connections with Jewish work he hangs on. He is after all a sentimentalist who has not the heart to spurn an old love of his." [56] Magnes, however, waited only for a propitious moment to resign. Meanwhile, he chaired executive committee meetings and conventions, addressed Kehillah gatherings, and participated in all policymaking decisions. No other Jew in New York could have continued to hold the chairmanship of the Kehillah under these circumstances, Bernard Semel, a distinguished figure in the immigrant community, told a meeting of the executive committee in December of 1919. Semel's tribute did not, however, change the fact that Magnes ceased being an asset to the Jewish community the moment he became a dissident in the greater, American community.[57]

The burden of administration passed to the shoulders of Samson Benderly, chief of the Kehillah's Education Bureau. From the beginning of 1917 until the fall of 1919, it was he who directed the major effort to revamp the organization.[58]

Henceforth, the 1917 convention decided, the Kehillah would devote its energies to one central task: the creation of a "mighty Jewish public opinion" which would shape the course of communal development. How can we find out from the one and a half million Jews of New York what kind of community they want? This was the question, according to Benderly, to which the Kehillah had to address itself in the months ahead. The first step to be taken was the removal of the encumbrances to the search for new forms. We noted earlier how the convention had voted to detach the bureaus and establish them on an independent basis. No longer saddled with bureau finances or with controversies connected with their operation, so the argument had gone, the "democratization" of the Kehillah would proceed apace.[59]

From June, 1917, until January, 1918, when a special convention was convened, Benderly used his staff at the Bureau of Education to prepare the plan of reorganization. The major phase of this preparatory work consisted of a comprehensive, demographic, economic, and institutional survey of New York Jewry. This massive 1,600-page inventory, published as the *Jewish Communal Register*, represented for Benderly and his young proteges the application of scientific method to the building of the "Good Community." Members of this circle, like Alexander Dushkin and Julius Drachsler, considered themselves social engineers providing the data and analysis which assured rational action. Once the Jewish public knew its liabilities and assets, Meir Isaacs, a Bureau staffman, wrote in the *Register*, its "communal consciousness" would awaken, and it would create the "well-ordered, well-organized Jewish community." Isaacs echoed the social philosophy of his progressive elders. The *Register*, Magnes wrote to Schiff, "will be an indispensable factor in helping us understand and create and guide the Jewish public opinion without which the community must always be an unorganized mass of diversified units." [60]

When Benderly presented his plan to the special convention, the delegates had the *Register* before them with its graphs, tables, maps, and diagrams. It contained, he noted in his opening address, information on 3,697 organizations (for an estimated 300 more, data were unobtainable). For the first time, Benderly claimed, the community had a reliable estimate of its strengths and weaknesses. The *Register* revealed, for example, that Jews had spent in 1916 a total of $17,-657,000 for local Jewish purposes alone. Yet for every dollar so expended, coordinating and research institutions had received only one cent. An elaborate population study estimated that the city contained one and a half million Jews. (The research staff then went further. It reduced these figures to neighborhood statistics, correlated them with the number and type of local institutions, and projected boundaries for viable subcommunities.) The communal portrait that emerged confirmed well-known facts about the prevailing situation: on the one hand, institutional complexity and confusion, parochialism, and extreme decentralization; on the other hand, the existence of vast resources and an abundance of communal weal.[61]

The blueprint of reorganization, which also appeared in the *Register*, contained two radical proposals for democratizing the Kehillah. The first suggested decentralizing the Kehillah's structure by dividing the city into eighteen districts (each with its local board) and subdividing the districts into one hundred neighborhoods. The second recommendation proposed a new category of membership. Along with its constituency of organizations, the Kehillah would also recruit individuals. (The city contained 300,000 Jewish families: surely the Kehillah could enroll 100,000 members and charge them a one-dollar communal tax, Benderly declared.) These notions were given institutional form in a perplexingly elaborate electoral system, which few at the convention fully understood, despite Benderly's long lecture and use of visual aids.[62]

The central feature of the system dealt with the methods of selecting the 550 delegates to the annual convention. By means of parallel electoral procedures on a neighborhood, district, and city level, Benderly endeavored to give fair weight to central organizations, local societies, and individual members of the Kehillah. The plan also established the structure and governing procedures for the neighborhood and district units.[63]

While Benderly translated the new emphasis into bureaucratic terms, Mordecai Kaplan discussed its substance. Heretofore, he explained, the Kehillah had united within itself two forces, one financial, the other moral. In establishing the Federation of Philanthropies, the community's leaders had, in fact, made it the repository of "financial power" and left the development of "moral power" to the Kehillah. Moral power could be exercised only through the instrumentality of a great body of public opinion which depended upon, Kaplan contended, individuals becoming "communally minded." Indeed, the emphasis on soliciting individual membership—the 100,000

Benderly spoke of—touched the essence of the reorganization scheme. Joining the Kehillah would now entail a deliberate act on the part of the individual. It represented recognition of the existence of a Jewish communal polity. Though not explicitly stated, Kaplan's formulation placed the didactic obligation above all others. One had to be "won over" to kehillah and inculcated with a "sense of community." (Months later, Benderly remarked that in the course of the membership drive many found it difficult to "grasp the meaning of kehillah." Every campaign worker, therefore, "had to be not only a soliciter but also a teacher.") [64]

In brief, Kaplan postulated a kehillah movement whose major assignment was preaching the gospel of community. The more conversions, the sooner a new consensus would arise and transcend partisan groupings. Eventually the Kehillah-as-consensus—the crucible of Jewish public opinion—would monitor the vast institutional activity of the community, including that of the Federation of Philanthropies.

During the spring of 1918, all district boards were nominally established. In fourteen districts, assemblies met and elected a total of 840 delegates, who represented 547 organizations. "It was an inspiring sight," Benderly reported, "to see the new life, the new thought." But few had any conception of neighborhood needs. Most had "never discussed anything but their own synagogue or their own school or their own relief society or lodge, and for the first time they came together to discuss the whole life of their district." In May, the membership drive took place. Twelve hundred volunteers, mostly young people, enrolled 17,000 members. Benderly had hoped for better results. But following closely upon "the more concrete human appeals of War Relief, Charity, and Liberty Bonds, the appeal of the Kehillah seemed abstract and far off." Finally, the end of May, Kehillah individual elections took place. The vote by mail brought a return of 7,000. June 1, 1918, the ninth and largest convention of the Kehillah opened at Carnegie Hall.[65]

Once again, as in 1917, the gathering afforded the Jewish group an opportunity to publicly declare itself (and, from the tone of the proceedings, to clear itself). Jacob Schiff offered the loyalty resolution in the name of delegates "representing large numbers of Jews in the eighteen Kehillah districts of New York City." Marshall extolled the manner in which the city's Jewish youth had responded to the call to national service. They had exhibited the same spirit as that "possessed by the sons of those who landed on Plymouth Rock." As a result of a careful investigation, moreover, the AJC was now able to prove that "our contribution to the Army and Navy of the United States is greater in proportion than that of any other part of our population." For those who had doubted the loyalty of the American Jew, "these facts will prove how unjustly we have been maligned and misjudged." Friedlaender, who praised Britain's Palestine policy, concluded his address by linking Zionist aspirations with American doctrine. To us, he said in his peroration, "Palestine represents the same ideals for which our country, for which the United States, is fighting for, . . . ideals of justice and righteousness, the ideals that right stands above might, that spirituality stands above materialism." [66]

That the demonstrative function of the convention outweighed all other considerations became immediately apparent. For the first time, a major figure of the Jewish labor movement, Joseph Schlossberg, addressed a Kehillah convention. His theme was "The Jewish Workman and an Organized Jewish Community." Two or three conventions before, the episode might well have been celebrated as a turning point in the community's development. His talk, however, went unreported in the press. Nor did Magnes' address receive coverage. By the time the Kehillah chairman's turn came, the hour was too late for more than a brief review of the organization's activities. Measured on the scale of a Carnegie Hall opening, Kehillah matters obviously did not seem newsworthy.[67]

In two working sessions on the following day, the convention—under Benderly's management—approved a set of extravagant objectives. The feasibility of the "democratic plan of representation," he explained at great length, had been satisfactorily tested. The next phase included achieving the goal of 100,000 members, increasing the number of affiliated organizations to 1,000, raising a sum of $200,000, and establishing the local districts on a sound basis. ("Representation without taxation is as unfair as taxation without representation," Benderly commented.) The delegates accepted the goals as well as a series of resolutions which called for the publication of a monthly journal, the creation of a department of speakers, the opening of district information centers, and the formation of standing committees in each district for religious affairs, philanthropy, recreation, education, legislation, correctional affairs and more, each committee to have a paid secretary.[68] Thus Benderly completed his theoretical construction of a kehillah, convinced that his quotas and tables of organization would move sensible men to activate the group's latent resources.

But like so much of Benderly's work, the plan was utopian rather than practical, inspirational rather than operational—hence misleading and injurious. The *Tageblat* captured something of the incongruity of the situation when it noted that fewer delegates than at the opening, and none of the uptown notables, attended the business sessions. A "strange listlessness" marked the deliberations. They were "colorless" and "cold." When a motion was submitted to discuss the Kehillah's activities during the past year, it was roundly defeated.[69]

Nevertheless, the balance sheet of the Kehillah in June, 1918, though unfavorable, did include assets of consequence. There were Kehillah stalwarts like Bernard Semel, William Fischman, and Samuel Rottenberg, the affluent and moderate men who headed the immigrant community's most important institutions. Benderly's dedicated and able staff, though unsettled by the uncertainty which surrounded the Kehillah and the Education Bureau, was still available. Friedlaender, Kaplan, and Magnes carried intellectual weight, and they still preached Kehillah. Finally, the cumulative effect of nine years of activity constituted a claim to survival. But June, 1918, was surely the moment least suitable for innovation and rash experimentation on so vast a scale. The grand convention, product of a year of preparation, merely underscored the Kehillah's infirmities.

The convention, in fact, was the last major undertaking of the Kehillah. At an executive committee meeting in May, 1919, Magnes conceded that none of the resolutions had been implemented. The eyes of New York Jewry were fixed elsewhere—on the ending of the war, on the peace conference, and on overseas conditions—and neither sufficient funds nor sufficient public interest were forthcoming. In the light of these circumstances, he recommended that a committee review Kehillah policies. Discussions continued for a year, with nearly ninety communal leaders participating. By the spring of 1920, four programs had crystallized, and these were presented to two well-attended conferences in April and May.[70]

The "minimum or secular program" excluded all "controversial questions," such as Jewish education and religious affairs. Combating anti-Semitism, Americanization, group relations, arbitration, and the gathering and disseminating of information, constituted the proposed fields of interest. Since the spring of 1919, a secretary for civic affairs had been handling problems of discrimination. The program's supporters therefore proposed, in essence, continuing the Kehillah's office as it was. A second program called for the reconstitution of the original "bureau-type" Kehillah. The discussion, however, centered on the two remaining plans.[71]

The first of these recommended devoting exclusive attention to Jewish education, which it defined as the single, most fateful issue in Jewish life. Once the education problem was in hand, in a decade's time perhaps, the Kehillah would extend its activities. Alexander Dushkin of the Bureau of Education, who formulated the plan, and Samuel Rottenberg, a lay leader and its sponsor, conceived of their "Kehillah-for-education" as the counterpart of the Federation of Philanthropies. The latter had made its mark by centralizing the raising of funds for major charities; the Kehillah would do the same for educational institutions. "Just as the Federation of Charities," Magnes summarized,

is an attempt to unite all kinds of philanthropic institutions dealing with the abnormal life of the Jews, with the sick, with the weak, with the defective, so this Kehillah might be a federation of all kinds of positive institutions among the Jews: all those forces interested in the spiritual life rather than in the material or . . . charity life of the Jews.[72]

Mordecai Kaplan prepared the fourth proposal which was presented to the conference under the rubric, "The Positive Kehillah Program." It alone, Magnes explained, established criteria for membership. Kaplan offered two tenets as tests for affiliation and as the basis for organization: a commitment to the continuity of Jewish group life in the Diaspora—understood in broad, cultural terms; and the acceptance of diversity as characteristic of Jewish communal life.

To the Kehillah he assigned the responsibilities of encouraging the establishment of social and cultural centers, promoting Jewish education, and fostering the celebration of Sabbaths and festivals. He also placed within its purview such social and economic problems as industrial disputes, anti-Semitism, and Jewish criminality. The Kehillah polity he conceived of as operating "on the lines of party"—"Orthodox, Reformed, Conservative, Radical, or any other party that may arise"—with each endeavoring to further the above program in its own way, cooperating where possible. Finally, Kaplan sought to lift the debate above bald institutional considerations. The plan to turn the Kehillah into an educational federation, the Rottenberg-Dushkin program, he attacked as conceptually unacceptable, for it focused only on the "child question of Jewish life." Hence it was a "distortion of the community idea." Moreover, Jewish education would bear fruit only if the entire communal climate changed. Educational efforts would succeed only if they were part of an integrated, all-inclusive Kehillah program.[73]

The version adopted by the second conference, in May of 1920, syncretized features of the four proposals. Grafted onto Kaplan's programmatic statement with its listing of "spiritual aims" and "civic aims" were the ideas of a separate educational federation, of associations of "like-minded" groups operating within the Kehillah, and of departments for civic affairs, industrial relations, religious affairs, education, and organization. The conference also set the figure of $35,-000 as the minimum sum needed for the first year of operation. As proof of intent, delegates pledged half that amount before the meeting closed.[74]

In June, 1920, Magnes tendered his resignation and requested that a small committee be appointed to act upon it. The recent conferences, he wrote, had convinced those who attended that "the Kehillah idea had taken deep root," and all indications pointed to a revival of Kehillah activity. The organization, however, required "new blood and new enthusiasm," and he himself was in a "rut." Now that current expenses were being met, he could in good conscience withdraw. (The Kehillah's income for 1920 amounted to $13,707; most of the sum derived from annual subscriptions channeled through the Federation of Philanthropies.) Furthermore, those public considerations which had dissuaded him from resigning during the war period no longer held.[75]

For nearly two more years, Magnes' resignation was held in abeyance. The tragic death of his close collaborator, Israel Friedlaender (murdered on a JDC mission in the Ukraine in July, 1920), and Benderly's temporary withdrawal from communal work, Magnes explained, necessitated postponing his final retirement. In the meantime he "warmed the chair of the chairman" and also eliminated nearly the entire indebtedness of the organization. However, the 1920 conference decisions, he remarked, remained dead letters.[76]

This appraisal of the situation was not entirely fair. The long period of consultation, negotiations, and conferences begun with such earnestness in 1919 did bear fruit, but in the form of a new agency which, in effect, superseded the Kehillah. The Jewish Education Association, formally established in late 1921, "to awaken the community conscience to the need of Jewish education," resembled in design and intent the Rottenberg-Dushkin plan of Kehillah. Although this program had not been adopted by the 1920 conference, the delegates nevertheless agreed that the "great need of the hour is a concentration of forces upon [the education] problem." The Kehillah, they declared should "lay special emphasis upon the need of an independent Educational Federation," since the problem was "in itself so large and so complicated." [77]

Thus the same circle of communal functionaries and lay leaders supported, in principle, two endeavors. For seven years, from 1910 to 1917, the group had poured its energies into the Kehillah, whose most notable achievement was its educational work. (Magnes often remarked that the creation of the Bureau of Education, by itself, justified the Kehillah.) Now parallel agencies existed. One—for education—promised a renewed, single-minded assault on the preeminent deficiency in American Jewish life: or so the Kehillah had been contending. The other agency, the Kehillah itself, lingered on—shorn, as many believed, of its *raison d'être*. In this situation it was not difficult to pay homage to the Kehillah idea, pray for its institutional restoration, and at the same time functionally support the Jewish Education Association. Magnes himself did precisely that; while "warming the Kehillah chair" and asserting that the organization would one day again embrace bureaus, boards, and associations, he served as chief promotor and behind-the-scenes negotiator in the creation of the Jewish Education Association.[78]

One other factor skewed the institutional alignment to the Kehillah's disadvantage. By 1919 the young career men of the Bureau of Education wielded considerable influence. They were "educational scientists" and administrators. They devised the programs and prepared the data which served as the basis for the discussions. As professional Jewish educators, moreover, they had a clear stake in maintaining and strengthening the central educational institutions of the community. In 1917 and 1918, Benderly had used them to revamp the Kehillah. That experiment had failed dismally. Now the young doctors of education, men like Alexander Dushkin and Isaac Berkson, reversed the priority and treated the Kehillah, at best, as an ancillary to the Bureau and the new Association.[79]

On April 30, 1922, the executive committee met for the last time in order to act upon Magnes' resignation. At the meeting he listed the Kehillah's assets: a tradition of Kehillah existed; the organization had a contributing membership and no debts; some agencies associated with the Kehillah or closely identified with it still functioned —the Milah Board, the Bureau of Industry, the Bureau of Education; nothing had replaced the Kehillah conventions, and their communal platform was sorely needed; the tie to the AJC could be turned, once again, to advantage. His own removal, Magnes felt, would bring salutary results: the overdependence on one person and the lingering effects of his position on the war would be eliminated. The meeting, which accepted his resignation, appointed a committee with instructions to form a "council of seventy." In May, 1922, Magnes and his family sailed for Europe and then Palestine. Planned as a trip for a year or two to find spiritual refreshment, they extended it for a lifetime. The Committee on Organization continued to function as an ad hoc executive. In 1925, this final remnant ceased to exist.[80]

§ CHAPTER ELEVEN §

The Limits of Community

IN 1908, WHEN THE ADVOCATES OF THE KEHILLAH USED THE BING-
ham incident to raise the spectre of "communal anarchy,"
they sounded an alarm which stirred a troubled Jewish public.
Striving for acceptance in the larger community yet committed to the preservation of its ethnic life, the Jewish group reacted in a variety of ways. Those who understood Police Commissioner Bingham's charge as a dangerous anti-Semitic attack—and they
were primarily the immigrant Jews—accepted the argument that
communal disunity had prevented an effective rebuttal and marred
their image as an upstanding and industrious group. Since all Jews
were vulnerable, the entire group had to support a body capable of
defending the Jewish name. Others, mostly uptowners, admitted the
existence of criminality. It was, they declared, a symptom of the social
disorganization of the immigrant quarter, and it called for an extraordinary communal effort. But more than the efficient organization
of the community was necessary, a group of young intellectuals
added. Social amelioration to be meaningful and enduring had to go
hand in hand with the promotion of a Jewish cultural revival and
the bolstering of the traditional values of Judaism. Thus spokesmen
of the Kehillah proposal plumbed the depths of the group's fears,
touched its sensitive defense mechanism, and appealed to its idealism.

The Kehillah's sponsors also employed a progressive rhetoric which legitimized the venture in American terms. The project promised to activate wide circles of the Jewish quarter, coordinate and expand its services, foster self-help, and absorb immigrants into the life of the community. Here was a civic contribution of the first magnitude. Moreover, the give and take of the democratic process led to "intelligent social action," to a high order of "enlightened self-discipline," and to "social efficiency." Thus democratic organization and "constructive social engineering," in Dewey's terms, or a combination of the "democratic method and the scientific method," as Magnes stated it, would enable New York Jewry to create an American kehillah.[1] These general objectives, the movement's leaders hastened to add, carried a workaday, pragmatic importance for the host of small, independent associations to whom the majority of Jews owed their first allegiance. The officials and constituencies of such institutions would benefit from a central agency able to provide services of specialists, and plan a more rational use of existing resources.

The protagonists of the Kehillah used these disparate arguments to induce a significant cross-section of the Jewish public to join the new venture. But their outstanding feat consisted of winning over the American Jewish Committee. Brilliantly, Magnes used downtown's tumultuous protests against the criminality charge to compel uptown to enter the Kehillah despite its fears that the organization would encourage self-segregation. Only if they affiliated, he warned the notables, might the volatility of the Jewish quarter be controlled and their own influence maintained. Without their wealth, prestige, and experience in public service no major communal undertaking could in fact have survived. Collaboration by Schiff, Warburg, Marshall, and Sulzberger, then, immediately transformed the Kehillah from a visionary scheme to a major enterprise.

Their joining the Kehillah carried additional significance. Affiliation, indeed sponsorship, changed their view of Jewish communal life. At the founding convention of the Kehillah, when AJC leaders united with moderate Russian-Jewish circles and champions of an American ethnic pluralism, they announced a long-range strategy which projected the establishment of a network of AJC-sponsored democratically-run, kehillahs. For the AJC, such a program promised the popular base needed to establish itself as the coordinating body of American Jewry. But the process was to be gradual and organic, guided by the combined wisdom of the elders of both segments of the community and executed in strict accord with American practice. Conceptually, these old-stock worthies were abandoning, at least for a time and undoubtedly for tactical reasons, a Protestant-congregational model of communal polity for a broadly functional, pluralistic structure. Instead of employing a confessional definition of Jewish identity, they were reluctantly acknowledging that an operationally useful definition had to embrace a group splintered by dogma, culture, localism, and class. To reach and, hopefully, to control the radical, the Orthodox, the Zionist, and the *landsmanshaft* Jew demanded a conception of community which coincided with the bounds of a multifarious ethnicity.

For a time the strategy succeeded. The Kehillah's service bureaus were promising enough to win the approbation of the community. In regard to education, the Kehillah could indeed claim some remarkable achievements. In other instances—as in the case of the industrial bureau's mediation activities and the rabbinical board's kashruth supervision efforts—limited or fleeting success did not disprove the need for these agencies nor invalidate their conceptual basis. And the annual conventions gave every indication of evolving into a popular tribunal for reviewing the community's needs and policies. True, the Kehillah had failed to encompass the majority of societies which made up the immigrant community. Some important patrician-supported institutions like the Educational Alliance had also remained aloof. Nevertheless, even judged by level of participation the achievements were notable. Represented at the 1915 convention were aproximately 10 to 15 percent of the total number of Jewish organizations in the city.[2] Kehillah leaders quite correctly claimed that member organizations embraced a high proportion of the larger institutions and that the delegates included the more influential leaders of the Jewish quarter. As the only body of its kind in the community, the Kehillah's weight exceeded the sum total of enrolled societies.

But the Kehillah did not fulfill its founders' goals. For the uptowners, it was to control the unruly ghetto. The "moneyed powers," Mordecai Kaplan wrote in his journal, were eager to maintain the status quo, and they were using the Kehillah, the Jewish Theological Seminary, and the Bureau of Education as "nothing but Jewish social pacifiers." [3] By 1917, an alternative to the Kehillah existed, one which it had, in fact, been instrumental in creating. The wealthy contributors now turned to the Federation of Jewish Philanthropies as a more convenient means of "social pacification." Russian-Jewish leaders also lost interest in the Kehillah as the gap between commitments and performance widened. Beginning in 1917, the Kehillah stood, shorn of its bureaus, unable to claim a mass following and overshadowed by the newly established Federation of Philanthropies. The grand design of the founders—the transformation of an amorphous public into an organic community—had not been realized.

First, the Kehillah was overwhelmed by the circumstances of the time. Its struggle for existence coincided with the high tide of Jewish immigration, the moment of New York Jewry's greatest fragmentation. In 1914, the mid-point of the Kehillah's life, probably the majority of Jews living in the city had been in the country less than ten years. Eager to prove the utility of the Kehillah, its leaders committed the organization to an unprecedented scale and range of activity, arousing expectations that all too often were disappointed. Orthodox rabbis, bewildered by the New World, supported the Kehillah, expecting to be invested once again with their traditional authority. Zionists battled at conventions to win majority votes for their policy proposals, only to be ruled out-of-order. And when scores of small, hard-pressed Talmud Torahs applied to the Kehillah's education bureau for relief, they were refused for lack of funds. Conceivably, had greater resources been available, the Kehillah might have provided the support and created the stable structure it promised—one sufficiently strong to contain even the dissenters. But though financial aid came from uptown, mass support from downtown failed to materialize. Yet at the same time, Russian Jews were devoting their resources to their local institutions and associations.

In part, the Kehillah's newness and its experimental quality explains downtown's reserve, for despite the immigrants' familiarity with traditional "kehillah," the New York version was different. The size of the Jewish community and the complexity of the questions it faced made collaboration difficult. The American idiom of the Kehillah's spokemen, moreover, further strengthened downtown's ambivalence. But perhaps most important, synagogues and fraternal orders with their Old Country attachments and benefits, and trade unions and social movements offering economic amelioration and intellectual satisfaction, already crowded the communal world of the immigrant Jews. Ardent party men and competing functionaries polemicised, organized, and kept the quarter in turmoil. In this setting, critics attacked the Kehillah as either irrelevant, utopian, or an uptown intrusion.

Granted this catalog of encumbrances and failures, the fact remains that during its early years the Kehillah did make headway. It defined the problems facing the community and laid the groundwork for meeting them. So long as a modicum of goodwill and stability existed, the Kehillah registered gains. But by the end of 1914 new issues agitated the community upsetting communal priorities and disturbing the power structure upon which the Kehillah depended. Time had run out.

The outbreak of war turned the attention of the Jewish public to the ordeal of European Jewry and soon a call for extraordinary measures persuaded people, hitherto quiescent or disaffected, to come forward and challenge the established leadership. The new group, mostly of Russian-Jewish origin and of a Zionist persuasion, joined the Jewish congress movement to contest the hegemony of the AJC. In the name of popular control and activism leaders like Brandeis, Wise, and Lipsky assailed the AJC for its "paternalism and timidity." They rejected its gradualism and mounted a bitter attack against the "tutelage of the grand moguls."

Could the Kehillah, the congress faction asked, maintain its democratic integrity while continuing to be tied to an oligarchic body? In 1915 when it moved its dispute with the AJC over the organization of Jewish communal life to the Kehillah convention, it recognized the fact that the Kehillah offered the one open forum where issues could be debated and a consensus of sorts recorded. For a triumphant moment it appeared as though the Kehillah had contained the quarrel and produced a compromise, only to have the agreement vetoed by the AJC. At the 1916 convention, when Magnes declared national issues out-of-bounds, he may have insulated the organization against an acrimonious debate (and saved the AJC from further embarrassment), but he also isolated the Kehillah from the critical issues of the time. He seemingly confirmed what critics were stressing, that the Kehillah was no more than an appendage of one party to the dispute. A key change had occurred in the Jewish community and with startling speed: the AJC's hegemony had been challenged, upsetting existing arrangments; the Kehillah's patron was no longer the informal but nonetheless uncontested arbiter of Jewish communal life.

The Kehillah had been caught, observers at the time explained, in the crossfire of a struggle between a patrician Old Guard and a rising immigrant community. And in no small measure their view was accurate. But other elements also exacerbated the situation and took their toll of the Kehillah. Jewish radicals, for example, regularly denounced the AJC as the class enemy and belittled the Kehillah as an uptown plot to dominate the Jewish quarter. In the controversy over the establishment of a Jewish congress these same radicals allied themselves with the AJC "plutocrats" (Nachman Syrkin called it "the unholy alliance between Hester Street and Wall Street").[4] The Congress party behaved no differently. It finally agreed to confine the Congress to the specific issue of formulating postwar demands for Jewish rights abroad and to disband once it fulfilled this function, a far cry from its declared purpose. In the first instance a common abhorrence for the Zionists who dominated the Congress party had brought the Jewish socialists and the AJC magnates together. The "democratic" faction, the Congress men, on the other hand, compromised their declared goals in order to reach an accommodation with the numerically insignificant but financially and politically powerful AJC. If the Zionists justified their action as heardheaded compromising, obviously for them the Kehillah in 1916 was not worth a similar sacrifice of principle. The one institution dependent upon the collaboration of all parties could hardly survive this brand of Realpolitik.

The crowning blow for the Kehillah was Magnes' withdrawal from active leadership. He had been, until the Congress issue forced him to choose sides, the mediator par excellence, the one public figure with an entree to all groups in the community. In the years prior to World War I, Magnes was, in all likelihood, the most popular figure in Jewish public life. To the Kehillah he had brought much goodwill, a considerable personal following, and a virtuosity of leadership which went far to lift the organization to the stand it reached. The Kehillah became his cause and remained inextricably bound up with him. His pacifism, therefore, dealt a double blow to the Kehillah, vitiating his effectiveness as chairman, and casting a heavy pall upon the organization with which he was so closely identified.

The total impact of the Congress controversy, the effect of the war on the community, and then Magnes' pacifism proved to be disastrous for a fragile institution. Yet though the Kehillah failed to achieve its primary objective of molding New York Jewry into a single, integrated community, it did leave behind a considerable legacy. Now a Federation of Philanthropies existed with a wider sense of communal responsibility. A Bureau of Jewish Education and a Jewish Education Association carried on the tradition of communal responsibility for education. Interest in community planning and research as well as in the training of professional communal workers had developed. And the Kehillah had raised disciples. The young college men who had been induced by Benderly to make a career of Jewish education held key positions in the community. They were in turn raising up another generation of disciples. These products of the Kehillah idea continued to work for community collaboration despite the lack of a formal framework.

The Kehillah left its impress in other ways as well. It had provided a common meeting ground for the leaders of New York Jewry in all its ethnic, social, and ideological diversity. Cyrus Sulzberger described well the Kehillah's efforts to bring "some semblance of order" to the community. With just a touch of exaggeration, he wrote in 1915:

See, now, what a few years have wrought. The conventions of the Kehillah bring together the most varied assemblage of Jews that can be imagined. Side by side with the extremest orthodox—men with long beards and side curls, men who not for a moment have their heads uncovered—are members of the most reformed temples. Rich men and men practically penniless; extreme socialists and extreme conservatives gather together and under parliamentary methods discuss the subjects they have in common.[5]

The convention addresses of Louis Marshall, Magnes' state-of-the-community messages, the debates on the activities of the Kehillah's

bureaus, the parliamentary maneuverings, and the elections to office
—all gave the participants a broader view of the community and
more tolerant understanding of each other. For the immigrant leaders, the Kehillah democracy also provided a prime education in
American civics. It contributed to their quick assimilation of American ideology which included, significantly, learning the limits of ethnic community.

Magnes defined these limits in his remarks to the special convention of the Kehillah in January, 1918:

The European notion of a uniform, . . . all-controlling . . . kehillah
cannot strike root in American soil . . . because it is not in conso-
nance with the free and voluntary character of American religious, social,
educational, and philanthropic enterprises. . . . The only power that
the kehillah can exercise is moral and spiritual in its nature, the power
of an enlightened public opinion, the power of a developed community
sense.[6]

One had to agitate for community, then, by persuading individuals to
affiliate with the organized communal body; joining entailed an act of
personal self-identification. In the early days of the Kehillah
movement, the emphasis had been different. Magnes had assumed
the existence of an ethnic solidarity which, grounded in the group's
minority experience and the national-religious quality of Judaism, led
to collective responses to outside threats. He had proposed channeling these group sentiments into the creation of an integrated community—the Kehillah. Its utility and reasonability, he believed, would
bring the institution stability and recognition. This process fitted his
understanding of the thrust of American society, which he saw as
evolving into a "republic of nationalities." But in the declining period of the Kehillah, Magnes came to understand that under the free
conditions of American life, ethnicity was but one of many attachments shared by group and individual. Only some leaders would
continue the elusive pursuit of "organic community." Indeed,
Magnes' coworker in the Kehillah, Mordecai Kaplan, would make
this goal a central feature of his philosophy of Jewish life. But most
Jews remained interested in the minimum of separation from the
larger society necessary for maintaining their Jewish identity. They
would be content with a more modest vision of community.

Notes

Abbreviations Used in the Notes

AH	*American Hebrew*
AJA	*American Jewish Archives*
AJHQ	*American Jewish Historical Quarterly*
AJYB	*American Jewish Year Book*
ANAD	*American Newspaper Annual and Directory*
ARK	*Annual Reports to the Convention of the Jewish Community (Kehillah) of New York City*
CUOHP	Columbia University Oral History Project
Globe	*New York Globe and Commercial Advertiser*
HS	*Hebrew Standard*
JC	*Jewish Charities*
JCD	*Jewish Communal Directory*
JCR	*Jewish Communal Register*, New York, Kehillah (Jewish Community), 1917–1918
JE	*Jewish Education*
JHI	*Journal of the History of Ideas*
JPAS	Jewish Protectory and Aid Society
JSS	*Jewish Social Studies*
JT	*Jewish Teacher*
MA	Judah L. Magnes Archives, Jewish Historical General Archives, Jerusalem, Israel

Min ACK   Minutes of the . . . Annual Convention of the Kehillah

Min BDEA   Minutes of the Board of Directors of the Educational Alliance (microfilm), 1908–1916, YIVO Archives, New York

Min CCJC   Minutes of the Constituent Convention of the Jewish Community of New York City

Min ECK   Minutes of the Executive Committee of the Kehillah

Min JCC   Minutes of the Joint Conference Committee of Twenty-Five and the New York City Members of the American Jewish Committee

MJ   *Morgen Journal*

NEA   National Education Association

PAJHS   *Publications of the American Jewish Historical Society*

Tageblat   *Yiddishes Tageblat*

YIVO Annual   *YIVO Annual of Jewish Social Science*

Notes

I. THE TRADITION OF COMMUNITY

1. In addition to Handlin's *The Uprooted*, see his *American People*, pp. 58–72; "Historical Perspectives," in *Daedalus*, pp. 220–32; and "Immigration in American Life," in *Immigration and American History*, pp. 11–25. See also Glazer, in *Freedom and Control*, pp. 158–73; Gordon, pp. 105–14, 132–36; Fitzpatrick, pp. 5–15; Vecoli, pp. 404–17; Park and Miller, pp. 119–32.

2. Baron, I, 25–27; Elbogen, pp. 439–40; Bentwich, pp. 95–96.

3. Magnes, *Emanu-El Pulpit*, II, 1–10; III, 10. For brief statements on the intellectual climate of progressivism, see Wiebe, pp. 145–63; Mowry, pp. 17–37; Hofstadter, *Age of Reform*, pp. 176–86, 202–14, 241–44, 257–71; Hays, pp. 71–115; Clarke A. Chambers, pp. 201–4. White's *Social Thought in America* is a full-length treatment of the intellectual history of the period. For the functional expression of progressivism most relevant for the Kehillah leaders, see the discussions on the settlement house movement, charity movement, and social efficiency in Bremner, pp. 131–39, 149–53; Yellowitz, pp. 40–70; Cremin, pp. 58–75; Allen F. Davis, pp. 8–39, 84–94; Samuel Haber, pp. 77–82, 93–98.

4. Baron, I, 242–82, 348–74; Jacob Katz, *Tradition and Crisis*, pp. 11–28, 43–111, 157–244; Dubnow, I, 103–31, 188–98, 262–78.

5. Levitats, *Jewish Community in Russia*, pp. 31–68, 105–39, 147–72, 178–207, 218–40, 246–67; Dubnow, I, 366–71; II, 18–22, 59–66, 190–98, 206–14, 247–58, 265–69, 276–80, 324–33; Greenberg, I, 63–72; II,

19–58, 141–54, 160–69, 172–81; Pinson, in *JSS*, pp. 234–64. For examples of such developments within individual communities, see Shatsky, III, 27–67, 110–91, 351–405; Hershberg, I, 41–153, 249–268, 272–76, 318–27; II, 28–53, 74–95; Perlow, pp. 20–24, 28–34, 47–52, 71–72, 101–2, 173–75; Mahler, pp. 20–28, 50–52; Israel Cohen, pp. 333–57.

6. Kober, pp. 196–201, 211–15, 220–22; Wilhelm, pp. 47–53; Weinryb, pp. 113–26; Gartner, in *Journal of World History*, pp. 301–8; Glanz, *Jews in the Cultural Milieu*, pp. 26–48, and in YIVO *Annual* (1956–1957), pp. 15–23.

7. Rischin, *Promised City*, pp. 51–53; Supple, pp. 143–66; Handlin, *Adventures in Freedom*, pp. 78–79; Glazer, *American Judaism*, pp. 46–56; Elbogen, p. 344.

8. Rischin, *Promised City*, pp. 96–97; *AJYB* (1900–1901), p. 358; Rosenstock, pp. 31–32.

9. Rischin, *Promised City*, pp. 98–104; Nevins, pp. 13–14, 35; Adler, in *AJYB*, pp. 44–45; *Times*, Aug. 27, 1930, p. 21; Hirsh and Doherty, pp. 116–17; *AH*, Apr. 26, 1912, p. 782; Sulzberger, pp. 226–27; Lurie, *A Heritage Affirmed*, pp. 37–42; Gartner, in *Conference on Acculturation*, pp. 14–16.

10. Adler, in *AJYB*, pp. 21–29, 48–49; Waldman, p. 323.

11. Stein, pp. 15–36; Lurie, *A Heritage Affirmed*, pp. 62–64; *AH*, Oct. 9, 1903, pp. 675–76; *Fifty Years of Social Service*, pp. 66–69; Bogen, *Jewish Philanthropy*, pp. 226–31; Adler, *Jacob H. Schiff*, I, 292–93, 360–61, 393; Wischnitzer, pp. 30, 48, 50; Rubinow, pp. 111–22.

12. Oppenheim, pp. 32, 40–42; Laidlaw, pp. 52–53, 243, 292; Joseph, *Jewish Immigration*, pp. 43, 95, 117; Dushkin, in *JCR*, pp. 87–89; Rosenstock, pp. 14–15; Rischin, *Promised City*, pp. 93, 270.

13. Rischin, *Promised City*, pp. 64–67; Pope, pp. 49–53, 61–70; Hyman Berman, "Era of the Protocol," p. 18; Markens, pp. 151–52; Joel Seidman, pp. 33–34.

14. Rischin, *Promised City*, pp. 56–57, 68–69, 73; Isaac M. Rubinow, "Economic and Industrial Condition: New York," in Charles S. Bernheimer, ed., *The Russian Jew in the United States*, pp. 104, 106–21.

15. Rischin, *Promised City*, pp. 124–27, 151–68; Herberg, pp. 12–15, 25–30; Bloom, pp. 63–68.

16. Alexander M. Dushkin, *Jewish Education in New York City*, p. 189; B. Rivkin, "Di sotziale role fun di landsmanshaftn," in Rontch, pp. 68–108; Rischin, *Promised City*, pp. 64–65, 182–83; Handlin, *Adventure in Freedom*, pp. 114–15.

17. Handlin, *Adventure in Freedom*, 144–51, 191–201; Panitz, in *AJHQ*, LII (Dec. 1963), 118, 125–30; Rischin, *Promised City*, pp. 95–98.

18. Schachner, pp. 7–28; Reznikoff, pp. 18–25; Lipsky, pp. 34–35; Rogoff, p. 24; Szajkowski, in *JSS*, p. 14.

19. *AH*, Dec. 20, 1907, p. 173; May 8, 1908, pp. 7, 13; Margoshes, *JCR*, 1328–35; *JCD*, pp. 56, 63, 66; *AH*, May 18, 1906, pp. 777, 785; May 25, p. 813; June 8, p. 860; Moshe Davis, *Emergence of Conservative Judaism*, pp. 322–26; Rischin, *Promised City*, pp. 239–40; Dawidowicz, in *JSS*, pp. 102–25.

20. *AH*, Jan. 25, 1907, p. 311; Friedlaender, *Past and Present*, pp. 274–78, 399–422; Moshe Davis, in *YIVO Annual*, IX, 9–12; Shapiro, "Leadership of the American Zionist Organization: 1897–1930," pp. 23–59, 86–96.

II. THE EMERGENCE OF THE KEHILLAH MOVEMENT

1. *Tageblat*, p. 1; *Warheit*, p. 4; *Forward*, p. 1; *MJ*, p. 8.

2. *North American Review*, CLXXXVIII (Sept. 1908), 383–94. Bingham introduced his statistics on crime to prove the need for a secret service specially trained to deal with foreign-born criminals; see *ibid.*, Oct. 1908, pp. 639–40 and *Times*, Sept. 17, 1908, p. 16.

3. *American*, Sept. 2, 1908, p. 16; Sept. 14, p. 1; Sept. 16, p. 6; Sept. 18, p. 16; *Evening Post*, Sept. 16, 1908, pp. 1, 4; *Globe*, Sept. 2, 1908, p. 1; Sept. 3, p. 2; Sept. 4, p. 5; Sept. 8, pp. 3, 6; Sept. 16, p. 1; Sept. 17, p. 6; *Times*, Sept. 2, 1908, p. 6; Sept. 7, p. 5; Sept. 11, p. 8; Sept. 16, pp. 8, 16; Sept. 17, p. 16; Sept. 18, p. 16; *World*, Sept. 1, 1908, p. 7; Sept. 3, p. 6; Sept. 7, p. 6; Sept. 15, p. 3; Sept. 16, p. 20; Sept. 17, p. 7.

4. Syrett, pp. 296–97; *Warheit*, Sept. 2, 1908, p. 4; Sept. 3, p. 4; Sept. 4, p. 1; Sept. 13, p. 1; Sept. 15, p. 1; Sept. 17, pp. 1, 4; *Tageblat*, Sept. 2, 1908, p. 1; Sept. 3, p. 1; Sept. 4, p. 1; Sept. 16, p. 1; Sept. 17, p. 4; *Forward*, Sept. 4, 1908, p. 4; Sept. 17, p. 4; *MJ*, Sept. 2, 1908, p. 4; Sept. 4, p. 1.

5. *Tageblat*, Sept. 2, 1908, p. 4; Sept. 4, p. 6; Sept. 7, p. 4; *Warheit*, Sept. 2, 1908, p. 4.

6. The count is based upon statements appearing in the English and Yiddish press; see nn. 3 and 4.

7. *Tageblat*, Sept. 6, 1908, p. 6; *World*, Sept. 7, 1908, p. 6; *Times*, Sept. 7, 1908, p. 5; *Warheit*, Sept. 7, 1908, p. 1.

8. Sarasohn Papers: Publishers, *Jewish Daily News* [*Yiddishes Tageblat*], to Hon. George B. McClellan, Sept. 4, 1908.

9. *American*, Sept. 14, 1908, p. 1; *World*, Sept. 15, 1908, p. 3; Sept. 16, p. 20; *Forward*, Sept. 14, 1908, p. 1; *Tageblat*, Sept. 14, 1908, p. 1; *Warheit*, Sept. 14, 1908, p. 1.

10. *Globe*, Sept. 2, 1908, p. 1; *World*, Sept. 3, 1908, p. 6; *Federation Review*, II (Apr. 1908), 15; II (June 1908), 3, 4; II (July 1908), 3.

11. For a number of years Lauterbach was president of the board of trustees of the City College of New York, and from 1895 to 1898, chairman of the Republican County Committee of New York; see *Times*, Mar. 5, 1923, p. 15. It is noteworthy that Lauterbach was a member of the AJC's seventy-man general committee but not of its thirteen-man executive committee.

12. *Tageblat*, Sept. 3, 1908, p. 4; *Maccabean*, XV (Oct. 1908), 150. For an analysis of the *Maccabaean's* view of the American Jewish Committee and its "undemocratic" behavior, see Naomi Cohen, in *JSS*, pp. 166–69.

13. *Warheit*, Sept. 2, 1908, p. 4; *Tageblat*, Sept. 3, 1908, p. 4.

14. *AH*, Sept. 4, 1908, p. 419.

15. *AH*, Sept. 11, 1908, p. 444.

16. *Tageblat*, Sept. 14, 1908, p. 4.

17. *MJ*, Sept. 4, 1908, p. 1; Sept. 6, p. 14; Sept. 8, p. 4; Sept. 18, p. 4; Shifman, in Gladstone, Niger, and Rogoff, pp. 64–65.

18. Bardoness to Magnes, Sept. 8, 1908, in Gorenstein, *YIVO Annual*, pp. 208–10. See also: *American*, Sept. 5, 1908, p. 7; *Forward*, Sept. 4, 1908, p. 1; Sept. 6, p. 1; *Tageblat*, Sept. 4, 1908, p. 1; Sept. 6, p. 6; *Warheit*, Sept. 6, 1908, p. 1; Richards, in *Zukunft*, pp. 84–85. The Jewish League had been in existence only a short time; see *HS*, Aug. 21, 1908, p. 6. On Barondess see: Magidoff, pp. 55–62; Julius Haber, pp. 45–56; Epstein, *Profiles of Eleven*, pp. 111–34. On Blaustein's role in Jewish communal affairs see: Blaustein, pp. 33–65, 80–85; Bogen, pp. 231–36.

19. *Forward*, Sept. 6, 1908, p. 1; *Tageblat*, Sept. 6, 1908, p. 6; Barondess to Magnes, Sept. 8, 1908, in Gorenstein, *YIVO Annual*, pp. 208–9.

20. *Warheit*, Sept. 7, 1908, p. 1; Lipsky, in *HS*, Jan. 10, 1913, p. 3.

21. Barondess to Magnes, Sept. 8, 1908, in Gorenstein, *YIVO Annual*, pp. 209–10; *Times*, Sept. 7, 1908, p. 5.

22. *Warheit*, Sept. 7, 1908, p. 1.

23. The Dorf, Rosalsky, Goldfogle position should be viewed against the background of the controversies which led to the formation of the American Jewish Committee two years before. That debate was widely followed and was still fresh to the participants of the Clinton Hall meeting; see Schachner, pp. 9–28.

24. Barondess to Magnes, Sept. 8, 1908, in Gorenstein, *YIVO Annual*, p. 210.

25. Judge Rosalsky, a leading opponent of the Barondess plan during

the conference, later announced his support; he pledged himself to reintroduce the proposals before the conference committee. *Warheit*, Sept. 7, 1908, p. 1.

26. *MJ*, Sept. 8, 1908, p. 4; *Warheit*, Sept. 7, 1908, p. 4; *Tageblat*, Sept. 7, 1908, p. 4.

27. *Tageblat*, Sept. 13, 1908, p. 4; Blaustein, p. 83.

28. Schiff to Abelson, Sept. 6, 1908, Abelson Papers; Marshall to Radin, Sept. 8, 1908, Marshall Papers.

29. *Tageblat*, Sept. 13, 1908, p. 1; *Forward*, Sept. 13, 1908, p. 1; *Warheit*, Sept. 13, 1908, p. 1; Marshall to Woods, Sept. 15, 1908, Marshall to Magnes, Sept. 15, 1908, Marshall to Schiff, Sept. 18, 1908, in Gorenstein, *YIVO Annual*, pp. 210–12.

30. *Times*, Sept. 17, 1908, pp. 16, 17; Sept. 18, p. 16; *Tageblat*, Sept. 16, 1908, p. 1; *Forward*, Sept. 17, 1908, p. 1; *Warheit*, Sept. 17, 1908, p. 1.

31. *Tageblat*, Sept. 18, 1908, p. 6. The letter was later published in *AH*, Sept. 25, 1908, p. 502. The quotations are from this English version, which was most likely the original draft of the letter.

32. *Tageblat*, Sept. 18, 1908, p. 6.

33. *Ibid.*

34. *Times*, Sept. 18, 1908, p. 16.

35. For Magnes' career from his arrival in New York in 1903 until the founding of the Kehillah in 1909, see Bentwich, *For Zion's Sake*, pp. 32–75. See also: Waldman, pp. 392–95; Lipsky, *A Gallery of Zionist Profiles*, pp. 175–80; Lipsky, *Thirty Years of Zionism*, pp. 23, 35–36; interview with Bernard G. Richards, June 24, 1959 and Apr. 10, 1965; Rubenovitz, pp. 22, 24–25.

36. Interview with Mrs. Judah Magnes, Mar. 12, 1964, June 17, 1964, Jerusalem; interview with Baruch Zuckerman, Apr. 9, 1959, Jerusalem; interview with Benjamin Koeningsberg, Dec. 1, 1964, New York; Richards, CUOHP, pp. 9–10; Moshe Davis, in *Mordecai M. Kaplan Jubilee Book*, pp. 159–71; Bentwich, *For Zion's Sake*, pp. 48–50. Sixty-six letters from Schechter to Magnes, from Sept. 1906 to Aug. 1911 (MA, SP 62) reflect their relationship. In two letters, Mar. 25, 1908 and Mar. 31, 1908, Schechter criticized Magnes for representing the Zionists at the Gershuni memorial meeting. See also: Julius Haber, *Odyssey*, pp. 52–54; Richards, in *Zukunft*, pp. 82–83; Shpizman, I, 152–54; Parzen, *JSS*, pp. 243–46, 248–50, 261–62.

37. *Times*, Dec. 5, 1905, p. 6; *AH*, Dec. 8, 1905, pp. 62, 73; *AH*, Jan. 31, 1908, p. 334; Feb. 7, p. 351; *Warheit*, Jan. 30, 1908, pp. 1, 4; *Forward*, Jan. 30, 1908, p. 1; Julius Haber, *Odyssey*, pp. 58–59; Marshall to Schiff, Feb. 14, 1908, in Reznikoff, II, 836–38; Schiff to Marshall, Mar. 5, 1908, Marshall Papers.

38. Barondess to Magnes, Sept. 8, 1908, in Gorenstein, *YIVO Annual*, pp. 208–10. Magnes also aided Barondess in organizing the Zionist fraternal order, Sons of Zion; see Bentwich, *For Zion's Sake*, p. 63.

39. *General Jewish Conference, An Appeal to the Jewish Organizations of New York City to send Delegates to a Conference to be held at Clinton Hall, October 11th, and October 12th, 1908, 8 P.M.* (New York, [Sept. 1908], leaflet in Marshall Papers). Nissim Behar also signed the *Appeal*. Though executive director of the rival Federation of Jewish Organizations, he participated in the committee but later disclaimed membership in it. The *Appeal* was also printed in Yiddish; see *Idishe organization fun new york, oifruf zu der konferentz* . . . , MA, F48— L135; the text also appeared in *AH*, Oct. 2, 1908, p. 535.

40. *Ibid.; Warheit*, Sept. 22, 1908, p. 4; Sept. 28, p. 2; Oct. 6, p. 4; Oct. 9, p. 4; *Forward*, Sept. 18, 1908, p. 1; *Tageblat*, Sept. 23, 1908, p. 1; Oct. 1, p. 4; *Globe*, Sept. 30, 1908, p. 5; *Preliminary Draft of Constitution of the Jewish Organization of New York* (leaflet in the Archives of YIVO Institute, New York).

41. *Tageblat*, Oct. 1, 1908, p. 4; published later in *AH*, Oct. 2, 1908. The quotation is from the English text in *AH* which is most likely the original.

42. *AH*, Oct. 16, 1908, p. 583; *Tageblat*, Oct. 12, 1908, pp. 1, 4; Oct. 13, p. 1; Oct. 14, p. 4; *Warheit*, Oct. 12, 1908, p. 1; Oct. 13, p. 4; *MJ*, Oct. 12, 1908, p. 1; Oct. 13, p. 1; *HS*, Oct. 16, 1908, pp. 4, 8.

43. For the platform of the Federation see: *In Protest of Restrictive Immigration Legislation, Official Program, Mass Meeting, Cooper Union, June 4, 1906* (Federation of Jewish Organizations of the State of New York). See also: Szajkowski, in *PAJHS*, p. 406–36; *AH*, May 18, 1906, pp. 777, 785; Oct. 16, 1908, p. 587; *Maccabaean*, XV (Oct. 1908), 17; interview with Hyman Reit, Nov. 23, 1964. The Federation claimed four hundred affiliated organizations in 1907 (*AJYB* [1907–1908], p. 331).

44. *AH*, Oct. 16, 1908, p. 584. The wording was the same as the paragraph, "Purpose and General Duties," in the *Preliminary Draft of Constitution* which was presented to the opening session and tabled.

45. The *Globe* quoted Drachman as demanding a vote on his amendment so that all might see "whether delegates representing two hundred Jewish societies will be willing to vote to kill the Jewish religion." Oct. 13, 1908, p. 4. See also *AH*, Oct. 16, 1908, p. 584; *Tageblat*, Oct. 13, 1908, p. 1.

46. *AH*, Oct. 16, 1908, p. 584; *Maccabaean*, XV (Nov. 1908), 213.

47. *Tageblat*, Oct. 14, 1908, p. 4; Bernard Semel, secretary, Jewish Organization of New York, n.d., MA, F48–L135; *AH*, Oct. 23, 1908, p. 615.

III. THE FOUNDING CONVENTION

1. Magnes to Dr. Herbert Friedenwald (secretary, AJC), Oct. 6, 1908, MA, F1–L62. The absence of the prominent uptown Jews was a matter of wide comment. See: *Warheit*, Oct. 12, 1908, p. 1; *MJ*, Oct. 12, 1908, p. 1; *Maccabaean*, XV (Nov. 1908), 185. On the evening of October 12 the board of directors of the Educational Alliance met (Minutes, Oct. 12, 1908, YIVO Archives). Louis Marshall and others from uptown invited to Clinton Hall attended the Educational Alliance meeting. On Schiff's letter to the conference, see *AH*, Oct. 16, 1908, p. 583; Marshall's letter has been published in Reznikoff, I, 31–35. In the letter Marshall defended the AJC against the criticism of undemocratic behavior and criticized Magnes for encouraging separatism by emphasizing the East Side character of the meeting. He undoubtedly had in mind Magnes' letter in the *Tageblat* calling on the "Great East Side" to organize itself.

2. Reznikoff, I, 35–37 (published originally in the *AH*, Jan. 15, 1909, p. 282).

3. *AH*, Feb. 2, 1906, pp. 345–48; May 25, 1906, pp. 805–6; Naomi Cohen, in *JSS*, pp. 166–69.

4. *AH*, Nov. 13, 1908, p. 43, Jan. 15, 1909, pp. 282, 288; *AJYB* (1909–1910), p. 241.

5. Memorandum of a Tentative Agreement, Oct. 31, 1908, Marshall Papers; Marshall to Magnes, Nov. 2, 1908, MA, SP30; *AJYB* (1909–1910), pp. 253–54; *AH*, Nov. 13, 1908, p. 43; Min JCC Dec. 1 and Dec. 14, 1908, Jan. 13, and Feb. 18, 1909, MA, F48–L135. MA, F1–L62, contains three drafts of the constitution, apparently the revisions made by the successive meetings.

6. Draft of Constitution, MA, F1–L62. See also Tentative Memorandum of Apportionment of Delegates, MA, F1–L62; Min JCC, Dec. 1, 1909, MA, F48–L135. For criticism of the articles on representation, see *Forward*, Mar. 5, 1909, p. 5.

7. Min JCC, Feb. 18, 1909, MA, F48–L135.

8. *AH*, Dec. 25, 1908, p. 207; Feb. 19, p. 430; *Tageblat*, Feb. 28, 1909, p. 1; *Warheit*, Mar. 3, 1909, p. 4; *Forward*, Mar. 5, 1909, p. 5; Zuckerman, in *Yiddisher Kempfer*, pp. 44–46. See also: Min CCJC, Feb. 27–29, 1909, MA F48–L135; Mendes to Magnes, Jan. 20, 1909, MA, SP34.

9. *HS*, Dec. 11, 1908, p. 6.

10. *AH*, Oct. 9, 1908, p. 560.

11. Min JCC, Feb. 18, 1909, and Dec. 1, 1908, MA, F48–L135.

12. Magnes, *Emanu-El Pulpit*, II, 5.

13. *Ibid.*, pp. 5–6.
14. *Ibid.*, p. 7.
15. *Ibid.*, p. 8.
16. *Ibid.*, p. 10.
17. The Rev. Frederick Lynch, pastor of Pilgrim Church, in a sermon, "Christians and Jews in New York City: A Warning," said shortly after the establishment of the Kehillah: "Our Hebrew friends are continually complaining of being treated as a race apart and yet they often seem to be doing their best to separate themselves from the rest of the community." *Times*, Apr. 19, 1909, p. 9.

Magnes replied: "The Jews have the right and duty to organize themselves into as strong a body as is possible. They must be organized both for the sake of their Judaism and for the sake of the country in which they live. Their Judaism requires of them that they be a race apart. . . . The destruction of historic races is . . . not the highest conception of the future in America. [The Rev. Lynch] might consider the possibility of a variety of races dwelling peacefully together, and each of them contributing its share to the sum total of American culture."

After expressing these nationalist, separatist sentiments, Magnes shifted to the religious component of his definition of Judaism. "Judaism, as the religion of a minority of the people, must, as must any other minority religion, have minority interests. . . . We Jews shall continue to insist upon the rights of Judaism just as we trust that Christians may insist upon the rights of Christianity." *Evening Post*, Apr. 26, 1909, p. 7.

To which Lynch replied: "If Rabbi Magnes thinks, as he seems to, that as a race Italians, Irish, Jews, or any other foreign race can be at the same time foreigners and Americans, he will find it can not be in America. . . . One cannot be a Jew (except in religion) and a real American at the same time." *Globe*, May 8, 1909, p. 8. For a favorable non-Jewish view of the establishment of the Kehillah, see *The Survey*, Aug. 21, 1909, pp. 694–95.

18. The Cincinnati *American Israelite*, spokesman for Reform Judaism, described the Kehillah as advancing "that crazy nationalism which is the latest form of Jewish hysteria." The Kehillah's leaders were "unsafe men of narrow, distorted views . . . without understanding of the proper relation of a religious community to the American nation." Mar. 11, 1909, p. 4.

19. *Tageblat*, Jan. 28, 1909, p. 4; *AH*, Jan. 29, 1909, p. 337; untitled brochure, Jan. 14, 1909, MA, F48–L135. On the problems of contacting groups see: Marshall to Dr. Herbert Friedenwald, Jan. 14, 1909 and Marshall to Magnes, Jan. 30, 1909, Marshall Papers. A "propaganda committee" is mentioned and a person may have been hired to visit organizations (*AH*, Mar. 5, 1909, p. 468). This could not have altered the situation materially.

20. *AH*, Jan. 29, 1909, p. 337.

21. *Ibid.*, Mar. 5, 1909, p. 467; *AJYB* (1909–1910), p. 47; *MJ*, Feb. 28, 1909, p. 1.

22. On Moskowitz, see Schapiro, pp. 446–49; *Times*, Dec. 18, 1937, p. 23.

23. Magnes, *The Jewish Community; AH*, Mar. 5, 1909, p. 467.

24. Magnes, *The Jewish Community; Tageblat*, Feb. 29, 1909, p. 1; *AH*, Mar. 5, 1909, p. 467.

25. Min CCJC, Feb. 27–28, 1909, MA, F28–L135; *Tageblat*, Feb. 28, 1909, p. 1; *AH*, Mar. 5, 1909, p. 467.

26. Min CCJC, Feb. 27–28, 1909, MA, F48–L135.

27. *AH*, Mar. 5, 1909, p. 468; see also *Tageblat*, Feb. 28, 1909, p. 1.

28. Min CCJC, Feb. 27–28, 1909, MA, F48–L135; *AH*, Mar. 5, 1909, p. 468; *Tageblat*, Feb. 28, 1909, p. 1.

29. Min CCJC, Feb. 27–28, 1909, MA, F48–L135; *AH*, Mar. 5, 1909, p. 468; *Warheit*, Mar. 1, 1909, p. 4; Mar. 3, p. 4; Mar. 14, p. 4.

30. *AH*, Mar. 5, 1909, p. 468.

31. *Tageblat*, Mar. 1, 1909, p. 1; *Warheit*, Mar. 1, 1909, pp. 1, 4; *Wochenblat*, Feb. 12, 1909, p. 6; *Times*, Mar. 1, 1909, p. 16; *AH*, Mar. 12, 1909, p. 463.

32. Marshall to Schechter, Mar. 4, 1909, Marshall Papers.

33. *AH*, Mar. 5, 1909, p. 469; see also the *Maccabaean*, XVI (Jan., 1909), 3; *HS*, Mar. 5, 1909, p. 8; *Warheit*, Mar. 1, 1909, p. 1.

34. *Maccabaean*, XVI (Mar. 1909), 111; Min CCJC, Feb. 27–28, 1909, MA, F48–L135.

35. *MJ*, Mar. 7, 1909, p. 1; *AH*, Mar. 12, 1909, p. 493. The constitutional provision is Article IV, *Constitution of the New York Jewish Community (Adopted Feb. 28, 1909)*. The Constitution was also published in *AJYB* (1909–1910), pp. 50–54.

36. *Tageblat*, Mar. 28, 1909, p. 1; Minutes of the Meeting of the Jewish Community, Mar. 27, 1909, MA, F48–L135; *Globe*, Mar. 29, 1909, p. 3; *Times*, Mar. 28, 1909, p. 11.

37. *AH*, Apr. 2, 1909, p. 569; Vote for the Executive Committee, Jewish Community of New York, Mar. 27, 1909, MA, F48–L135. For the Miller vote, see copy in Marshall Papers. The five members of the AJC's executive committee who were on the ballot placed among the six highest on the list. They were Schiff, Magnes, Marshall, Joseph H. Cohen, and Sulzberger. Cohen was a Russian Jew. See also *MJ*, Mar. 28, 1909, p. 4.

38. *AH*, Apr. 2, 1909, p. 569; Drachman, pp. 206–8, 275–80.

39. *Globe*, Mar. 29, 1909, p. 3; *Times*, Mar. 28, 1909, p. 11. On Wise's earlier favorable attitude, see *Free Synagogue Pulpit*, I, Dec. 1909, and Min CCJC Feb. 27–29, 1909, MA, F48–L135. In later years

Wise vigorously opposed the attempt of the Kehillah to procure a charter from the New York legislature (*AH*, Apr. 12, 1912, p. 730).

40. *Globe*, Mar. 1, 1909, p. 7; *Dos Yiddishe Folk*, Feb. 26, 1909, p. 4; Mar. 5, p. 4; *Times*, Feb. 28, 1909, p. 6; Richards, CUOHP, pp. 14–20.

41. Samuel Dorf, "To the Officers and Members of Your Worthy Lodge," Feb. 8, 1909 (brochure in English and Yiddish), Marshall Papers.

IV. POLITY, PHILANTHROPY, AND RELIGION

1. *4th ARK*, Apr. 12 and 13, 1913, p. 8; Magnes, address, opening of the Constituent Convention of the Jewish Community of New York, Feb. 27, 1909, Marshall Papers.

2. Richards, in *American Zionist*, LV, 17.

3. Min ECK, Apr. 17, 1909, MA, F1–L62; Magnes to executive committee of the Kehillah, June 3, 1920, MA, F41–L49.

4. Min ECK, Apr. 17, 1909 and Apr. 12, 1910, MA, F1–L62; Min ECK, Jan. 14, 1913 and Aug. 11, 1914, MA, F48–L159.

5. Min ECK, May 11, 1909 and June 9, 1909, MA, F1–L62; Magnes, *What the Kehillah Has Given*, pp. 11–14.

6. Magnes, address delivered at dinner in honor of Herbert L. Lehman, Mar. 8, 1915, MA, F17–L231; Bureau of Education, Staff, 1915, MA, F28–L36; Min 7th ACK, June 3 and 4, 1916, MA, F2–L1a.

7. Min ECK, Apr. 12, 1910, MA, F1–L62; Min ECK, May 12, 1914, MA, F46–L22b; Min ECK, May 3, 1917, MA, F10–L31. Magnes, Address to meeting of delegates of the Kehillah, Jan. 24, 1915, MA, F17–L231; Magnes, *Plan of Jewish Communal Organization in New York City*, Apr. 24 and 25, 1915, (pamphlet), MA, F48–L148.

8. Min 6th ACK, Apr. 24 and 25, 1915, MA, F28–L7; Min 7th ACK, June 3 and 4, 1916, MA, F2–L1a; *MJ*, Feb. 26, 1911, p. 1; Apr. 29, 1912, p. 8; *Maccabaean*, XXII (Dec. 1912), 188.

9. Magnes, Address to meeting of delegates of the Kehillah, Jan. 24, 1915, MA, F17–L231.

10. *MJ*, Feb. 21, 1911, p. 4.

11. Min ECK, May 11, 1909, MA, F1–L62; Min ECK, Aug. 10, 1909 and Sept. 14, 1909, MA, F48–L155; Min ECK, Jan. 11, 1910, MA, F48–L156; Min ECK, June 9, 1910, MA, F1–L62; Min ECK, Oct. 8, 1912, MA, F10–L6; Magnes, address, opening of the Constituent Convention, Feb. 27, 1909, Marshall Papers.

12. Dr. Samson Benderly to Magnes, July 13, 1914, MA, SP156; Felix Warburg to Magnes, July 14, 1914, MA, F48–L120. Aaron E. Nussbaum, the treasurer-designate, brother-in-law of Julius Rosenwald,

promised $5,000 to the General Education Fund (Benderly to War-burg, June 23, 1914, MA, SP156). Two years later Nussbaum con-tributed $1,000 to the Kehillah (Report of Finance Committee, Apr. 11, 1916, F48–L162); see also: Nussbaum to Magnes, Nov. 9, 1915, MA, F29–L114.

13. Magnes to Daniel Guggenheim, Feb. 16, 1916, MA, F30–L4.

14. Min ECK, Jan. 11, 1910, MA, F1–L62, Min ECK, Sept. 9, 1912, MA, F1–L27; Min ECK, Nov. 12, 1912, MA, F10–L7; Min ECK, May 12 and Sept. 8, 1914, MA, F46–L22b; Min ECK, Mar. 3 and 14, 1916, MA, F28–L98; Min 7th ACK, June 3 and 4, 1916, MA, F2–L1a; Report of the Committee on Organization and Propaganda, William Liebermann, chairman, n.d., MA, F7–L96.

15. Magnes to Lehman, Apr. 27, 1915, Lehman to Magnes, Apr. 30, 1915 and Magnes to Lehman, Nov. 19, 1915, MA, F28–L83; Min ECK, Nov. 9, 1915, MA, F28–L103. Together with Jacob Wertheim, retired president of the United Cigar Company, Lehman shared the financial burdens with Magnes until he resigned a year later; see Chairman [Lehman], Finance Committee to Executive Committee, Apr. 11, 1916, MA, F48–L162; Financial Committee Report, Min 7th ACK, June 3, 1916, MA, F2–L1a; Min ECK, Dec. 12, 1916, MA, F7–L59.

16. Lipsky, in *Maccabaean*, pp. 185–88; Min 7th ACK, June 3 and 4, 1916, MA, F2–L1a.

17. See, for example, *Tageblat*, Apr. 28, 1912, p. 1; Apr. 29, p. 2; Apr. 25, 1915, p. 1; Apr. 26, p. 1; May 24, p. 1; *MJ*, Apr. 28, 1912, p. 4; Apr. 29, p. 4; *AH*, Mar. 4, 1910, pp. 455, 458; June 9, 1916, pp. 140–43, 148, 150–51.

18. Cf. membership lists of the executive committee, ARK, 1910–1914; *JCR*, p. 72. Most changes were due to resignations for reasons of ill-health or "other obligations."

19. Magnes, *What the Kehillah Has Given*, pp. 8–10.

20. *Ibid.*, p. 15.

21. 3d *ARK*, Apr. 27 and 28, 1912, p. 10.

22. Lurie, A *Heritage Affirmed*, pp. 34–58.

23. Min 5th ACK, Apr. 25 and 26, 1914, MA, F48–L160. See also *Jewish Charities*, II (May 1912), 21.

24. *AH*, Jan. 22, 1909, p. 317. The institutions were Montefiore Home, Mount Sinai Hospital, Hebrew Benevolent and Orphan Asylum Society, Hospital for Chronic Invalids, Educational Alliance, Home for Aged and Infirm Hebrews, and United Hebrew Charities.

25. *Ibid.*, Apr. 9, 1909, p. 605.

26. Waldman, pp. 388, 390.

27. 3d ARK, Apr. 27 and 28, 1912, pp. 10–11; see also: 4th ARK, Apr. 12 and 13, 1913, pp. 17–18; *Jewish Charities*, II (Dec. 1911), 3.

28. The primacy given to Jewish education is the most striking ex-

ample of the social and cultural emphasis and is discussed in chapters 5 and 6. See also Cyrus Sulzberger's presidential address before the National Conference of Jewish Charities, *Jewish Charities*, IV (May 1914), 15.

29. Min ECK, May 9 and Sept. 12, 1911, MA, F1–L58; Min ECK, Jan. 14, 1913, MA, F48–L159. The employment office was transferred to the Bureau of Industry in 1915 and is discussed in chapter 9.

30. Min ECK, Sept. 9, 1912, MA, F1–L27; *4th ARK*, Apr. 12 and 13, 1913, pp. 13, 15–16; Min ECK, Aug. 11, 1914, MA, F48–L159; *JCR*, p. 647, 1339.

31. *Times*, Aug. 1, 1914, p. 16; Aug. 4, p. 4; Aug. 5, p. 4; Aug. 7, p. 11; Aug. 30, p. 10; Sept. 27, p. 8; Min ECK, Aug. 11, 1914, MA, F48–L159; Magnes to Sulzberger, Aug. 7, 1914, MA, F46–L59; Charles Dushkind to Magnes, Aug. 11, 1914, MA, F46–L59. The four banks were Adolf Mandel, Max Kobre, M. and L. Jamulowsky, and Deutsch Brothers. Meyer Jarmulowsky was a member of the executive committee of the Kehillah.

32. Minutes of Meeting at Office of Louis Marshall, Aug. 10, 1914, MA, F46–L59. (Among those present were Schiff, Herbert Lehman, Albert Bing, Joseph H. Cohen, and Israel Unterberg.) Magnes to Eugene Lamb Richards, Aug. 11, 1914, MA, F46–L59; Announcement No. 3, Depositors Protective Committee, Aug. 18, 1914 and, Statement, Depositors Protective Committee, Oct. 16, 1914, MA, F46–L59.

33. Depositors Protective Committee, Aug. 31, 1914, MA, F46–L59; Magnes to Harris Mandelbaum, Aug. 18, 1914, MA, F46–L59; Mandlebaum to Magnes, Sept. 4, 1914, MA, F46–L59; Magnes to Sulzberger, Mar. 16, 1915, Mortimer Schiff to Sulzberger, Mar. 16, 1915, Daniel Guggenheim to Sulzberger, Mar. 18, 1915, and Sulzberger to Felix Adler, Mar. 22, 1915, MA, F46–L23.

34. Report of the Committee on Plan and Scope of the Bureau of Philanthropy and, Minutes of the Advisory Committee of the Bureau of Philanthropic Research, Feb. 16, 1916, Abelson Papers; *JCR*, pp. 1160–62; Minutes of the Meeting of the Bureau of Philanthropic Research, Apr. 11, 1916, Apr. 26, 1916, Oct. 17, 1916, and Report of the Advisory Committee of the Bureau of Philanthropic Research on the Plan for Federation, MA, F2–L136.

35. Waldman to Magnes, Mar. 4, 1914 and Apr. 3, 1914, MA, F17–L251; Magnes to Cyrus Sulzberger, May 27, 1914, MA, F2–L72; Magnes to Warburg, Nov. 1, 1915, MA, F28–L97b; *5th ARK*, Apr. 25 and 26, 1914, pp. 18–19, 61.

36. *5th ARK*, Apr. 25 and 26, 1914, p. 18.

37. Magnes to Sulzberger, May 27, 1914, MA, F2–L72.

38. Magnes to Warburg, Nov. 1, 1915, MA, F28–L97b; Min BDEA, Oct. 11, 1915 and Dec. 13, 1915.

39. *AH*, Mar. 26, 1909, p. 551; William Salomon to Magnes, Mar. 23, 1916, MA, F30–L4; Min BDEA, Dec. 13, 1915. In 1912 when the Kehillah sought incorporation by the legislature, Stephen S. Wise and Lee Kohns joined hands with Greenbaum and Jacob Saphirstein, publisher of the *Morgen Journal*, to prevent passage of the bill. The title— "Jewish Community of New York City"—they claimed, was a misnomer since the Kehillah represented in fact "a very small percentage of the Jewish population of New York." Saphirstein warned that the uptown Jews would use the state charter bearing so inclusive a name to control Orthodox institutions. In 1914, the Kehillah submitted a bill for incorporation substituting "the Kehillah of New York City" for "Jewish Community of New York City." The bill passed the legislature and was signed into law. *AH*, Apr. 12, 1912, p. 730; Mar. 27, 1914, p. 623; Reznikoff, I, 37–38; Louis Marshall to Hon. Henry W. Pollak, Jan. 15 and Apr. 24, 1913, and Louis Marshall to Jacob Saphirstein, Jan. 23, 1913, Marshall Papers.

40. Min BDEA, Dec. 13, 1915.

41. Goldwasser, pp. 114–16, 118–19, 122, 134–35, 141–42.

42. Min ECK, May 10, 1916, MA, F48–L162; Min 8th ACK, Apr. 29, 1917, MA, F18–L33.

43. Goldwasser, pp. 116, 125–26, 135, 139–41; JCR, pp. 1304–11.

44. Goldwasser, pp. 142, 146; Kaplan Journal, Sept. 15, 1915.

45. 7th ACK, June 3 and 4, 1916, MA, F2–L1a; JCR, pp. 1163–65; Waldman, pp. 452–53, 455; Brief Summary of the History and Activities of the School for Jewish Communal Work, c. 1919, MA, F13–L112; Kaplan Journal, Sept. 15, 1915; Bogen, *Jewish Philanthropy*, p. 252.

46. Summary of School for Jewish Communal Work, MA, F13–L112; Minutes of the Administrative Committee of the School for Jewish Social Work, June 13, 1917, and Paul Abelson to Max Pine (manager, United Hebrew Trades), Nov. 5, 1917, Abelson Papers; Winter, pp. 90–92.

47. Summary of School for Jewish Communal Work, MA, F13–L112.

48. Waxman, pp. 3–13; Rischin, *Promised City*, pp. 145–48.

49. A Kehillah census in 1917 counted 503 synagogues on the lower East Side and 71 more operated only on the High Holy Days (JCR, pp. 122, 145). On the various factions, see [Isaac Allen], Answers to Questions on Kashruth [c. 1915], MA, F46–L24; Benjamin Koeningsberg to Magnes, May 26, 1915, MA, F29–L134.

50. Karp, pp. 129–87.

51. Monroe Goldstein (counsel, National Desertion Bureau) to Magnes, Apr. 5, 1914, MA, F46–L25; Min ECK, Oct. 8, 1912, MA, F10–L6.

52. Min ECK, Dec. 12, 1911, MA, F48–L158; Marshall to Magnes, July 24, 1912, MA, F46–L18; Min ECK, Nov. 17, 1913, and Aug. 11, 1914, MA, F48–L159; Dr. Moses Hyamson, "The Milah Board of the Jewish Community," *JCR*, pp. 324–25.

53. Jeremiah J. Berman, *Shehitah*, pp. 83–132.

54. *JCR*, p. 319; H. Pereira Mendes, Suggestions for the Organization of Jewish Ritual Affairs in New York City by the Kehillah [c. Nov. 1909], MA, F1–L48. See also Williams, pp. 20–24.

55. J. Berman, *Shehitah*, pp. 49–72, 141–55, 167–69, 170–207.

56. [Allen], Answers to Questions on Kashruth, MA, F46–L24; Isaac Allen to Magnes, Oct. 15, 1915, MA, F46–L24.

57. Allen to Magnes, Oct. 15, 1915, MA, F46–L24.

58. [Allen], Answers to Questions on Kashruth, MA, F46–L24; "A Few Remarks in Kashruth," *JCR*, pp. 312–19; interview with Isaac Allen, Jan. 20, 1965. On various strikes and boycotts, see *MJ*, June 11, 1912, p. 5; June 14, p. 1; June 24, p. 1; May 26, 1918, p. 1; *Times*, Dec. 24, 1914, p. 1; *Forward*, July 21, 1918, p. 1. On crime see especially material on the Barnet Baff murder: *Times*, Nov. 25, 1914, p. 1; Nov. 26, pp. 6, 12; Nov. 27, p. 1; Dec. 3, p. 7; Feb. 13, 1916, p. 1; Harold Seidman, pp. 187–88. E. B. Goodman, The Rule of Gangsters, Sept. 1913, Mitchel Papers, Location 196.

59. *4th ARK*, Apr. 12 and 13, 1913, p. 9.

60. Mendes, Suggestions for the Organization of Jewish Ritual Affairs, MA, F1–L48.

61. *Report fun di Kehillah*, Feb. 26, 1910, pp. 8–10; Min ECK, Feb. 8, 1910, MA, F1–L62.

62. Report of the Religious Committee, Feb. 8, 1910, MA, F1–L53b; [Allen], Answers to Questions on Kashruth, MA, F46–L24; interview with Isaac Allen, Jan. 20, 1965.

63. Min ECK, Jan. 10, June 13, and Oct. 10, 1911, MA, F48–L158; *3d ARK*, Apr. 27 and 28, 1912, p. 7.

64. On Reb Velvele, see *Der Tog*, Sept. 1, 1935, p. 1; *Times*, Sept. 9, 1935, p. 19; interview with Benjamin Koeningsberg, Dec. 1, 1964. Saphirstein was outraged at the Kehillah's attempt to arbitrate between himself and the Chief Rabbinate of England. The latter accused him of pirating an English edition of the prayerbook for the High Holy Days (Min ECK, Oct. 11, 1910, MA, F48–L156 and Jan. 10, 1911, MA, F48–L158); see also Y. Fishman, "Fir und fertzig yohr Morgen Journal," in Gladstone et al., pp. 62–66. On the meat speculators see: [Allen], Answers to Questions on Kashruth, MA, F46–L28 and J. Berman, *Shehitah*, p. 305.

65. *MJ*, Dec. 18, 1912, p. 4.

66. Min ECK, Jan. 10, June 13, and Oct. 10, 1911, MA, F48–L158; *3rd ARK*, Apr. 27 and 28, 1912, p. 7; Magnes to Walter Blumenthal,

Sept. 3, 1912, Magnes to Leo Joseph, Sept. 5, 1912, Magnes to Sulz-berg & Sons, Sept. 5, 1912, and Magnes to Edward Kohn, Sept. 6, 1912, MA, F1–L53a; Plan to New York Wholesalers to Standardize Kosher Meat Trade, MA, F1–L53b; interview with Bernard G. Richards, Apr. 10, 1965.

67. Magnes to Adler, Sept. 23, 1912, MA, F21–L7.

68. *4th ARK*, Apr. 12 and 13, 1913, pp. 9–10, 25; Min ECK, June 9 and Dec. 9, 1913, MA, F48–L159.

69. Min ECK, June 9, 1913, MA, F48–L159; *Times*, Dec. 6, 1916, p. 17.

70. Meeting at Ohab Zedek Congregation of Representatives of Orthodox Hebrew Congregations, Dec. 15, 1912, MA, F10–L15; Magnes to Jarmulowsky, Feb. 11, 1913 and Apr. 15, 1913, MA, F10–L15.

71. *5th ARK*, Apr. 25 and 26, 1914, p. 8–9.

72. Benjamin Koeningsberg to Magnes, May 26, 1915 and Jan. 14, 1916, MA, F28–L3; Min ECK, June 8 and Aug. 10, 1915, MA, F28–L108; J. Berman, *Shehitah*, pp. 304–5, 328–29.

73. Min ECK, Oct. 12, 1909, MA, F48–L155; Min ECK, Jan. 11, 1910, MA, F1–L62; Min ECK, May 9, 1911, MA, F1–L58; Min ECK, Dec. 10, 1912, MA, F10–L8; Min ECK, Jan. 14, 1913, and Aug. 11, 1914, MA, F48–L159; Min 7th ACK, June 2 and 3, 1916, MA, F2–L1a.

74. *4th ARK*, Apr. 12 and 13, 1913, p. 10; Min ECK, Sept. 14, 1909, MA, F48–L155; Min ECK, Oct. 10, 1911, MA, F1–L58; Min ECK, Oct. 13, 1914, MA, F46–L22b; Min ECK, Nov. 21, 1916, MA, F7–L60.

75. David de Sola Pool to Magnes, Feb. 1, 1912, MA, F47–L99; Minutes of Milah Board Physicians, Sept. 24 and Nov. 7, 1913, MA, F48–L131; Moses Hyamson, Report, Apr. 23, 1915, MA, F29–L142; *Methods to be Employed by Mohelim*, 1915 (Hebrew and Yiddish section entitled *Sefer habrith*, Rabbi Yaacov Eskolsky, ed.); Haven Emerson to Magnes, Nov. 24, 1916, MA, F29–L142; Hyamson, *JCR*, pp. 321–29.

76. Magnes to Sulzberger, May 29, 1914, MA, F48–L105; Min ECK, Aug. 11, 1914, MA, F48–L159; *Survey*, Apr. 18, 1914, p. 77; Aug. 28, 1915, p. 482.

77. Rabbi Samuel H. Glick (secretary of the Board of Rabbis) to Magnes, June 24, 1913, MA, F1–L53b; Min ECK, Aug. 14, 1913, MA, F48–L159; Memorandum of *Ghet* [divorce] Committee Meeting, Mar. 9, 1914, MA, F46–L25; B. H. Hartogensis to Magnes, Nov. 4, 1914, MA, F46–L25.

V. EDUCATION AS A COMMUNAL RESPONSIBILITY

1. Three studies deal, in part, with the Kehillah's Bureau of Education. Dushkin, *Jewish Education*, pp. 100–28; Scharfstein, *Toldot*, II, 200 ff.; Winter, pp. 65–99.

2. The fullest development of this view is that of Berkson, *Theories of Americanization*.

3. Cremin, pp. 66–75, 85–89; Magnes, *Emanu-El Pulpit*, II; Benderly to Magnes, Mar. 9, 1910, published in *JE*, XX (1949), 110–13.

4. Draft of a letter by Magnes to Schiff (c. Jan. 1910), MA, F1–L23.

5. Magnes, *Jewish Community*.

6. Dubnow, I, 114–31; Levitats, *Jewish Community in Russia*, pp. 69–86, 188–90; Baron, I, 356–60, II, 169–207; Gamoran, pp. 60–89, 104–21, 138–42; Greenberg, II, 141–47, 155–57, 172–73, 179–85; Scharfstein, *Toldot*, I, 362–85; Scharfstein, *Ha'heder*, pp. 52–59, 217–46.

7. Dushkin, *Jewish Education*, pp. 63–79; Jeremiah J. Berman, in *YIVO*, IX (1954), 272–75.

8. Min ECK, Sept. 14, Nov. 9, and Dec. 14, 1909, Jan. 11, 1910, MA, F1–L62; *Report fun di Kehillah*, pp. 10–12.

9. Some limited surveys had been done previously: Gartner, in *AJHQ*, LIII, 264–84, and Blaustein, p. 140. For contemporary response to the Kehillah study, see *MJ*, Feb. 27, 1910, p. 1; Feb. 28, pp. 1, 4; *Tageblat*, Feb. 27, 1910, p. 1; Feb. 28, p. 1.

10. Mordecai M. Kaplan and Bernard Cronson in *JE*, XX (1949), 113–16. See also, *AH*, Mar. 4, 1910, pp. 458–59. The estimated number of Jewish children of school age (6 to 16) was little more than a crude estimate. Kaplan used the figure 170,000. The figure of three-quarters unschooled did not take into account children who at one time or another attended a religious school. Few children went to religious school beyond their thirteenth year. The best statistics are those of Dushkin for the year 1916. For the ages 5 to 14, he arrived at a total Jewish population of 275,000. Of this total, 65,000 (23.5 percent) were receiving some kind of Jewish education. Dushkin, *Jewish Education*, pp. 152–56. On the heder in America, see Scharfstein, *Toldot*, II, 181–87; Dushkin, *Jewish Education*, pp. 211–17. Kaplan in his report acknowledged that there were some modern *hadarim*.

11. Konovitz, pp. 114–16; Benderly, in *JE*, XX (1949), 94; Dushkin, *Jewish Education*, p. 155; Masliansky, pp. 173–74; Handler, in *Sheviley hahinuch*, XXIII (Autumn, 1962), 40.

12. Kaplan and Cronson, in *JE*, XX, 115.

13. *Ibid.*, pp. 114–15. Seventeen "institutional schools" such as the

Educational Alliance, Hebrew Orphan Asylum, and Jewish Protectory, served 4,650 students. For the early development of these "institutional schools" as media for Americanizing the immigrant children, see Jeremiah J. Berman, in *YIVO*, IX, 253–71. Immigrants often sent their girls to these schools and the boys to the *hadarim*.

14. Kaplan and Cronson, in *JE*, XX (1949), 113–14; Scharfstein, *Ha'heder*, pp. 130–32.

15. Dushkin, *Jewish Education*, pp. 66–72; Scharfstein, *Toldot*, II, 187–90.

16. Kaplan and Cronson, in *JE*, XX (1949), 115; Benderly, A *Survey of the Financial Status*, pp. 8, 12.

17. Galician Jews predominated among the supporters of the downtown Talmud Torah, Russian Jews among supporters of the uptown Talmud Torah, and Lithuanian Jews among supporters of the Machzikey Talmud Torah.

18. Benderly, in *JE*, XX (1949), 110–12.

19. Kaplan and Cronson, *JE*, XX, 113–15; Konovitz, *Sefer Ha'yovel*, p. 118. Most Talmud Torah teachers taught from 4 to 8 P.M. on weekdays except for Friday. On Sunday they taught from 9 to 3 P.M. Each taught two classes. Thus the student attended class eleven hours a week. The eight largest Talmud Torahs in 1910 averaged eleven teachers a school and the remaining sixteen Talmud Torahs, five teachers per school. Benderly, A *Survey of the Financial Status*, pp. 5, 7.

20. Scharfstein, *Toldot*, II, 194–98; "Hamishim shnot hinuch yehudi b'amerika," *Sefer ha'yovel*, pp. 156–57.

21. Grinstein, in *PAJHS*, XXXV (1939), 61–62; Konovitz, *Sefer Ha'yovel*, pp. 131–32; Margolis, pp. 70–74; Min ECK, June 9, 1909, MA, F1–62.

22. *Tageblat*, Feb. 28, 1910, p. 1; *MJ*, Feb. 28, 1910, p. 1; *Times*, Feb. 28, 1910, p. 9; *AH*, Mar. 4, 1910, pp. 455–56.

23. Benderly to Magnes, Mar. 9, 1910, published in *JE*, XX, 110; Kaplan and Cronson, in *JE*, XX, 116.

24. *MJ*, Feb. 28, 1910, p. 1. When Magnes first approached Schiff prior to the convention, he suggested that the philanthropist establish a foundation like the Rockefeller Fund. Schools of a certain standard applying for subvention would receive aid. This approach was abandoned in favor of the idea of a bureau of education. Minutes of the Committee on Education, Apr. 18, 1910, MA, F1–L22.

25. Benderly to Magnes, Mar. 9, 1910, *JE*, XX, 111. At the first meeting of the education committee and later at the executive committee, a demand was made for direct aid to schools. Minutes of the Committee on Education, Apr. 18, 1910, MA, F1–L22; Min ECK, May 10, 1910, MA, F48–L156.

26. Benderly to Magnes, Mar. 9, 1910, *JE*, XX, 111–12.

27. *MJ*, Mar. 2, 1910, p. 4; *Tageblat*, Mar. 1, 1910, p. 4.

28. Min ECK, Apr. 12, 1910, MA, F1–L62a. Bluestone was a key figure of the oldest Russian Jewish Talmud Torah, Machzikey Talmud Torah. Rabbi Margolies was chairman of the education committee of the uptown Talmud Torah. Also on the committee were Isidore Hershfield, secretary of uptown Talmud Torah and an organizer of the Central Board of Talmud Torah schools, and Dr. Solomon Neuman, active in the downtown Talmud Torah. Margolies, Hershfield, and Neuman were not on Magnes' slate but were proposed from the floor.

29. Minutes of the Committee on Education, Apr. 18, 1910, MA, F1–L22.

30. Min ECK, Apr. 28, 1910, MA, F48–L156; Minutes of the Committee on Education, May 9, 1910, MA, F1–L22; *New York Foundation, Forty Year Report: 1909–1949* (New York, 1950), pp. 5, 57; Felix Warburg to Magnes, Apr. 25, 1911, MA, F1–L23. The contribution was for $5,000.

31. Min ECK, Sept. 22, 1910, MA, F1–L22; Minutes of the Board of Trustees, Nov. 29, 1910, MA, F1–L23. The committee of education retained jurisdiction over all other educational activities like the adult education program and the attempts to establish community centers. See Minutes of the Committee on Education, June 6, 1910, MA, F1–L22.

32. Friedlaender and Kaplan were members of the faculty of the Seminary. Marshall was chairman of the board of trustees. Szold and Magnes were socially and intellectually close to the Seminary's president, Solomon Schechter, and to members of the faculty. At the time of the establishment of the Bureau of Education, Schechter was abroad. He later opposed the Bureau. See also: Moshe Davis, *The Emergence of Conservative Judaism*, pp. 322–26; Sklare, p. 165.

33. Schechter, pp. 93, 101; Parzen, in *JSS*, XXIII (Oct. 1961), 246–64; Shapiro, "Leadership," pp. 86–96.

34. Rischin, in *PAJHS*, XLIX (Mar. 1960), 189–90.

35. The fear that so large a gift would carry undue influence of the donor was voiced by the Orthodox immediately after the Schiff gift was announced (*MJ*, Feb. 2, 1910, p. 4). The Orthodox opposition is discussed in ch. 6.

36. Benderly, *JE*, XX, 110; Minutes of the Committee on Education, Apr. 18, 1910, MA, F1–L22. Magnes read of Benderly's work in the Hebrew periodical *Hashiloah* in 1902 while a student in Germany. He later visited Benderly in Baltimore a number of times ("Tribute from Dr. J. L. Magnes, Aug. 13, 1944," *JE*, XX [1949], 4–5). One of Kaplan's first acts as principal of the Teachers Institute in 1909 was to visit Benderly's Baltimore school (Kaplan, "The Impact of Dr. Benderly's Personality," *JE*, XX, 16). Benderly's educational views were well known from an essay published in the Philadelphia *Jewish Exponent*,

Jan. 17, 1908 and reprinted in *JE*, XX, 80–86 ("Jewish Education in America"). See also Dushkin, in *JE*, pp. 6–7; Brickner, p. 53; Winter, pp. 31–38.

37. Dushkin, in *JE*, pp. 7–8; Brickner, pp. 56–57; Winter, pp. 38–44.

38. Benderly, *JE*, XX, 80–86.

39. *Ibid.*, pp. 81–82, 110–11.

40. *Ibid.*, p. 110; Winter, pp. 48–49.

41. Cremin, pp. 71–75; Rischin, *The Promised City*, pp. 199–200.

42. The Rabbi Jacob Joseph Yeshiva was established in 1903 and had about 500 students in 1910. Dushkin, *Jewish Education*, pp. 73–76, 95–96. Minutes of the Committee on Education, Apr. 18, 1910, MA, F1–L22.

43. Minutes of the Committee on Education, May 9, 1910, MA, F1–L22; Min ECK, Sept. 22, 1910, MA, F48–L156; Minutes of the Board of Trustees, Nov. 29, 1910, MA, F1–L23.

44. *MJ*, Oct. 10, 1910, p. 4. See also: *MJ*, Oct. 9, 1910, p. 4. For other friendly press reactions, see *Tageblat*, Oct. 9, 1910, p. 5, Oct. 16, p. 4; *AH*, Oct. 7, 1910, pp. 571–72, 578.

45. Minutes of the Board of Trustees, Nov. 29, 1910, MA, F1–L23.

46. *Ibid.*; Benderly to Magnes, Jan. 19 and Feb. 8, 1911, MA, F1–L23. When no printer would risk publication, Benderly ordered the textbooks printed on his own responsibility. He then asked Magnes to procure a commercial loan of $10,000 to finance the project. Magnes procured the loan from the National Committee for the Relief of Sufferers from Russian Massacres through Schiff, who was the treasurer. Min ECK, Feb. 14, 1911, MA, F48–L158. See also Mordecai Kaplan, in *JE*, XX, 18–19; Chipkin, in *JE*, XX, 21. The apprenticeship program is discussed in ch. 6. On Benderly's curriculum reforms, see Minutes of the Board of Trustees, Nov. 29, 1910, MA, F1–L23; Min ECK, May 9, 1911, MA F1–L58.

47. Benderly to Magnes, Feb. 8, 1911, MA, F1–L23. The study was published in the summer of 1911 as *A Survey of the Financial Status.* . . . On the principals' conferences, see Benderly, *Brief Survey of Thirty-One Conferences*; Handler, in *Sheviley Hahinuch*, XXIII, 38–46.

48. Benderly to Magnes, Feb. 8, 1911, MA, F1–L23.

49. Magnes to Schiff, Mar. 9, 1911 and Schiff to Magnes, Mar. 20, 1911, MA, F1–L23. Schiff at first made his contribution of $10,000 contingent on Magnes raising $90,000 and then lowered the requirement to $40,000 (Schiff to Magnes, Mar. 24, 1911 and Magnes to Schiff, Apr. 28, 1911, MA, F1–L23).

50. Magnes to Schiff, Mar. 23, 1911, MA, F1–L23. Magnes was thirty-four years old, Friedlaender and Benderly were thirty-five, and Kaplan was thirty.

51. Of the German Jews asked to contribute, Daniel Guggenheim

and Adolph Lewisohn refused. They later became heavy contributors. Lewisohn to Magnes, May 12, 1911 and Guggenheim to Magnes, May 22, 1911, MA, F1–L23. Magnes approached the Cloak and Suit Manufacturers Association through some of the Arverne group who belonged to the Association and through Louis Marshall, who, together with Schiff, had taken a prominent part in settling the 1910 cloakmaker's strike. Benderly to Magnes, Sept. 8, 1911, MA, F1–L23.

52. Warburg to Magnes, Apr. 25, 1911, MA, F1–L23; Complete List of Subscriptions to Education Fund, 1911–1912, 1912–1913, 1913–1914, MA, F46–L75. Eighty-four subscriptions came from members of the Cloak and Suit Manufacturers Association, 127 from the Arverne group (the primary fund-raising activity took place in Arverne in Aug. of 1911), and sixteen were from the German-Jewish group. Besides Schiff and Felix Warburg, the larger contributions came from Paul M. Warburg ($2,500), Jacob Wertheim ($1,000), Isaac N. Seligman ($1,000), I. M. Stettenheim ($1,500), William Fischman ($1,000), and J. H. Rubin ($1,000). The Baron de Hirsch Fund, controlled by German Jews, contributed $3,500 for one year.

53. Times, Jan. 31, 1912, p. 1; Tageblat, Jan. 31, 1912, p. 1; MJ, Feb. 1, 1912, p. 1; AH, Feb. 2, 1912, pp. 409, 418; Min ECK, Jan. 31, 1912, MA, F48–L158. The original subvention to the Bureau by Schiff and the New York Foundation amounted to $75,000 for five years. A $10,000 loan for text books was obtained. Of the $335,000 subscribed and borrowed, members of Kuhn, Loeb, and Company accounted for $162,000.

54. Times, Jan. 31, 1912, p. 1. The Society for the Advancement of Judaism should not be confused with the organization by the same name associated with Mordecai Kaplan and organized in the 1920s. The society associated with Magnes was created, essentially, to assure his salary. At the Society's annual meeting he would deliver a report on Jewish communal affairs. Magnes did not receive compensation from the Kehillah. The arrangement was formalized in 1913. He was then presented with a scroll that read: "for the next five years the sum of Ten Thousand Dollars per annum will be placed at [Magnes] disposal with the distinct understanding that this will be for his personal use and that of his family." The address was signed by Felix Warburg and Israel Unterberg, Apr. 1, 1913, MA, unclassified.

55. Maccabaean, XXI (Feb. 1912), 222. Magnes had resigned his position in Temple Emanuel in 1910 because the membership refused to accept his more conservative position on religious matters. He then occupied the pulpit of Congregation Bnai Jeshurun. For an account of his ministry, see Bentwich, For Zion's Sake, pp. 48–50.

56. Benderly to Magnes, Dec. 31, 1912, MA F10–L18; Minutes of the Board of Trustees, Feb. 20, 1913 and July 16, 1913, Friedlaender

Papers, Warburg to Benderly, June 11, 1914, MA, SP156; Magnes to Marshall, Mar. 12, 1915, MA, F10–L22; List of Contributors to the Education Fund, 1911–1916, MA, F2–L17; Complete List of Subscriptions to the Education Fund, Bureau of Education, MA, F46–L75; Deficit Account, Bureau of Education, for period from Oct. 1, 1910 to Jan. 31, 1916, MA, F28–L38; Textbook Fund, Bureau of Jewish Education, Jan. 31, 1916, MA, F28–L38.

57. Benderly, *JE*, XX, 106 and *Some of the Activities*, pp. 6–7; Minutes of the Board of Trustees, Nov. 29, 1910, MA, F1–L23; and Nov. 27, 1911, Friedlaender Papers; Sept. 19, 1913, MA, F10–L20; Benderly to Magnes, Dec. 31, 1912, MA, F10–L18; Textbook Fund, Jan. 31, 1916, MA, F28–L38. On the problem of textbooks for Jewish religious schools, see Aharon Klein, pp. 76–81.

58. Benderly to Schiff, Feb. 10, 1914, in Jerusalem p. 17; Minutes of the Board of Trustees, Mar. 28, 1912, Friedlaender Papers, Bureau of Education, Staff, 1915, MA, F28–L36; *5th ARK*, Apr. 25 and 26, 1914, p. 3; Dushkin, *Jewish Education*, p. 116; Scharfstein, *Arba'im shanah b'amerika*, pp. 156–58. The English weekly was called *The Jewish Child* and the Hebrew monthly was called *Shachruth*. Of those employed in the publication department, Simon and Pesach Ginzburg became Hebrew poets of note; Zevi Scharfstein became professor of education at the Teachers Institute of the Jewish Theological Seminary, a prolific writer and editor. Dr. Herman Seidel served for many years as president of the Labor Zionist Organization; Dr. Samuel Margoshes became editor of the Jewish daily, *Der Tog*; Dr. Alexander M. Dushkin edited *The Jewish Child* and later headed the Jewish Education Committee of New York; Maurice Samuel, the author, was a contributor to *The Jewish Child*. Benderly's success in attracting this caliber staff is discussed in ch. 6.

59. Scharfstein, in *Sheviley Hahinuch*, XIV (Sept. 1954), 208; Interview with Dr. Samuel Margoshes, Nov. 24, 1965. According to Margoshes and Scharfstein many left the Bureau and the field of Jewish education because of irregular salaries, especially as the younger men married and raised families; see also Benderly to Magnes, June 23, 1914, MA, SP156; Warburg to Magnes, June 15, 1914, MA, F48–L120; Benderly to Friedlaender, July 3, 1914, Friedlaender Papers; Dushkin *et al.* to Magnes, May 2, 1917, MA, F10–L22.

60. Szold to Friedlaender, Feb. 2, 1913, Friedlaender Papers; Szold to Benderly, Feb. 2, 1913, Friedlaender Papers. Marshall to Magnes, Mar. 13, 1914, MA, F48–L132.

61. Friedlaender to Magnes, Dec. 12, 1915, Magnes to Friedlaender, Dec. 27, 1915, MA, SP277. Magnes prevailed upon Friedlaender to remain as chairman. In 1916 Friedlaender again asked to be relieved of the chairmanship. Friedlaender to Magnes, June 5, 1916, Friedlaender

Papers. In a memo to the dormant board of trustees in 1918, Fried-laender presented a biting critique of the Bureau's management. Statement to Meeting of Trustees of the Board of Education, Apr. 6, 1918, Friedlaender Papers.

62. Lehman to Magnes, Apr. 30, 1915, MA, F28–L83; Min ECK, Nov. 9, 1915, MA, F28–L103; Magnes to Lehman, Nov. 19, 1915, MA, F28–L83; Min ECK, Dec. 12, 1916, MA, F7–L59. On one occasion Lehman wrote to Magnes: "I think it is of the highest importance that you shape the work of the Kehillah, not in accordance with your very proper aims and ideals, but with the available resources. . . . I have talked this matter over at great length and very seriously with Mr. [Jacob] Wertheim, Mr. Schiff, and Mr. Warburg, and we all agree that there would be very little encouragement in the situation if we could not confidently expect that in the future the expenditures of the Kehillah will be kept absolutely within its resources. I mention this at length and seriously, as I consider it of great importance." Mar. 2, 1916, MA, F28–L83.

63. Magnes to Schiff, July 14, 1915, MA, F46–L21b.

64. Mortimer Schiff explained that he was already contributing heavily to the Kehillah's employment bureau. Two years earlier he refused to contribute because the "East Side community" was not giving its share nor paying its subscriptions. Mortimer Schiff to Magnes, July 17, 1913, MA F20–L14. See also Magnes to Jacob Schiff, July 3, 1916, MA F31–L161.

65. Honor, in *Sefer hayovel*, pp. 347–48; interview with Isaac B. Berkson, Oct. 28, 1965.

66. Schiff to Friedlaender, Feb. 16, 1914, Friedlaender Papers.

67. Magnes to Warburg, Feb. 13, 1913, MA, F20–L139; Benderly, in *JE*, XX, 105.

68. Kaplan Journal, Oct. 4, 1914; Israel Friedlaender, *Past and Present*, pp. 269–278, 412–422; Friedlaender to Magnes, Apr. 7, 1910, MA, SP102; interview with Isaac B. Berkson, Oct. 28, 1965.

69. 3d ARK, Apr. 27 and 28, 1912; Louis Marshall to the Editor of the *American Israelite*, May 4, 1912, in Charles Reznikoff, pp. 41–42.

70. Lee Kohns to Friedlaender, June 4, 1914, Friedlaender Papers.

71. 3d ARK, Apr. 27 and 28, 1912, pp. 5–6.

72. Min 7th ACK, June 3, 1916, MA, F2–L1a.

73. Benderly, in *JE*, XX, 110.

74. Invitation to Mid-Day Club, May 29, 1914, MA, F48–L120; Statement of Committee [circa June 1914], MA, F46–L75.

75. Friedlaender to Lee Kohns, June 15, 1914, Friedlaender Papers. From Oct. 1, 1910 until Jan. 31, 1916, the Bureau had received $267,473 (*see above*, n.61). At that time the debt was $72,330, which was written off during the following three years as contributions. Thus in

Jan., 1916, the Bureau had received $339,803. No budgets were found for the years 1916 and 1917. However, for the calendar year of 1918, the Bureau's income was $57,578.18 (Educational Fund of the Bureau of Education, Jan. 1, 1918 to Dec. 31, 1918, MA, F24–L105). Thus its total income by 1917 was most likely higher than the $380,000 figure.

76. Constitution of the Board of Jewish School Aid, MA, F24–L10; Min 8th ACK, Apr. 29, 1917, MA, F18–L33.

77. Goldwasser, pp. 118–19; Committee Representing Jewish Educational Institutions to Hon. William N. Cohen, chairman, Committee of Seven of the Federation for Support of Jewish Philanthropic Societies, Mar. 9, 1917, MA, F2–L33. For a brief summary of the negotiations, see Winter, pp. 97–99.

VI. EDUCATION: THE PROFESSIONALS AND THE ORTHODOX

1. The most comprehensive exposition of Benderly's program is Benderly, *Aims and Activities*. The pamphlet has been republished in *JE*, XX (1949), 92–109, which is the source hereafter cited. For aspects of the educational thought of the period which apparently influenced Benderly, see Callahan, pp. 47–125.

2. Scharfstein, *Toldot*, II, 194–98; Brickner, p. 58.

3. Minutes of the Board of Trustees, Sept. 19, 1912, MA, F10–L20; *JCR*, p. 371.

4. Benderly, in *JE*, XX, 107–108; Dushkin, *Jewish Education*, pp. 107, 116–17, 212; Friedlaender, in *Report of the Commissioner*, I, 387–88.

5. Scharfstein, *Arba'im shanah b'amerika*, pp. 167–68.

6. Benderly, in *JE*, XX, 100, 102, 107; Friedlaender, *Report of the Commissioner*, I, 391; Honor, in *Hebrew Union College Annual*, pp. 631–38.

7. Brickner, p. 58; Benderly, in *JE*, XX, 102; Minutes of the Board of Trustees, Feb. 20, 1913, Friedlaender Papers; *5th ARK*, Apr. 25 and 26, 1914, pp. 24, 46; Min 6th ACK, Apr. 24 and 25, 1915, MA, F28–L7; Min ECK, June 8, 1915, MA, F28–L108; Honor, in *Hebrew Union College Annual*, pp. 363–38.

8. Benderly, in *JE*, XX, 108; *4th ARK*, Apr. 12 and 13, 1913, p. 36.

9. *Ibid.* Felix Warburg, on Benderly's prompting, won the Commissioner of Education's approval to recruit Jewish public school teachers for volunteer work in the Bureau's extension program (Magnes to Warburg, Sept. 3, 1912; William H. Maxwell to Warburg, Sept. 7, 1912; Magnes to Warburg, Sept. 18, 1912; Magnes to Warburg, Sept.

20, 1912, MA, F47–L98). See also, *4th ARK*, Apr. 12 and 13, 1913, p. 36.

10. Soltes, in *JE*, XX, 30–31; Minutes of the Board of Trustees, Sept. 19, 1912, MA, F10–L20; Feb. 20, 1913, Friedlaender Papers; Dushkin, *Jewish Education*, pp. 112–113, 123–26, 174–76, 352–57.

11. Benderly, in *JE*, XX, 97. By insisting that a Talmud Torah have at least a third of its students on full tuition and another third on half-tuition, Benderly intended to remove the obloquy of a charity school. *Ibid.*, pp. 97–98. The eight largest Talmud Torahs averaged 881 pupils and eleven teachers per school. Benderly, *Survey of the Financial Status of Jewish Religious Schools*, pp. 5–6.

12. Min 6th ACK, Apr. 24 and 25, 1915, MA, F28–L7; see also Benderly, in *JE*, XX, p. 98 and *AJYB* (1916–1917), p. 358.

13. *4th ARK*, Apr. 12 and 13, 1913, p. 35; *AJYB* (1916–1917), p. 358.

14. Benderly, in *JE*, XX, 98–100.

15. *Ibid.*, p. 101; Minutes of the Board of Trustees, Sept. 19, 1912, MA, F10–L20; Friedlaender to Schechter, Jan. 24, 1912, Friedlaender Papers.

16. Benderly, in *JE*, XX, 99; Benderly, in *Brief Survey of Thirty-One Conferences*, pp. 6–7.

17. Benderly, in *Brief Survey of Thirty-One Conferences*, p. 7.

18. *Ibid.*, p. 8. The *Brief Survey* is a 14-page summary of a 35-page Hebrew report. Both are bound as one pamphlet. For the fuller discussion, see the Hebrew version, Israel Konovitz, *Kitzur din v'cheshbon shel v'eedat m'nahaley batey t"t*. For recollections of the meetings, see Handler, in *Sheviley Hahinuch*, pp. 38–46.

19. See series of articles by Rabbi Shmarya Hurwitz on the conferences: *Tageblat*, Dec. 11, 1911, p. 5; Dec. 20, p. 4; Dec. 26, p. 4; Jan. 2, 1912, p. 4. Tension, nevertheless, did exist between Benderly and some of the *maskilim*. Scharfstein claims that since Benderly could not dominate the Europeans as he did his American novices, and since the philanthropists were more impressed by American collegians than European intellectuals, he favored the Americans. Scharfstein, *Arba'im shanah b'amerika*, pp. 161–66.

20. Benderly, in *JE*, XX, 96–97.

21. Brickner, pp. 57–58; Benderly, *Some of the Activities*, p. 5.

22. Min 6th ACK, Apr. 24 and 25, 1915, MA, F28–L7; Minutes of the Board of Trustees, Feb. 20, 1913, Friedlaender Papers.

23. Minutes of the Board of Trustees, Nov. 29, 1910, MA, F1–L24; Mordecai M. Kaplan, in *JE*, p. 17.

24. Mordecai Kaplan, in *JE*, p. 18; Albert P. Schoolman, in *JE*, XXVIII (1957), 14–15; Interview with Isaac B. Berkson, Oct. 28, 1965; Dushkin, *Jewish Education*, pp. 85–90; interview with Alexander Dush-

kin, Dec. 23, 1965; Dushkin, in *AJA*, pp. 117–26; Kaplan Journal, Oct. 4, 1914.

25. Dushkin, in *JE*, XX, 7; Kohn, pp. 66–69; Bentwich, *For Zion's Sake*, pp. 50–51; Eisenstein and Kohn, pp. 293–96; Kaplan Journal, Dec. 15, 1913, Oct. 29, 1914; Eisenstein, p. 15; interview with Alexander Dushkin, Dec. 23, 1965.

26. Honor, in *JE*, XX, 29; Honor, in Scharfstein, *Sefer hayovel*, pp. 347–48; interview with Isaac B. Berkson, Oct. 28, 1965.

27. Dushkin, in *JE*, XX, 10–11; interview with Alexander Dushkin, Dec. 23, 1965. For a similar apprenticeship, see Chipkin, in *JE*, XX, 22–23.

28. Mordecai Kaplan, in *JE*, XX, 18–19; Benderly, in *JE*, XX, 101; Minutes of the Board of Trustees, Jan. 1, 1912 and Feb. 15, 1912, Friedlander Papers; Minutes of the Board of Trustees, Sept. 19, 1912, MA, F10–L20; Kaplan Journal, Oct. 4, 1914.

29. Interview with Alexander Dushkin, Dec. 23, 1965; Dushkin, in *AJA*, p. 126; Kaplan would have preferred that the trainees pursue their higher studies at the JTS (Kaplan, *JE*, XX, 18–19). Kaplan also confided in his journals his objection to Benderly's secularism (Kaplan Journal, Oct. 4, 1914). The published dissertations are: Alexander M. Dushkin, *Jewish Education in New York City*; Isaac B. Berkson, *Theories of Americanization, A Critical Study with Special Reference to the Jewish Group*; Emanuel Gamoran, *Changing Conceptions in Jewish Education*; Mordecai Soltes, *The Yiddish Press: An Americanizing Agency*; Leo L. Honor, *Sennacherib's Invasion of Palestine*. Honor's special interest was the teaching of Jewish history. On the Bureau workers as a group at Teachers College, see interview with Alexander Dushkin, Dec. 23, 1965. I identified eighteen persons who were on the staff of the Bureau and graduate students at Teachers College in the period 1911 to 1918.

30. Tenenbaum, p. 299; interview with Alexander Dushkin, Dec. 23, 1965. On Kilpatrick's influence on Jewish education, see Blumenfield, pp. 184–94. On Dewey's influence on Jewish education, see Blumenfield, pp. 173–83; also Dushkin, in Scharfstein, *Sefer ha'yovel*, pp. 104–13.

31. Hofstadter, in *Anti-Intellectualism in America*, pp. 359, 372–90, examines the anti-intellectual tendencies and consequences of "certain ideas to which Dewey gave by far the most influential expression." Jewish education, where the intellectual-traditionalist element weighs so heavily, was especially vulnerable to this tendency in progressive education. The main effects were felt after 1918, a period beyond the limits of this study. See, for example, Hurwich, III, 320–28; Blumenfield, pp. 175–76.

32. *The Jewish Teacher*, I, 1; Alexander Dushkin, the first editor, was assisted by Isaac B. Berkson, Samuel Margoshes, Albert Schoolman, Meir Isaacs, and Judith Ish-Kishor. *JCR*, p. 459.

33. Cremin, pp. 117–18; cf., Samson Benderly, "The Fundamental Elements in the Solution of the Problem of Jewish Education in America," *The Jewish Teacher*, I, 17–27.

34. *The Menorah Journal*, III (Apr. 1917), 92. Dewey, in giving the school the educational function once performed by family, neighborhood, or shop, Cremin writes, gave "classic statement to this notion of the school as a *legatee* institution." Cremin, p. 117. On the psychological necessity of the Jewish teacher *in loco parentis*, see A. A. Brill, "Mental Adjustment in Jews," *Jewish Teacher*, I, 141–50, and the editorial on Brill's article, *ibid.*, pp. 138–39.

35. Dewey, *Democracy and Education*, pp. 53, 241, 248–49.

36. Dushkin, *Jewish Education*, p. 317.

37. Dewey, *Democracy and Education*, pp. 20–22; Cremin, pp. 121–23; Dushkin, *Jewish Education*, p. 384.

38. Dewey, *Democracy and Education*, p. 85.

39. *Ibid.*, p. 87.

40. Interview with Isaac B. Berkson, Oct. 28, 1965; Berkson, in *JE*, XXVII, 8.

41. Berkson, *Theories of Americanization*, p. 39; Solomon Grayzel, "Memorial on Leo Honor," *JE*, XXVIII (1957), 9.

42. Dewey, *Democracy and Education*, pp. 87–99.

43. Berkson, *Theories of Americanization*, pp. 162–63; Dushkin, *Jewish Education*, pp. 140, 382. Dushkin saw place for a select group receiving its education in the Jewish parochial school. "One per cent of [Jewish] children will be specially selected for the periods of intermediate and secondary schooling to be trained as the 'priest class,' as the centers of energy for intense Jewish life," *ibid.*, p. 331. Berkson polemicized at length with the Catholic position. Berkson, *Theories of Americanization*, pp. 152–67. See also Kallen, pp. 124–25. This chapter of the book originally appeared in *The Nation*, Feb. 18 and 25, 1915. Gordon, pp. 149–52, 154–55, discusses Berkson's criticism of Kallen.

44. Dushkin, *Jewish Education*, pp. 21–22, 382–83. For Dushkin, the sacrifice entailed in maintaining the school was in itself a democratic and moral act of the highest order (p. 385); Berkson enlarges on this point: "Ethnic community loyalty to a minority becomes a severe mental and moral discipline. . . . Trained to seek below the surface of his own tradition, he will tend to look for what is exalted in American life." *Theories of Americanization*, pp. 127–28.

45. Berkson, *Theories of Americanization*, pp. 98–106.

46. Berkson, *Theories of Americanization*, p. 118. The memoir literature and interviews create the impression that the Teachers College experience had a profound emotional impact on these young students. Note Berkson's rhapsodic lines: "Democracy is not only something political and institutional; its real essence is spiritual. . . . It reaches upward, too, towards unattained heights of the spirit; it is essentially an

urge—a dynamic force in life. Democracy is a religious aspiration as well as a form of social organization." *Theories of Americanization,* p. 13. See above, n.29 for Kaplan's criticism of their secularism.

47. Dewey, in *Menorah Journal,* III, 205–206. Though Dewey attacked the anti-hyphenate campaign, his description of the "genuine American" as a "hyphenate" of all immigrant cultures comes close to the melting-pot image. Dewey, in *National Education Association: Addresses and Proceedings,* LIV, 183–89. For a review of Dewey's article in the *Menorah Journal* see *Evening Post,* Oct. 12, 1917, p. 8.

48. Simon, pp. 94–95, 223–30; Berkson, *Theories of Americanization,* p. 109. See also, Friedlaender, *Past and Present,* pp. 415–22.

49. Dushkin, *Jewish Education,* pp. 384–85.

50. *MJ,* Mar. 2, 1910, p. 4; *Tageblat,* Mar. 1, 1910, p. 4.

51. *MJ,* Feb. 21, 1911, p. 4.

52. *Tageblat,* Apr. 29, 1912, p. 1; Apr. 24, p. 4. Though members of the Central Board were individually coopted to the Kehillah's committee on education, Magnes turned down an official request to give the Central Board corporate membership (Minutes of the Committee on Education, Apr. 18, 1910, MA, F1–L22). Nevertheless, the Central Board declared its readiness to cooperate with the Kehillah's Bureau. *AH,* June 24, 1910, p. 208.

53. Min ECK, Oct. 10, 1911, MA, F1–L58, and Nov. 14, 1911, MA, F48–L158; *Tageblat,* Dec. 11, 1911, p. 5; Dec. 26, p. 4; Jan. 31, 1912, p. 7; *MJ,* Mar. 18, 1912, p. 4; Aug. 9, p. 5; Jan. 3, 1913, p. 4; Jan. 10, p. 4; *AH,* May 3, 1912, p. 7; Min 3d ACK, Apr. 27 and 28, 1912, MA, F10–L3.

54. See above, Chap. 4.

55. Herbert S. Goldstein, pp. 31–32; Drachman, pp. 208–14, 275, 278–79. Some of the leading synagogues and their rabbis were Bernard Drachman (Ohev Zedek), Herbert S. Goldstein (Kehillat Yeshurun and later the West Side Institutional Synagogue), and Moses Hyamson (Orach Chayim). Of the lay leaders, Semel headed the Galician Federation, Unterberg the Society for the Advancement of Judaism, Fischel the Hebrew Free Loan Society. Other key members of the group were Joseph H. Cohen (Beth Israel Hospital) and Sender Jarmulowsky (Union of American Orthodox Congregations). The synagogue, Derech Emunah, was established in Arverne, Long Island, in 1905 and became the focal point of various fund-raising activities on behalf of the Kehillah and other causes. Israel Unterberg was the first president. *AH,* July 28, 1911, p. 361; Aug. 25, p. 485.

56. Benderly, in *JE,* XX, 95, 97; *Yehrlicher report fun der downtown talmud torah,* pp. 7, 17–18. On the mediation roles of the Orthodox friends of the Kehillah, see *MJ,* Feb. 10, 1911, p. 5; Apr. 29, 1912, p. 8; May 22, 1914, p. 4; *4th ARK,* Apr. 12 and 13, 1913, p. 32.

57. *MJ,* Nov. 13, 1911, p. 7; Nov. 27, p. 1; Dec. 11, p. 8; Jan. 2,

1912, p. 4; Jan. 5, p. 4; Feb. 1, 1912, p. 5; *AH*, Nov. 17, 1911, p. 79; Dec. 1, p. 139; Dec. 15, p. 207; Jan. 5, 1912, p. 294.

58. *MJ*, Nov. 8, 1911, p. 5.

59. *MJ*, Nov. 27, 1911, p. 1. The story may have had its origin in the fact that Benderly studied at the American College in Beirut, a Protestant institution. Orthodox circles were extremely sensitive to Christian missionary activities on the East Side. Rabbi Shalom Rabinowitz of Brooklyn made the accusation. On the book incident see, *MJ*, Nov. 27, 1911, p. 1. Benderly had purchased a lot of secondhand books. Some Bureau worker chose a thick book, which happened to be about Lutheranism, and labeled it in Hebrew, "ze sefer 'aveh ve'gadol" ("this is a thick and big book"). The "exhibit" was to be used as a visual aid in teaching Hebrew through the "natural method." Rabbi Rabinowitz who led the attack later said: "For a long time I knew that in the heder where charts with dogs and cats on them [the reference was to language charts with pictures explaining the Hebrew words] are introduced, there the Pentateuch becomes a rare article." *MJ*, Dec. 3, 1911, p. 5; see also *AH*, Dec. 1, 1911, p. 139.

60. *MJ*, Dec. 13, 1912, p. 4. Gedaliah Bublick made a similar accusation at the Kehillah's 1912 convention. Pictures of a beardless Isaiah and a Jeremiah were being hung on the walls of the Talmud Torahs by order of the Bureau. *Ibid.*, Apr. 29, 1912, p. 8. Dushkin tells of Bureau opponents who cut the electric wires to prevent showing slides of Bible stories. *JE*, XX, 10.

61. *MJ*, July 26, 1912, p. 5.

62. Min ECK, Dec. 12, 1911, MA, F48–L158.

63. *MJ*, Nov. 8, 1911, p. 5; Nov. 24, p. 5; Nov. 23, p. 5; Nov. 17, p. 1.

64. *Ibid.*, Dec. 11, 1911, p. 8; *Tageblat*, Dec. 13, 1911, p. 5; *AH*, Dec. 1, 1911, pp. 139, 145; Lipsky, in *Maccabaean*, XXII, 185–89. See also *Tageblat*, Sept. 8, 1911, p. 1; Isaac Allen to Magnes, July 24, 1911, MA, F1–L59; Minutes of the Committee on Permanent Organization, July 7, 1911; Minutes of Meeting of Kehillah Delegates and the Council of Seventy, Nov. 26, 1911, MA, F1–L59.

65. *MJ*, Nov. 8, 1911, p. 5; Nov. 26, p. 5. *American Hebrew* commented that Benderly's reforms were resented "by those who fear that they may not come up to the standard which the reforms will establish. The old-fashioned *melamed* [teacher] naturally fears that he will be reformed out of existence, and this accounts for most of the outcry that is being made." Nov. 17, 1911, p. 74.

66. *MJ*, Nov. 26, 1911, p. 5.

67. *Ibid.*, Nov. 27, 1911, p. 5; *AH*, Nov. 17, 1911, p. 79.

68. *MJ*, Dec. 11, 1911, p. 8; Apr. 29, 1912, p. 8; *Tageblat*, Dec. 16, 1912, p. 6; *Maccabaean*, XXI (May 1912), 296; Rabbi I. J. Estherson

to Magnes, Sept. 1912, MA, F1–L53b; Rabbi Samuel H. Glick to Magnes, July 22, 1912, MA, F1–L53b.

69. *MJ*, Nov. 27, 1911, p. 5; Minutes of the Board of Trustees, Jan. 8, 1912, Friedlaender Papers; Min ECK, May 14, 1912, MA, F10–L2; Min ECK, June 11, 1912, MA, F10–L7.

70. Rabbi Samuel H. Glick to Magnes, July 18, 1912, Magnes to Glick, July 21, 1912, MA, F1–L53b; Min ECK, Dec. 10, 1912, MA, F10–L8.

71. *Tageblat*, May 22, 1914, p. 10; *MJ*, May 22, 1914, p. 4. The Kehillah considered bringing libel charges against the rabbis. Marshall to Magnes, May 29, 1914, MA, F48–L132.

72. *MJ*, May 22, 1914, p. 4.

73. *Ibid.*; *Tageblat*, May 24, 1914, p. 6. Harry Fischel the Orthodox lay-leader, accused the rabbis of never having been truly interested in the Talmud Torahs. *MJ*, May 22, 1914, p. 4.

74. Benderly, *Some of the Activities*, Apr. 24, 1915, p. 7; *JCR*, pp. 371–72; Budget of Amount Required for Jewish Education Fund, 1916–1917, MA, F2–L17.

VII. CRIME IN THE JEWISH QUARTER

1. Myers, pp. 278–79; Moss, II, 366 81, III, 54–66, 159–240; Cyrus L. Sulzberger, "New York's Responsibility: A Chapter of Civic History," *AH*, Nov. 29, 1912, pp. 127–28.

2. *First Annual Report: Hawthorne School of the Jewish Protectory and Aid Society* (New York, Jan. 1, 1908); *JCR*, p. 1142; *AH*, Nov. 5, 1909, p. 9; *Year Book: New York Section of Council of Jewish Women* (New York, 1907–1908), pp. 9, 22–26, 50–54; Mayer, III, 88–90; Frankel, IV, 31–32; Bogen, in *Jewish Charity*, IV, 126–29.

3. *Evening Post*, Sept. 18, 1908, p. 6.

4. *Independent*, Sept. 24, 1908, p. 731; *World*, Sept. 17, 1908, p. 8; *Globe*, Sept. 17, 1908, p. 6; *Times*, Sept. 16, 1908, p. 8.

5. *Times*, June 2, 1909, p. 2; July 2, p. 6; July 3, p. 6; *World*, July 1, 1909, p. 8; July 2, p. 6; *Outlook*, July 10, 1909, p. 573. For the background of Gaynor's criticism of Bingham, see Hochman, pp. 55–60. Bingham had been retired from the Army with the rank of Brigadier General.

6. *Times*, July 3, 1909, p. 2; *Outlook*, July 17, 1909, p. 617; on the brief Bingham boom for mayor, see *World*, July 3, 1909, p. 1; *Warheit*, July 4, 1909, p. 1.

7. Filler, pp. 287–91; Stowe, pp. 73–78.

8. Nevins and Krout, pp. 73–87; Smith, p. 130. On Whitman, see Binkerd, CUOHP, p. 41 and *Times*, Mar. 30, 1947, p. 1. Others who

benefited politically were Emory R. Buckner, Henry H. Curran, John Purroy Mitchel, and Samuel Seabury.

9. On Kid Twist, see *Times*, May 15, 1908, p. 1; on Yuski Nigger, see *Times*, Mar. 25, 1913, p. 24; on Big Jack Zelig, see *Times*, Oct. 6, 1912, p. 1; on Dopey Benny, see *Times*, May 12, 1915, p. 6; May 13, p. 24; on Kid Dropper, see *Times*, Aug. 29, 1923, p. 1; see also Asbury, pp. 274–95, 325–36, 339–43, 359, 373.

10. U.S. Immigration Commission, *Importing Women for Immoral Purposes*, pp. 23–24; New York State, *Report of the Commission of Immigration*, p. 16.

11. Rischin, *Promised City*, pp. 198–200.

12. For a racial explanation of crime, see McClure, pp. 117–28; Bingham, in *Hampton's* Magazine, pp. 289–300. More striking is the absence of such views in the editorials of the metropolitan press during the period under study.

13. Rischin, *Promised City*, pp. 195–220; Roy Lubove, pp. 43–48, 57–58, 66–80, 130–32, 137–39; Handlin, *The Uprooted*, pp. 155–64, 227–58; Rudoph Glanz, in YIVO *Annual*, IX, 308–31; Miner, pp. 53–87.

14. Turner, in *McClure's* Magazine, June 1909, pp. 117–34; McClure, pp. 117–28.

15. In addition to McClure's own article, Turner and Theodore A. Bingham contributed. The articles are discussed below. On the stress given to the prostitution problem as a means of shocking the public into more general reforms, see King, pp. 46, 73, 113.

16. *Sun*, Oct. 21, 1909, p. 3; *Times*, Oct. 24, 1909, p. 12; Oct. 27, 1909, p. 4; *Evening Post*, Oct. 24, 1909, pp. 1, 6; *American*, Oct. 16, 1909, p. 4; Oct. 28, 1909, pp. 1, 2.

17. Bingham, in *McClure's* Magazine, pp. 62–67; McClure, p. 124.

18. *McClure's* pp. 45–61; *Sun*, Oct. 29, 1909, p. 6. For the historical context of the concern over prostitution, see Feldman, pp. 192–206.

19. The newspapers examined (the *Times*, *World*, *Sun*, *Evening Post*, *American*) made no editorial comment on the exaggerations and offensive writing in Turner's article.

20. *MJ*, Oct. 22, 1909, p. 4; Oct. 25, p. 4; Oct. 26, p. 4; Oct. 31, p. 1; *Tageblat*, Oct. 31, 1909, p. 1; *Warheit*, Oct. 24, 1909, p. 4. Among those quoted were Police Commissioner William F. Baker, ex-Police Commissioner William McAdoo, and Thomas M. Mulry, head of the St. Vincent de Paul Society. Affidavits were also published containing statements by persons claiming to have provided information to Turner and stating that Turner had misrepresented them.

21. *McClure's* Magazine, Nov. 1909, p. 45; *Warheit*, Oct. 31, 1909, p. 4; *MJ*, Oct. 25, 1909, p. 4.

22. *MJ*, Oct. 25, 1909, p. 4.

23. *MJ*, Oct. 22, 1909, p. 4; Oct. 27, p. 4; *Warheit*, Oct. 28, 1909, p. 4; *Tageblat*, Oct. 29, 1909, p. 4.

24. *Warheit*, Oct. 28, 1909, p. 4.

25. *Ibid.*, *Forward*, Oct. 22, 1909, p. 4; Oct. 26, p. 1; Oct. 28, p. 4; Oct. 29, p. 4; Oct. 30, p. 4; Oct. 31, pp. 1, 4.

26. *Times*, Oct. 27, 1909, p. 4; Oct. 29, p. 2; Oct. 30, p. 6.

27. Min ECK, Oct. 26, 1909, MA, F48–L155.

28. *Times*, Oct. 28, 1909, p. 3; *Tageblat*, Oct. 29, 1909, p. 10. Min ECK, Nov. 9, 1909, Dec. 14, 1909, Jan. 1, 1910, Feb. 8; MA, F48–L155; *Report fun di Kehille*, Feb. 26, 1910, pp. 16–18; *MJ*, Feb. 27, 1910, p. 1.

29. AH, Feb. 4, 1910, p. 360.

30. Magnes, *Emanu-El Pulpit*, III, 4–7; *Times*, Nov. 7, 1909, p. 9; *MJ*, Nov. 7, 1909, p. 1. Magnes also inveighed against "do-gooders" who pried into the "houses of the poor" and prevented the East Side from working out its own problems.

31. Charles S. Whitman was the exception. Whitman is discussed below.

32. Louis Marshall to the editor of the *Warheit*, Apr. 30, 1910, Marshall Papers; *Federation Review*, II (Oct. 1908), 8; *Third Annual Report: Hawthorne School of the Jewish Protectory and Aid Society*, Mar. 14, 1910.

33. U.S. Immigration Commission, *Importing Women for Immoral Purposes*, pp. 3–13, 23–24. The report led to the passage of the Mann Act.

34. U.S. Immigration Commission, *Immigration and Crime*. For a highly critical view of the Immigration Report as "never very meaningful" and "often misleading," see Handlin, in *Race and Nationality*, pp. 99–102.

35. *Times*, Jan. 4, 1910, p. 5; Apr. 30, p. 1; *Outlook*, July 16, 1910, pp. 545–46; *McClure's* Magazine, Aug. 1910, pp. 471–73; Waterman, p. 85.

36. Kneeland, *Commercialized Prostitution in New York City*.

37. Committee of Fourteen, *Annual Report for 1912*, pp. 1–32; Waterman, pp. 90–116. The Committee of Fourteen was originally organized as the Committee of Fifteen. It was reestablished in 1907 as the Committee of Fourteen to fight the "Raines Law Hotels" in New York City.

38. Committee of Fifteen, *The Social Evil* (1902); Committee of Fourteen, *The Social Evil* (1910); Edwin R. A. Seligman, ed., *The Social Evil, with Special Reference to Conditions Existing in the City of New York* (New York, 1912.)

39. Committee of Fourteen, *Annual Report for 1912*, pp. 1–21;

Annual Report for 1913, p. 41; Waterman, pp. 102–11; Israels, pp. 486–97.

40. *Warheit*, Oct. 28, 1912, p. 1; Oct. 29, p. 1; Oct. 30, p. 1.

41. Robison, pp. 19–20, 122–26, 157; Mark J. Katz, July, 1908, p. 5.

42. Dr. Paul Abelson to Edward Lauterbach, Sept. 4, 1908; Lauterbach to Abelson, Sept. 12, 1908, Abelson Papers; U.S. Immigration Commission, *Immigration and Crime*, p. 304; Rischin, *Promised City*, pp. 90–91.

43. *Warheit*, Oct. 27, 1909, p. 4; Sellin, pp. 71–73.

44. Robison, pp. 162–64; Knowland, pp. 175, 190–92, 215; U.S. Immigration Commission, *Importing Women for Immoral Purposes*, pp. 12–13.

45. *AH*, Sept. 25, 1908, p. 502.

46. *World*, July 13, 1912, p. 1; July 17, p. 8; *Times*, July 16, 1912, p. 1; *Evening Post*, July 16, 1912, p. 6; *Forward*, July 18, 1912, p. 4; New York *Herald*, July 18, 1912, p. 4; New York *American*, July 17, 1912, p. 1, July 18, pp. 1, 2, 20; July 23, p. 18.

47. *Times*, July 18, 1912, p. 1.

48. *Times*, Aug. 21, 1912, p. 1; Sept. 15, p. 3; Oct. 13, pp. 1, 2; Oct. 20, p. 1; Oct. 16, p. 1. Henry H. Klein, who reported the Rosenthal murder for the *American*, was convinced of Becker's innocence. He has written extensively on the case. See entries under Klein in Bibliography. Klein interpreted the murder as an attempt by rival gambling interests to prevent Rosenthal from testifying before the grand jury. He portrayed Whitman, consumed by ambition, as accepting the perjured stories of the rival gamblers who received immunity in return.

49. Dr. Felix Adler, Frank Moss, Eugene Outerbridge, William J. Schieffelin, Jacob Schiff, Eugene Philbin, Dr. Charles Parkhurst, and James B. Reynolds are the outstanding examples.

50. The attempt on Roosevelt's life occupied the entire front page on Oct. 15, 1912.

51. See, for example, *Times*, May 13, 1913, p. 1; Nov. 30, p. 1; Feb. 25, 1914, pp. 1, 2; Feb. 26, p. 1; Feb. 28, p. 1; Mar. 23, p. 1; Mar. 31, p. 1; Apr. 12, pp. 1, 2; Apr. 13, pp. 1–2; May 23, p. 1; July 27, 1915, p. 1; July 29, p. 1; July 30, p. 1; July 31, p. 1; Aug. 2, p. 1.

52. William J. Gaynor to John D. Maher, Aug 8, 1912, Gaynor Papers; Stephen S. Wise to Charles H. Parkhurst, Nov. 15, 1912, Wise to Charles S. Whitman, Nov. 21, 1912, Parkhurst to Wise, Dec. 2, 1912, Wise Papers; Hochman, pp. 91–92, 267, chs. xi, xii; Smith, pp. 136–40, 168–71; *Times*, July 23, 1912, p. 8; Sept. 11, p. 1. On the reformers' views, see Committee of Fifteen, pp. 147–50; Waterman, pp. 80–87; King, pp. 85–87; Hochman, pp. 270–73, 462–69; Fosdick, pp. 114–43. A dissenting group held that the police should be limited to constabulory functions and not attempt to enforce moral precepts.

Hutchins Hapgood wrote in his column in the *Globe*, "It was puritanism that killed Rosenthal" (July 18, 1912, p. 6). See also *ibid.*, Aug. 1, 1912, p. 6.

53. Hochman, pp. 75–104; Pink, pp. 130–32.

54. *Report of the Special Committee of the Board of Aldermen of the City of New York To Investigate the Police Department Submitted June 10, 1913*, p. 2; Curran, pp. 152–73. *Report of the Citizens Committee Appointed at the Cooper Union Mass Meeting, Aug. 14, 1912, submitted Feb. 26, 1913*; *Times*, July 29, 1912, p. 2; Aug. 4, p. 2; Aug. 6, p. 4; Aug. 8, p. 2; Aug. 13, p. 2; Aug. 15, pp. 1–2; Aug. 17, p. 2; Aug. 29, p. 2.

55. Hochman, pp. 55–58; Smith, pp. 41–43; Pink, pp. 95–96, 100–4; *MJ*, June 3, 1909, p. 1; July 2, p. 4; *Tageblat*, June 3, 1909, p. 4; *Times*, June 2, 1909, p. 1; June 3, p. 2; *Forward*, July 2, 1909, p. 4; *World*, Oct. 22, 1909, p. 6; Oct. 25, p. 1; Oct. 26, pp. 4, 5; Oct. 31, p. 5; *Tageblat*, Oct. 22, 1909, p. 1.

56. *Report of the Special Committee of the Board of Alderman*, p. 107. Hochman, pp. 246, 274, 462–69. Total number of arrests in 1911 were 27 percent less than 1909 and 42 percent less than 1908 for the city as a whole. Hochman, p. 248.

57. Werner, p. 407. On Wise's criticism of Gaynor's policy, see *Times*, Oct. 25, 1909, p. 2 and Wise, *Challenging Years*, pp. 12–13; for Gaynor's reply, see Pink, p. 222; *Times*, Aug. 2, 1912, p. 2; see also Louis Miller to Gaynor, Sept. 17, 1912, Gaynor Papers, Location 127.

58. *Sun*, Oct. 20, 1909, p. 2; Oct. 24, p. 2; *World*, Oct. 26, 1909, p. 4. On Moss, see above, p. 134. Reynolds was a member of the Committee of Seventy in 1893, chairman of the Citizens Union Campaign Committee in 1897, member of the New York State Tenement House Committee in 1900, and wrote the chapter on tenement-house prostitution in *The Tenement House Problem*, eds., Robert W. De Forest and Lawrence Veiller (New York, 1903). He was a member of the New York State Immigration Commission, 1908–1909. On Whitman, see *Outlook*, Sept. 28, 1912, p. 223–24; *American Bar Association Journal* (May 1947), pp. 473–74; Henry H. Klein, *My Forty Year Fight for Justice*, pp. 7–9.

59. Smith, pp. 130–32, 139–40; *Times*, July 17, 1912, p. 2; July 18, pp. 1–2; July 19, pp. 1–2; July 28, p. 2; Aug. 2, p. 2; Aug. 16, p. 2; Aug. 17, p. 2; Aug. 22, p. 1; Aug. 27, pp. 1–2; Sept. 1, p. 1. For a contemporary view of the investigations as biased, see *Times*, Sept. 24, 1912, p. 1; Oct. 1, p. 24.

60. *Forward*, Aug. 15, 1912, p. 8; *Times*, Aug. 15, 1912, p. 1; Aug. 16, p. 8; *Outlook*, Aug. 24, 1912, pp. 900–1. Morse M. Frankel to Judah Magnes, Aug. 16, 1912, and Judah Magnes to Morse M. Frankel, Aug. 19, 1912, MA, F46–L10. The *Evening Post* (July 31,

1912, p. 1) reported that the Progressive Party was "looking Whitman over" for the gubernatorial nomination. The *Warheit* continued to see Whitman's handling of the Rosenthal case as part of his drive for the gubernatorial nomination. Aug. 20, 1912, p. 4; Aug. 21, p. 4; Aug. 25, p. 4. On a Whitman boom for the mayoralty nomination and criticism of his use of the Rosenthal affair for political ends, see *Current Literature*, Dec. 1912, pp. 635–36 and Nov. 1912, p. 491. For the mayor's bitter letter to the chairman of the committee, see *Times*, Aug. 29, 1912, p. 2; see also, *ibid.*, Aug. 20, 1912, p. 3, and *Forward*, Aug. 20, 1912, p. 8.

61. *Warheit*, Aug. 17, 1912, pp. 1, 4.

62. *Times*, Jan. 28, 1912, p. 7; Feb. 4, p. 1; Feb. 5, p. 1; Feb. 22, p. 2; Feb. 24, p. 1; Feb. 27, p. 1; Apr. 1, p. 1; June 11, p. 6; Jan. 10, 1913, pp. 1, 10; Jan. 18, p. 1; Magidoff, pp. 164–66; *American*, Jan. 24, 1913, p. 1; Jan. 25, p. 1; Jan. 26, p. 1; Jan. 27, p. 1; *World*, Jan. 26, 1912, p. 1; Feb. 7, p. 1; Feb. 8, pp. 1, 8; Feb. 9, pp. 1, 8; Feb. 10, p. 1.

63. *Times*, July 27, 1912, p. 2; *Warheit*, Aug. 15, 1912, p. 4; Aug. 17, pp. 1, 4; Louis Miller to Gaynor, Aug. 21, 1912, Miller to Schiff, Aug. 21 (copy sent to Gaynor), Miller to Gaynor, Aug. 26, Gaynor Papers, Location 127. Schiff's support of Gaynor's bid for reelection is discussed in chapter 8.

64. For a sampling of the English and Yiddish press which stresses the human interest side, see *Warheit*, July 25, 1912, p. 4; Aug. 3, p. 4; Dec. 13, p. 4; Apr. 11, 1914, p. 6; Apr. 13, p. 4; *MJ*, Aug. 1, 1912, p. 4; Oct. 7, p. 5; *Tageblat*, July 28, 1912, p. 4; July 30, p. 4; Dec. 6, p. 4; *Times*, July 22, 1912, p. 2; Aug. 21, p. 2; Sept. 13, p. 1; Sept. 14, p. 1; Oct. 6, pp. 1, 2; Apr. 13, 1914, p. 2; *Globe*, July 29, 1912, p. 6; *AH*, Nov. 29, 1912, p. 127; *American*, Aug. 21, 1912, p. 4; Lane, pp. 13–16. The prime area of gambling and prostitution was the Tenderloin, which stretched from the thirties to Columbus Circle, and not the East Side. Jewish operators, however, were beginning to move into the Tenderloin. See George J. Kneeland, *Commercialized Prostitution*, pp. 4, 25, 36, 42–43, 53, 65–66.

65. *MJ*, July 23, 1912, p. 5; *Tageblat*, July 29, 1912, p. 4.

66. *Warheit*, July 25, 1912, p. 4; July 22, p. 4; *MJ*, July 22, 1912, p. 4; July 27, p. 4; July 30, p. 4.

67. *Warheit*, July 17, 1912, p. 4; July 18, p. 4; July 22, p. 4; July 25, p. 4; *Tageblat*, July 21, 1912, p. 4; July 26, p. 4; July 30, p. 4.

68. *Forward*, July 20, 1912, p. 4; July 21, p. 4; July 27, p. 4; July 31, p. 4.

69. *Forward*, July 23, 1912, p. 4.

70. *MJ*, July 29, 1912, p. 4; Aug. 1, 1912, p. 4; Aug. 2, p. 4.

71. *AH*, Aug. 9, 1912, p. 396; Aug. 23, p. 444. See also *Maccabaean*, XXII (Aug. 1912), 39.
72. Marshall to Magnes, July 24, 1912, MA, F46–L18.
73. Marshall to Orthodox Rabbis, July 23, 1912 (handwritten draft), MA, F46–L18.

VIII. CRIME FIGHTING

1. Min ECK, July 28, 1912, MA, F10–L4; Magnes to David Pinski, Aug. 2, 1912, MA, F46–L11. The press featured the Kehillah statement prominently. *Times*, July 29, 1912, p. 2; *American*, July 29, 1912, p. 1; *Globe*, July 29, 1912, p. 2; *Evening Post*, July 29, p. 2.
2. Minutes of conference called by virtue of resolution of the Executive Board and Advisory Council of the Jewish Community, Aug. 1, 1912, MA, F46–L9. Among others present were Dr. Hebert Friedenwald, secretary of the American Jewish Committee, and Abraham Goldberg, of the Federation of American Zionists.
3. On Mrs. Charles H. Israels (Belle Moskowitz), see *Times*, Jan. 3, 1933, p. 1; *Dictionary of American Biography*, XXI, 567–77. On Henry Moskowitz, see Schapiro, pp. 446–49; *Times*, Dec. 18, 1937, p. 23. On London, see Epstein, *Profiles of Eleven*, pp. 161–74; Gorenstein, in *PAJHS*, pp. 222–26.
4. Alexander H. Kaminsky to Magnes, July 28, 1912, MA, F46–L11. Jonah J. Goldstein to Dr. Henry Moskowkitz, Sept. 11, 1913, MA, F6–L1a. On Goldstein, see Binkerd, p. 31 and *Times*, July 23, 1967, p. 60; interview with Jonah J. Goldstein, Oct. 24, 1964 and Feb. 4, 1965. In 1931 Goldstein was appointed city magistrate and in 1936 judge of General Sessions. He was elected to that post in 1939 and in 1945 was a Fusion candidate for the mayoralty. On the Young Men's Benevolent Association, see *Federation Review*, IV (Apr. 1910), 101–3; interview with Hyman Reit, Nov. 23, 1964; on the Jewish Big Brother Movement, see *ibid.*, II (Oct. 1908), 8; on Kaminsky, see *Times*, Sept. 27, 1937, p. 1.
5. Magnes to David Pinski, Aug. 2, 1912, MA, F46–L11; Min ECK, Sept. 9, 1912, MA, F1–L27.
6. *Tageblat*, Aug. 20, 1912, p. 1; *Forward*, Aug. 20, 1912, p. 8; *AH*, Aug. 23, 1912, p. 439.
7. Report to the Temporary Committee on Organization of Vigilance Committee, Aug. 4, 1912, MA, F46–L9.
8. *Times*, Aug. 20, 1912, p. 3; MA, F46–L11 contains miscellaneous letters with information on criminal activities. *World*, Aug. 21, 1912, p. 3.

9. Jonah J. Goldstein to Magnes, Sept. 2 and Sept. 18, 1912, MA, F6–L1a.

10. Cyrus Sulzberger to Magnes, Aug. 11 and Sept. 4, 1912, Magnes to Sulzberger, Aug. 22, 1912, MA, F47–L95. Warburg contributed $1,000. The sum of Schiff's contribution is not mentioned.

11. Min ECK, Sept. 9, 1912, MA, F1–L27; Magnes to Goldstein, Oct. 23, 1912, Nov. 14, 1912, MA, F6–L1a.

12. Interviews with Abe Shoenfeld, Jan. 6 and Feb. 6, 1965. For examples of the way the Kneeland study was conducted, see Kneeland, pp. 18, 21, 109, 127–28, 140–46, 149.

13. AH, Feb. 9, 1913, p. 415; MJ, Feb. 6, 1913, p. 1.

14. Interview with Shoenfeld, Jan. 6, 1965; Magnes to Gaynor, Oct. 23, 1912, Gaynor Papers, Location 127. MA (SP125–SP139) contains about 1,900 case histories of Jewish criminals prepared by the Kehillah's chief investigator and based on information supplied by his informers and agents covering the period Aug. 1912 to Sept. 1917. For the initial six weeks of activities, see Stories #4, #6, #29, MA, SP126, and Stories #54, #66, #83, MA, SP127.

15. Magnes to Gaynor, Oct. 23, 1912, Gaynor Papers, Location 127.

16. Magnes to Robert N. Adamson (secretary to the mayor), Oct. 21, 1912, Gaynor Papers, Location 127.

17. Magnes to Gaynor, Oct. 23, 1912, Gaynor Papers, Location 127; Gaynor to Magnes, Oct. 24, 1912, Gaynor Papers, Location 154.

18. Gaynor to Magnes, Nov. 11, 1912, MA, F6–L1c.

19. Min BDEA, Nov. 11, 1912, Jan. 5 and Feb. 10, 1913, YIVO Archives; Magnes to Greenbaum, Jan. 10, 1913, MA, F46–L16; Magnes to Warburg, Jan. 12, 1913, and Magnes to Schiff, Jan. 29, 1913, MA, F20–L139.

20. Min BDEA, Jan. 13, 1913, Mar. 10, 1913, YIVO Archives. Judah Magnes to Samuel Greenbaum, Jan. 12, 1914, MA, F46–L16. Among other new contributors were Adolph Ochs, George Blumenthal, Jesse Straus, and Lucien Littauer (Magnes to Greenbaum, Mar. 10, 1914, MA, F46–L16). Eighteen persons pledged $22,500 at the meeting. Schiff and Lewisohn pledged $5,000 each. See also Min BDEA, May 12, 1913, Oct. 13 and Dec. 14, 1914, Feb. 8, 1915, Apr. 12, 1915, YIVO Archives.

21. Warheit, Dec. 13, 1912, p. 4; The Guild Journal (published by the clubs of the University Settlement), III (Oct. 1912), 11; ibid., (Jan. 1913), p. 52; AH, Dec. 20, 1912, pp. 224, 231. Interview with Judge Jonah J. Goldstein, Oct. 24, 1964, and Feb. 4, 1965.

22. Goldstein to Magnes, Sept. 2 and Sept. 18, 1912, Nov. 25, 1913, MA, F6–L1a; Goldstein to Moskowitz, Sept. 11, 1913, MA, F6–L1a.

23. Goldstein to Moskowitz, Sept. 11, 1913, MA, F6–L1a; Morse M. Frankel to Goldstein, Sept. 11, 1913, MA, F6–L1a; Magnes to

Warburg, Sept. 15, 1913 ("not sent"), MA, F6–L1a. Harry W. Newburger to Magnes, Nov. 11, 1913, MA, F46–L16; Shoenfeld, Report on Rader Case, Dec. 27, 1912, MA, F6–L1a; Magnes to Moskowitz, Dec. 27, 1913 ("not sent") MA, F6–L1a; Story #54, MA, SP127; Story #772, MA, SP134. Interview with Abe Shoenfeld, Jan. 6, 1965.

24. Dr. E. W. Krackowicer, Goldstein's club leader at the Educational Alliance ten years earlier, attempted to convince Magnes of Goldstein's integrity and leadership potential. He stressed the influence of Dr. David Blaustein (formerly executive director of the Educational Alliance) on Goldstein in his youth. "He needs guidance," Krackowicer wrote, "now as he got it then. You should take Blaustein's place." Krackowicer to Magnes, Mar. 19 and Mar. 23, 1915, MA, F46–L19. Magnes failed to respond.

25. Magnes to Warburg, Sept. 1, 1913, MA, F46–L19. Magnes to Moskowitz, Dec. 27, 1913 ("not sent"), MA, F6–L1a; Krackowicer to Magnes, Apr. 15, 1915, MA, F46–L19. Magnes, Memo of Meeting with Jonah J. Goldstein, Nov. 27, 1912, MA, F6–L1a. In Sept. 1913, a confidential letter Magnes wrote to Warburg describing Goldstein's behavior unintentionally reached Goldstein, who brought a libel suit against Magnes. It was settled in March, 1916, after Magnes reluctantly apologized for defaming Goldstein's name. Magnes' utter implacability, despite the advice of his closest advisers, to soften his harsh judgments, stands out. Magnes to Schiff, July 14, 1914, MA, F46–L19; Newburger to Magnes, Mar. 5, 1915, MA, F47–L121. Newburger, upon whose information Magnes had originally formed his low opinion of Goldstein, wrote to Magnes in 1916 that he had come to know Goldstein better and understood "the East Side type which Goldstein represents." He was ambitious but honest. Newburger to Magnes, Jan. 17, 1916, MA, F47–L106.

26. Goldstein to Magnes, MA, Nov. 25, 1912, F6–L1a.

27. *Ibid.* In two interviews with Judge Goldstein he stressed two themes: Newburger belonged to Magnes' uptown social group, and therefore Magnes had confidence in him rather than in an East Sider who was "too close to the source"; and, Newburger and his staff were getting salaries while Goldstein and his helpers were all volunteers. Interview with Jonah Goldstein, Oct. 24, 1964 and Feb. 4, 1965. For Goldstein's account of these events, see *MJ*, Mar. 29, 1940, pp. 7–8.

28. Jonah J. Goldstein to John P. Mitchell, Jan. 12, 1914 (copy of letter from James G. Wallace Jr., Commissioner of Licenses, to James Matthews, executive secretary to the mayor, Dec. 27, 1913, attached), Mitchel Papers, Location 245. Krackowicer to Magnes, Apr. 15, 1915, MA, F46–L19; Goldstein to Newburger, Jan. 22, 1916, MA, F47–L106. Goldstein to Dr. Henry Moskowitz, Sept. 11, 1913, MA, F6–L1a; *Stenographer's Minutes of the Special Committee of the Board of Alder-*

men, V, 4234–37; Goldstein to Felix Warburg, July 8, 1913, MA, F46–L19. Interview with Jonah Goldstein, Feb. 4, 1965.

29. Goldstein to Moskowitz, Sept. 11, 1912, MA, F6–L1a; University Settlement Society of New York, *26th Annual Report*, 1912, pp. 40–41; *AH*, Dec. 20, 1912, p. 224; *Warheit*, Dec. 13, 1912, p. 4; *MJ*, Dec. 18, 1912, p. 5; *Times*, Aug. 12, 1913, p. 4. Magnes and Newburger challenged the claims of the ESNA (Magnes to Warburg, Sept. 1, 1913, MA, F46–L19; Newburger, Memorandum: Analysis of List of Complaints of ESNA from Jan. 1, 1913 to Sept. 12, 1913, MA, F6–L2). On the East Side Forum, see *Times*, June 14, 1915, p. 13.

30. *Warheit*, Dec. 13, 1912, p. 4; *MJ*, Dec. 18, 1912, p. 5; June 6, 1913, p. 2. Settlement house workers on the executive committee of the ESNA were Alice P. Gannet, Robbins Gilman, George Landy, and Richard Neustadt.

31. See above, n. 20; interview with Abe Shoenfeld, Feb. 6, 1965. A budget for the year Jan. 1, 1914, to Dec. 31, 1914, entitled "Vice Account" (MA, F47–L112) lists five investigators on per annum salary. No other budget was found. Shoenfeld asserted that this staff was hired by the beginning of January, 1913. Lawrence Greenbaum later became senior partner of the law firm Greenbaum, Wolff, and Ernst. In 1942, he was appointed chairman of the New York State Board of Social Welfare. *Times*, Aug. 29, 1951, p. 25; interview with Edward S. Greenbaum, Jan. 5, 1965. On Greenbaum's work for the Kehillah, see Magnes to Greenbaum, Feb. 27, 1913, and Greenbaum to Magnes, Mar. 13, 1913, MA, F6–L3; Greenbaum, p. 36.

32. MA, F46–L7 contains considerable material on this office. See also *Warheit*, Aug. 2, 1913, pp. 1, 4; Aug. 4, p. 1; Aug. 5, p. 1; *AH*, Aug. 3, 1913, p. 386.

33. Newburger to Gaynor, Dec. 3, 1912, Gaynor Papers, Location 127; Gaynor to Newburger, Dec. 3, 1912, Location 155; Newburger to Gaynor, Dec. 16, 1912, Location 127; Newburger to Gaynor, Jan. 18, 1913, Location 132; Gaynor to Newburger, Jan. 22, 1913, and Jan. 23, MA, F6–L2; Newburger to Magnes, Jan. 25, 1913, MA, F6–L2; Magnes to Gaynor, Apr. 9, 1913, MA, F6–L1c; Magnes to Gaynor, May 20, 1913, Gaynor Papers, Location 132; Gaynor to Magnes, June 10, 1913, Location 157; "Vice Report" (mimeographed), Nov. 14, 1913, pp. 3, 14, MA, F46–L16.

34. "Vice Report" (mimeographed), Nov. 14, 1913, pp. 55–58, MA, F46–L16. Toblinsky confessed to poisoning three hundred horses. *Times*, Mar. 25, 1913, p. 24; Aug. 24, p. 7.

35. Interview with Abe Shoenfeld, Jan. 6, 1965. Shoenfeld exhibited a remarkable ability for recalling details, which were confirmed by the written reports from 1912 to 1917 in MA.

36. "Vice Report" (mimeographed), Nov. 14, 1913, p. 60, MA, F46–L16.

37. *Ibid.*, p. 5.
38. *Ibid.*, p. 3.
39. *Ibid.*, p. 4.
40. *Ibid.*, p. 13; see also *Times*, Feb. 4, 1913, p. 6; Feb. 21, p. 3; Mar. 11, pp. 1, 2; Mar. 14, p. 3.
41. "Vice Report" (mimeographed), Nov. 14, 1913, pp. 25 ff. MA, F46–L16.
42. *Ibid.*, p. 30.
43. *MJ*, Feb. 6, 1913, p. 1; Magnes to Warburg, Sept. 15, 1913, MA, F6–L1a; interview with Abe Shoenfeld, Jan. 6, 1965.
44. Magnes to Greenbaum, June 20, 1913, MA, F6–L3; Newburger to Magnes, Nov. 11, 1913, and Magnes to Greenbaum, Nov. 5, 1913, MA, F6–L3.
45. Interview with Abe Shoenfeld, Jan. 6 and Feb. 6, 1965.
46. *Times*, Feb. 7, 1913, p. 2; Feb. 12, p. 1. In this capacity Newburger clashed with District Attorney Whitman. Gaynor evidently saw in Newburger a lawyer and investigator of unimpeachable integrity who would conduct the department's own investigations and thereby check Whitman's continuous probing.
47. Magnes to Judge Samuel Greenbaum, May 11, 1913, MA, F46–L16; Magnes to Harry Newburger, June 2, 1913, MA, F6–L2. *Report of the Citizens Committee* was published Feb. 26, 1913. The Aldermanic Investigating Committee (the Curran Committee) issued a preliminary report on Mar. 11, 1913, and a final report on June 10, 1913. Gaynor ignored both reports. See the Fusion platform for the Mayoralty campaign, *Times*, Aug. 1, 1913, p. 2.
48. Newburger to Magnes, July 19, July 26, and Aug. 19, 1913; Judge Samuel Greenbaum to Magnes, Aug. 28, 1913; draft of letter to Mayor Gaynor sent to Committee of Nine for comments, Aug. 20 and Sept. 1, 1913 (includes comments of Judge Greenbaum), MA, F6–L5. Magnes to Gaynor, Sept. 1, 1913 (penciled note, "to have been given to the Mayor on Sept. 3, 1913"), MA, F6–L1c. Magnes to Judge Samuel Greenbaum, Sept. 25, 1913, MA, F46–L16.
49. Magnes to Acting Mayor Ardolph Kline, Sept. 25, 1913, MA, F46–L16; Magnes to Kline, Sept. 26, Oct. 8, and Nov. 7, 1913, Gaynor Papers, Location 132; Magnes to Judge Samuel Greenbaum, Nov. 14, 1913, MA, F46–L16.
50. Magnes to Judge Samuel Greenbaum, Nov. 20, 1913, MA, F46–L16; William Salomon to Judge Samuel Greenbaum and Marshall, Jan. 16, 1914, MA, F47–L116.
51. For the year 1914, $15,400 was subscribed. Magnes to Judge Samuel Greenbaum, Mar. 10, 1914, MA, F46–L16. Salomon reduced his contribution from $2,500 to $500. Magnes to Judge Samuel Greenbaum, Jan. 6, 1915, MA, F46–L16.
52. Lewinson, pp. 110–11, points to Mitchel's "aloofness," his fear

of contact with the public, and his frequent canceling of appointments with delegations. Marshall invited Mitchel to address a meeting at Carnegie Hall sponsored by the American Jewish Relief Committee. The mayor failed to reply and Marshall sent a second invitation. On the evening of the meeting, the mayor sent a note excusing himself because of illness and failing to include a word of greeting to the gathering. Marshall to Mitchel, Dec. 22, 1915, Marshall Papers. Marshall viewed Mitchel's behavior as "shabby" and as indicative of the mayor's attitude toward Jews. Marshall to Charles H. Brodek, Dec. 30, 1915, Marshall Papers.

53. Bertram D. Cruger (executive secretary to the mayor) to Magnes, Jan. 10, 1914, Mitchel Papers, Location 172; Magnes to Mitchel, Jan. 14, 1914, MA, F46–L15.

54. Times, Dec. 23, 1913, p. 18.

55. AH, Feb. 6, 1914, p. 435.

56. Mitchel was trying to convince Col. George W. Goethals to serve as police commissioner. Lewinson, pp. 118–20.

57. See, for example, Woods to Newburger, Jan. 30, 1914, MA, F47–L120; Magnes to Mitchel, Feb. 6, 1914, MA, F46–L15; Woods to Magnes, Feb. 16, 1914, Mitchel Papers, Location 172; Magnes to Mitchel, Feb. 27, 1914, MA, F46–L15; Bertram Cruger to Magnes, Mar. 3, 1914, and Bertram Cruger to Newburger, Aug. 17, 1914, Mitchel Papers, Location 172; Bertram Cruger to Newburger, Aug. 17, 1914, Mitchel Papers, Location 173; Magnes to Mitchel, Oct. 25, 1914, MA, F46–L15.

58. Times, Apr. 7, 1914, p. 3; Apr. 8, p. 9; Apr. 12, 1914, p. 1; May 13, 1942, p. 19. In 1916 Woods married the granddaughter of J. Pierpont Morgan. On Woods's death, the Times editorialized: "A Police Commissioner concerned about social problems was something new . . . He so won the confidence of his men, that his administration became not only effective but smooth; . . . a great change in policy had been carried out quietly and almost without notice (May 14, 1942, p. 18). See his Crime Prevention and Policeman and Public. For a brief appraisal of his administration see Lewinson, pp. 120–21.

59. Magnes to Woods, Feb. 6, 1914, Mitchel Papers, Location 248. Newburger to Woods, June 16, 1914, and Newburger to Mitchel, June 16, 1914, Mitchel Papers, Location 248. On Newburger's monthly lists, see for example, Newburger to Mitchel, May 5, 1914, MA, F46–L15; Newburger to Woods, June 16, 1914, Mitchel Papers, Location 248.

60. Newburger to Magnes, July 6, 1914, MA, F47–L120; Magnes to Woods, Aug. 14, 1914, MA, F47–L110; Newburger to Magnes, Sept. 16, 1914, MA, F47–L120.

61. Magnes to Woods, Dec. 29, 1914, MA, F47–L100.

62. Magnes to Judge Samuel Greenbaum, Jan. 6, 1915, MA, F46–L16. Magnes to Marshall, Jan. 8, 1915, MA, F48–L132.

63. Newburger to Magnes, Jan. 18, 1915, MA, F47–L121.

64. Magnes to Schiff, Apr. 29, 1915, MA, F47–L116.

65. Salomon to Magnes, May 4, 1915 and Schiff to Magnes, May 4, 1915, MA, F47–L116; Marshall to Magnes, May 7, 1915, MA, F28–L86; Magnes to Judge Samuel Greenbaum, Oct. 20, 1915, MA, F46–L16.

66. Judge Samuel Greenbaum, Oct. 21, 1915, MA, F46–L16.

67. Magnes to Woods, Dec. 29, 1914, MA, F47–L100.

68. Pink, pp. 245–48.

69. *Times*, July 16, 1913, p. 1; Lewinson, p. 89; *Warheit*, July 16, 1913, p. 1. Both the *Times* and the *Warheit* expressed surprise when Schiff publicly urged Gaynor's candidacy, since he was considered a supporter of McAneny.

70. McAneny married the daughter of Dr. Abraham Jacobi, the famous German-Jewish pediatrician. On McAneny, see Lewinson, pp. 83–85; *Times*, July 30, 1953, p. 23. On the subway construction issue, see Pink, pp. 171, 197–98; Smith, pp. 122–23; Lewinson, pp. 67–71, 85, 91–92. The *Times*, Sept. 10, 1913, p. 2, reported that Hearst's Independence League was planning to offer its nomination for mayor to Mitchel.

71. Mitchel won the Fusion nomination with a one vote plurality over Whitman. *Times*, Aug. 8, 1913, p. 1. The *Warheit* claimed that a number of Jewish members of the nominating committee voted against Whitman because of his role in the Brandt affair and his unpopularity on the East Side (Aug. 3, 1913, p. 1). The central figures in the Gaynor movement besides Schiff were R. Ross Appleton, Herman Ridder, and Joseph Johnson. *Times*, Sept. 4, 1913, p. 1. See also, Adler, *Schiff: Life and Letters*, I, 339.

72. *Times*, Sept. 13, 1913, pp. 1, 2. The account mentions Schiff's "repugnance" for Mitchel's "mud-slinging campaign" against Gaynor. See also Adler, *Schiff: Life and Letters*, I, 340.

73. *Times*, Aug. 5, 1913, p. 2; Aug. 7, p. 3; *Warheit*, Aug. 5, 1913, p. 1; Magnes to Barondess, Sept. 2, 1913, MA, F23–L83.

74. *Times*, Aug. 1, 1913, pp. 1, 2. Mitchel appointed Moskowitz chairman of the Civil Service Commission. On Wise, see *Times*, Aug. 30, 1913, p. 2; Wise to Whitman, Nov. 4, 1914, Wise Papers. Once Mitchel won the Fusion nomination Wise supported him. On Saphirstein, see *MJ*, July 16, 1913, p. 4; Aug. 1, p. 4; Aug. 3, p. 4.

75. Adler, *Schiff: Life and Letters*, I, 340.

76. Abe Shoenfeld to Magnes, June 15, 1915, MA, F46–L4; Minutes of Conference Called by Police Commissioner Woods with representative citizens of associations of the East Side, Jan. 15, 1915, MA, F47–L110. No one connected with the Kehillah's vice work was present. The idea of a neighborhood conference was discussed by Woods and Moskowitz shortly before Woods became police commissioner. Thus ten months passed before Woods took any steps. Goldstein to Woods, Mar. 31, 1914, Mitchel Papers, Location 245; Cruger to Landy, May 20,

1914, Mitchel Papers, Location 172. Moskowitz, a close adviser of Mitchel, was still president of the ESNA. Woods's neighborhood conference brought no results. See also *MJ*, Jan. 18, 1915, p. 2.

77. Vice Fund, May 1915, MA, F47–L116; Magnes, *Address*, Apr. 24, 1915, p. 15.

78. Magnes to Newburger, Mar. 16, 1916, MA, F47–L106; Address of Judah Magnes to Seventh Convention, June 3, 1916, MA, F2–L1a; Newburger to Magnes, Apr. 7, 1916, MA, F47–L106. The reduced activity is indicated by the less frequent reports. Shoenfeld still had several agents in his employ. Shoenfeld to Magnes, May 4, 1915, MA, F46–L4. Newburger was on a part-time basis. Newburger to Magnes, Jan. 10, 1916, MA, F47–L106.

79. Magnes to Schiff, Apr. 26, 1917, MA, F31–L161; Herbert Lehman promised one-fourth of all money raised up to $20,000. Magnes to Newburger, Mar. 5, 1917, MA, F2–L127. Warburg contributed $2,500 and Schiff $1,000. Magnes to Schiff ("Vice Fund Subscriptions" attached), May 2, 1917, MA, F31–L161.

80. MA, SP127; *Times*, Dec. 5, 1916, p. 4; Dec. 6, p. 6; Dec. 11, p. 8; Jan. 25, 1917, p. 17; Apr. 29, p. 5; Aug. 9, p. 2; Sept. 7, p. 7; Dec. 26, p. 11. Shoenfeld recalls undertaking investigatory work for the Narcotics Division of the U.S. Department of Justice through Magnes' intercession, for which he received $10,000 as compensation. The assignment permitted Shoenfeld to continue during the same period to serve as the Kehillah's chief investigator. Interview with Abe Shoenfeld, Feb. 6 and June 6, 1965.

81. Newburger to Magnes, Apr. 7, 1916, MA, F47–L106.

IX. THE JEWISH LABOR MOVEMENT AND THE KEHILLAH

1. Meeting of Kehillah Delegates, Jan. 24, 1914, MA, F17–L231; Rischin, *Promised City*, pp. 202–5, 244. For a dissenting view on Kehillah intervention in industrial problems, see Cyrus Sulzberger to Magnes, Nov. 19, 1912, MA, F47–L95.

2. Rischin, *Promised City*, pp. 250–52; Herberg, pp. 17–21.

3. Soon after the founding convention of the Kehillah, 2,000 bakery workers struck the 150 Jewish bakeries of the East Side. It presaged the militant trade union activity that began in the fall of 1909. Bernard Weinstein, pp. 424–35.

4. Rischin, *Promised City*, pp. 247–57; Joel Seidman, pp. 104–13, 118–30; Stolberg, pp. 59–92; Levine, pp. 144–207, 218–319; Hoffman, *Fuftzig yohr cloakmacher union*, pp. 173–275; Hyman Berman, "Era of the Protocol"; Dubofsky, *When Workers Organize*, pp. 23–25, 97–101. Irwin Yellowitz describes the ambivalent stand of the "social prog-

ressives" toward labor's demands in *Labor and the Progressive Movement*, pp. 88–127.

5. *Forward*, July 27, 1910, p. 4.

6. Abraham Rosenberg, *Di cloak-macher un ze'ire union* (New York, 1920), quoted in Levine, p. 182.

7. Levine, p. 157. Levine cites such contemporary periodicals as *Survey, Outlook, The World To-day, The World, Evening Journal;* see *ibid.*, pp. 152–56, 158–60, 226–28.

8. Herberg sees the period of 1909–1916 as the time of "transformation of the Jewish labor movement from the European to the American model" (*AJYB*, 1952, p. 24). Hyman Berman suggests that the workers were "emotional and not ideological socialists" and hence accepted business unionism ("Protocol," pp. 199–200). Though both insights are valid, the transition was possible because nontrade union activities permitted posturing as a revolutionary movement. In relation to the American political scene and the Jewish community, union leaders were as radical as the editors of the socialist Yiddish press. These developments are indicated below. See also Dubofsky, *When Workers Organize*, pp. 32–36.

9. *Zukunft*, XV (Jan. 1910), 65.

10. *Ibid.*

11. The phrase is Will Herberg's. See *AJYB*, 1952, p. 16 and especially pp. 29–30 where he briefly discusses "the emergence of a self-contained Jewish labor community." See also Rischin, in *Labor History*, IV, 233, 235–36, 247.

12. Epstein, *Jewish Labor*, I, 273–97, 327–34; Niger, IV, 300–4; Rischin, *Promised City*, pp. 117–38, 152–61, 166–67. N. W. Ayer and Sons' ANAD, p. 1129, records the *Forward* circulation as 52,190. Ayers' ANAD for 1917, p. 661, lists a circulation for the *Forward* of 198,982. However, Ayers' ANAD for 1918, p. 676, shows a figure of 130,380. The loss reflected the rise in the price of the paper and the war situation, during which time the *Forward*, as a socialist, foreign-language newspaper, lost readers. However, beginning with the 1918 edition of Ayers' ANAD, the *Forward* joined the Audit Bureau of Circulation (ABC) which provided a more precise estimate of circulation. The figure of 200,000 is generally used as the high-point of the *Forward's* circulation; 150,000 seems to be closer to the truth. The Yiddish paper with the second largest circulation in 1917 was the *Morgen Journal*, with 82,270. Ayers' ANAD, 1918, p. 676.

13. *Evening Call*, Nov. 25, 1910, p. 6; Dec. 15, p. 6; Rogoff, p. 60; Rischin, *Promised City*, p. 235; Gorenstein, in *PAJHS*, pp. 202–26.

14. Rogoff, pp. 16, 57–59.

15. Herberg, pp. 14–15, 26.

16. Hertz, *Fuftzig yohr arbeiter ring*, pp. 98–108, 52–57; Leo Wolf-

son, "Jewish Fraternal Organizations," *JCR*, pp. 865–68; Frank F. Rosenblatt, "Mutual Aid Organizations," *ibid.*, pp. 732–34; B. Rivkin (B. A. Weinrebe), in Rontch, pp. 75–77.

17. Hertz, *Fuftzig yohr arbeiter ring*, pp. 150, 158; *Forward*, Mar. 22, 1909, p. 1; List of Delegates to the Constituent Convention of the Jewish Community of New York, Feb. 27, 28, Mar. 6, 27, 1909, MA, F48–L135.

18. Quoted in Hertz, *Fuftzig yohr arbeiter ring*, p. 123.

19. *Eighth Annual Report of the Workmen's Circle, 1908* (New York, 1909), pp. 5, 77–81; *JCR*, p. 869.

20. Rischin, *Promised City*, pp. 166–67, 235; M. Osherowitch, "Di geschichte fun forvets: 1897–1947" (typescript, New York Public Library), pp. 136–40.

21. Levine, p. 192; Epstein, *Jewish Labor*, I, 323; Cahan, IV, 549–50; V, 240, 341–42; Rogoff, pp. 58–59; Rich, pp. 27–29.

22. Rischin, *Promised City*, pp. 148–62; Epstein, *Jewish Labor*, II, 7–10, 364–90; Hertz, *Sotzialistishe bavegung*, pp. 100–2, 123–28; Bloom, pp. 42–68. For the European background, see Pinson, in *JSS*, pp. 233–64. On the language controversy, see Hoffman in *Zukunft*, XIV (May 1909), 274–81; *ibid.*, XVI (July 1911), 382–85; Feigenbaum, pp. 392–97; Niger, pp. 294–99.

23. Cahan, IV, 398–411, 414–19, 424–27, 431–55; Hertz, *Sotzialishtishe bavegung*, pp. 124–27; Rogoff, pp. 23–27; Hertz, *Fuftzig yohr arbeiter ring*, pp. 65–69; Menes, pp. 360–65.

24. Rischin, *Labor History*, IV, 233–47; Berman, "Protocol," 178–79; Levine, 196–97, 235–36, 310–11.

25. Levine, pp. 153, 156, 159–61; Rischin, *Promised City*, p. 248; Dubofsky, *When Workers Organize*, pp. 54–55; *Times*, Jan. 22, 1913, p. 1.

26. Shannon, pp. 47–50; Kipnis, pp. 206, 276–88; Budin, pp. 303–5. London, pp. 401–3; Hertz, *Sotzialistishe bavegung*, pp. 91, 100–14, 116–18, 127.

27. *Evening Call*, Sept. 13, 1908, p. 3.

28. Hoffman, *Far fuftzig yohr*, pp. 157–65; Hertz, *Sotzialistishe bavegung*, pp. 91–107, 112, 118, 142–44.

29. *Tzeitgeist*, Jan. 25, Feb. 22, and Apr. 12, 1907, quoted in Hertz, *Sotzialistishe bavegung*, pp. 101–2.

30. *Ibid.*

31. Hertz, *Fuftzig yohr arbeiter ring*, pp. 109–19, 131–46.

32. Glazer, *American Judaism*, p. 67; Sherman, p. 168.

33. *JCR*, p. 144; *Report fun arbeiter ring zu der tzenter yehrlichen convention*, May 4–7, 1910, p. 107; Lamed Shapiro, in Rontch, p. 32. For a discussion of socialism and *landsmanshaftn*, see Rivkin in Rontch, pp. 83–84.

34. *Forward,* Mar. 4, 1909, p. 8. Twice the *Forward* softened its outright rejection of the Kehillah mentioning the desirability of a Jewish communal framework but rejecting the existing Kehillah as dominated by uptown philanthropists and downtown rabbis. *Forward,* Mar. 5, 1909, p. 4; Aug. 14, p. 4.

35. Hoffman in *Zukunft,* XVII (Jan. 1912), 64–65.

36. Levine, pp. 161–62, 204–5, 260, 283; Green, pp. 8–11, 62–73, 79, 83, 87–89, 147–50, 300, 329; National Civic Federation, *Monthly Review,* I (July 1904), 17, 19; Strauss, pp. 194–201; Naomi W. Cohen, *Dual Heritage,* pp. 114–20; Mason, pp. 146–49; Berman, in *Essays,* p. 81; Schapiro, pp. 446–49; Forcey, pp. 66–70; Rischin, *Promised City,* p. 244.

37. Berman, in *Essays,* pp. 75–92; Levine, pp. 200, 467; Mason, pp. 301–2; Reznikoff, I, 1127–30.

38. Julius Henry Cohen, p. 182. Berman sees the origin of the protocol and its labor philosophy not in the religious background of the framers but rather in the peace and progressive movements ("Protocol," pp. 231–32); cf. Budish and Soule, p. 66 and Seidman, pp. 49–50.

39. Baron, II, 208–43; Jacob Katz, *M'soret u'mashber,* pp. 119–24.

40. Menashe, "Landsmanshaftn far'n idishn gericht," in Rontch, pp. 127–30; Levitats, in *Essays,* p. 343; Rischin, *Promised City,* pp. 147–48.

41. The Committee on Conciliation consisted of Rabbi Moses Z. Margolies, chairman, Rabbi Philip Klein, William Fischman, Sender Jarmulowsky, and Abraham S. Schomer. Min ECK, Apr. 12, 1910, MA, F1–L62; see also Min ECK, Sept. 14 and Oct. 12, 1909, Apr. 12, 1910, MA, F1–L62; Isaac Allen to Magnes, Sept. 9, 1909, Bernard G. Richards to Abraham S. Schomer, Dec. 5, 1909, MA, F1–L62c; Min ECK, June 9 and Dec. 4, 1909, MA, F1–L62; Min ECK, May 9, 1911, MA, F1–L58; Min ECK, Sept. 9, 1912, MA, F1–L27; Min ECK, Jan. 14, 1913, MA, F48–L159; Min ECK, Apr. 9, 1913, MA, F10–L2; Min ECK, May 3, 1917, MA, F10–L31.

42. Magnes to Barondess (proposed constitution for court of arbitration attached to letter), Aug. 5, 1913, MA, F23–L83; Report by William Lieberman to Kehillah Convention, Apr. 25, 1914, MA, F17–L138; Magnes to Sol M. Stroock, May 13, 1914, Abelson Papers; Lieberman to Magnes, Mar. 16, 1915, MA, F17–L131; [William Lieberman], Draft, Kehillah Arbitration Courts, Rules for conduct of Kehillah Arbitration Courts [Mar. 1919], MA, F47–L22; Counsel (William Lieberman) to Dr. H. Peirera Mendes, Apr. 4, 1919, MA, F12–L13.

43. Adler, *Schiff: Life and Letters* I, 393–94. For Schiff's interest in the immigrant worker, see *ibid.* 292–94, 388–89. For the Industrial Removal Office, see Joseph, *History of the Baron de Hirsh Fund,* pp. 184–96. By 1910 the diversion of immigrants directly to Galveston,

Texas—the "Galveston movement"—was in deep trouble. Government and labor charged that the project violated the law against importing contract labor. Joseph, *ibid.*, pp. 205–9; Adler, *Schiff: Life and Letters*, II, 94–114. This may in part account for Schiff's keen interest in labor mediation at this time.

44. *Times*, Jan. 22, 1913, p. 2.

45. *Times*, July 2, 1915, p. 22; Magnes to Schiff, May 25, 1915, Schiff to Magnes, May 26, 1915, MA, F46–L21b; Ralph M. Easley to Isaac N. Seligman, June 2, 1915; Schiff to Easley, June 3, 1915; Schiff to Magnes, June 17, 1915; Magnes to Straus, June 29, 1915; all are in MA, F30–L31. Magnes expected the signatories to be selected to serve as a council of conciliation. Magnes to Straus, July 7, 1915, MA, F30–L31. See also Levine, pp. 279–91; Berman, "Protocol," pp. 403–19.

46. Adler, *Schiff: Life and Letters*, I, 354–57; Zborowski and Herzog, pp. 74–76, 194–96, 206–7; Supple, pp. 143–45, 158–66; Herbert S. Goldstein, pp. 52–55, 92–93, 98–100, 108–11; Waldman, pp. 323, 325–28, 352–53.

47. Julius Cohen, p. 205.

48. Some members of the Kehillah's executive committee at first opposed the idea of Kehillah mediation. It was "beyond the Kehillah's competence," they felt, and would be misconstrued by the unfriendly Jewish labor movement. Min ECK, Dec. 4, 1909, MA, F1–L62; *Report fun di kehille*, Feb. 26, 1910, p. 23; Min ECK, May 9, 1911, MA, F1–L58. In early 1912, the Kehillah intervened in an incident involving Jewish longshoremen who complained of religious discrimination, Min ECK, Mar. 12, 1912, MA, F10–L2. The arbitration achievements in the apparel trades from 1910 to 1912 and the role played by Kehillah members probably contributed to the change in policy.

49. Bernard Weinstein, pp. 444–46; Rischin, *Promised City*, 65–66; Foner, pp. 39–41.

50. Bernard Weinstein, pp. 443–44; Foner, pp. 24–26, 41–42; *Forward*, June 21, 1912, pp. 1, 4.

51. Bernard Weinstein, p. 449, writes that Rosenfeld's poem, especially written for the purpose, was sung at the strikers' meetings. See also Foner, p. 43–45.

52. Bernard Weinstein, pp. 446–52; Dubofsky, *When Workers Organize*, pp. 68–72; Rogoff, pp. 50–51; *Times*, Sept. 9, 1912, p. 20; *Forward*, July 9, 1912, pp. 1, 5; July 11, p. 1; Aug. 5, p. 1; Aug. 18, p. 1; Aug. 23, p. 1; Sept. 1, p. 1; Sept. 9, pp. 1, 5. The union spent $60,000 during the strike. The *Forward* raised $20,000, the Cloakmakers Union $20,000, street collections, picnics, and theater benefits netted $10,000. Mutual aid societies were asked to provide benefits for their members who were on strike. Foner, pp. 46–48; *Forward*, July 21, 1912, p. 1; July 19, p. 1; Aug. 1, p. 1; Aug. 6, p. 1; Aug. 29, p. 1.

53. Min ECK, Sept. 9, 1912, MA, F1–L27; Foner, p. 49.

54. Memorandum of Agreement, Nov. 1912, MA, F22–L42; Minutes of Furriers Conference Committee, Nov. 6 and Dec. 3, 1912, Feb. 6, Mar. 13, and May 5, 1913, MA, F22–L45; *The Fur Worker* (Joint Board, Furriers Union of Greater New York), Jan. 1914, p. 1.

55. Memorandum of Agreement between the Associated Fur Manufacturers and the Furriers Union, 1914–1917, July 13, 1914, MA, F29–L35; Foner, pp. 53–55; Bernard Weinstein, pp. 452–53.

56. Memorandum of Agreement between Associated Fur Manufacturers and Joint Board of Furriers, Mar. 1917, MA, F22–L45; Magnes (untitled address), July 16, 1919, MA, SP253; Bernard Weinstein, p. 453.

57. *Survey*, XXIX (Jan. 18, 1913), 492; *Forward*, Jan. 9, 1913, p. 1; Jan. 15, p. 1; Levine, pp. 219–20, 222–28; Zaretz, pp. 85–88; Bernard Weinstein, pp. 285–90; Dubofsky, *When Workers Organize*, pp. 72–85.

58. *Times*, Jan. 14, 1913, p. 7 (quoted in Mann, p. 58). For the character of the strike, see *Times*, Jan. 6, 1913, p. 1; Jan. 7, p. 1; Jan. 24, p. 7; *Forward*, Jan. 11, 1913, p. 4; Jan. 14, p. 1; Jan 30, p. 6; Cahan, V, 251–76; Bernard Weinstein, pp. 290–93.

59. Epstein, *Jewish Labor*, I, 416; Bernard Weinstein, pp. 294–96; Levine, p. 227; *Forward*, Jan. 13, 1913, p. 1; Jan. 19, p. 1; Jan. 23, p. 1; Feb. 15, p. 1; *Survey*, XXIX (Feb. 15, 1913), 661.

60. Agreement between United Garment Workers and East Side Retail Clothing Manufacturers Association, Feb. 14, 1913, MA, F22–L42. The settlement contained better terms than those in the final industry-wide agreement and contributed to the eventual break between the local unions and the national United Garment Workers. Min ECK, Feb. 9, 1915, MA, F48–L161.

61. *Times*, Mar. 1, 1913, p. 1; Mar. 3, p. 20; Mar. 8, p. 10; Mar. 13, p. 22; *Forward*, Mar. 2, pp. 1, 4; Mar. 11, p. 1; Cahan, V, 254–55, 257–66, 276–78; Zaretz, pp. 89–90. Paul Abelson claimed that "the general strike in the clothing industry in 1913 was settled through the mediating efforts of the Chairman [Judah Magnes] of the Jewish Community." Notes on the Organization of the Committee on Industrial Relations of the Jewish Community [Oct. 1914], MA, F22–L42.

62. Zaretz, pp. 105–10; Epstein, *Jewish Labor*, II, 40–46, 48–50; Memo of Agreement between American Clothing Manufacturers Association and Amalgamated Clothing Workers, July 20, 1915, MA, F22–L42; Minutes of Meeting of Council of Moderators, Jan. 12, MA, F29–L27.

63. A connection also existed between industrial turmoil and Jewish criminality. Manufacturers and unions employed criminal gangs. One veteran of the Jewish labor movement writes: "Some of the so-called Jewish unions . . . fell early in their careers upon evil days: under-

world characters, gangsters, got a foothold in the organization. . . . It all came as a desperate effort to secure protection on picket lines . . . against sluggers employed by the other side and against the police. . . . Unfortunately, the element engaged to help would refuse to clear out when their services were no longer wanted. They would be engaged by some unconscionable officers or office-seekers as praetorian guards and vote-getters." Hardman (Salutzky), pp. 373–74. See also *AH*, Jan. 15, 1915, pp. 267–68; *Times*, May 12, 1915, p. 6, May 13, p. 24, May 14, p. 22; Foner, pp. 45–46; Asbury, p. 361; Story #282, MA, SP131; Story #719, MA, SP134; Memorandum from E. B. Goodman, n.d., Mitchel Papers, Location 200.

64. MA, F21–L57.

65. Hertz, *Fuftzig yohr arbeiter ring*, pp. 126–27.

66. *Forward*, June 10, 1915, p. 8; Report of the Director of the Bureau of Industry, Aug. 10, 1915, MA, F28–L106.

67. *5th ARK*, Apr. 25 and 26, 1914, p. 17.

68. Magnes to Lehman, May 6, 1914, MA, F46–L37; Magnes to Lehman, June 1, 1914 and Lehman to Magnes, June 23, 1915, MA, F28–L83; Lehman to Magnes, May 15, 1914 and Magnes to Lehman, May 17, 1914, Lehman to Magnes, May 19, 1914, Abelson Papers; Min ECK, Aug. 11, 1914, MA, F48–L159; Notes on the Organization of the Committee on Industrial Relations [Oct. 1914], MA, F22–L42; Magnes to Warburg, May 29, 1914, MA, F48–L120; Magnes to Adolph Lewisohn, Jan. 5, 1916 and Jan. 14, 1916, MA, F28–L84.

69. Magnes, *Address*, pp. 6–7; Min ECK, June 8, 1915, MA, F28–L108.

70. Magnes to Sulzberger, May 29, 1914, MA, F48–L105.

71. *Times*, Nov. 5, 1953, p. 31; Biographical Sketch, Abelson Papers and Abelson to Members of the Organization Committee, Dec. 7, 1901, Abelson Papers; Levine, pp. 204–5; Rischin, *Promised City*, p. 240.

72. *AJYB*, 5664 (1903–1904), p. 78; *Times*, Apr. 17, 1913, p. 2; Apr. 19, p. 9; Mannheimer, *Address*, Apr. 18, 1913.

73. Memorandum, Division of Industrial Relations, Bureau of Industry for October and November 1915, MA, F22–L42; Monthly Bulletin of Association of Fur Manufacturers, Mar. 1, 1916, p. 1; Min ECK, Feb. 9, 1915, F48–L161; Abelson to Magnes, Feb. 9, 1915, MA, F22–L42.

74. Report of the Director of the Bureau of Industry, Aug. 10, 1915, MA, F28–L106. See also, Zaretz, pp. 108–9, 178.

75. Magnes to Adolph Lewisohn, Jan. 14, 1916, MA, F28–L84; Report of the Bureau of Industry, Feb. 8, 1916, MA, F22–L42; Report of the Bureau of Industry, Apr. 11, 1916, MA, F7–L66; Zaretz, p. 110.

76. Foner, pp. 55–57; Memorandum of Agreement, May 10, 1915, MA, F22–L42; Michael Hollander to Magnes, May 11, 1915, Hollander

to Mannheimer, Sept. 4, 1915, MA, F29–L36; Report of Bureau of Industry, Apr. 11, 1916, MA, F7–L66; Memorandum of Agreement between Muff Bed Manufacturers and Muff Bed Workers Local #51 of International Fur Workers Union, Aug. 10, 1916, MA, F22–L42.

77. Report of Bureau of Industry, Feb. 8, 1916, MA, F22–L42; Report of Bureau of Industry, Apr. 11, 1916, MA, F7–L66. Magnes to Adolph Lewisohn, Jan. 5, 1916, MA, F28–L84; Epstein, *Jewish Labor*, I, 413.

78. Report of the Bureau of Industry, Apr. 11, 1916, MA, F7–L66. Memorandum of Bureau of Industry, Dec. 9, 1915, MA, F22–L42; Mannheimer to Magnes, Dec. 23, 1915, MA, F29–L10; Memo of Settlement of Strike of New York Swiss Embroidery Works, June 14, 1915, MA, F29–L11; Master Bakers Federation to Magnes, July 8, 1915, MA, F29–L22; Mannheimer to Magnes, Oct. 20, 1915, MA, F29–L33; Min ECK, Nov. 10, 1914, MA, F48–L159; Min ECK, Feb. 9, 1915, and Sept. 14, 1915, MA, F48–L161; Min ECK, Sept. 8, 1914, MA, F46–L22b.

79. Abelson, *Activities*, Apr. 24 and 25, 1915. For a general statement of Abelson's view see, "Industrial Problem of the Jew in New York City," *JCR*, pp. 637–40.

80. Meeting of Committee on Industrial Education and Vocational Guidance, Nov. 8, 1915, Abelson Papers; Memorandum of Plan of Work of the Division of Vocational Guidance, Nov. 30, 1915, MA, F22–L42; Outline of Work of the Division of Surveys of the Bureau of Industry, Aug. 1915, MA, F22–L42; Report of the Bureau of Industry, Dec. 13, 1915, Abelson Papers.

81. Memorandum of Plan of Work of the Division of Vocational Guidance and Industrial Education, MA, F29–L13.

82. Min ECK, June 9 and Nov. 9, 1909, MA, F1–L62; Nov. 8, 1910, MA, F48–L156; Report of an Investigation and Appraisal of the Work of the Employment Bureau of the Jewish Community, Mar. 15, 1915, MA, F22–L42; 2d ARK, Feb. 25–26, 1911, p. 12; 4th ARK, Apr. 12–13, 1913, p. 13–14; 5th ARK, Apr. 25–26, 1914, p. 14.

83. Abelson, Plan for Federating the Jewish Philanthropic Employment Bureaus, Jan. 7, 1916, Abelson Papers; Abraham M. Reis to Magnes, Apr. 19, 1912, MA, F2–L81; Min ECK, Feb. 8, 1916, MA, F48–L162; Abelson, Annual Account of the Work of the Employment Bureau of the Jewish Community for year ending Mar. 31, 1917, MA, F22–L42.

84. Abelson to Magnes, Nov. 8, 1918 and Jan. 7, 1920, Abelson Papers; Magnes to Conference Committee of the Fur Industry, May 17, 1920, MA, F41–L34. For a critical view of the Bureau of Industry at this time by a Jewish radical, see Hoffman (Zivyon), in *Zukunft*, XXII (Jan. 1917), 40–43.

85. Abelson to Magnes, Mar. 15, 1923, and Magnes to Abelson, May 9, 1923, Abelson Papers.

X. DECLINE: THE WAR AND THE DEMOCRACY

1. Rappaport, "Jewish Immigrants," pp. 212–55; Shapiro, "Leadership," pp. 132–223, 262–69.
2. Handlin, *American People*, pp. 109–35; Higham, *Strangers in the Land*, pp. 194–233.
3. *AJYB* (1917–1918), p. 198. The communal politics of relief work is treated by Szajkowski, in *YIVO Annual*, pp. 99–158.
4. *AJYB* (1917–1918), p. 199. The AJC was undoubtedly aware of the proposal made at the extraordinary conference of Zionist leaders in August, 1914, that the Zionists call "a convention of Jewish organizations" for the purposes of creating a relief fund, of maintaining Jewish institutions in Palestine, and of discussing the "Jewish situation . . . in the changed condition of the world after the war." Minutes, extraordinary conference, Federation of American Zionists, MA, unclassified. See also Szajkowski, *YIVO Annual*, pp. 101–5.
5. *AJYB* (1917–1918), pp. 200–1: Szajkowski, *YIVO Annual*, 108–10.
6. Zuckerman, in *Geschichte*, I, 33–46; Lipsky, *Thirty Years of Zionism*, pp. 49–50; *JCR*, pp. 1473–75; Szajkowski, in *Yearbook of the Leo Baeck Institute*, X (1965), 33 and in, *YIVO Annual*, pp. 115, 118, 152.
7. Marshall to Warburg, Oct. 26, 1916, Marshall Papers.
8. Zuckerman, *Zichronos*, II, 123–26; *AJYB* (1917–1918), p. 202.
9. *Times*, Dec. 22, 1915, pp. 1–2; Bentwich, *For Zion's Sake*, p. 99; *AJYB* (1916–1917), p. 91; *AH*, Feb. 4, 1916, p. 363, Feb. 11, p. 402, May 26, p. 92, Dec. 29, p. 262.
10. *AJYB* (1917–1918), pp. 201, 209–11, 241; Bentwich, *For Zion's Sake*, pp. 99–102; Brandeis to Magnes, Sept. 9, 1915, Magnes to Brandeis, Sept. 13, 1915, MA, F28–L97a; Harry Friedenwald to Warburg and Magnes, June 20, 1916 and Friedenwald to Magnes, July 10, 1916, MA, F5–L83. For criticism of Magnes' relief activities, see *Maccabaean*, XXVIII (June 1916), p. 123; XXIX (Oct. 1916), 50; XXIX (Dec. 1916), 97–98; *Tageblat*, Dec. 16, 1916, p. 4. Stephen S. Wise to Bernard G. Richards, July 27, 1916, Wise Papers. See also Szajkowski, in *Yearbook of Leo Baeck Institute*, X, 36–43.
11. *AH*, June 9, 1916, p. 150; interview with Isaac B. Berkson, Oct. 28, 1965.
12. For general accounts of the movement for an American Jewish

Congress, see Janowsky, *Jews and Minority Rights*, pp. 161–90; and Shapiro, "Leadership," pp. 181–270.

13. Jewish Congress Organization Committee, pp. 3–4.

14. Min 6th ACK, Apr. 24 and 25, 1915, MA, F28–L7; Jewish Congress Organization Committee, pp. 6, 10–14; Brandeis to Cyrus Adler, Aug. 10, 1915, *ibid.*, pp. 21–22; Minutes, Provisional Executive Committee for General Zionist Affairs, May 9, 1915, MA, unclassified. Richard Gottheil to Stephen S. Wise, Aug. 26, 1915, Wise Papers; *MJ*, Mar. 25, 1916, p. 4; Zuckerman, *Zichrones*, II, 57–59, 64; *Maccabaean*, XXVI (May 1915), 101; XXX (June 1917), 276–77. Lipsky told Friedlaender that he and his associates wanted "to put the AJC out of existence." Friedlaender to Brandeis, Sept. 2, 1915, Friedlaender Papers. Shapiro ("Leadership," pp. 206–10) writes that while Brandeis sought an understanding with his AJC opponents, the East European intellectuals among the Zionist leaders wished to annihilate them.

15. *AH*, Feb. 25, 1916, p. 439; Jan. 28, p. 319; Mar. 31, p. 587. See also Syrkin, "Di problem fun congress," *Idishe congress*, Aug. 6, 1915, p. 4; and Voss, *Stephen S. Wise*, pp. 71–72.

16. Friedlaender to Brandeis, June 20, 1915, Friedlaender Papers; Min 6th ACK, Apr. 24 and 25, 1915, MA, F28–L7; Kaplan Journal, July 16, 1916.

17. Marshall to Adler, Sept. 22, 1915, Marshall Papers; *AH*, Mar. 3, 1916, p. 472; Schiff to Magnes, Mar. 22, 1916, MA, F31–L161; Jewish Congress Organization Committee, p. 6, 15–20; Rischin, in *PAJHS*, XLIX (Mar. 1960), 188–201.

18. Jewish Congress Organization Committee, pp. 15–16; Magnes to Adler, July 29, 1915, MA, F31–L2.

19. Schiff to Magnes, May 21, 1915, MA, F46–L21b; see also Schiff's remarks in *AH*, Mar. 3, 1916, p. 471 and *AJYB* (1916–1917), p. 423. Adler considered the congress movement "insincere propaganda, which, taking advantage of the terrible distress of our brethren abroad, is endeavoring to consolidate the Jews of America into a separate nationalistic group." *AH*, Mar. 24, 1916, p. 558.

20. Marshall to Magnes, May 21, 1915, MA, F28–L86.

21. Alice D. Menken, Dr. S. Newman, Joshua Sprayregen (memorandum, *circa* Jan. 1915), MA, F31–L2; Isaac Allen, Isaac A. Hourwich, Bernard G. Richards, *et al.*, [Call to Delegates' Caucus], Apr. 19, 1915, MA, F28–L18; Minutes of the Provisional Executive Committee for Zionist Affairs, May 9, 1915, Friedlaender Papers.

22. Magnes to Marshall, Jan. 31 and Feb. 22, 1915, MA, F31–L2; Friedlaender to Brandeis, June 20, 1915, Friedlaender Papers. As early as November 1914 Magnes warned of the necessity of democratizing the AJC "if the AJC expects really to lead an organized Jewry in this country." Magnes to Judge Julian W. Mack, Nov. 24, 1914, MA F17–L216.

23. Magnes to Marshall, Jan. 31, 1915, MA, F31–L2; Magnes to the president and members of the executive committee of the AJC, May 9, 1915, MA, F31–L2; Magnes to Marshall, Schiff, and Oscar Straus, May 21, 1915, MA, F46–L21b.

24. Friedlaender to Brandeis, June 20, 1915, Friedlaender Papers. The 23-page letter was published, in somewhat revised form, in Friedlaender, *Past and Present*, pp. 331–52 after appearing in the *Menorah Journal*, Dec. 1915.

25. Analysis of Organizations and Delegates Sent to the Kehillah Conventions in 1915 and 1916, MA, F18–L64.

26. Min 6th ACK, Apr. 24 and 25, 1915, MA, F28–L7; Magnes, *Address*, Apr. 24, 1915.

27. Remarks, Apr. 25, 1915, MA, F28–L64.

28. *Maccabaean*, XXVI (May 1915), 81. Several weeks after the convention, obviously stung by the criticism, Marshall responded to a decision of the Kehillah's executive committee which declared that the committee on legislation, of which he was chairman, was to take no action on any subject unless authorized by the executive. In a letter withdrawing from the committee, he wrote to Magnes: "I am not accustomed to have my hands tied in this manner. In all matters of legislation in which the Kehillah has thus far been concerned, my action has not been thus circumscribed. . . . The Committee on the Amendment of the Law of the Association of the Bar of the City of New York, of which I am the chairman . . . is not required to confer with anybody in the Association, but has absolute authority. As President of the American Jewish Committee I have assumed to act in matters of legislation without first consulting the executive committee. . . . Now that democracy is rampant, it would be just as well to leave all matters of legislation to the action of the quarterly conventions [of the Kehillah]. That would be in accordance with the ancient Greek model, which seems now so popular. So long as the idea has now become triumphant, that one man knows just as much an another upon every subject which may arise, there is no need that I shall devote any further attention to matters of legislation in which the Jewish community is concerned." May 17, 1915, MA, F28–L86.

29. Min 6th ACK, Apr. 24 and 25, 1916, MA, F28–L9; Magnes, Memorandum for the Executive Committee of the AJC, May 9, 1915, MA, F28–L64; Magnes to Isaac Hourwich, Meyer L. Brown, Solomon Suffrin, Joseph Barondess, May 12, 1915, MA, F31–L2; Magnes to Marshall, May 13, 1915, MA, F28–L86; Min ECK, May 11, 1915, MA, F48–L161; Magnes to Schiff, May 21, 1915, MA, F28–L86.

30. Minutes of the Session of May 23, 1915, MA, F28–L9a.

31. *Ibid.*; Schiff to Magnes, May 26, 1915, MA, F46–L21b; *Maccabaean*, XXVI (June 1915), 101.

32. Min 7th ACK, June 3 and 4, 1916, MA, F2–L1a; AH, June 2, 1916, p. 118, June 9, p. 142.

33. Min 7th ACK, June 3 and 4, 1916, MA, F2–L1a; see also *Maccabaean*, XXVIII (June 1916), 122–23; AH, June 9, 1916, pp. 142–3, 147.

34. Schiff to Magnes, May 21, 1915, MA, F46–L21b; Kaplan Journal, May 30, 1915.

35. Friedlaender to Brandeis, Sept. 2, 1915, Friedlaender Papers; Kaplan Journal, July 13, 1915; Magnes to Brandeis, June 30, 1915, Sept. 2, 1915, MA, SP215; *Maccabaean*, XXVII (July 1915), 11–12; Friedlaender to Stephen S. Wise, July 3, 1916, Friedlaender Papers; AH, Dec. 29, 1916, p. 266; Janowsky, *Minority Rights*, pp. 186–89.

36. Janowsky, *Minority Rights*, pp. 171–72.

37. AH, Dec. 29, 1916, p. 266; Apr. 27, 1917, p. 863; May 11, p. 20; *Der Tog*, Jan. 13, 1918, p. 6; Goldwasser, pp. 140–46; JCR, pp. 1304–11, 1479–90; "Proceedings, National Conference of Jewish Charities, May 15, 1918," *Jewish Charities*, IX (Mar. 1919), section two (unpaginated).

38. *Forward*, Mar. 20, 1917, p. 1; AJYB (1917–1918), p. 238.

39. AH, May 4, 1917, p. 893; May 18, p. 45; Adler, *Schiff: Life and Letters*, II, 307–308.

40. Rappaport, "Jewish Immigrants," pp. 265–89, 292–95; Higham, *Strangers*, 204–17; Rosenstock, pp. 102–3; AH, Mar. 30, 1917, p. 646; AJYB (1917–1918), p. 244; *Jewish Charities*, VIII (Nov. 1917), p. 135; Adler, *Schiff: Life and Letters*, II, 181–93, 201–7; Wise, in *Free Synagogue Pulpit*, IV (1916–17; sermon delivered Apr. 8, 1917); Wise to Dr. F. E. Hirschland, Sept. 16, 1914, and Wise to H. M. Kallen, Sept. 24, 1917, Wise Papers; Marshall to Schiff, June 1, 1917, Schiff Papers; Marshall to Cyrus Sulzberger, Aug. 16, 1917, MA, F16–L80.

41. Wise, in *Free Synagogue Pulpit*, IV (1916–17), 109.

42. AH, May 4, 1917, pp. 892–93, 911.

43. *Ibid.*, pp. 893, 900.

44. For a general treatment of Magnes's pacificsm see, Bentwich, *For Zion's Sake*, pp. 97–118; and Szajkowski, *Conservative Judaism*, pp. 36–55.

45. Magnes to Schiff, Nov. 27, 1916, MA, F8–L32; Magnes to George Kirchway, Feb. 28, 1917, MA, F5–L127; *Evening Call*, Mar. 25, 1917, p. 1; *Times*, Mar. 25, 1917, p. 1; Magnes to Schiff, Mar. 26, 1917, Schiff Papers; Schiff to Magnes, Mar. 27, 1917, MA, F8–L32; Rebecca Shelly to Magnes, Apr. 5, 1917, MA, SP159; Jordan, II, 717–18, 730.

46. *Times*, Apr. 17, 1916, p. 20; Villard, pp. 323–24; interview with Norman Thomas, July 14, 1966; Johnson, pp. 1–9. Among seventy pacifist ministers active during the war years, Ray H. Abrams found only

three rabbis (pp. 196–97). Abrams mentions no names. Emil Hirsch of Chicago was an active pacifist until America's entry into the war. Mervis, p. 200–1. Besides Magnes, only Abraham Cronbach in Akron, Ohio (Mervis, p. 215) and Professor Goddard Deutsch of the Hebrew Union College (Stuart R. Bolin to the U.S. Attorney General, July 30, 1917, General Records of the U.S. Department of Justice, Record Group 60, File 186233–20–21) openly criticized United States policy.

47. Christopher Lasch has categorized the progressives who were critical of Allied policy as "anti-imperialist liberals" in contradistinction to "war liberals." A distinguishing mark of the former, he points out, was their praise of the Russian revolution as democratic and socially progressive. Lasch, pp. vii–xiii. For Magnes' activities, see Minutes of Conference of Members of Various Peace Groups (Judah Magnes in the chair), Apr. 5, 1917, Emergency Peace Federation Papers; Rebecca Shelly to Magnes, Apr. 20, 1917, MA, SP159; Minutes of the Organizing Committee of the People's Council, June 8, 1917, June 21, July 3, People's Council Papers; Johnson, pp. 18–24; Norman Thomas, p. 23. Magnes' "Observer" articles appeared in Evening Post, Nov. 14, 1917, p. 13, Nov. 27, p. 9, Dec. 3, p. 11, Dec. 6, p. 9; Jan. 7, 1918, p. 9, Feb. 6, p. 11, Feb. 20, p. 18. For the meeting with Palmer, see Albert De Silver to Magnes, Apr. 15, 1919, MA, F25–L150; Memorandum of Conference with Attorney General, Apr. 17, 1919, MA, F25–L158.

48. Evening Call, May 31, 1917, p. 1; June 1, p. 1; Times, June 1, 1917, p. 1; Survey, XXXVIII (June 9, 1917), 246 and Aug. 4, p. 411; Magnes, in War-Time Addresses, pp. 10–18. See also Lasch, pp. 40–41; Peterson and Fite, pp. 74–76, 184–85; Grubbs, pp. 22–35.

49. Magnes, War-Time Addresses, pp. 10, 46; Times, June 1, 1917, p. 1; Peterson and Fite, pp. 76–78; Grubbs, pp. 58–65; Evening Post, Sept. 9, 1917, p. 4; J. L. Magnes, Let the Peace Conference Convene, Address Delivered at Constituent Meeting, People's Council of America, Chicago, Sept. 2, 1917 (pamphlet, MA, F16–L130); Times, May 26, 1919, p. 17. 26,000 copies of the Chicago speech were mailed to professors, clergymen and others. MA F16–L130. On Magnes' moderate position within the People's Council, see Magnes to Scott Nearing, Jan. 23, 1918, MA F16–L155 and Apr. 26, 1918, MA F14–L56. See also Minutes, executive committee of People's Council, Oct. 16, 1917, People's Council Papers.

50. New York State Senate, Revolutionary Radicalism, I, 960–63.

51. Marshall to Magnes, in Reznikoff, II, 971–74.

52. [Memoir], July 18, 1919, MA, SP302.

53. Wise, Free Synagogue Pulpit, IV (1917–1918), 159 [delivered Sept. 23, 1917]. The sermon was reprinted in Advocate of Peace, LXXX (Jan. 1918), 14–19. Norman Thomas recalls how Wise's former co-workers in the peace movement were angered by Wise's calling those

who criticized the war pro-German (interview, July 14, 1966). See also *Times*, June 4, 1917, p. ii; Marshall to Sulzberger, Aug. 16, 1917, MA, F16–L80; Pool, pp. 383–84.

54. *AH*, Mar. 15, 1918, p. 505.

55. Kaplan Journal, Apr. 9, 1918. In private discussions, coworkers like Friedlaender and Barondess urged Magnes to quit the Kehillah, but they did not press the matter or raise it formally. Kaplan Journal, July 28, 1919; Barondess to Wise, Jan. 2, 1924, Wise Papers.

56. Magnes to executive committee of the Kehillah, June 3, 1920, Ma, F41–L49; interview with Harry Sackler, Feb. 4, 1965; Marshall to Gottheil, May 31, 1917, Gottheil Papers; Kaplan Journal, July 28, 1919.

57. Magnes to executive committee, May 27, 1919. MA, F24–L78; Min ECK, Dec. 11, 1919, MA, F24–L77. Two contemporaneous episodes provide contrasting examples of the way in which ethnic leaders dealt with dissenters. See Dawidowicz, in *For Max Weinreich*, pp. 31–43, and Herbert Parzen's description of Gottheil's and Wise's roles in preventing Friedlaender's appointment to a position of government trust in *JSS*, XXIII (Oct. 1961), 253–57.

58. For a brief statement of Benderly's role in the reorganization of the Kehillah, see Winter, pp. 100–3.

59. *AH*, May 4, 1917, pp. 900, 911; Min 8th ACK, Apr. 28–29, 1917, MA, F18–L33.

60. *JCR*, pp. 91–98; Bernard G. Richards, CUOHP, pp. 49–50; interview with Henry Sackler, Feb. 4, 1965; interview with Alexander M. Dushkin, Dec. 23, 1965.

61. Minutes of the Special Convention, Jan. 13, 1918, MA, F18–L24; *JCR*, maps, tables, and graphs facing pp. 75, 81, 99, 103, 105, 107; *AH*, Jan. 18, 1918, p. 314.

62. *AH*, Jan. 18, 1918, pp. 314–15; *Tog*, Jan. 14, 1919, p. 1; *Tageblat*, Jan. 14, 1918, p. 1, Jan. 15, p. 4.

63. *JCR*, 63–71.

64. Minutes of the Special Convention, Jan. 13, 1918, MA, F18–L24.

65. *Ninth Annual Convention of the Kehillah*, June 1 and 2, 1918, pp. 25–34; Min 9th ACK, June 1 and 2, 1918, MA, F12–L75; interview with Harry Sackler, Feb. 4, 1965. In his democratization plan, Benderly had undoubtedly been impressed by the elections to the American Jewish Congress which had taken place in June, 1917. Nearly 120,000 participated in New York City. The Federation of Charities had shown similar success in a membership campaign enrolling 51,000 during a brief period in early January 1918. *AH*, June 8, 1917, p. 124; June 15, p. 152; Feb. 1, 1918, p. 406; *JCR*, pp. 1304–11.

66. Min 9th ACK, June 1 and 2, 1918, MA, F12–L75; *AH*, June 7, 1918, pp. 114–15; *Tageblat*, June 2, 1918, p. 1.

67. *AH*, June 7, 1918, pp. 114–15.

68. Min 9th ACK, June 1 and 2, 1918, MA, F12–L75; *Ninth Annual Convention of the Kehillah*, pp. 15–17, 19–24, 35–44, 48–49.

69. *Tageblat*, June 4, 1918, p. 4.

70. Min ECK, May 28, 1919, MA, F24–L78; Min ECK, Oct. 13 and Dec. 11, 1919, MA, F24–L79; Memorandum of Four Plans Submitted to the Executive Committee of the Kehillah, Mar. 11, 1920, MA, F41–L39; Minutes of Conference of Kehillah District Chairmen, Apr. 4, 1920, MA, F41–L44.

71. Minutes of the Special Conference of Kehillah Delegates, Apr. 25, 1920, MA, F41–L42; Statement of Civic Activities of the Kehillah [c. 1920], MA, F41–L20.

72. Dushkin, A Plan for the Organization of the Educational and Religious Needs of the Jewish Community of New York, Nov. 15, 1919, MA, F47–L5; Minutes of the Special Conference, Apr. 25, 1920, MA, F41–L42.

73. Minutes of the Special Conference, Apr. 25, 1920, MA, F41–L42. Marshall was among those who supported the educational-federation plan of Kehillah.

74. *Ibid.*; Statement Concerning Kehillah Policies and Activities, adopted May 16, 1920, MA, F41–L42; Minutes of the Second Conference of Kehillah Delegates, May 16, 1920, MA, F41–L40.

75. Magnes to executive committee of the Kehillah, June 3, 1920, MA, F41–L49; Magnes to Bernard Semel, Feb. 14, 1921, MA, F41–L13.

76. Min ECK, Apr. 30, 1922, MA, F24–L77; Kehillah Statement of Income and Expenditures for Jan. 1 to Apr. 30, 1922, MA, F47–L44. On Benderly see, Winter, pp. 105–6.

77. Isaac B. Berkson to Magnes, Mar. 15, 1921 and Mar. 29, 1921 (with attached "Plan for Temporary Organization Committee for Jewish Education"), MA, F47–L80; draft of letter (by Magnes) from Israel Unterberg to Arthur Lehman, May 17, 1921, MA, F47–L6; Chipkin, JE, X11, 136–45; Statement Concerning Kehillah Policies and Activities, adopted May 16, 1920, MA, F41–L42.

78. Magnes to Benderly, Aug. 14, 1921, MA, F47–L63; Magnes, Memorandum on Conversation with Dr. Dushkin, Oct. 27, 1921, MA, F47–L5; Magnes, Memorandum on Conversation with Dr. Benderly, Nov. 7, 1921, MA, unclassified; Magnes to Warburg, Jan. 23, 1922, MA, F47–L63.

79. Benderly to Marshall, Aug. 19, 1919, Various Plans Proposed for the Organization of Jewish Educational Work, Sept. 9, 1919, MA, F24–L105; Isaac Berkson to Magnes, May 19, 1920, MA, F41–L7; interview with Isaac B. Berkson, Oct. 28, 1965. MA F47–L80 contains correspondence and reports for the period March–December, 1921, concern-

ing plans for a new educational agency. Isaac Berkson was especially active on the "Plan and Scope Committee" which functioned at this time.

80. Min ECK, Apr. 30, 1922, MA, F24–L77; Kaplan Journal, May 10, 1922; William Lieberman to Magnes, Nov. 29, 1922 and Lieberman (?) to Marshall, Jan. 28, 1925, MA, F47–L45; Bentwich, *For Zion's Sake*, pp. 127–28; Chairman, Organization Committee to Jacob Sperber, Joseph P. Plaut, Herbert H. Lehman, Herman Conheim, J. M. Proskauer, Sept. 9, 1924, MA, F41–L38a.

XI. THE LIMITS OF COMMUNITY

1. Dewey, *Characters and Events*, II, 820–30.
2. Analysis of Organizations and Delegates Sent to the Kehillah Convention in 1915 and 1916, MA, F18–L64.
3. Kaplan Journal, July 13, 1915.
4. *Labor Zionist Handbook*, p. 216.
5. Cyrus Sulzberger to Oscar Straus, Oct. 29, 1915, MA, F30–L31.
6. Minutes of the Special Convention of the Kehillah, Jan. 13, 1918, MA, F18–L24.

Bibliography

A Note on Sources

THIS NOTE DESCRIBES THE UNPUBLISHED MATERIALS I FOUND MOST USEFUL in my research. The secondary literature which I relied upon for general background is cited in the notes for those pages where I introduce the major themes of the book. One recent study, however, deserves special mention: Moses Rischin's impeccably researched book, *The Promised City*, an invaluable guide to the complex world of New York Jews.

The Judah L. Magnes Archives in Jerusalem contains an outstanding collection of sources for the study of Jewish life in New York and Jewish communal politics in America from 1908 to 1922. Some 1500 files bear upon this period. The largest part of this material consists of the Kehillah's records which contain a wealth of sources on Jewish education, religious life, philanthropic organization, industrial conditions, and crime. Since Magnes was a central figure in the important national Jewish associations of his day, his archives contains reports, minutes, and correspondence of the American Jewish Committee, American Jewish Relief Committee, Federation of American Zionists, Joint Distribution Committee, Menorah Intercollegiate Association, and the Provisional Executive Committee for General Zionist Affairs. Among his correspondents were Sholom Asch, Samson Benderly, Israel Friedlaender, Herbert H. Lehman, Louis Marshall, David Pinski, Solomon Schechter, Jacob Schiff, Cyrus Sulzberger, Felix Warburg, and Chaim Weizman. The collection also reflects Magnes' liberal interests. There are minutes, bulletins, and reports of the People's Council, National

Civil Liberties Bureau and its successor, the American Civil Liberties Union, as well as correspondence with Morris Hillquit, Norman Thomas, Scott Nearing, and Oswald Garrison Villard, among others.

I used the manuscript collections of Louis Marshall, Jacob Schiff, and Stephen S. Wise to supplement the Magnes Archives on such subjects as the Kehillah, labor relations, and Jewish communal politics. The Paul Abelson Papers provided valuable insights into life on the Jewish East Side. They contained as well material on the Kehillah's Bureau of Industry, labor arbitration, vocational training, and employment agencies. The William J. Gaynor and John Purroy Mitchel Papers proved to be an important source for the anti-crime activities of the Kehillah and for relations between the Jewish community and the two mayors. The Israel Friedlaender Papers contained minutes of the Board of Trustees of the Kehillah's Bureau of Education missing in the Magnes Archives and a number of long letters—essays, in fact—addressed to Brandeis, Greenbaum, Magnes, and Schiff, which are important for understanding the educational policy of the Kehillah and Jewish communal politics in general.

Mordecai M. Kaplan's journal, which he began keeping in December, 1913, is a fascinating source for the period. His astute and pungent account of events and personalities is a delight for the historian.

Of the unpublished studies I used, the following are particularly noteworthy: Hyman Berman's "Era of the Protocol," Joseph Rappaport's "Jewish Immigrants and World War I," and Yonathan Shapiro's "Leadership of the American Zionist Organization," which tells a great deal more about American Jews than its title indicates.

Interviews supplemented the usual historical sources frequently illuminating particular episodes, often providing clues and nearly always giving events a sense of immediacy. Bernard G. Richards and Mrs. Judah L. Magnes discussed the Kehillah, its leaders, and Jewish life in general for many hours. The Isaac B. Berkson, Alexander M. Dushkin, and Samuel Margoshes interviews dealt primarily with Jewish education. Jonah J. Goldstein discussed crime and politics on the East Side and relations between uptown and downtown. Abe Shoenfeld described with great precision the details of Jewish crime and the seamier side of the Police Department. Hyman J. Reit recalled pre-Kehillah developments, Harry Sackler the Kehillah's demise, and Benjamin Koeningsberg the Orthodox Jewish community. Norman Thomas cast interesting light on Magnes' pacificism and radicalism. These interviews are on deposit in the William E. Wiener Oral History Library of the American Jewish Committee. An important interview with Mordecai M. Kaplan is on deposit in the Oral History Project of the Institute for Contemporary Jewry at the Hebrew University in Jerusalem. The "Reminiscences" of

William H. Allen, Robert Binkerd, Samuel S. Koenig, Bernard G. Richards and William Jay Schieffelin—all part of the Columbia University Oral History Collection—were helpful in understanding the New York City setting.

Bibliography

ARCHIVAL SOURCES

Cincinnati, Ohio. American Jewish Archives
    Paul Abelson Papers
    Louis Marshall Papers
    Kasriel and Ezekiel Sarasohn Papers
    Jacob H. Schiff Papers

Jerusalem, Israel. Central Zionist Archives
    Richard Gottheil Papers
    ——Jewish Historical General Archives
    Judah L. Magnes Archives (including the files of the New York Kehillah)

New York City. Columbia University Oral History Project
    William H. Allen, "Reminiscences," 1950
    Robert Binkerd, "Reminiscences," 1949
    Samuel S. Koenig, "Reminiscences," 1950
    Bernard G. Richards, "Reminiscences," 1960
    William J. Schieffelin, "Reminiscences," 1949
    Norman Thomas, "Reminiscences," 1950
    ——Jewish Theological Seminary
    Israel Friedlaender Papers
    ——Municipal Archives and Records Center

William J. Gaynor Papers
John Purroy Mitchel Papers
——YIVO Archives
Minutes of the Board of Directors of the Education Alliance, 1908–1916 (microfilm)
——in the possession of Professor Kaplan
Journals of Mordecai M. Kaplan

Swarthmore, Pennsylvania. Swarthmore College Peace Collection
Emergency Peace Federation Papers
People's Council Papers

Waltham, Massachusetts. Brandeis University
Stephen S. Wise Papers

Washington D.C. National Archives
General Records of the U.S. Department of Justice

PERIODICALS, 1903–1922

American. New York, 1908–1913, 1917–1918.
American Hebrew. New York, 1905–1922.
Current Literature. New York, 1909–1913.
Emanu-El Pulpit. New York, 1908–1910.
Evening Call. New York, 1908–1910, 1917–1918.
Evening Post. New York, 1908–1913, 1917–1918.
Federation Review. New York, 1907–1910.
Forward. New York, 1908–1920.
Free Synagogue Pulpit. New York, 1908–1918.
Globe and Commercial Advertiser. New York, 1908–1913.
The Guild Journal. New York, 1911–1915.
Hebrew Standard. New York, 1908–1913.
Herald. New York, 1908, 1912.
Der Idisher Congress. New York, 1915.
The Independent, 1908–1913.
Jewish Charity. New York, 1903–1906.
Jewish Charities. New York, 1910–1920.
The Jewish Child. New York, 1912–1915.
The Jewish Teacher. New York, 1916–1918.
The Maccabaean. New York, 1908–1920.
Morgen Journal. New York, 1908–1920.
The Outlook. New York, 1909–1913.
The Searchlight. New York, 1911–1913.

Survey and Common Welfare, New York, 1909–1918.
Times. New York, 1908–1922.
Der Tog. New York, 1917–1920.
Tribune. New York, 1908–1909.
Warheit. New York, 1908–1914.
Dos Yiddishe Folk. New York, 1909–1910.
Yiddisher Kemfer. New York, 1910–1914.
Yiddishes Tageblat. New York, 1908–1917.
Yiddishe Wochenblat. New York, 1909.
World. New York, 1908–1913.
Zukunft. New York, 1908–1920.

PUBLISHED REPORTS AND SECONDARY SOURCES

Abelson, Paul. *Activities and Plans of the Bureau of Industry Presented to the Sixth Annual Convention of the Kehillah, Apr. 24–25, 1915.* New York, The Kehillah (Jewish Community) of New York City, 1915.
Abrams, Ray H. *Preachers Present Arms*. New York, Round Table Press, 1933.
Adler, Cyrus. *Jacob Henry Schiff: A Biographical Sketch*. New York, American Jewish Committee, 1921.
——*Jacob H. Schiff: His Life and Letters*. 2 vols. New York, Doubleday, 1929.
Agar, Herbert. *The Saving Remnant*. New York, Viking, 1960.
Ahad Ha'am. *Igrot ahad ha'am*. Vol. IV. Jerusalem, Yavne, 1924.
——*Selected Essays*. Philadelphia, Jewish Publication Society, 1912.
Ahad Ha'am: Essays, Letters, Memoirs. Leon Simon, ed. London, Phaidon, 1946.
American Jewish Year Book. Philadelphia, Jewish Publication Society, 1900–1968.
American Newspaper Annual and Directory. Philadelphia, N. W. Ayer, 1908, 1909, 1917, 1918.
Antonovsky, Aaron and Elias Tcherikower, eds. *The Early Jewish Labor Movement in the U.S.* New York, YIVO Institute for Jewish Research, 1961.
Asbury, Herbert. *The Gangs of New York: An Informal History of the Underworld*. New York, Knopf, 1928.
Baron, Salo W. *The Jewish Community*. 3 vols. Philadelphia, Jewish Publication Society, 1948.

Bell, Daniel. "Crime as an American Way of Life," *The End of Ideology*. Glencoe, Ill., Free Press, 1960.

Benderly, Samson. *Aims and Activities of the Bureau of Education, 1912* (Bulletin No. 5, Bureau of Education of the Jewish Community [Kehillah], 1912). Reprinted in *Jewish Education*, XX (Summer, 1949), 92–109.

——*Brief Survey of Thirty-One Conferences Held by Talmud Torah Principles in New York City*. New York, Bureau of Education of the Jewish Community of New York, 1912.

——*The Bureau of Education of the Jewish Community of New York City* (Bulletin No. 1, Bureau of Education of the Jewish Community [Kehillah]). Reprinted in *Jewish Education*, XX (Summer, 1949), 110–12.

——*Some of the Activities of the Bureau of Education*. Presented to the Sixth Annual Convention of the Kehillah, Apr. 24, 1915. New York, Kehillah (Jewish Community) of New York City, 1915.

——*A Survey of the Financial Status of the Jewish Religious Schools of New York City*. New York, Bureau of Jewish Education of the Jewish Community (Kehillah) of New York City, 1911.

——"Can a System of Jewish Education in America be Self-Supporting?" *Jewish Teacher*, I (Dec., 1917), 204–210.

——"The Fundamental Elements in the Solution of the Problem of Jewish Education in America," *Jewish Teacher*, I (1916), 17–27.

——"The Gary Plan and Jewish Education," *Jewish Teacher*, I (Jan., 1916), 41–47.

——"Jewish Education in America," *The Jewish Exponent* (Jan. 17, 1908). Reprinted in *Jewish Education*, XX (Summer, 1949), 80–86.

——"The Present Status of Jewish Religious Education in New York City," *Jewish Communal Register of New York City*, 1917–1918, pp. 349–57. New York, Kehillah (Jewish Community), 1918.

Bentwich, Norman. *For Zion's Sake: A Biography of Judah L. Magnes*. Philadelphia, Jewish Publication Society, 1954.

——*Solomon Schechter*. Philadelphia, Jewish Publications Society, 1938.

Berger, Morris Isaiah. "The Settlement, the Immigrant, and the Public School." Ph.D. dissertation, Teachers College, Columbia University, 1956.

Berkson, Isaac B. *Theories of Americanization: A Critical Study with Special Reference to the Jewish Group*. New York, Teachers College, Columbia University, 1920.

——"The Community Idea for Jewish Education," *Jewish Education*, XXIV (Fall, 1953), 35–38.

——"Education and the Jewish Renaissance," *Jewish Education*, XXXIII (Summer, 1963), 198–208.

Berman, Hyman. "The Cloakmakers' Strike of 1910," in Joseph L. Blau et al., eds., *Essays on Jewish Life and Thought Presented in Honor of Salo Wittmayer Baron*. New York, Columbia University Press, 1959.

——"Era of the Protocol: A Chapter in the History of the International Ladies' Garment Workers' Union, 1910–1916." Ph.D. dissertation, Columbia University, 1956.

Berman, Jeremiah J. *Shehitah: A Study in the Cultural and Social Life of the Jewish People*. New York, Bloch, 1941.

——"Jewish Education in New York City, 1864–1900," YIVO *Annual of Jewish Social Science*, IX (1954), 247–75.

Berman, Myron. "A New Spirit on the East Side: The Early History of the Emanu-El Brotherhood, 1903–1922," *American Jewish Historical Quarterly*, LIV (Sept., 1964), 53–81.

Bernheimer, Charles S., ed. *The Russian Jew in the U.S.* Philadelphia, Winston, 1905.

Bingham, Theodore A. "Foreign Criminals in New York," *North American Review*, CLXXXVII (Sept., 1908), 383–94.

——"The New York Police in Politics," *Century Magazine*, LXXVII (Sept., 1909), 725–32.

——"The Organized Criminals of New York," *McClure's Magazine*, XXXIV (Nov., 1909), 45–61.

——"Patrolling 3095 Miles of Streets: New York's Unique Police Problem, and the Means to Its Solution," *Harper's Weekly*, LI (Nov. 9, 1907), 1648–1656.

——"Policing Our Lawless Cities," *Hampton's Magazine* (Sept., 1909), pp. 289–300.

——"Why I Was Removed as Police Commissioner, Part One." *Van Norden Magazine*, V (Sept., 1909), 591–96.

——"Why I was Removed as Police Commissioner, Part Two," *Van Norden Magazine*, VI (Oct. 1909), 19–28.

Birmingham, Stephen. *"Our Crowd": The Great Jewish Families of New York*. New York, Harper and Row, 1967.

Blaustein, Miriam (Mrs. David). *Memoirs of David Blaustein: Educator and Communal Worker*. New York, McBride, Nast, 1913.

Bloom, Bernard H. "Yiddish-Speaking Socialists in America: 1892–1905," *American Jewish Archives*, XII (1960), 34–68.

Blumenfield, Shmuel M. *Chevra v'chinuch b'yahadut amerika*. Tel Aviv, Israel, M. Newman, 1965.

Bogen, Boris D. *Born a Jew*. New York, Macmillan, 1930.

Bogen, Boris D. *Jewish Philanthropy*. New York, Macmillan, 1917.
––––"The Jewish Boy Criminal," *Jewish Charity*, IV (Oct., 1904), 126–29.
Bourne, Randolph. *War and the Intellectuals: Essays, 1915–1916*. Edited with an introduction by Carl Resek. New York, Harper and Row, 1964.
Bremner, Robert H. *From the Depths: The Discovery of Poverty in the United States*. New York, New York University Press, 1956.
Brickner, Rebecca A. "As I Remember Dr. Benderly," *Jewish Education*, XX (Summer, 1949), 53–59.
Brody, David. *The Butcher Workmen: A Study of Unionization*. Cambridge, Harvard University Press, 1964.
Budin, L. B. "Di natzionale convention fun der sotzialistishe partey," *Zukunft*, XV (May, 1910), 303–5.
Budish, J. M. and George Soule. *The New Unionism in the Clothing Industry*. New York, Harcourt, Brace, 1920.
Cahan, Abraham. *Bleter fun mein leben*. 5 vols. New York, Forward, 1926–1931.
Callahan, Raymond E. *Education and the Cult of Efficiency: A Study of the Social Forces that Have Shaped the Administration of the Public Schools*. Chicago, University of Chicago Press, 1965.
Chaikin, J. *Yidishe bleter in amerika*. New York, privately published, 1946.
Chambers, Clarke A. "The Belief in Progress in Twentieth-Century America," *Journal of the History of Ideas*, XIX (Apr., 1958), 197–224.
Chambers, Walter. *Samuel Seabury: A Challenge*. New York, Century, 1932.
Chipkin, Israel S. "Dr. Samson Benderly, Reminiscences and Reflections," *Jewish Education*, XX (Summer, 1949), 21–23.
––––"The Jewish Education Association of New York City," *Jewish Education*, XII (January, 1941), 136–45.
––––"Twenty-Five Years of Jewish Education in the U.S.," *American Jewish Year Book* (1936–1937), pp. 27–116. Philadelphia, Jewish Publication Society, 1936.
Clemen, Rudolf Alexander. *The American Livestock Industry*. New York, Ronald Press, 1923.
Cohen, Israel. *Vilna*. Philadelphia, Jewish Publication Society, 1943.
Cohen, Julius Henry. *They Builded Better Than They Knew*. New York, Julian Massner, 1946.
Cohen, Naomi W. *A Dual Heritage: The Public Career of Oscar S. Straus*. Philadelphia, Jewish Publication Society, 1969.

——"The *Maccabaean's* Message: A Study in American Zionism until World War I," *Jewish Social Studies*, XVIII (July, 1956), 163–78.
——"The Reactions of Reform Judaism in America to Political Zionism: 1897–1922," *Publications of the American Jewish Historical Society*, XL (June, 1951), 361–94.
Committee of Fifteen. *The Social Evil, with Special Reference to Conditions Existing in the City of New York*. New York, Putnam, 1902.
——*The Social Evil, with Special Reference to Conditions Existing in the City of New York*. 2d ed., revised with new material edited by Edwin R. A. Seligman. New York, Putnam, 1912.
Committee of Fourteen in New York City. *Annual Reports*. New York, 1913–1918.
——*The Social Evil in New York City: A Study of Law Enforcement by the Research Committee of the Committee of Fourteen*. New York, Kellogg, 1910.
Cowen, Philip. *Memories of an American Jew*. New York, International Press, 1932.
Cremin, Lawrence A. *The Transformation of the Schools: Progressivism in American Education, 1876–1957*. New York, Knopf, 1961.
Croly, Herbert D. *The Promise of American Life*. New York, Macmillan, 1912.
Curran, Henry H. *Pillar to Post*. New York, Scribner's, 1941.
Davis, Allen F. *Spearheads for Reform: The Social Settlements and the Progressive Movement, 1890–1914*. New York, Oxford University Press, 1967.
Davis, Moshe. *The Emergence of Conservative Judaism: The Historical School in 19th Century America*. Philadelphia, Jewish Publication Society, 1963.
——"Israel Friedlaender's Minute Book of the Achavah Club, 1909–1912," *Mordecai M. Kaplan Jubilee Volume*. New York, Jewish Theological Seminary, 1953, pp. 157–213.
——"Jewry, East and West (The Correspondence of Israel Friedlaender and Simon Dubnow)," *YIVO Annual of Jewish Social Science*, IX (1954), 9–62.
Davis, Moshe and Isidore S. Meyer, eds. *The Writing of American Jewish History*. New York, American Historical Society, 1957.
Dawidowicz, Lucy S. *The Golden Tradition: Jewish Life and Thought in Eastern Europe*. Boston, Beacon Press, 1968.
——"From Past to Present: Jewish East Europe to Jewish East Side," *Conservative Judaism*, XXII (Winter, 1968), 19–27.
——"Louis Marshall and the *Jewish Daily Forward*: An Episode in War-

time Censorship," *For Max Weinreich on his Seventieth Birthday.* The Hague, Mouton, 1964.

——"Louis Marshall's Yiddish Newspaper *The Jewish World," Jewish Social Studies,* XXV (Apr., 1963), 102–25.

Dewey, John. *Characters and Events* (Joseph Ratner, ed.), 2 vols. New York, Holt, 1929.

——*Democracy and Education.* New York, Macmillan Paperbacks Edition, 1963.

——"Nationalizing Education," *National Education Association: Addresses and Proceedings of the Fifty-Fourth Annual Meeting,* LIV (1916), 183–89.

——"The Principle of Nationality," *The Menorah Journal,* III (Apr., 1917), 203–8.

——"Universal Service as Education," *New Republic* (Apr. 22, 1916), pp. 309–10.

Dinin, Samuel. *Judaism in a Changing Civilization.* New York, Teachers College, Columbia University, 1933.

Drachman, Bernard. *The Unfailing Light: Memories of an American Rabbi.* New York, Rabbinical Council of America, 1948.

Drachsler, Julius. *Democracy and Assimilation: The Blending of Immigrant Heritages in America.* New York, Macmillan, 1920.

——"The Juvenile Court and the Jewish Community," *Jewish Charities,* VI (Mar., 1916), 143–48.

Dubnow, Simon M. *History of the Jews in Russia and Poland.* 3 vols. Philadelphia, Jewish Publication Society, 1916.

Dubofsky, Melvyn. *When Workers Organize: New York City in the Progressive Era.* Amherst, University of Massachusetts Press, 1968.

——"Organized Labor and the Immigrant in New York City, 1900–1918," *Labor History,* II (Spring, 1961), 182–201.

——"Success and Failure of Socialism in New York City, 1900–1918: A Case Study," *Labor History,* IX (Fall, 1968), 361–75.

Dushkin, Alexander M. *Jewish Education in New York City.* New York, Bureau of Jewish Education, 1918.

——"Antaeus, Autobiographical Relections," *American Jewish Archives,* XXI (Nov., 1969), 113–39.

——"Hashpa'at ha'chinuch ha'amerikani al ha'chinuch ha'yehudi b'amerika," in Zevi Scharfstein, ed., *Sefer hayovel shel agudat ha'morim ha'ivrim b'new york.* New York, Modern Linotype, 1944, pp. 93–113.

——"The Jewish Population of New York," *Jewish Communal Register of New York City, 1917–1918,* New York, Kehillah (Jewish Community), 1918, pp. 75–89.

——"The Personality of Samson Benderly," *Jewish Education*, XX (Summer, 1949), 6–15.

——"The Profession of Jewish Education, Part One," *Menorah Journal*, III (Apr., 1917), 90–97.

——"The Profession of Jewish Education, Part Two," *Menorah Journal*, III (June, 1917), 174–81.

Eisenstein, Ira. "Alexander M. Dushkin at Seventy-Five," *Reconstructionist* (Jan. 7, 1966), pp. 15–23.

Eisenstein, Ira and Eugene Kohn, eds. *Mordecai M. Kaplan: An Evaluation*. New York, Jewish Reconstructionist Foundation, 1952.

Elazar, Daniel J. "The Pursuit of Community: Selections from the Literature of Jewish Public Affairs, 1965–1966," *American Jewish Year Book* (1967), pp. 178–229. Philadelphia, Jewish Publication Society, 1967.

Elbogen, Ismar. *A Century of Jewish Life*. Philadelphia, Jewish Publication Society, 1946.

Epstein, Melech. *Jewish Labor in U.S.A.* 2 vols. New York, Trade Union Sponsoring Co., 1950–1953.

——*Profile of Eleven*. Detroit, Wayne State University Press, 1965.

Eskolsky, Jacob, ed. *Methods To Be Employed by Mohelim in the Performance of Circumcision* (with Hebrew section, *Sefer ha'brith*). New York, Kehillah of New York, 1915.

Feigenbaum, Benjamin. "Idish in der sotzialishtishe bavegung in amerika," *Zukunft*, XVII (June, 1912), 392–97.

Feldman, Egal. "Prostitution, the Alien Woman, and the Progressive Imagination, 1910–1915," *American Quarterly*, XI (Summer, 1967), 192–206.

Fifty Years of Social Service: The History of the United Hebrew Charities of the City of New York. New York, Jewish Social Service Association, 1926.

Filler, Louis. *Crusaders for American Liberalism*. Yellow Springs, Ohio, Antioch Press, 1961.

Fitzpatrick, Joseph P. "The Importance of 'Community' in the Process of Immigrant Assimilation," *The International Migration Review*, I (Fall, 1966), 5–16.

Foner, Philip S. *The Fur and Leather Workers Union: A Story of Dramatic Struggles and Achievements*. Newark, Norden Press, 1950.

Forcey, Charles. *The Crossroads of Liberalism*. New York, Oxford University Press, 1961.

Fosdick, Raymond B. *Chronicle of a Generation: An Autobiography*. New York, Harper, 1958.

Frankel, Lee K. "The Problem of Dependent and Delinquent Jewish Children," *Jewish Charity*, IV (Oct., 1904), 27–32.

Friedlaender, Israel. *Past and Present: A Collection of Jewish Essays.* Cincinnati, Ark Publishing, 1919.

——"The Problem of Jewish Education in America and the Bureau of Education of the Jewish Community of New York City," *Report of the Commissioner of Education for the Year Ended June 30, 1913,* Vol. I, ch. 6. Washington D.C., 1914.

Friedman, Jacob A. *The Impeachment of Governor William Sulzer.* New York, Columbia University Press, 1939.

Gamoran, Emanuel. *Changing Conceptions in Jewish Education.* New York, Macmillan, 1924.

Gannes, Abraham P. *Central Community Agencies for Jewish Education.* Philadelphia, Dropsie College, 1954.

Gartner, Lloyd P. "The Jewish Community in America Transplanted and Transformed," *Conference on Acculturation.* New York, American Federation of Jews from Central Europe, 1965, pp. 7–16.

——"The Jews of New York's East Side, 1890–1893: Two Surveys by the Baron de Hirsch Fund," *American Jewish Historical Quarterly,* LIII (Mar., 1964), 264–81.

——"Immigration and the Formation of American Jewry, 1840–1925," *Journal of World History,* XI (1968), 297–312.

General Executive Committee of the Workmen's Circle [Arbeiter Ring]. *Eighth Annual Report for the Year 1908.* New York, 1909.

Gladstone, Jacob et al., eds. *Finf und zibtzig yor yidishe prese in amerika.* New York, Y. L. Peretz Writers Union, 1945.

Glanz, Rudolf. *Jews in the Cultural Milieu of the Germans in America Up To the Eighteen Eighties.* New York, Marstin Press, 1947.

——"German Jews in New York City in the Nineteenth Century," *YIVO Annual of Jewish Social Science,* XI (1956–1957), 9–38.

——"The Immigration of German Jews up to 1880," *YIVO Annual of Jewish Social Science,* II–III (1948), 81–99.

——"Jewish Social Conditions As Seen by the Muckrakers," *YIVO Annual of Jewish Social Science,* IX (1954), 308–31.

Glazer, Nathan. *American Judaism.* Chicago, University of Chicago Press, 1957.

——"Ethnic Groups in America: From National Culture to Ideology," in Morroe Berger et al., eds., *Freedom and Control in Modern Society.* New York, Van Nostrand Co., 1954.

Goldberg, Abraham. *Pioneers and Builders*. New York, Abraham Goldberg Publications Committee, 1943.

Goldberg, David B. "Attitudes Toward the New York Kehillah as Reflected in the Yiddish and Anglo-Jewish Press of New York City, 1908–1917." Master's thesis, Graduate School of Jewish Social Work, 1937, on deposit in the New York Public Library.

Goldberg, Nathan. "The Jewish Population in the United States," *The Jewish People, Past and Present*, II, 25–34. New York, Jewish Encyclopedic Handbooks, 1948.

Goldman, Eric F. *Rendezvous with Destiny: A History of Modern American Reform*. New York, Vintage Books, 1956.

Goldstein, Herbert S., ed. *Forty Years of Struggle for a Principle: The Biography of Harry Fischel*. New York, Bloch, 1928.

Goldstein, Israel. *A Century of Judaism in New York*. New York, Congregation B'nai Jeshurun, 1930.

Goldwasser, I. Edwin. "Federation for the Support of Jewish Philanthropies of New York City," *American Jewish Year Book* (1918–1919), pp. 113–46. Philadelphia, Jewish Publication Society, 1918.

Gordon, Milton M. *Assimilation in American Life*. New York, Oxford University Press, 1964.

Gorenstein (Goren), Arthur. "The Commissioner and the Community: The Beginnings of the New York City 'Kehillah' (1908–1909)," *YIVO Annual of Jewish Social Science*, XIII (1965), 187–212.

——"A Portrait of Ethnic Politics: The Socialists and the 1908 and 1910 Congressional Elections on the East Side," *Publications of the American Jewish Historical Society*, L (Mar., 1961), 202–38.

Green, Marguerite. *National Civic Federation and the American Labor Movement: 1900–1925*. Washington, Catholic University of America Press, 1956.

Greenbaum, Edward S. *A Lawyer's Office, In Court, In the Army, In the Office*. New York, Harcourt, Brace and World, 1967.

Greenberg, Louis. *The Jews in Russia: The Struggle for Emancipation*. 2 vols. New Haven, Yale University Press, 1944–1951.

Greenstone, Julius H. "Jewish Education in the United States," *American Jewish Year Book* (1914–1915), pp. 90–127. Philadelphia, Jewish Publication Society, 1914.

Grinstein, Hyman B. *The Rise of the Jewish Community of New York, 1654–1860*. Philadelphia, Jewish Publication Society, 1947.

——"The Efforts of East European Jewry to Organize Its Own Community in the United States," *Publications of the American Jewish Historical Society*, XLIX (1959), 73–89.

——"The Memoirs and Scrapbook of the Late Dr. Joseph Isaac Bluestone of New York City," *Publications of the American Jewish Historical Society*, XXXV (1939), 53–64.

Grubbs, Frank L., Jr. *The Struggle for Labor Loyalty: Gompers, the A.F. of L., and the Pacifists, 1917–1920*. Durham, N.C., Duke University Press, 1968.

Haber, Julius. *The Odyssey of an American Zionist*. New York, Twayne, 1956.

Haber, Samuel. *Efficiency and Uplift: Scientific Management in the Progressive Era, 1890–1920*. Chicago, University of Chicago Press, 1964.

Halpern, Benjamin. *The American Jew: A Zionist Analysis*. New York, Theodor Herzl Foundation, 1956.

——*The Idea of the Jewish State*. Cambridge, Harvard University Press, 1961.

Handbook of Settlements. Robert A. Woods and Albert J. Kennedy, eds. New York, Charities Publications Committee, 1911.

Handler, Zevi. "Yisud agudat ha'm'nahalim," *Sheviley Hahinuch*, XXIII (Autumn, 1962), 38–46.

Handlin, Oscar. *Adventure in Freedom: Three Hundred Years of Jewish Life in America*. New York, McGraw-Hill, 1954.

——*The American People in the Twentieth Century*. Cambridge, Harvard University Press, 1954.

——*The Dimensions of Liberty*. Cambridge, Harvard University Press, 1961.

——*Race and Nationality in American Life*. New York, Doubleday Anchor, 1957.

——*The Uprooted: The Epic Story of the Great Migrations that Made the American People*. Boston, Little, Brown, 1951.

——"American Views of the Jews at the Beginning of the Twentieth Century," *Publications of the American Jewish Historical Society*, XL (June, 1951) 323–44.

——"Historical Perspectives on the American Ethnic Group," *Daedalus* (Spring, 1961), 220–32.

——"Immigration in American Life, A Reappraisal," in Henry Steel Commager, ed., *Immigration and American History: Essays in Honor of Theodore C. Blegen*. Minneapolis, University of Minnesota Press, 1961.

Hapgood, Hutchins. *The Spirit of the Ghetto: Studies of the Jewish Quarter of New York*. New York, Funk and Wagnalls, 1902.

Hardman, J. B. S. "Interrelationship of the Jewish and the General American Labor Movement," *YIVO Annual of Jewish Social Science*, IX (1954), 373–76.

Harlow, Alvin F. *Old Bowery Days: The Chronicles of a Famous Street*. New York, D. Appleton, 1931.

Hartmann, Edward George. *The Movement to Americanize the Immigrant*. New York, Columbia University Press, 1948.

Hays, Samuel P. *The Response to Industrialism: 1885–1914*. Chicago, University of Chicago Press, 1957.

Herberg, Will. "The Jewish Labor Movement in the U.S.," *American Jewish Year Book* (1952), pp. 3–74.

Hershberg, A. A., ed. *Pinkos Bialystok*, 2 vols. New York, Bialystok Jewish Historical Association, 1949.

Hertz, Jacob S. *Di yidishe sotzialistishe bavegung in amerika*. New York, Der Wecker, 1954.

——*Fuftzig yor arbeiter ring in yidishn leben*. New York, National Executive Committee of the Arbeiter Ring, 1950.

Higham, John. *Strangers in the Land*. New Brunswick, Rutgers University Press, 1955.

——"Social Discrimination Against Jews in America, 1830–1930," *Publications of the American Jewish Historical Society*, XLVII (Sept., 1957), 1–33.

Hillquit, Morris. *Loose Leaves from a Busy Life*. New York, Macmillan, 1934.

Hirsh, Joseph and Beka Doherty. *The First Hundred Years of Mount Sinai*. New York, Random House, 1952.

Hirshler, Eric E., ed. *Jews from Germany in the United States*. New York, Farrar, Straus and Cudahy, 1955.

Hochman, William Russell. "William J. Gaynor: The Years of Fruition." Ph.D. dissertation, Columbia University, 1955.

Hoffman, Ben Zion (Tzivyon). *Far fuftzig yor*. New York, Elias Laub, 1948.

——*Fufzig yor cloak-macher union*. New York, Cloakmakers Local 117, 1936.

——"Di entviklung fun arbeiter ring un di idisher arbeiter," *Zukunft*, XVII (Jan., 1912), 64–65.

——"Di idishe agitatzi'as bureau," *Zukunft*, XIV (May, 1909), 274–81.

——"Idishkeit," *Zukunft*, XVI (July, 1911), 382–85.

334   BIBLIOGRAPHY

Hoffman, Ben Zion (Lzivyou). "Di kehille, ir industrial department un der chicken trust," *Zukunft*, XXII (Jan., 1917), 40–43.

Hofstadter, Richard. *The Age of Reform*. New York, Vintage, 1960.

——*Anti-Intellectualism in American Life*. New York, Knopf, 1963.

Honor, Leo L. (Aryeh). "Educating Teaching Personnel for Jewish Schools: 1897–1918," *Hebrew Union College Annual*, XXIII (1950–1951), Part Two, 617–47.

——"Jewish Education in the United States," *The Jewish People, Past and Present*, II, 151–71. New York, Jewish Encyclopedic Handbooks, 1948.

——"Jewish Elementary Education in the United States: 1901–1950," *Publications of the American Jewish Historical Society*, XLII (Sept., 1952), 1–42.

——"Our Professional Debt to Dr. Benderly," *Jewish Education*, XX (Summer, 1949), 27–29.

——"Shlosha she'hish'piyu," in Zevi Scharfstein, ed., *Sefer hayovel shel agudat ha'morim ha'ivrim b'new york*, pp. 343–51. New York, Modern Linotype, 1944.

Hourwich, Isaac A. *Immigration and Labor*. New York, B. W. Huebsch, 1922.

Hurwich, Aryeh Leb. *Zichronot m'chanech ivri*. Vol. III. Boston, Bureau of Jewish Education, 1960.

Israels, Belle Lindner. "The Way of the Girl," *Survey and Common Welfare*, XII (July 3, 1909), 486–97.

Jacobs, Joseph. "The Federation Movement in American Jewish Philanthropy," *American Jewish Year Book* (1915–1916), pp. 159–98. Philadelphia, Jewish Publications Society, 1915.

Janowsky, Oscar I., ed. *The American Jew: A Reappraisal*. Philadelphia, Jewish Publication Society, 1964.

——*The Jews and Minority Rights*. New York, Columbia University Press, 1933.

Jerusalem, Edmond. "The Kehillah." Study of the Kehillah on deposit in SP 320, Magnes Archives, Jerusalem.

Jewish Communal Directory. New York, Jewish Community (Kehillah), 1912.

The Jewish Communal Register of New York City, 1917–1918. New York, Kehillah (Jewish Community), 1918.

Jewish Congress Organization Committee. *To the Jews of America: The Jewish Congress versus the American Jewish Committee, A Complete*

Statement, with the Correspondence between Louis D. Brandeis and Cyrus Adler. New York, Aug., 1915.

Jewish Protectory and Aid Society. *Fifth Annual Report of the Hawthorne School.* Jan. 1, 1908.

——*First Annual Report for the Year Ending Dec. 31, 1911.*

Johnson, Donald. *The Challenge to American Freedoms: World War I and the Rise of the American Civil Liberties Union.* Lexington, University of Kentucky Press, 1963.

Jones, Maldwyn A. *American Immigration.* Chicago, University of Chicago Press, 1960.

Jordan, David Starr. *The Days of Man.* 2 vols. Yonkers, World, 1922.

Joseph, Samuel. *History of the Baron De Hirsch Fund: The Americanization of the Jewish Immigrant.* Philadelphia, Jewish Publication Society, 1935.

——*Jewish Immigration to the U.S. from 1881 to 1910.* New York, Columbia University, 1914.

Kallen, Horace M. *Culture and Democracy in the United States.* New York, Boni and Liveright, 1924.

Kaplan, Mordecai M. *Judaism as a Civilization: Towards a Reconstruction of American-Jewish Life.* New York, Macmillan, 1934.

——"The Impact of Dr. Benderly's Personality," *Jewish Education,* XX (Summer, 1949), 16–20.

——"A Program for the Reconstruction of Judaism," *Menorah Journal,* VI (Aug., 1920), 181–96.

——"The Society of the Jewish Renascence," *The Maccabaean,* XXXIV (Nov., 1920), 110–13.

Kaplan, Mordecai M. and Bernard Cronson. "First Community Survey of Jewish Education in New York City, 1909; Presented at the First Annual Convention of the Kehillah, Feb. 27, 1910," *Jewish Education,* XX (Summer, 1949), 113–16.

Kaplan, Sidney. "Social Engineers as Saviors: Effects of World War I on some American Liberals," *Journal of the History of Ideas,* XVIII (June, 1956), 347–69.

Karp, Abraham. "New York Chooses a Chief Rabbi," *Publications of the American Jewish Historical Society,* XLIV (Mar., 1955), 129–98.

Katz, Jacob. *Bayn y'hudim la'goyim.* Jerusalem, Bialik Institute, 1960. Translated as *Exclusiveness and Tolerance: Studies in Jewish–Gentile Relations in Medieval and Modern Times.* London, Oxford University Press, 1961.

Katz, Jacob. *M'soret u'mashber*. Jerusalem, Bialik Institute, 1958. Translated as *Tradition and Crisis: Jewish Society at the End of the Middle Ages*. New York, Free Press, 1961.

Katz, Mark J. "Jewish Criminality in New York in 1907," *Federation Review*, II (June, 1908), 3–5; (July, 1908), 3–5; (Nov., 1908), 8.

King, Helene Feldman. "The Banishment of Prudery: A Study of the Issue of Prostitution in the Progressive Era." Master's thesis, Department of History, Columbia University, 1956.

Kipnis, Ira. *The American Socialist Movement, 1897–1912*. New York, Columbia University Press, 1952.

Klaperman, Gilbert. "Yeshiva University: Seventy-Five Years in Retrospect," *American Jewish Historical Quarterly*, LIV (Sept., 1964), 5–50.

Klein, Aharon. "Toldoth sifre ha'limud l'batei sefer ha'yehudim b'amerika," *Sheviley Hahinuch*, XVII (Winter, 1957), 76–81.

Klein, Henry H. *My Forty-Year Fight for Justice: The Story of the Judicial Framing and Execution (Murder) of Police Lieutenant Charles Becker of New York City*. New York, published by the author, 1953.

——*My Last Fifty Years: An Autobiographical History of "Inside" New York*. New York, published by the author, 1935.

——*Police Lieutenant Charles Becker: Framed for the Murder of Herman Rosenthal*. New York, published by the author, 1939.

——*Sacrificed: The Story of Police Lieutenant Charles Becker*. New York, published by the author, 1927.

Kneeland, George J. *Commercialized Prostitution in New York City*. New York, Century, 1913.

Kober, Adolf. "Jewish Communities in Germany from the Age of Enlightenment to Their Destruction by the Nazis," *Jewish Social Studies*, IX (July, 1947), 195–238.

Kohn, Jacob. "Israel Friedlaender: A Biographical Sketch," *American Jewish Year Book* (1921–1922), pp. 65–79. Philadelphia, Jewish Publications Society, 1921.

Konovitz, Israel. "B'reyshit ha'chinuch ha'ivri b'amerika," in Zevi Scharfstein, ed., *Sefer hayovel shel agudat ha'morim ha'ivrim b'new york*. New York, Modern Linotype, 1944.

Labor Zionist Handbook. New York, Poale Zion Zeire Zion of America, 1939.

Landesman, Alter F. *Brownsville: The Birth, Development, and Passing of a Jewish Community in New York*. New York, Bloch, 1969.

Lane, Winthrop D. "The Four Gunmen," *The Survey*, XXXII (Apr. 4, 1914), 13–16.

Lasch, Christopher. *American Liberals and the Russian Revolution*. New York, Columbia University Press, 1962.

Leuchtenburg, William E. *The Perils of Prosperity, 1914–1932*. Chicago, University of Chicago Press, 1958.

Levine, Louis. *The Women's Garment Workers: A History of the International Ladies' Garment Workers' Union*. New York, B. W. Huebsch, 1924.

Levitats, Isaac. *The Jewish Community in Russia, 1772–1844*. New York, Columbia University Press, 1943.

——"The Jewish Association in America," in Joseph L. Blau *et al.*, eds., *Essays on Jewish Life and Thought Presented in Honor of Salo Wittmayer Baron*. New York, Columbia University Press, 1959.

Lewinson, Edwin R. *John Purroy Mitchel, the Boy Mayor of New York*. New York, Astra Books, 1965.

Liebman, Charles S. "Orthodoxy in American Jewish Life," *American Jewish Year Book* (1965), pp. 21–92. Philadelphia, Jewish Publication Society, 1965.

Lifschitz, E. "Jewish Immigrant Life in American Memoir Literature," YIVO *Annual of Jewish Social Science*, V (1950), 216–31.

Lippmann, Walter. *Drift and Mastery*. Introduction and Notes by William E. Leuchtenburg. Englewood Cliffs, Prentice-Hall, 1961.

Lipsky, Louis. *A Gallery of Zionist Profiles*. New York, Farrar, Straus and Cudahy, 1956.

——*Thirty Years of Zionism*. New York, Nesher, 1927.

——"What Ails the New York Kehillah," *The Maccabaean Magazine*, XXII (Dec., 1912), 185–89.

London, Meyer. "Der schicagener partey congress," *Zukunft*, XV (July, 1910), 401–3.

Lubove, Roy. *The Progressives and the Slums: Tenement House Reform in New York City*. Pittsburgh, University of Pittsburgh Press, 1962.

Lurie, Harry L. *A Heritage Affirmed: The Jewish Federation Movement in America*. Philadelphia, Jewish Publications Society, 1961.

——"Jewish Communal Life in the United States," *The Jewish People, Past and Present*, IV, 187–242. New York, Jewish Encyclopedic Handbooks, 1955.

Magidoff, Jacob. *Der shpigl fun der istsayd*. New York, published by the author, 1923.

Magnes, Judah L. *Address at the Opening of the Sixth Annual Conven-*

338 BIBLIOGRAPHY

tion of the Jewish Community (Kehillah), April 24, 1915. New York, Kehillah, 1915.

——*For Democracy and Terms of Peace: Address at Opening of First American Conference for Democracy and Terms of Peace, New York City, May 30–31, 1917.* New York, 1917.

——*The Jewish Community of New York City: Address Delivered at Constituent Convention.* New York, Jewish Community (Kehillah), 1909.

——*War-time Addresses, 1917–1921.* New York, Thomas Seltzer, 1923.

——*What the Kehillah Has Given New York Jewry: Presented to the Eighth Annual Convention of the Kehillah.* New York, 1917.

——"Evidences of Jewish Nationality," *The Emanu-El Pulpit,* Vol. I. New York, 1908.

——"The Melting Pot," *The Emanu-El Pulpit,* Vol. III. New York, 1909.

——"A Republic of Nationalities," *The Emanu-El Pulpit,* Vol. II. New York, 1909.

Mahler, Raphael, ed. *Czenstochover Yidn.* New York, United Czenstochover Relief Committee, 1947.

Mandel, Irving Aaron. "Attitudes of the American Jewish Community Toward East-European Immigration, 1880–1890," *American Jewish Archives,* III (June, 1950), 11–36.

Mann, Arthur. *LaGuardia: A Fighter Against His Times, 1882–1933.* Philadelphia, Lippincott, 1959.

Mannheimer, Leo. *Shall the Minister Lead or Follow? An Address, April 18, 1913.* Paterson, N.J., 1913.

Margolis, Isidor. *Jewish Teacher Training Schools in the U.S.* New York, National Council for Torah Education, 1964.

Margoshes, Samuel. "The Verband Movement in New York City," *Jewish Communal Register of New York City, 1917–1918,* pp. 1328–36. New York, Kehillah (Jewish Community), 1918.

Markens, Isaac. *The Hebrew in America.* New York, privately published, 1888.

Markowitz, Eugene. "Henry Pereira Mendes: Architect of the Union of Orthodox Jewish Congregations of America," *American Jewish Historical Quarterly,* LV (Mar., 1966), 364–84.

Masliansky, Zevi. *Kitve masliansky.* New York, published by the author, 1920.

Mason, Alpheus Thomas. *Brandeis: A Free Man's Life.* New York, Viking, 1946.

Mayer, Julius M. "The Problem of the Delinquent Child," *Jewish Charity*, III (Jan., 1904), pp. 88–90.

McClure, Samuel S. "The Tammanyizing of a Civilization," *McClure's Magazine* (Nov. 1909), pp. 117–28.

Menes, Abraham. "The Jewish Labor Movement," *The Jewish People, Past and Present*, IV, 264–307. New York, Jewish Encyclopedic Handbooks, 1955.

Mervis, Leonard J. "The Social Justice Movement and the American Reform Rabbi," *American Jewish Archives*, VII (June, 1955), 171–227.

Miner, Maude E. *Slavery of Prostitution: A Plea for Emancipation.* New York, Macmillan, 1916.

Mitgang, Herbert. *The Man Who Rode the Tiger: The Life and Times of Judge Samuel Seabury.* Philadelphia, Lippincott, 1962.

Morris, Robert and Michael Freund, eds. *Trends and Issues in Jewish Social Welfare in the United States, 1899–1952.* Philadelphia, Jewish Publications Society, 1966.

Moss, Frank. *The American Metropolis.* 3 vols. New York, Peter Fenelon Collier, 1897.

Mowry, George E. *The Era of Theodore Roosevelt.* New York, Harper, 1958.

Myers, Gustavus. *The History of Tammany Hall.* New York, Boni and Liveright, 1917.

National Conference of Jewish Charities. *Proceedings of the Biennial Session.* New York, 1902–1916.

Nevins, Allan. *Herbert H. Lehman and His Era.* New York, Scribner, 1963.

Nevins, Allan and John Krout, eds. *The Greater City: New York, 1898–1948.* New York, Columbia University Press, 1948.

New York City. *Report of the Special Committee of the Board of Aldermen of the City of New York Appointed Aug. 5, 1912 to Investigate the Police Department.* June 10, 1913.

——*Stenographer's Minutes of the Special Committee of the Board of Aldermen Appointed to Investigate the City's Police Department Pursuant to Resolution of Aug. 5, 1912.* 6 vols. New York, 1913.

New York Foundation. *New York Foundation: Forty Year Report, 1909–1949.* New York, 1950.

New York State, Senate Document No. 29. Apr. 5, 1909. *Report of the Commission of Immigration.*

New York State Senate, Joint Legislative Committee Investigating Seditious Activities. *Revolutionary Radicalism: Its History, Purposes and Tactics,* 4 Vols. Albany, N.Y., J. B. Lyon Co., 1920.

Niger, Samuel. "Yiddish Culture," *The Jewish People, Past and Present,* IV, 264–307. New York, Jewish Encyclopedic Handbooks, 1955.

Ninth Annual Convention of the Kehillah of New York City: June 1, 1918. New York, Kehillah, 1918.

Oppenheim, Samson D. "The Jewish Population of the U.S.," *American Jewish Year Book* (1918–1919), pp. 2–74. Philadelphia, Jewish Publication Society, 1918.

Panitz, Esther. "In Defense of the Jewish Immigrant (1891–1924)," *American Jewish Historical Quarterly,* LV (Sept., 1965), 57–97.

——"The Polarizing of American Jewish Attitudes Towards Immigration (1870–1891)," *American Jewish Historical Quarterly,* LII (Dec., 1963), 99–130.

Park, Robert E. and Herbert A. Miller. *Old World Traits Transplanted.* New York, Harper, 1921.

Parzen, Herbert. *Architects of Conservative Judaism.* New York, Jonathan David, 1964.

——"Conservative Judaism and Zionism (1896–1922)," *Jewish Social Studies,* XXIII (Oct., 1961), 235–64.

Perlman, Selig. "Jewish-American Unionism, Its Birth Pangs and Contribution to the General American Labor Movement," *Publication of the American Jewish Historical Society,* XLI (1952), 297–338.

Perlow, Yitzchak, ed. *Sefer Radom.* 2 vols. Tel Aviv, Irgun Yotzey Radom, 1961.

Peterson, Horace C. and Gilbert C. Fite. *Opponents of War: 1917–1918.* Madison, University of Wisconsin Press, 1957.

Pink, Louis Heaton. *Gaynor: The Tammany Mayor Who Swallowed the Tiger.* New York, International Press, 1931.

Pinson, Koppel. "Arkady Kremer, Vladimir Medem, and the Ideology of the Jewish 'Bund,' " *Jewish Social Studies,* VII (July, 1945), 233–64.

——, ed. *Dubnow: Nationalism and History.* Philadelphia, Jewish Publication Society, 1958.

Pool, David and Tamar de Sola. *An Old Faith in the New World: Portrait of Shearith Israel, 1654–1954.* New York, Columbia University Press, 1955.

Pupil's Series: A Course in Hebrew for Sunday Schools, First Book. New York, Bureau of Education of the Kehillah, 1913.

Rappaport, Joseph. "The American Yiddish Press and the European

Conflict in 1914," *Jewish Social Studies*, XIX (July–Oct., 1957), 113–28.

——"Jewish Immigrants and World War I: A Study of American Yiddish Press Reaction." Ph.D. dissertation, Columbia University, 1951.

Report fun di Kehillah zu der ershte yehrlicher convention, Feb. 26, 1910. New York, Jewish Community (Kehillah) of New York City, 1910.

Report of the Citizen's Committee Appointed at the Cooper Union Mass Meeting, Aug. 14, 1912.

Reznikoff, Charles, ed. *Louis Marshall, Champion of Liberty: Selected Papers and Addresses*. 2 vols. Philadelphia, Jewish Publication Society, 1957.

Rich, J. C. "Sixty Years of the *Forward*," *New Leader* (June 3, 1957), Section Two, pp. 24–36.

Richards, Bernard G. "The Address of the Jewish People," *The American Zionist*, LV (June, 1965), 17–18.

——"The American Jewish Congress," *Jewish Communal Register of New York City, 1917–1918*, pp. 1385–1400. New York, Kehillah (Jewish Community), 1918.

——"Amol iz geven a kehile," *Zukunft*, L (Feb., 1945), 80–87.

Rischin, Moses. *An Inventory of American Jewish History*. Cambridge, Harvard University Press, 1954.

——*The Promised City: New York's Jews, 1870–1914*. Cambridge, Harvard University Press, 1962.

——"The Early Attitude of the American Jewish Committee to Zionism: 1906–1922," *Publications of the American Jewish Historical Society*, XLIX (Mar., 1960), 188–201.

——"The Jewish Labor Movement in America: A Social Interpretation," *Labor History*, IV (Fall, 1963), 227–47.

Robison, Sophia Moses. *Can Delinquency Be Measured*. New York, Columbia University Press, 1936.

Rogoff, Harry. *An East Side Epic: The Life and Work of Meyer London*. New York, Vanguard, 1930.

Rontch, Isaac E., ed. *Di yidishe landsmanshaftn fun new york*. New York, Y. L. Peretz Shreiber Farein, 1938.

Rosenstock, Morton. *Louis Marshall: Defender of Jewish Rights*. Detroit, Wayne State University Press, 1965.

Rubenovitz, Herman H. and Mignon L. *The Waking Heart*. Cambridge, Nathaniel Dame, 1967.

Rubinow, Isaac Max. "The Jewish Question in New York City (1902–1903)," *Publications of the American Jewish Historical Society*, XLIX (Dec. 1959), 90–136.

Rudavsky, David. "The Bureau of Jewish Education after 1918," *Jewish Education*, XX (Summer, 1949), 36–52.

Rudens, S. P. "A Half Century of Community Service: The Story of the New York Educational Alliance." *American Jewish Year Book* (1944–1945), pp. 73–85. Philadelphia, Jewish Publication Society, 1944.

Sackler, Harry. "A Brief History of the Kehillah," *The Jewish Communal Register of New York City*, 1917–1918, pp. 45–56. New York, Kehillah (Jewish Community), 1918.

Sanders, Ronald. *The Downtown Jews: Portraits of an Immigrant Generation*. New York, Harper and Row, 1969.

Sayre, Wallace S. and Herbert Kaufman. *Governing New York City: Politics in the Metropolis*. New York, Russel Sage Foundation, 1960.

Schachner, Nathan. *The Price of Liberty: A History of the American Jewish Committee*. New York, American Jewish Committee, 1948.

Schapiro, J. Salwyn. "Henry Moskowitz: A Social Reformer in Politics," *Outlook* (Oct. 26, 1912), pp. 446–49.

Scharfstein, Zevi. *Arba'im shana b'amerika*. Tel Aviv, Masada, 1956.

——*Ha'cheder b'chaye a'maynu*. New York, Histadrut Ha'ivrit, 1943.

——*Toldot ha'chinuch b'yisrael*. 3 vols. Jerusalem, Reuven Mas, 1960–1962.

——"Samson Benderly," *Sheviley Hahinuch*, XIV (Sept., 1954).

——, ed. *Sefer ha'yoval shel agudat ha'morim ha'ivrim b'new york*. New York: Modern Linotype, 1944.

Schechter, Solomon. *Seminary Addresses and Other Papers*. Cincinnati, Ark Publishing, 1915.

Schoolman, Albert P. "Emanuel Gamoran: His Life and Work," *Jewish Education*, XXXIV (Winter, 1964), 69–79.

——"Leo Lazarus Honor: 1894–1956," *Jewish Education*, XXVIII (Fall, 1957), 14–23.

Sefer ha'talmid. New York, Bureau of Education of the Kehillah, 1914.

Seidman, Harold. *Labor Czars: A History of Labor Racketeering*. New York, Liveright, 1938.

Seidman, Joel. *The Needle Trades*. New York, Farrar and Rinehart, 1942.

Sellin, Thorsten. *Culture Conflict and Crime*. New York, Social Science Research Bulletin No. 41, 1938.

Shannon, David A. *The Socialist Party of America.* New York, Macmillan, 1955.

Shapiro, Yonathan. "American Jews in Politics: The Case of Louis D. Brandeis," *American Jewish Historical Quarterly,* LV (Dec., 1965), 199–211.

——"Leadership of the American Zionist Organization: 1897–1930." Ph.D. dissertation, Columbia University, 1964.

Shatsky, Jacob. *Di geshikhte fun yidn in varshe,* 3 vols. New York, Yiddish Scientific Institute, 1953.

Sherman, C. Bezalel. *The Jew Within American Society: A Study in Ethnic Individuality.* Detroit, Wayne University Press, 1961.

Shpizman, L. *Geschichte fun der tzionistisher arbeiter bavegung in tzfon amerika.* 2 vols. New York, Yiddisher Kemfer Publishing, 1955.

Simon, Leon. *Ahad Ha'am: A Biography.* Philadelphia, Jewish Publication Society, 1960.

Sklare, Marshall. *Conservative Judaism.* Glencoe, Ill., Free Press, 1955.

Smith, Mortimer. *William Jay Gaynor, Mayor of New York.* Chicago, Regnery, 1951.

Soltes, Mordecai. *The Yiddish Press: An Americanizing Agency.* New York, Teachers College, Columbia University, 1925.

——"Dr. Benderly's Projects in Extension Education," *Jewish Education,* XX (Summer, 1949), 30–32.

Steffens, Lincoln. *The Shame of the Cities.* New York, Sagamore Press, 1957.

Stein, Herman D. "Jewish Social Work in the United States," *American Jewish Year Book* (1956), pp. 3–98. Philadelphia, Jewish Publication Society, 1956.

Stolberg, Benjamin. *Tailor's Progress: The Story of a Famous Union and the Men Who Made it.* New York, Doubleday, Doran, 1944.

Stowe, Lyman Beecher. "Vice, Crime, and the New York Police," *American Review of Reviews,* XLVIII (July, 1913), 73–78.

Straus, Oscar S. *Under Four Administrations.* Boston, Houghton Mifflin, 1922.

Strong, Earl D. *The Amalgamated Clothing Workers of America.* Grinnell, Iowa, Herald-Register, 1940.

Sulzberger, Cyrus L. "Morris Loeb," *Publications of the Jewish Historical Society,* XX (1914), 225–27.

Supple, Barry E. "A Business Elite: German-Jewish Financiers in 19th-Century New York," *Business History Review,* XXXI (Summer, 1957), 143–77.

Swanberg, W. A. *Citizen Hearst: A Biography of William Randolph Hearst.* New York, Scribners, 1961.

Syrett, Harold C., ed. *The Gentleman and the Tiger: The Autobiography of George B. McClellan, Jr.* Philadelphia, Lippincott, 1956.

Szajkowski, Zosa. "The Alliance Israelite Universelle in the U.S.," *Publications of the American Jewish Historical Society,* XXXIX (June, 1950), 389–436.

——"Concord and Discord in American-Jewish Overseas Relief, 1914–1924," *YIVO Annual of Jewish Social Science,* XIV (1969), 99–158.

——"Jewish Relief in Eastern Europe, 1914–1917," *Year Book of the Leo Baeck Institute,* X (1965), 24–51.

——"The Pacificsm of Judah Magnes," *Conservative Judaism,* XXII (Spring, 1968), 36–55.

——"Paul Nathan, Lucien Wolf, Jacob H. Schiff, and the Jewish Revolutionary Movements in Eastern Europe," *Jewish Social Studies,* XXIX (Jan., 1967), 3–26.

The Tenement House Problem. Including Report of the New York State Tenement House Committee of 1900. Edited by Robert W. DeForest and Lawrence Veiller. 2 vols. New York, Macmillan, 1903.

Tenenbaum, Samuel. *William Heard Kilpatrick: Trail Blazer in Education.* New York, Harper, 1951.

Thomas, Alan M. Jr. "American Education and the Immigrant," *Teachers College Record,* LV (Feb., 1954), 254–65.

Turner, George Kibbe. "The Daughters of the Poor," *McClure's Magazine,* XXXIV (Nov., 1909), 45–61.

——"Tammany's Control of New York by Professional Criminals: A Study of a New Period of Decadence in the Popular Government of Great Cities," *McClure's Magazine,* XXXIII (June, 1909), 117–34.

United Hebrew Charities. *Annual Reports.* New York, 1900–1911.

U.S. Immigration Commission. *Immigration and Crime.* Senate Document No. 750, 61st Cong., 3d Sess., Dec. 5, 1910 (Vol. 36 of Reports of the Immigration Commission). Washington D.C., 1911.

——*Importing Women for Immoral Purposes: A Partial Report.* Senate Document No. 196, 61st Cong., 2d Sess., Dec. 10, 1909. Washington D.C., 1909. [Included with different pagination in Vol. 37 of Reports of the Immigration Commission, 1911.]

U.S. Industrial Commission. *Reports of the Industrial Commission on Immigration,* Vol. XV (Immigration and Education). Washington D.C., 1901.

University Settlement Society of New York. *Annual Report*. New York, 1912 and 1913.

Vecoli, Rudolph J. "*Contadini* in Chicago: A Critique of The Uprooted," *Journal of American History*, LI (Dec., 1964), 404–17.

Villard, Oswald Garrison. *Fighting Years: Memoirs of a Liberal Editor*. New York, Harcourt, Brace, 1939.

Voss, Carl Hermann. *Rabbi and Minister: The Friendship of Stephen S. Wise and John Haynes Holmes*. Cleveland, World, 1964.

——ed. *Stephen S. Wise, Servant of the People: Selected Letters*. Philadelphia, Jewish Publication Society, 1969.

Wald, Lillian D. *The House on Henry Street*. New York, Holt, 1915.

Waldman, Morris D. *Nor By Power*. New York, International Universities Press, 1953.

Waterman, Willoughby Cyrus. *Prostitution and Its Repression in New York City: 1900–1931*. New York, Columbia University Press, 1932.

Waxman, Meyer. "Hayahadut ha'ortedoksit b'amerika," *Luach achiever*. New York, Histadrut Achiever, 1918, pp. 3–13.

Weinryb, Bernard D. "The German-Jewish Immigrants in America," in *Jews from Germany in the United States*, Eric E. Hirshler, ed. New York, Farrar, Straus and Cudahy, 1955.

Weinstein, Bernard. *Di yidishe unions in amerika*. New York, United Hebrew Trades, 1929.

Weinstein, James. "Anti-War Sentiment and the Socialist Party, 1917–1918," *Political Science Quarterly*, LXXIV (1959), 215–39.

Werner, M. R. *Tammany Hall*. New York, Doubleday, Doran, 1928.

Weyl, Walter E. *The New Democracy*. New York, Macmillan, 1912.

White, Morton. *Social Thought in America: The Revolt Against Formalism*. Boston, Beacon Press, 1957.

Wiebe, Robert A. *The Search for Order, 1877–1920*. New York, Hill and Wang, 1967.

Wilhelm, Kurt. "The Jewish Community in Post-Emancipation Period," *Yearbook of the Leo Baeck Institute*, II (1957), 47–75.

Williams, Faith M. *The Food Manufacturing Industries in New York and Its Environs*. New York, Regional Plan of New York and Its Environs, 1924.

Winter, Nathan W. *Jewish Education in a Pluralistic Society: Samson Benderly and Jewish Education in the United States*. New York, New York University Press, 1966.

Wischnitzer, Mark. *To Dwell in Safety*. Philadelphia Jewish Publication Society, 1948.

Wise, James Waterman, ed. *The Personal Letters of Stephen Wise.* Boston, Beacon Press, 1956.

Wise, Stephen Samuel. *Challenging Years: The Autobiography of Stephen S. Wise.* New York, Putnam, 1949.

——"What We Are Fighting For," *Free Synagogue Pulpit,* IV (1917–1918), 151–78.

——"The World War for Humanity," *Free Synagogue Pulpit,* IV (1916–1917), 101–20.

Woods, Arthur. *Crime Prevention.* Princeton, Princeton University Press, 1918.

——*Policeman and Public.* New Haven, Yale University Press, 1919.

——"Police Administration," *Proceedings of the Academy of Political Science in the City of New York,* V (Apr., 1915), 532–39.

Yehrlicher report fun der downtown talmud torah zu der 19th yehrlicher mitglider ferzamlung. New York, 1912.

Yellowitz, Irwin. *Labor and the Progressive Movement in New York State, 1897–1916.* Ithaca, Cornell University Press, 1965.

Zaretz, Charles Elbert. *The Amalgamated Clothing Workers of America.* New York, Ancon, 1934.

Zborowski, Mark and Elizabeth Herzog. *Life Is With People: The Culture of the Shtetl.* New York, Schocken Books, 1962.

Zuckerman, Baruch. *Zichronos.* 2 vols. New York, Yiddisher Kemfer, 1962–1963.

——"Dos idishe leben in amerika in ershtn fertl fun tzvantzikstn yohrhundert," *Geschichte fun der tziyonistsher arbeter bavegung in tzfon amerika.* Vol. I. New York, Yiddisher Kemfer, 1955, pp. 1–80.

——"Der kamf far a fareinikt idisher kehile in new york," *Yiddisher Kemfer* (Apr. 13, 1962), pp. 44–48.

Index